# FLYING COLORS

# FLYING COLORS

Compiled by William Green and Gordon Swanborough

MBI Publishing Company

# A Salamander Book

This edition first published in 2001 by MBI Publishing Company,
729 Prospect Avenue, PO Box 1, Osceola, WI 54020-0001 USA

© Salamander Books Limited 2001

A member of the Chrysalis Group plc

MBI Publishing Company books are also available at discounts in bulk quantity for industrial or sales-promotional use. For details write to Special Sales Manager at Motorbooks International Wholesalers & Distributors,
729 Prospect Avenue, PO Box 1, Osceola, WI 54020-0001 USA.

Library of Congress Cataloging-in-Publication Data Available

ISBN 0-7603-1129-3

# The Compilers

### WILLIAM GREEN

William Green entered aviation journalism early in World War II with the *Air Training Corps Gazette* (Now *Air Pictorial*) and has gained an international reputation for his many works of aviation reference, covering both aeronautical history and the current aviation scene. Following RAF service, he was European correspondent to US, Canadian and South African aeronautical journals and British correspondent to several European publications. He was Technical Director to the RAF *Flying Review,* then Editorial Director when it became *Flying Review International.* In 1971 he and Gordon Swanborough jointly created the monthly *Air International,* now one of Europe's foremost aviation journals, and they have also produced a number of books under joint authorship.

### GORDON SWANBOROUGH

Gordon Swanborough has spent his working life as an aviation journalist and author, with the exception of a year-long appointment in 1964 as a Sales Publicity Officer with the British Aircraft Corporation. From 1943 until 1963 he was a member of the editorial staff of the weekly magazine *The Aeroplane,* specializing for much of that time in air transport affairs. In 1965 he became editor of *Flying Review International,* and in 1971 joined forces with William Green to create *Air International.*

# Credits

**Editor:** Ray Bonds
**Designers:** Philip Gorton, Lloyd Martin, Standley and Marritt Designs
**Artwork:**
**Pages 16-208:** John Weal, Richard Caruana and Brian Knight (© Pilot Press). **Pages 1-5:** Terry Hadler (© Salamander Books Ltd)

**Photographs:**
**Pages 6-7:** 1, Imperial War Museum (IWM); 2 and 3, Pilot Press; 4, IWM. **Pages 8-9:** 1, IWM; 2, Pilot Press; 3, Charles E. Brown; 4, IWM. **Pages 10-11:** 1 and 2, US Navy; 3, Messerschmitt Archiv; 4, IWM; 5, US Navy. **Pages 12-13:** 1 and 2, US Navy; 3, US Air Force; 4, J. G. Moore Collection. **Pages 14-15:** 1 and 2, US Air Force; 3, Lockheed; 4, Dassault-Breguet; 5, US Air Force

**Filmset by:** Modern Text Typesetting Ltd.
**Colour reproduction by:** Positive Colour Ltd., Bantam Litho Ltd, Magnum Graphics Ltd, and Graphic Affairs Ltd
**Printed in Spain**

# Compilers' Preface

Since, some 70 years or so ago, the first coats of drab-coloured dope were applied to the natural linen skinning of military aircraft in order that they would better blend with their backgrounds, a need was first seen for some means of endowing aircraft with a national identity, and air and ground crews first began to personalize their charges with emblems, the camouflage of aircraft has become a science and their decoration an art form.

In times of war and, indeed, during the periods of quasi peace between conflicts, military aircraft have worn camouflage schemes in infinite variety; schemes that have changed with extraordinary frequency to reflect differing ideas of means of concealment under specific circumstances, changing scenarios and enhanced performance capabilities.

The other side of the coin is provided by what may be termed as *anti-*camouflage intended to render an aircraft readily visible or positively identifiable at the greatest possible distance, perhaps to increase, for example, the likelihood of an aircraft being sighted after an enforced descent onto snow-covered terrain, or to ensure wide berth for an aircraft engaged in training activities.

*Flying Colours* surveys, by means of profile drawings of military aircraft, many of these camouflage and anti-camouflage schemes that have been applied over nearly 70 years, together with functional and theatre markings, and national, unit and personal markings. *Flying Colours* makes no pretence to being a definitive treatise on this exceedingly complex subject—virtually every air force of stature and, indeed, almost every major aircraft type, might well warrant a volume entirely to itself—being intended as a synoptic overview, a broad outline of the application of colour, for both utilitarian and decorative purposes, to military aircraft.

The compilers' selection of aircraft has been of necessity somewhat arbitrary, being primarily motivated by the desire to illustrate colour finishes and markings, both typical and atypical, across the entire spectrum. The following pages will reveal that these range from the manifestly pedestrian to the startlingly flamboyant.

# Contents

*Aircraft types are presented in the chronological sequence of their initial service introduction.*

# The history of FLYING COLOURS

*by **Bruce Robertson**, author, co-author, editor and compiler of some 20 major works on aeronautical subjects, former Improved Inspector of the Aeronautical Inspection Directorate of the British Air Ministry, and for more than 20 years a member of the recognition training policy team at the British Ministry of Defence.*

THE COLOURED finishes of service aircraft are as functional as their equipment. The range of their colouring is wide but, although there are admittedly only seven colours in the spectrum, for the purposes of this survey, flying colours cover every shade, including black and white. These colours can reflect the tenor of the times, with trends towards camouflage colours for concealment as international relationships deteriorate, while natural finishes and embellishment express a lack of tensions.

The early aeroplanes of World War I were built of wood, covered with fabric. This fabric was linen, flax or Egyptian cotton rendered air- and water-tight by covering with a thin acetyl cellulose film, that also tautened the covering, in an application process called doping. To protect this finish it was usually covered with a so-called clear varnish, which looked brown in bulk and bestowed a yellowish tinge to the fabric. No other colouring was then considered necessary and the only marking was a service identity number.

From the time that Bleriot had flown across the English Channel in 1909, the international implications of aviation became very apparent. During 1912, delegates of flying clubs of 13 countries pressed for national identity letters on aircraft, but governments and their military authorities saw no reason to pursue the matter—except the French.

## France takes the lead

France, leading the world in aviation at that time, led also in aircraft markings. The French Army decreed in July 1912 that its aircraft would bear on their wings an indication of French nationality using the colours of the Tricolour, the French national flag, in the form of a *cockade* of one metre diameter. So the roundel form was introduced, later to be adopted by most countries of the world using their own combinations of national colours.

All military and naval aircraft bore an indication of individual identity by a number or letter, but the French went further and made it mandatory for their aircraft to bear letters indicative of the manufacturer as well as an individual registration. Also made obligatory was an indication of maximum load *(Charge Maxima)* to which the aircraft had been satisfactorily tested. Many nations were to follow suit by marking the maximum loaded weight on their aircraft. For all these functional markings, black was appropriate as contrasting well on the light-coloured finishes of the day. Such were the main markings of aircraft of the belligerents when Europe went to war in August 1914.

The neutral Dutch, fearful that their wedge of land might become embroiled in the conflict, took steps to proclaim their nationality and neutrality. As early as 5 August 1914 they announced that their aircraft would have wings and fuselage marked with orange discs indicative of the House of Orange of the Dutch Royal Family. Orange remains at the core of the Dutch national marking today.

## Germany's "Iron Cross"

The Germans soon found a need to mark their aircraft to assure their own troops of their identity and the black "Iron Cross" marking chosen was suitably symbolic. The four squadrons of Britain's Royal Flying Corps, reaching France on 8 August 1914, found their aircraft fired upon by friend and foe alike and were quickly forced to paint Union Jacks under their wings. It was also found expedient to mark the national flag on lateral surfaces as protection from their Allies on the ground. Forced landings were frequent and an absence of markings, plus the barrier of language, led those in the locality of the landing to treat any stranded airmen as potentially hostile.

The fact was soon brought home that in the visibility of markings, shape is dominant to colour. At a distance the Cross of St George on the Union Jack was mistaken for the black Maltese style cross adopted by Germany. With the agreement of the French Allies, the Royal Flying Corps adopted in mid-December 1914 the French cockade, but with a reversal of the order of the colours. The Royal Naval Air Service, making its own rulings, had apparently reasoned that the diametric opposite to a black cross was a red nought and so adopted a red circle as its nationality marking. However, in one of the first of a series of unification measures that eventually were to result in the amalgamation of the air arms of the Army and Navy as the Royal Air Force in April 1918, the now familiar red, white and blue roundel became Britain's standard national aircraft marking from 1 November 1915. Earlier that year rudder striping in national colours, and the addition of roundels on the fuselage sides in place of any Union Jack markings, had come into use.

Even psychology has its place in aircraft markings. Pilots and observers took exception to the fact that the most

**1.** Understandably, flight crews felt some-what vulnerable with a "bullseye at their vitals", as represented by the roundel on this Royal Air Force D.H.9a.
**2.** A clear-doped Albatros C III sports the German Cross Patée.
**3.** Captain Eddie Rickenbacker (top American "ace" of World War I with 26 victories) who became Commander of 94th Aero Squadron American Expedition Force, poses with a Spad 13 dispaying standard late WWI French camouflage and famous "Hat-in-the-Ring" emblem.
**4.** S.E.5a's of No 85 Sqdn,Royal Air Force, at St. Omer in June 1918, showing the unit's hexagonal markings.

vulnerable part of an aircraft, its crew, sat beside a marking that most resembled, of all things, a target with the bullseye at their vitals. The unfeeling regulation to place the roundel at the centre of the fuselage was superseded by instructions to mark roundels aft of the cockpits.

Up to 1916 the object of markings, in the main, had been to call attention to national identity. During 1916, a new phase of concealment came into vogue. Aircraft on reconnaissance or bombing missions, sneaking over enemy-held territory, sought concealment from fighters patrolling against just such an incursion to their bases, which were at that time attractive bombing targets, where the light finishes of aircraft on the airfield were like a guiding beacon. The problem was in finding a colour or combination of colours that would blend with the background to render aircraft inconspicuous, both on the ground at its base and in the air when viewed from above. This took precedence over concealment in the air, primarily because fighter aircraft were of a greater menace in destroying aircraft than anti-aircraft guns.

The Germans and the Allies, both accepting the need of concealment from above, approached the method of the mass camouflaging of their aircraft in two very different ways. After an initial blotching by paints or distempers, usually in two or three different shades, the Germans in late 1916 introduced printed fabrics of irregular polygons in four to five shades. Advantages of this included the saving of man-hours in painting, and the printing dyes had less of a weight penalty than the pigment mixed with varnishes adopted by the Allies to achieve a uniform camouflage colour.

The British air arms, both dependent on the Royal Aircraft Factory for official innovations, were recommended to use a concoction called PC10 (Protective Covering No 10) produced initially by the Factory and then by industry. Its shade has been a subject of controversy, although chemically its ingredients cannot be disputed. No doubt its colouring varied from khaki-green to chocolate brown as reports and samples indicate. But its precise shade was not all that important. The covering had been introduced to protect, by its pigmented content, the fabric from deteriorating under the harmful actinic rays of the sun, which it did more efficiently than the clear varnish remaining in use for undersurfaces. It was logical to have the pigment in a camouflaging shade at this stage of the war in the air, and since khaki was the basic camouflage shade for uniforms and battlefield equipment, this was the basis for the shade originally chosen.

# The history of flying colours

Simultaneous with the trend towards camouflage came the very antithesis of concealment by some German fighter units which adopted colour schemes akin to the plumages of tropical birds. The leading ace of that war, Manfred von Richthofen, was colloquially known as the Red Baron from the all-red aircraft that he few, while others in his Geschwader flew red-painted fighters, but with some other distinguishing colour. Small wonder that his Geschwader and other similarly painted fighter units were called circuses by the Allies. Although the term originated from likening the gaudy colours to those of circus caravans, the term becomes even more apt when it is appreciated that the Geschwadern, the grouping of fighter units from mid-1917, was to provide units that could be switched to different locations along the front as required. One of the most incongruous aspects of this aircraft colouring was that it was often painted over the camouflage-patterned fabric.

## Unit markings introduced

The British military authorities, regarding uniformity as a military virtue, viewed the unorthodox in aircraft markings with as much distaste as variations in airmen's uniforms. Unit markings were also first introduced on a large scale in 1916. While French units in general and German fighter units in particular adopted large, colourful and symbolic motifs, the British squadrons were conditioned to simple geometric shapes or fuselage bands in black or white to contrast.

In April 1916, the Royal Flying Corps in the Field had introduced their unit marking scheme, black on the light finishes and white when camouflaging became general later that year. The marking scheme was extended to all British squadrons as they arrived on the Western Front, including naval squadrons temporarily under RFC tactical control. Bars, triangles, discs, rings, crescents and hexagons formed the basis of the markings, some of which can be seen to this day, perpetuated by squadrons which now bear the appropriate number. Changes were made occasionally to confuse enemy intelligence, but the most sweeping change came on 22 March 1918, the day following the launching of the massive German offensive. Some airfields were over-run and a re-grouping of squadrons took place. To mask these moves from German intelligence, fighter markings were changed and all other units were instructed to obliterate their squadron markings.

The gaudy schemes sported by some Sopwith Camels have tended to give a false picture of the rigid British standardisation. Snow-white and chequered Camels were on the strength of the 1st Australian (Training) Wing in Britain and some other embellished aircraft were flown by Canadians in Britain. The nationals of these countries had a reputation for non-conformity, but their handiwork was the exception, certainly not the rule.

During the 'twenties, with belief that World War I had been the war to end all wars and with faith in the League of

1

Nations, peace in Europe seemed assured. The League had given mandate to Britain and France to police Iraq and Syria respectively and both countries had colonial interests in other semitropical spheres. To give the increased protection to aircraft fabric from ultraviolet rays in sunny climes, red oxide was added to the pigment, but by the mid-'twenties this had been replaced by an overall standard scheme. Fabric was then initially doped with red oxide content, making red the basic colour of doped fabric showing on the inside, a practice that remains. The fabric was then covered with a powdered aluminium dope to reflect heat. This finish, loosely called silver, became standard on all RAF aircraft, whether at home or overseas, with proprietory dopes by Cellon, Emaillite and Titanine being used. To accord, metal cowlings were left in natural metal finish. The metal was sometimes clear varnished to give a sheen, but rarely polished as this could adversely affect the rather dull anodised finish of the duralumin sheeting.

During the mid-'twenties the fighter squadrons of the RAF adopted unofficial squadron markings along fuselage sides and top wing upper surfaces. The only official mandate on colouring was given in 1924, when flight colours of red for

"A", yellow for "B" and blue for "C" Flights were sanctioned in Air Ministry Weekly Orders that December for all aircraft. Later in the 'twenties the main RAF Command, Air Defences of Great Britain, regularised the fighter squadron markings and permitted, from August 1930, bomber squadrons to display their squadron numbers in flight colours.

The United States, having abandoned the League it was instrumental in inaugurating, pursued an isolationist policy and, with no worries other than those posed by her relatively weak Central American neighbours, abandoned camouflage for natural finishes with coloured embellishment. One exception, due no doubt to the fact that it was an *Army* Air Corps, was the camouflaging of aircraft by washable distempers in air exercises.

So far this survey has dealt with finishes in general by aircraft operating by day. An overall black for a night operating aircraft may seem fundamental, but it was proved that it is finish, not shade, that is all important. As early as May 1915, an Avro 504 was covered with blacklead at Eastchurch, Kent, to assess its effectiveness at night in a searchlight beam at 3,000 feet (914 metres) in comparison to a clear varnished standard Avro. In smoothing the blacklead down it had been polished to give a sheen and,

proving even easier to detect by reflected light than other aircraft, black was dismissed as unsuitable instead of a non-reflecting material like lampblack being tried. The RFC did use black varnish on night-bombing FE 2bs, but its Handley Page 0/400s were in standard PC10.

However, the Experimental Station, Orfordness, early in 1918, came up with a nitro-varnish of a grey-green shade that they called Nivo, promising good night "invisibility" in conditions of moonlight. It had a slight sheen, calculated to be equivalent to the reflection of calm sea. This became the standard overall finishing varnish for RAF bombers such as the Virginias, Hinaidis and Hendons, 1922 to 1938. Associated with this finish was the night roundel of red and blue. This roundel, excluding the white portion, became standard for all camouflaged upper surfaces on RAF and RCAF aircraft during World War II and is currently used on the camouflaged surfaces of RAF aircraft.

In 1936, with Britain committed to an expansion programme while Germany continued unremittingly a policy of "guns before butter", the gathering of war clouds was represented more literally on aircraft as bright finishes gave way to dull paints.

**1.** Believed photographed at Marckebeeke in August 1917, this Fokker Dr I prototype (F I 102/17) was the first of several of the triplanes flown by von Richthofen and painted bright red.
**2.** A restored example of the Sopwith Snipe as flown by 208 Sqdn.
**3.** A Beaufort (L9878) of No 217 Sqdn, RAF Coastal Command, operating from St. Eval, in the temperate land scheme of dark green and earth of the early WWII period.
**4.** A Mosquito B IV (DK338) on test, in dark green and ocean grey camouflage with medium sea grey undersurfaces adopted in 1942.

# The history of flying colours

Printed fabrics were out for the metal-covered German aircraft; indeed, it was the British with their fabric-covered Wellingtons coming into service that might have considered dyed fabrics. While most European countries at this time, or soon after, adopted disruptive camouflage patterns in varying colour tones, Britain and Germany differed widely on their application.

The British standardised on shades described as dark earth and dark green, merging into each other in curving lines. The Germans initially standardised on three colour tones meeting without merging, in a rather haphazard and jagged way, earning the name of splinter camouflage. To avoid having a line of aircraft with uniform patterns compromising camouflage, both countries had a reversal of the order of the colours by making alternate aircraft from production the mirrored image of each other.

## War clouds prompt camouflage

The Munich crisis of September 1938 provoked several emergency measures in Britain, including the hasty camouflaging of aircraft remaining silver in the industrial camouflage paints being used in aerodrome buildings. The disruptive patterning had applied only to operational aircraft on production, but this crisis heralded universal camouflage for aircraft based in South-Eastern and Eastern England. German aircraft, already in camouflage, were unaffected, but a significant change came in January 1939. Hitherto the swastika, displayed over fin and rudder, had been set in a white disc on a red band. The red and white setting was then removed and the last vestiges of peacetime disappeared from the appearance of German aircraft.

The German national marking was four white angles, and the British national marking in the early stages of the war was a yellow circle. The books on markings and the official decrees, or the interpretation of them, did not put it this way—but for all practical purposes of identification by the participants, these were the facts. The official German marking was a black cross on a dark setting; outlining the corners of the cross in white did not show up the cross, it merely indicated where it was. For a period in 1939, Britain withdrew white from the fuselage roundel but outlined both this and the conventional roundel later by a thick yellow outer circle that almost eclipsed the national markings within.

Both Germany and Britain were fairly uniform in the marking of coded unit and individual aircraft letters. In both cases the national marking provided the focal point for this display of coded characters, and in both cases the letter immediately aft of the cross or roundel was the aircraft's individual letter. The two letters (British) and two characters (German) in front of the marking comprised a coded reference to the unit or formation. The Germans had the refinement of two letters after with the final letter denoting its unit, as distinct from the higher formation letters.

At the time, the need for security by a coded reference seemed obvious. In retrospect, it is difficult to understand why. Unlike during World War I when the simple emblems were changed from time to time, the British and German codes were generally unvarying. Documents from both sides suggest that the opponents had a keener knowledge of the overall coded references than compatriots had of their own!

The Nivo finish for invisibility to night fighters by night bombers proved pointless when it came to operations. The possibilities of visual detection of any aircraft at night, until airborne radar became effective, was remote—except when aided by the revealing illumination of searchlights. As an anti-searchlight finish Nivo was ineffectual since it reflected light, and a new light-absorbing velvety black was introduced by Britain, under the official designation RDM2, for night bombers from 1937. The Germans adopted a similar finish. At first it was applied to undersurfaces only, by the RAF, but since searchlight techniques involved coning by a series of lights, considerable light concentration on the sides of the aircraft was likely to result. As a counter, by the end of 1940, the black was extended to the complete lower half of the aircraft and in the next year it was extended to all but the strict plan view. This was indicative of the growing bomber offensive, in that concealment of attacking bombers took precedence over their temperate land scheme colours for concealment at their bases, so endorsing Bomber Command's philosophy—"the best form of defence is attack".

As a matter of morale, American bombers crews in particular adorned the noses of their aircraft with various forms: voluptuous females, gruesome ogres and the screen and comic strip characters of the day. Such was the world-wide syndication of Walt Disney's art that Mickey Mouse and Donald Duck gave colour to the aircraft of friend and foe alike. The Americans in particular bestowed names upon their bombers such as: "Bat Outa

**1.** During World War II, mission symbols took various forms, but the most usual were bombs, as seen below being applied to a Douglas SBD-5.
**2.** As from June 1943, white rectangles augmented US insignia, as seen on these Grumman F6F-3 Hellcats.
**3.** Rather obvious away from the desert, these Bf 110Es of II Gruppe of Zerstörergeschwader 26 are in a sand finish for North African operations early in 1942. Note the white theatre bands toward the rear of the fuselages, and also that the aircraft at the rear lacks the nose emblem.
**4.** The unofficial embellishment of combat aircraft during World War II was widespread, one example being the "Shark's Nose" decoration of RAF No 112 Squadron's Kittyhawks.
**5.** Most B-17s bore decorative nose emblems, often very imaginative and sometime risqué, but tail decoration, such as this, was rare. Such adornment was regarded as a morale-booster for bomber crews.

**2**

Hell", "Boeing's Best", "Bugs Bunny", "Calamity Jane", "Fancy Nancy", "Flash Dodger", etc, often with an associated motif. Some were considered too outrageous and only recently has publication of photographs of such been permitted.

### Different theatres, differing camouflage

With war involving all five continents camouflage varied according to the theatre of war. Britain had five main schemes—Temperate Land of dark green and dark earth, Temperate Sea of dark slate grey and extra dark sea grey, Middle East of dark earth and middle stone, Command optional at discretion and Photographic Reconnaissance (PR) of various shades of blue initially—and later included even pink finishes. The PR scheme was overall single colouring, but all the others were in a disruptive scheme to six separate patterns according to the basic configuration of the aircraft, with undersurfaces in shades for concealment against the sky, varying from nondescript grey to blue in the Mediterranean area.

The United States, with commitments east and east, adopted olive drab as the most suitable camouflage shade for upper and side surfaces, with neutral grey or azure for undersurfaces in European and Pacific theatres respectively. Germany, fighting a war on several fronts, with a need for switching forces, changed to a variety of schemes, to suit the terrain, by using paints easily removed. The Soviet Union followed the German trend of supplying paints for local application, with dark green, earth brown and

white predominant to meet their seasonal requirements, but availability being a primary factor in the early stages of the conflict. For example, Lavochkin fighters built in a former tractor factory were given a disruptive camouflage pattern of black and green simply because large stocks of paint of these colours were available for the tractors formerly built by the factory!

During 1941, the British Temperate Land scheme for dark earth for fighters was changed to sea grey, so epitomising Britain's changing fortunes of war from the defensive role of the Battle of Britain to a colour appropriate to aiding the concealment of aircraft crossing the sea. Fighter Command aircraft were then flying across the Channel to do battle with the Luftwaffe over enemy-held territory.

### The Japanese influence

Japan brought into the war a variety of camouflage schemes, largely because the official schemes decreed in their temperate homeland had little relevance in the tropical spheres to which rapid advances were made, where local command schemes came into effect. A facet of Japanese military aircraft markings was that the fin and rudder was the area for unit and formation, as well as personal, markings. Because of their *Hinomaru* national marking, the red disc of the sun, red was excluded from the national markings of American and British aircraft in the Pacific and South-East Asian spheres to avoid mistaken identities. But mis-identifications did still occur, bringing home once again that shape is more important than colour, leading in mid-1943 to white bars being added to each side of the American insignia, which have remained to this day. Another ploy, still used, was the asymmetrical presentation of the US national markings on the wings, being placed on the upper surface of the port wing, and lower surface of the starboard wing.

Practically all countries, including Japan, agreed that yellow was the appropriate colour for trainers. A yellow flag in the International Code denotes "Fever", with the implication "keep well away" and the message conveyed by trainers was equally apt. Yellow would, of course, compromise the camouflage of airfields and so uppersurfaces of trainers were camouflaged in operational areas during World War II. But on the American continent, in Australia and South Africa, trainers were mainly an overall bright yellow.

One of the most surprising changes in 1943 was the transformation of RAF Coastal Command aircraft, by restricting their temperate sea scheme of ocean shades to strict plan view only and having the rest of the aircraft white. It was deemed, by experiment, to reduce their visibility from the submariners' point of view, and light shades are today in vogue for anti-submarine aircraft of all nations.

Since national markings were in matt finishes, to prevent them compromising camouflage, something more outstanding was needed for the assaulting aircraft of the Allied Expeditionary Air Forces for D-Day, planned for 5 June 1944, and executed the day following, when massive retaliation was anticipated. Five alternating white and black stripes around wings and fuselage proclaimed Allied aircraft. Similar striping was to be applied again where joint forces were concerned; by Fleet Air Arm aircraft operating in Korean waters and by British and French aircraft in the 1956 Suez operations.

Undoubtedly the most startling markings of all were the bizarre schemes of the American "assembly ships" of the US Eighth Air Force, around which formations took up station before flying over enemy-held territory. These exotic polka-dotted or striped B-24Ds did not accompany the formations on their missions, but conspicuously marked radar-equipped "lead-ships" did. The latter had to be conspicuous for the cue to others of their formation to drop their bombs when the leaders were seen to do so by acting on their superior locating aids. As part of a formation they were defended from enemy fighters by other bombers flying in box formation and, with German anti-aircraft fire being radar-predicted at this stage of the war, their conspicuous markings provided no additional hazard.

### Diminishing threat, no camouflage

From early 1944, the Americans saw little need to continue with camouflage. Bases in the Pacific were beyond the reach of the Japanese strikes and in Britain the threat from the Luftwaffe over Britain had greatly diminished. The absence of camouflage helped performance by reducing weight and surface drag, but of even greater importance was the saving in factory manhours. Fabric-covered portions of aircraft structures were then given "silver" doping to match the natural metal of the remainder.

The RAF did not follow suit until after hostilities had ended in Europe, except in the second half of 1944, when paint was scraped from some fighters to gain extra speed necessary to pursue and shoot down V-1 flying bombs.

Among the many smaller markings were those proudly announcing victories; roundels or swastikas, depending upon the side, to show the number of aircraft shot down by a pilot. But as only wing leaders normally retained a particular aircraft that they could temporarily call their own, it was a far from rigid system.

1

3

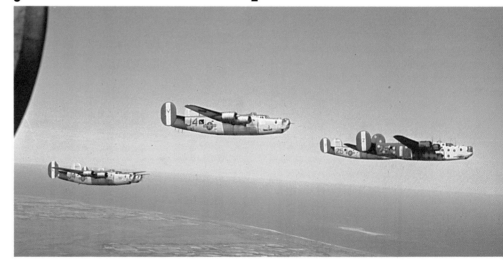

2

**1.** Markings are often applied not to hide an aircraft, but to make it more conspicuous. A perfect example of anti-camouflage during World War II is provided by these Bell P-39 Airacobras which were used to train gunners.
**2.** The normal US Navy method of recording "kills" is seen on this Hellcat of Lt. (j.g.) E.R. Hanks, who reportedly achieved five successes over Japanese aircraft in a single mission.
**3.** The extraordinarily flamboyant decoration of the B-24 Liberator assembly ships of the US 8th Army Air Force is typified by the B-24H lead aircraft in this 458th Bomb Group formation as it climbs out of St. Faith, Norfolk, England.
**4.** A remarkable example of suitable camouflage is provided by this Bf 109E-4/ Trop fighter of I Gruppe of Jagdeschwader 27 merging in with the Libyan desert over which it is here seen flying during the summer of 1941.

With bombers, however, it became something of a fetish to record with bomb silhouettes the number of sorties carried out. Lancaster B Mk III ED888 of No 103 Sqdn, RAF, is the accredited Bomber Command record holder with 140 bombing missions. American C-46 and C-47 transports on the Burma-China run over "the hump", as the lower reaches of the Himalayas were called, were marked with a camel silhouette for completing each loaded flight over this route. In a carry-over from bombing Japan to similar missions over Korea, one Boeing B-29 had 150 bomb silhouettes marked on its nose, topped by a MiG-15 profile silhouette representing a destruction claim by one of its gunners. Search and rescue aircraft, particularly

helicopters, have similarly recorded more peaceful missions—a matchstick man silhouette for each life saved and for some other emergency mission a stork silhouette was considered apt.

The 'fifties brought in new aircraft finishes. With the general introduction of jet aircraft, with their higher speeds, smooth finishes became essential, not only to reduce drag, but to prevent the paint from being torn from the structure. The ideal finishes had to be gloss-drying direct from the spray gun, eliminating the need for an additional transparent cellulose finish then being applied as an interim measure. This entailed an initial "filler", so that all joins in metal coverings and indentations were first smoothed over. Polyurethane, now in domestic use, was one such paint scheme introduced in the 'fifties that was sufficiently hard to resist the abrasive effects of dust-laden air.

Sophistication brought new ranges of coverings and exceptions to an overall colouring scheme. Some all-weather jet fighters had to be "tipped and tailed" in a different colour since resin/glass fibre radomes needed paints with special adherence and anti-tracking properties, while the jet tailpipe needed a special heat-resisting paint in black so that exhaust deposits were not so apparent.

With the coming of the new finishing schemes came a re-introduction of camouflage resulting from the "cold war". The intransigent attitude of the Soviet Union in blocking road access to Berlin, leading to the massive Anglo-American airlift in 1948 and then the Korean War in

1950, heightened tension between East and West. Britain reintroduced camouflage as early as 1947 and standardised in the mid-'fifties, but both the USA and the USSR resisted the trend and continued to operate aircraft in natural metal finish with transparent protective coverings. There were several reasons for this. Whatever lead Germany might have had in jet aircraft had been utterly destroyed, leaving Britain to lead the world for a brief period in this field and its associated factors, including finishes. Other countries did not then have available paints suitable for the high speeds being attained by jet fighters, and only Commonwealth countries displayed interest in importing from Britain. This was not the only reason. The USA had defence interests worldwide and the Soviet Union's own territory bordered on three continents, apart from its interests beyond its borders. So extended were their commitments that strength at all points was impossible and their true might was in their mobility—the ability to switch the forces. There was no camouflage colouring suitable at the construction stage for all the environments of their respective global commitments.

In the Korean conflict, Soviet fighter types, mainly MiG-15s, operating for North Korea did, however, adopt camouflage tactics. Since the United Nations air forces, primarily American, had air superiority with tactical as well as strategic bombers on call, North Korean aircraft were camouflaged both for concealment on their airstrips and against detection in the air from above. Their dark and light

13

# The history of flying colours

green patterned camouflage was deemed effective by their opposing F-86 Sabre pilots who, when they did spot and attack were at times themselves attacked from high-flying MiG-15s in an overall powder blue finish which might be considered the forerunner of the pale air superiority finishes of today. Distemper for such tactical camouflaging has been considered before and since, but because of the drag in high speed aircraft it is generally restricted to helicopters.

For the countries of the Middle East and Gulf areas, with large tracts of arid territory, variations on a mid-stone shade overall are general for what is loosely called "desert camouflage". Not only are the finishes of the various countries similar but so are their national markings, for this centre of the Islam world shows its cult in their markings—white for virtue, red for fierceness in battle, black for the era of the Caliphates and green, Mohammed's own colour. The country with Mecca as its capital, Saudi Arabia, has its service aircraft bearing the legend in Arabic, "There is no god, but God, and Mohammed is his prophet". In the Western World, only Portugal and Switzerland proclaim Christendom, by a cross, a symbol anathema to Islam so that their air ambulances display a red crescent instead of a red cross.

Army aviation rapidly expanded during the 'fifties, particularly in the US Army. The reconstituted Wehrmacht required eight different types of aircraft and Britain gave Corps status to its Army's air arm. From 1940 it had been usual to give army aircraft an overall ground camouflage scheme in matt (lustreless in American parlance) finishes.

## Colourful display teams

Mitigating the trend to dull colouring from the mid-'fifties were the service aerobatic teams, some coining names based on their unorthodox colour schemes, such as the "Black Arrows" and "Blue Diamonds", flying RAF Hunters, and "Diavoli Rossi" from Italy and "Golden Hawks" from Canada flying Sabres. Alternatively colour schemes in national colours were in vogue. In the 'sixties it was deemed extravagant to dress a front line squadron in this way and a mis-employment of operational aircraft. By the end of the 'sixties the national display teams were practically all of trainer aircraft types and are so today, although the USAF's "Thunderbirds" are to relinquish their T-38 trainers in favour of F-16 Fighting Falcon fighters in the future.

Another problem was the conflict between the dull operational finishes and a need for high visibility to avoid collision. For this reason fighter aircraft in particular have been allowed a certain degree of embellishment over small areas that could be quickly obliterated in an emergency. For trainers, except in war, bright colours have always been used and the introduction of Dayglo flexible finishes enabled trainers in natural finishes to have rashes of colour.

The US Navy, over the years, has shown how views on camouflage can change radically. A wartime scientific study advocated lighter finishes on areas

1

2

shaded by wings with meticulous definitions of shade intensity, but the scheme was impractical in temperate climes. In 1944, American carrier-borne aircraft, including those supplied to Britain under Lend-Lease, were given an overall dark "midnight blue" finish, which gave way to light greys after the war. With postwar patrol aircraft, Neptunes and early Orions, there was the extraordinary scheme of the lower half dark blue and upper half grey, the very reversal of colours for camouflage against sea and sky backgrounds! It originated from a need to have a lighter heat-reflecting surface than the wartime dark blue. From October 1964 this scheme gave place to white upper surfaces for the functional purpose of heat-reflecting and grey undersurfaces for concealment against the sky from naval vessels.

Perhaps the ultimate in light finishes were those of the RAF V-bombers in the 'sixties of high gloss white overall as an anti-radiation finish in their nuclear deterrent role. With the Navy taking over the nuclear role by submarine-launched Polaris missiles, the V-force was switched to conventional bombing and tanker roles, so once against disruptive patterned camouflage was reintroduced for bomber upper surfaces.

The trend for camouflage continued throughout the 'sixties with USAF aircraft in Europe adopting a disruptive patterned camouflage, a reduction in size of national insignia presentation and the toning down of unit and serial markings. In the 'seventies even the RAF's Lightnings went under the spray guns for camouflage shades. The Soviet Union continued to use natural finishes, except for some

5-256

**1.** US Air Force F-5E Tiger IIs painted in various "Aggressor" finishes apparently resembling genuine finishes applied to one or another operator of Soviet combat aircraft. These aircraft participate in Dissimilar Air Combat Training of USAF and other NATO air crews, to improve their air-to-air combat capability "by realistic simulation of the enemy threat".
**2.** Expected to operate at "tree-top" height, this Fairchild A-10A Thunderbolt II is therefore appropriately camouflaged in the USAF's so-called lizard scheme of two greens and charcoal.

**3.** Currently there are several variations of maritime aircraft finishes. That adopted for this P-3F Orion of the Iranian Islamic Air Force seems appropriate enough for operation over sea, but would render the aircraft somewhat conspicuous when it returned to its land base.
**4.** Another variation is the high-gloss sea blue-grey and white of the French Aéronavale Super Etendard.
**5.** The current USAF tactical camouflage of two shades of green and tan looks appropriate on this F-111E cruising against a terrain with similar colouring.

fighters in the 'seventies which were given an overall low-visibility grey finish as an air-to-air camouflage shade.

At the dawn of the 'eighties, when the Fairchild A-10A Thunderbolt II was introduced as a low-level anti-armour attack aircraft, a new overall three-tone camouflage of dark grey, light and dark green was applied. The patterning and shades are not far removed from those advocated for Sopwith Salamanders over 60 years earlier when they were being produced as trench strafing aircraft, although too late for operations.

A new development in the 'eighties, involving experimentation with both RAF and USAF aircraft, has been a revival of a low visibility grey overall camouflage scheme. But why in this sophisticated age of electronic detection should visual detection be considered at all? In an international emergency it is anticipated that there may be a period of "radar silence", meaning that detection equipment might be switched off to prevent defence radar latching on to the source of emissions and revealing redeployment of forces, so that at this most critical of times the human eye would again be the prime detector. Also, some of the modern air defence missile systems are tracked optically, under high magnification, where visibility of the target to the eye is of importance.

So once again we turn full circle until the trend is arrested and reversed for safety considerations of the collision risks. There are irreconcilable factors—the dull finishes of camouflage for concealment in operational posture and eye-catching colours to advertise presence in the interests of safety. Since the flying colours mirror the states of international tension over the years, let us hope for a trend towards brightness in the flying colours of the future.

# SPAD 7 (1916)

Remembered today as one of the most efficacious fighting scouts fielded by the Allies during WWI, the Spad 7 was created by the Société anonyme pour l'Aviation et ses Dérivés, the products of which were to become universally known by the acronym Spad (thus written). A shapely little aeroplane, it first flew (as the Type V) early in April 1916. It was not outstandingly agile, it offered rather restricted forward vision and it presented a dauntingly steep glide angle, but its speed performance and great structural strength were seen to offer a pronounced advance and it therefore immediately entered production. By 1 August 1917, 50 escadrilles de chasse were mounted on the Spad 7 and some 3,500 were built in France, with a further 220 being produced in the UK and 100 in Russia. (1) Spad 7 of Escadrille SPA 81 in the overall French Grey finish which was favoured by the Aviation militaire in 1917. The SPA 81 "Greyhound" emblem appeared in black on some aircraft. (2) Spad 7 of Lt de Turenne of Escadrille SPA 48. Note clear-doped fabric aft of cockpit and repetition of aircraft number on aft fuselage decking. (3) Spad 7 (A6662) of No 19 Sqdn, Royal Flying Corps, St Marie Cappille, France, in December 1917. Note the khaki-doped sides and top decking,

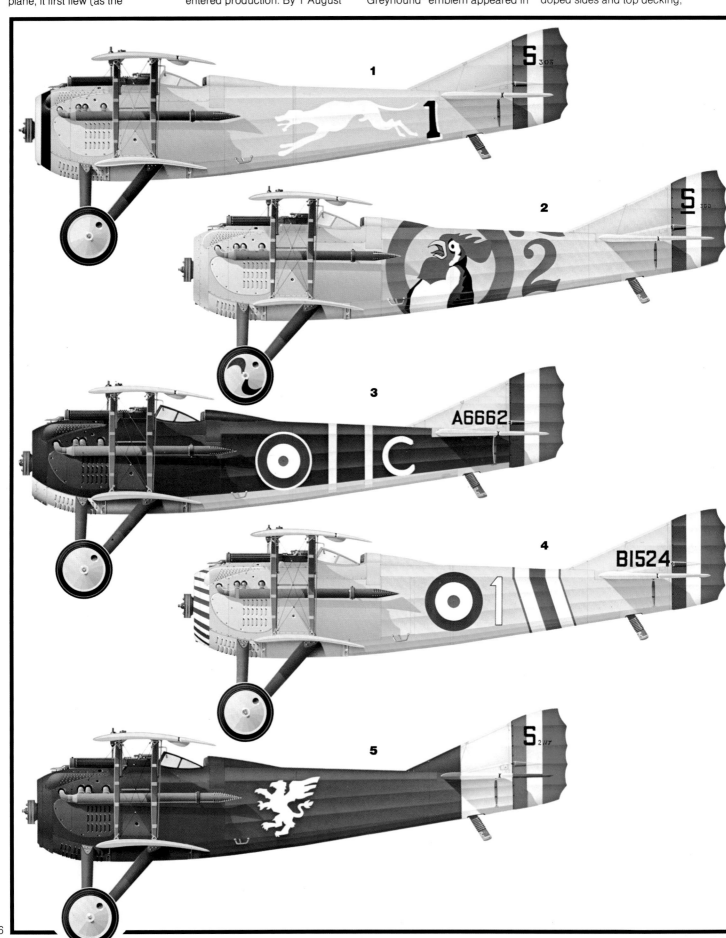

all other surfaces being clear doped. (**4**) Spad 7 (B1524) of No 23 Sqdn, RFC, La Lovie, France, July 1917. Note red-and-white front cowl striping and the aft fuselage bands. (**5**) Spad 7, 91ª Squadriglia, XXIII Gruppo, Italian Aeronautica del Regio Esercito, Centocelle, November 1923. Note olive fuselage, clear-doped wings, and white aft fuselage band incorporating fixed portion of tailplane, the rudder and elevators being striped in national colours. (**6**) Spad 7 of the Commandante of the XXIII Gruppo, Lonate Pozzolo, 1924. The shield on the fuselage contains the emblems of the four component squadriglie. (**7**) Spad 7 of the Czechoslovak Army Air Force, Cheb, Western Bohemia, circa 1920. (**8**) Duks-built Spad 7 of Finnish Ilmailuvoimien (Aviation Force), 1921. (**9**) In 1918, a standard camouflage was adopted for France's Aviation militaire; this comprised irregular segments of chestnut brown, dark green, light grey-green and beige, with yellowish-cream undersurfaces. The starboard side pattern of the Spad 7 is seen here, together with (**9a**) those for the upper surfaces and (**9b**) lower wing. (**10**) An ex-SPA 86 Spad 7 after capture and use at German fighter school at Valenciennes, 1918. Standard French camouflage is retained.

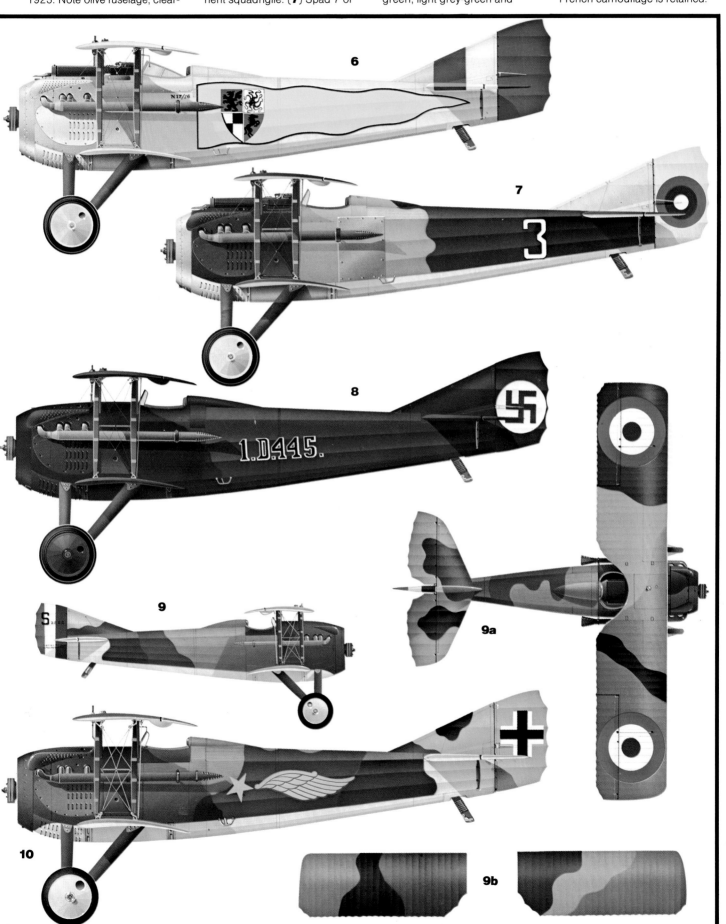

# Albatros D V (1917)

Backbone of the Jastas from late summer 1917 until early summer 1918, the D V and its more robust but externally similar derivative, the D Va, were built in large numbers, 900 of the former and 1,612 of the latter being produced by Albatros and OAW. The D V began to reach the Jastas in May 1917, but suffered structural deficiencies which led to the D Va, the latter providing almost half the total German front line fighter complement in April 1918. The Albatros fighters were elegantly streamlined and were remarkable in that they introduced twin-gun synchronised armament. When delivered, the D V and D Va fuselages were varnished natural wood (birch ply), but varied and frequently flamboyant colour schemes were subsequently applied at unit level. The irregular patches of drab mauvish purple and dark olive green originally applied to the fabric skinning of wings and tail (with pale blue undersides) gave place to a pattern of irregular polygons— widely known as "lozenge" fabric. This consisted of either a four- or a five-colour combination, that applied to the upper surfaces using darker shades than that printed for the undersides. Differing dye batches produced considerable shade variations, and supply sometimes dictated the use of a single type of fabric rather

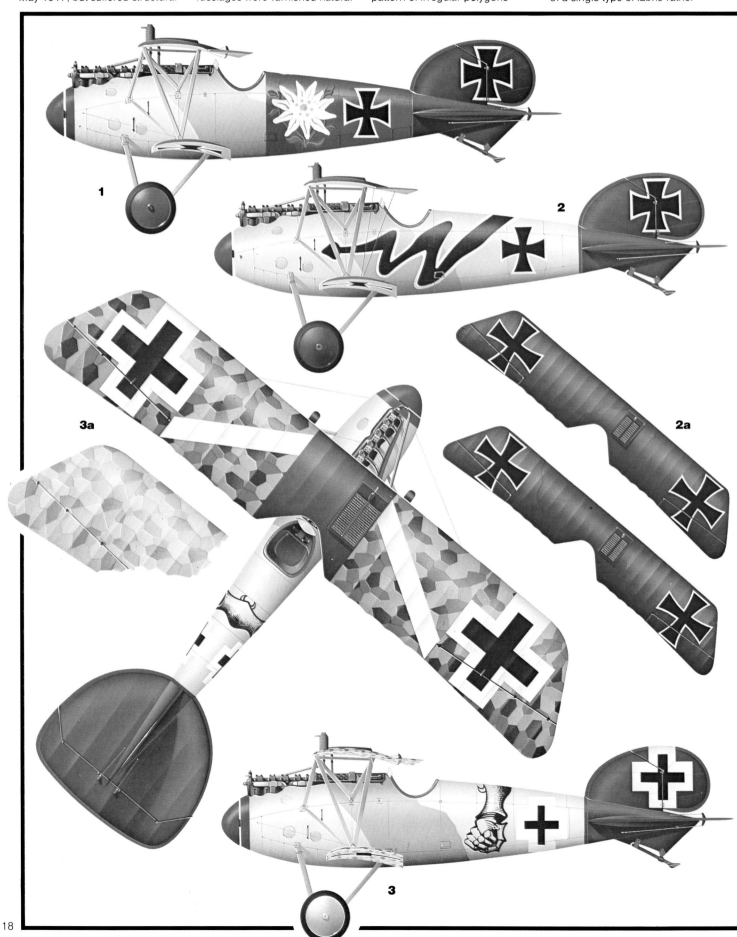

than the usual two. (**1**) D V with Edelweiss emblem flown successively by Obltn Paul Bäumer and Ltn Wilhelm Lehmann, Jastaführer of Jasta 5. (**2**) D Va "Blitz" flown by Ltn Hans J von Hippel, also of Jasta 5, in the spring of 1918, the upper wing surface being divided roughly half and half in mauvish purple and dark

olive green (**2a**), a three-segment arrangement (lower) of these colours being applied to some aircraft. (**3**) D V flown by Hptm Richard Flashar, predecessor of Lehmann as Jastaführer of Jasta 5, sporting "mailed gauntlet" motif, and (**3a**) illustrating lighter "lozenge" pattern applied to wing and tail undersides. Note early

style Balkankreuz. (**4**) D V flown by Ltn Dingel, executive officer of Jasta 15. (**5**) D V flown by Ltn Fritz Rumey of Jasta 5 who was to claim 45 "kills" before losing his life. The Iron Cross gave place to the Balkankreuz on this and other D Vs during early summer 1918. (**6**) D V flown in autumn 1917 by Vzfw Clausnitzer of Jasta 4. Note

the varnished natural plywood fuselage. (**7**) A D V (pilot unidentified) at Boistrancourt, summer 1917. This aircraft sported a similar chevron (in black) on upper wing to that of Flashar's aircraft. (**8**) D V (pilot unidentified) of Jasta 5 with an elaborately decorated fuselage and a stylised Bavarian Lion motif.

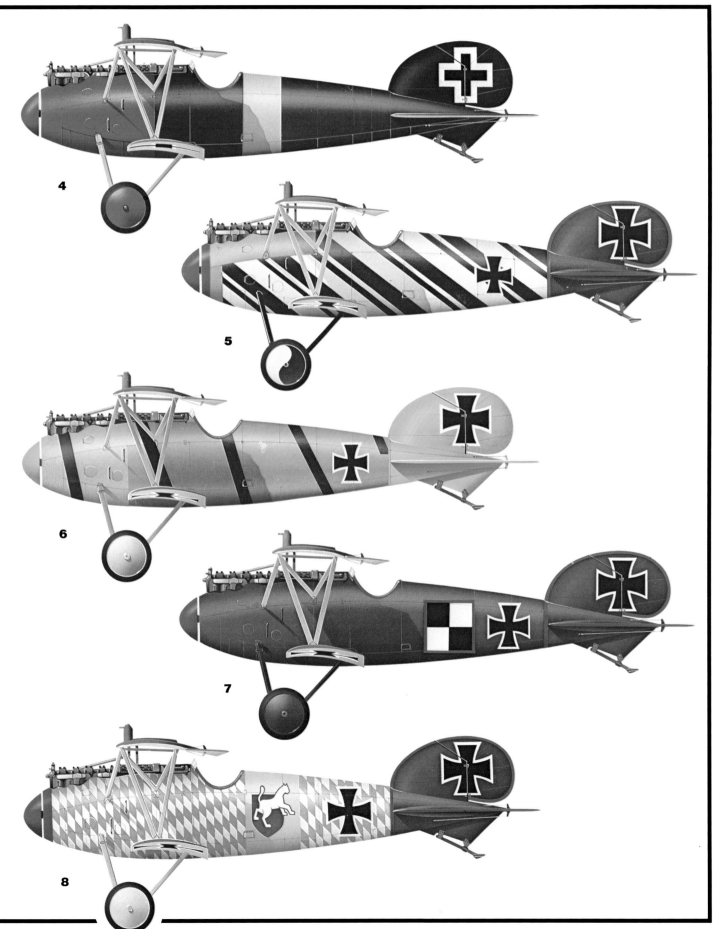

Closely related to the extremely successful Nie.17, the Nie.24 and 27 represented refined perpetuation of the basic Nieuport fighter formula. The Nie.24 was flown early in 1917, entering Aéronautique militaire service in the summer of that year. The climb and level speed performance were good, but the Nie.24 proved unpopular owing to heavy ailerons and poor control in turning. The Nie.27 followed closely behind the Nie.24, soon outnumbering its predecessor in service. Embodying some further aerodynamic improvement, performance was, from several aspects, inferior, neither type emulating the success of its progenitor.

(1) Nie.24 (N5024) of US Air Service construction (training) sqdn, France, early 1918. Note retention of French national insignia. (2) Nie.24 (N3961) of Escadrille N.91, French Aviation militaire, in 1917. (3) Nie.27 (B6768), No 1 Sqdn, Royal Flying Corps, Builleul, France, October 1917. Note retention of French three-tone camouflage. (4) Nie. 27 (B3637) as flown at Royal Aircraft Establishment, Farnborough, March 1919. Note the standard RAF PC10 overall finish. (5) Nie.27 (N5800) of the 81ª squadriglia, Italian Aeronautica Militare, summer 1917. Note the retention of French insignia and three-tone camouflage scheme.

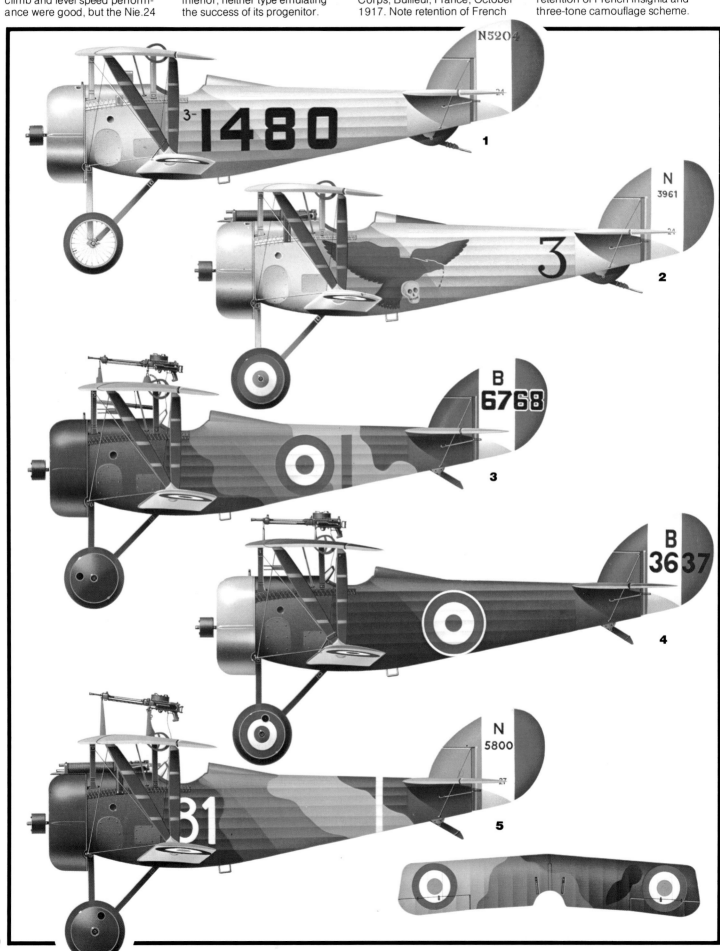

# S.E.5a (1917)

Created at the Royal Aircraft Factory, Farnborough, where the prototype first flew late in 1916, the S.E.5a was to emerge as one of the truly great combat aircraft of WWI. Its initial service career was marred by some structural weakness of the upper mainplane centre section, problems with the power plant reduction gear and troublesome gun synchronisation, but once these difficulties had been overcome, the S.E.5a was to prove itself a formidable and extremely robust fighter, easy to fly and popular with its pilots, and, most important, the equal of the superlative Fokker D VII when the German fighter appeared over the Western Front. First committed to combat in April 1917, the S.E.5a reached its production peak mid-1918 — 1,423 were built during the second quarter of the year — and more than 5,500 were built of which some 2,700 were on RAF strength at time of Armistice. (**1**) S.E.5a (E5808), No 56 Sqdn, RAF, Bethenecourt, France, in January 1919. (**1a**) Head-on and (**1b**) topside views of E5808. (**2**) S.E.5a (D276), No 74 Sqdn, RAF, Teteghem, France, April 1918. This was one of the S.E. 5as flown by "Mick" Mannock. (**3**) S.E.5a (F8010), "C" Flight, 25th Aero Sqdn, US Air Service, Langley Field, circa 1920.

# Fokker Dr I (1917)

The Dr I fighter triplane began to arrive at the front in October 1917, after operational trials with two prototypes in August-September, Ltn Werner Voss of Jasta 10 being shot down in one of these on 23 September. Very sensitive about all axes and most taxing to fly, the Dr I nevertheless possessed superb aerobatic qualities and the more skilled pilots considered it a joy to fly. It was a slow, low-altitude performer, however, and its measure was quickly taken by Allied fighter pilots who refused to engage the Dr I in the classic dogfight with their less agile but more powerful aircraft. A total of 320 Dr Is was built. When delivered by Fokker, the Dr Is were doped dark olive green overall, the method of dyeing the fabric resulting in an uneven, streaked effect. Many flamboyant finishes were applied to the Dr Is once delivered to the Jastas. These were mostly confined to fuselage and tail surfaces, but a number of triplanes were given decorative overall schemes, the best-known examples being the all-vermilion aircraft flown by Manfred Freiherr von Richthofen. Other examples were the all-black Dr I of Ltn Jacobs of Jasta 7 and the Dr I bedecked overall with black-and-white diagonal striping of Ltn Kirchstein of Jasta 6. (**1**) Dr I 213/17 of Ltn Fritz Kempf of Jasta Boelcke in finish of dark

olive green doped fabric as applied by factory. Ltn Kempf adopted the unusual practice of having his name on the top wing (**1a**) and the legend "kennscht mi noch?" (**1b**) painted on the mid wing, this literally translating as "still remember me?" (**1c**) Head-on view of Kempf's aircraft showing white-painted front cowl plate. (**2**) Rear fuselage of a Dr I of Jasta 12 with similar finish to that of Kempf's aircraft. Iron Cross marking may still be seen beneath diagonal striping. (**3**) Dr I of Jasta 26 on which the early-style crosses may again be seen beneath the later Balkankreuz on fuselage and tail. (**4**) The all-black Dr I flown by Ltn Josef Jacobs of Jasta 7, the ninth ranking German "Ace". Note non-standard white fuselage crosses which were repeated on the wings. (**5**) The overall vermilion Dr I 425/17 in which Rittmeister Manfred Freiherr von Richthofen lost his life on 21 April 1918. Note that the old-style Iron Cross may still be seen beneath the white outline of the Balkankreuz. (**6**) A Dr I operated by Jasta 18 and acquired by the French after the Armistice. (**7**) The rear fuselage of a Dr I operated by an unidentified Jasta. The remainder of this aircraft was similar to that flown by Kempf as seen on opposite page with streaked dark olive green dope.

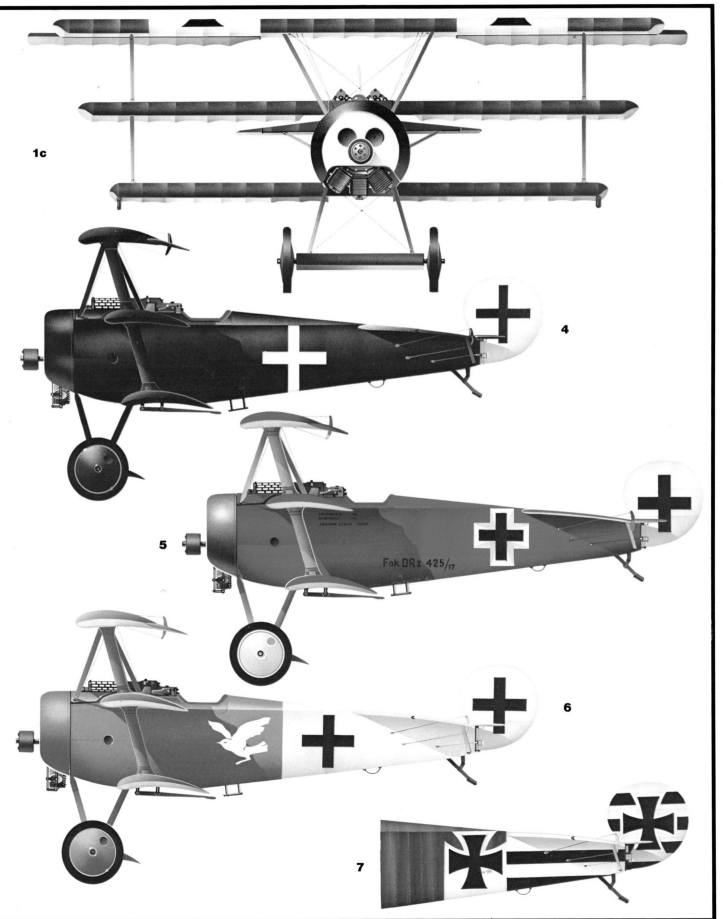

1c

4

5

6

7

# Fokker D VII (1918)

Reputedly capable of translating a mediocre pilot into a good pilot, and undoubtedly the most famous of all German fighters of World War I, the Fokker D VII was a comparatively easy aircraft to fly, extremely responsive and highly controllable at its ceiling, being able to "hang on its prop" and shoot at the enemy when other contemporary fighters would have stalled and spun. It was to soldier on in the inventories of a number of air forces for many years, in some cases into the 'thirties. Such was its awesome reputation that it was singled out for mention in the Armistice Agreement. Winner of the first D-type contest at Adlershof in January 1918, the D VII began to reach the Front in the following April, Fokker manufacturing 861 and Albatros at least as many again. Most first-line Jastas had received at least some of the agile D VIIs before the end of hostilities, operating them with considerable success. Early Fokker-built D VIIs had the same dark olive green fabric applied to their fuselages as was used overall by the Dr I (see pages 22-23), the so-called "lozenge" printed fabric being applied to wings and horizontal tail surfaces only. Albatros-built D VIIs had the "lozenge" fabric overall, as did some later Fokker-built examples. The metal nose

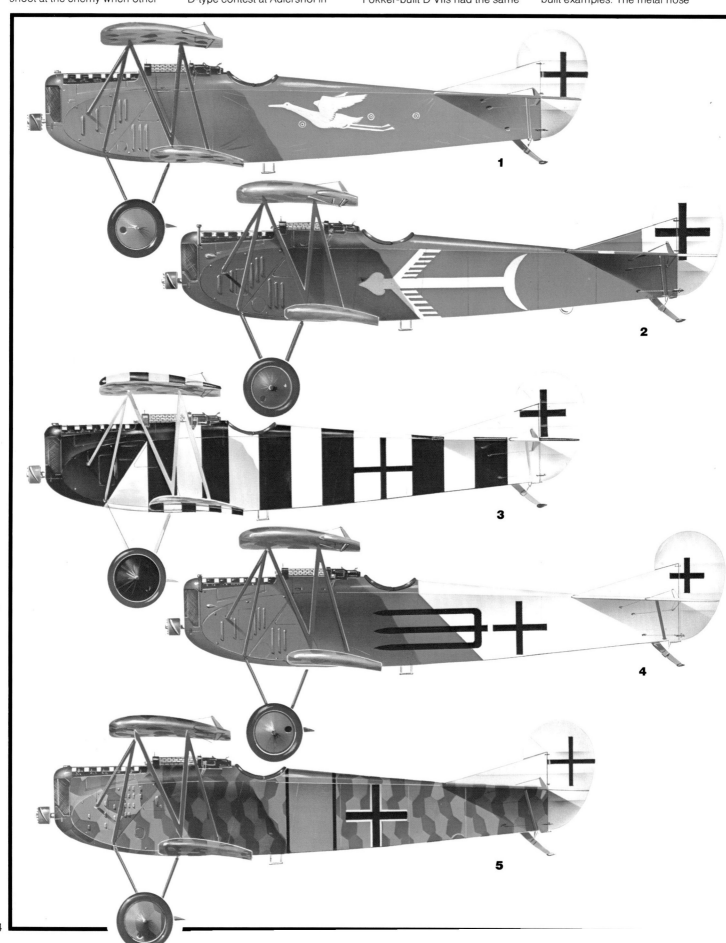

panelling and all strutting were painted dark grey-green or dark olive green before leaving the factory. Many D VIIs were later painted with both unit markings and insignia chosen by the pilot. (**1**) D VII flown by Uffz Piel of Jasta 13, this unit affecting green noses. The wings (as with all examples on this page apart from No 3) were covered by the so-called "lozenge" pre-printed fabric. (**2**) D VII flown by Ltn Veltejns when Jastaführer of Jasta 15. (**3**) D VII flown by Obltn Bruno Loerzer at Sissonne with Jagdgeschwader 3, late summer 1918. (**4**) D VII of Rudolph Stark, Jastaführer of Jasta 35 at Epinoy. (**5**) D VII of Josef Raesch, Jastaführer, Jasta 43. (**6**) MAG-built D VII with all armament removed as trainer with Czechoslovak Army Air Force, mid 'twenties. (**7**) One of 20 D VIIs of Netherlands Marineluchtvaart-dienst, 1919-20. (**8**) Swiss D VII purchased for Fliegertruppe in 1921 via the Allied Control Commission, this type serving until 1934. (**9**) D VII 6693/18 of the Belgian Aviation Militaire at Bruxelles-Evere, July 1919. Note "Le Chardon" emblem and retention of wartime German "lozenge"-type fabric. (**10**) D VII 6162/18 purchased by Victor Simonet in 1920, and the first aircraft to be listed on Belgian civil register. Note rudder striping.

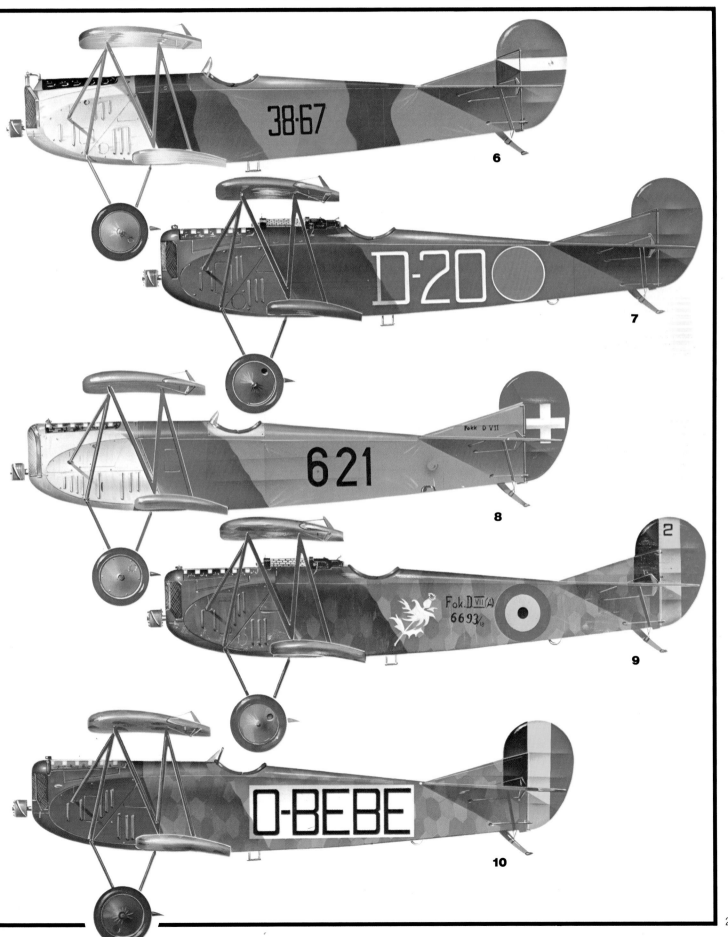

# Breguet Bre 19 (1924)

A sturdy, fabric-covered metal biplane, possessing what was at times to be described as a most alarmingly flexible structure, the Bre 19 was intended as a replacement for the outstandingly successful Bre 14 of World War I in the light bombing and recce roles. In the event, it was to eclipse its sire in almost every respect and be built in what were for its day and age phenomenal quantities. It was to establish innumerable records, be adopted by almost a score of air forces and become the world's best-known aircraft of its generation. The prototype Bre 19 was first flown in March 1922, deliveries to France's Aviation Militaire beginning in the autumn of 1924, by which time licence manufacture was also being undertaken by Farman and Amiot, despite which, the parent company's Bre 19 output was at times to peak at five daily, more than 1,800 Bre 19s leaving French factories in the first two-and-a-half years of production. There were two main versions, the Bre 19 A2 recce model and the Bre 19 B2 light bomber, licence production taking place in Belgium, Spain and Yugoslavia, a wide variety of engines being fitted. Before the production of the Bre 19 was phased out in 1932 by the parent company, several improved models, such as the Bre 19.7 and 19.8, appeared. Remarkably,

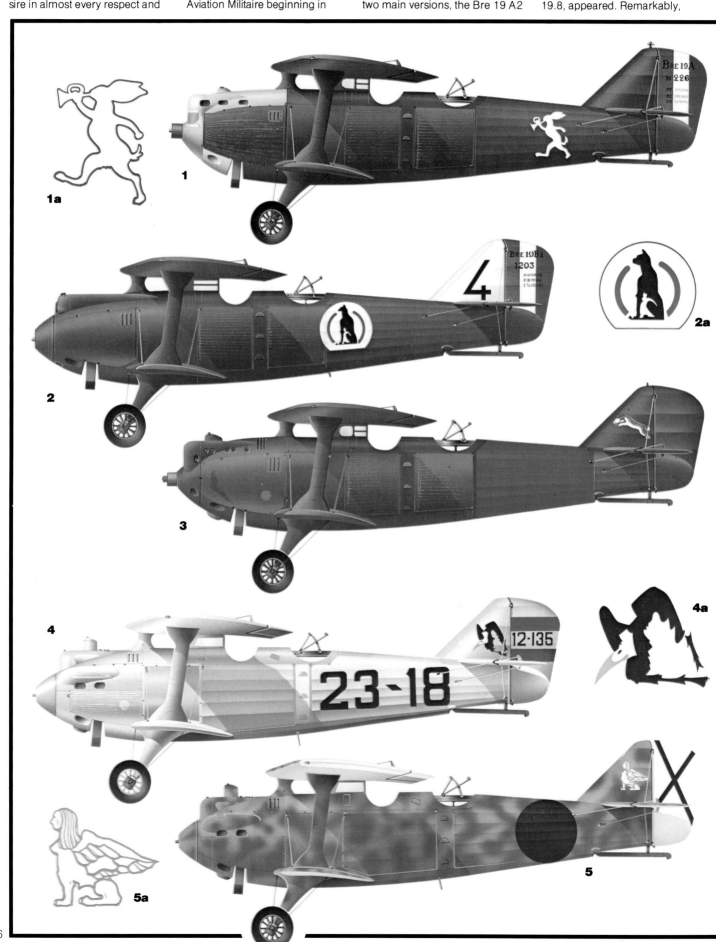

some Bre 19 aircraft survived to see service in WWII, notably with Croatia. (**1**) Bre 19 A2 (No 226) of the 2ᵉ Escadrille, 51ᵉ Escadre of the Aviation Militaire at Tours, early 1932. (**1a**) Emblem of the 2ᵉ Escadrille (ex-Sal 39). (**2**) Bre 19 B2 (No 1203) of 5ᵉ Escadrille, 11ᵉ Régiment, Metz-Frescaty, 1928, and (**2a**) emblem of the 5ᵉ Escadrille (ex-Bre 29). (**3**) CASA-built Bre 19 operated by Spanish Republican night flying school at El Carmoli, circa 1938. (**4**) CASA-built Bre-19 of Grupo Núm 23 of the Spanish Aviación Militar at Logroño, circa 1935, and (**4a**) the Grupo emblem. (**5**) CASA-built Bre 19 serving circa 1938 with a Spanish Nationalist obser-ver's school, and (**5a**) tail emblem retained from pre-Civil War Grupo. (**6**) A Yugoslav-built Bre 19.8 serving with Croatian Air Force on anti-partisan operations, circa 1943. (**7**) A Bre 19 A2 (No 1330) serving with the Yugoslav Air Force, circa 1935. (**8**) Bre 19.7 of the Turkish Air Force, 1934-35. (**9**) Bre 19 GR (Grand Raid = Large Endurance) flown by Cmdt Girier and Cmdt Weiss for a world speed record over a 5000km distance, 25 May 1929. (**10**) The Bre 19 GR "Point d'Interrogation" (Question Mark) in the form in which it was flown from Paris to New York, 1-3 September 1930. Note the "Stork" emblem.

# Hawker Fury (1931)

The Fury single-seat fighter set new standards in elegance when it entered service in May 1931 with No 43 Sqdn as the RAF's first frontline aircraft capable of a level speed in excess of 200mph (124km/h). Its delicacy of contour belied its sturdiness; its climb and dive characteristics were particularly good and it allegedly set new standards in control sensitivity for fighters of its generation. The prototype Fury — originally named Hornet by its manufacturer — first flew in March 1929, and 118 of the initial model for the RAF were delivered, these becoming known as Fury Is when a more powerful and refined version made its debut as the Fury II, the RAF receiving 112 of the later model. Small numbers were exported to Iran, Portugal, South Africa, Spain and Yugoslavia, the last two mentioned countries obtaining production licences, although, in the event, only Yugoslavia actually built Furies, the delivery of 50 commencing in August 1937. Their obsolescence notwithstanding, these Furies were flown against the Luftwaffe when Yugoslavia was invaded by the Wehrmacht in 1941. South African Furies also saw combat in 1940-41, flying against the Regia Aeronautica in East Africa. During 1938, all Furies remaining on RAF charge were hurriedly

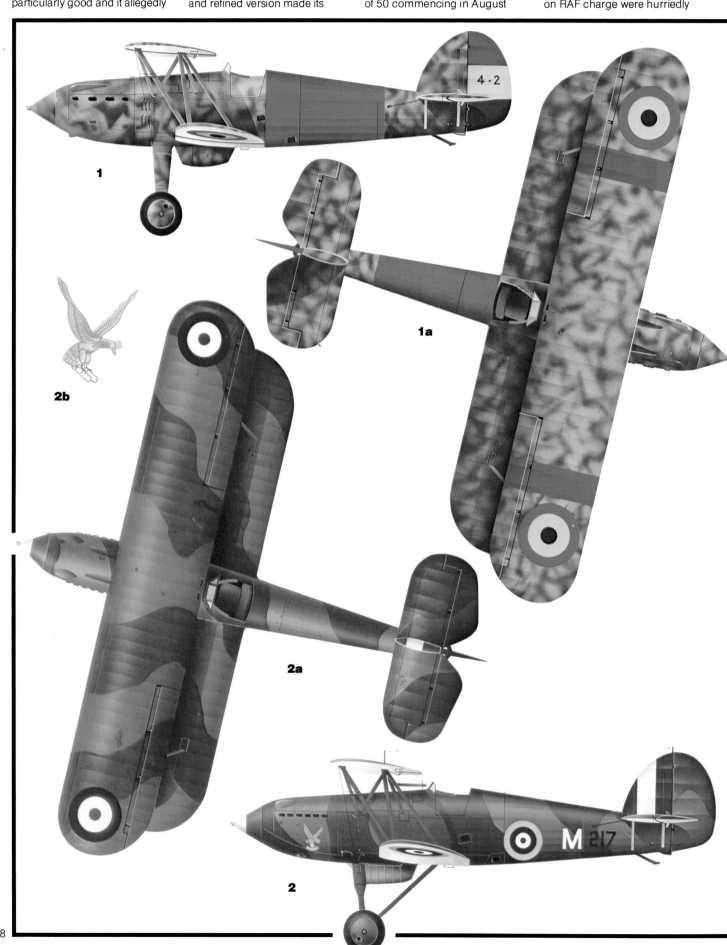

camouflaged with a disruptive pattern of dark green and dark earth over upper surfaces, the undersides being half black and half white (in a few cases the undersides of fuselage and tail-plane remained silver), but by the time WWII commenced, the Fury had all but disappeared from the RAF. (1) The second of three Spanish Furies in Republican colours, this aircraft having initially flown operationally painted aluminium overall with red wing bands and large red panels on the fuselage. (1a) Top side plan view of same aircraft. (2) Fury I of No 43 Sqdn, SAAF, 1942, with (2a) upper surfaces of same aircraft and (2b) emblem of No 3 Sqdn, SAAF. (3) Fury I (K5673) of No 1(F) Sqdn, at RAF Tangmere 1936-37, and (3a) the emblem of No 1 Sqdn. (4) One of three Furies of the Portuguese Arma da Aeronautica, 1935. Note "greyhound" unit emblem. (5) Fury II of No 43 Sqdn, RAF, 1938, and (5a) emblem of No 43 Sqdn, RAF. (6) Zmaj-built Fury of 35th Group, 5th Fighter Regiment, Royal Yugoslav Air Force, Kraljevo, April 1941. This aircraft was subsequently captured at Niksic by Italian forces. (7) A Fury captured by the Spanish Nationalists after having been rebuilt by Hispano-Suiza, and (7a) detail of the wing markings.

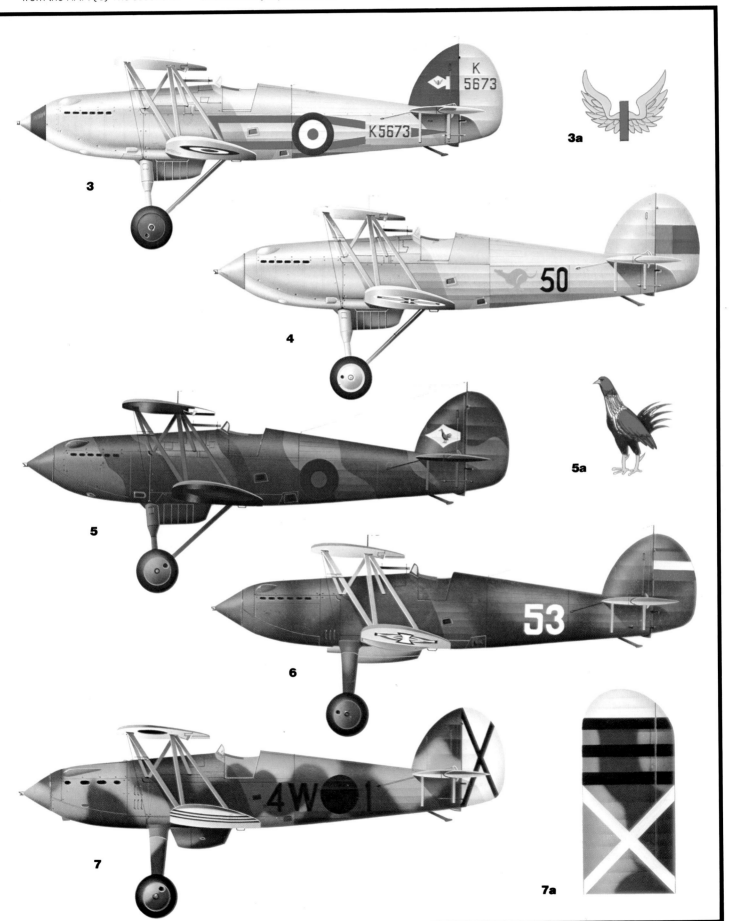

# Junkers Ju 52/3m (1933)

If any transport aircraft may lay claim to immortality then Germany's lusty, all-metal Ju 52/3m must surely be so entitled. With its heavily-braced undercarriage, between the rear legs of which an immense "dustbin" could be suspended to house bomb-aimer/gunner for the auxiliary bombing role, corrugated skinning and complex trailing flappery of the Junkers "double-wing" type, this angular trimotor had, as was to be expected, a sedate performance. It was exceptionally docile, very stable and could be flown virtually hands-off. But, if slow and noisy, it was supremely reliable, and the unpretentious and manifestly obsolescent Ju 52/3m was to play a greater role in shaping the course of World War II than was any first-line combat aircraft! The first Ju 52/3m was flown in April 1931, the type entering service with the still-clandestine Luftwaffe in 1933, and several hundred had been built by 1939, when really large-scale production began, a further 3,255 then being built until mid-1944. Viewed by the Luftwaffe with affection as "Tante Ju", the Ju 52/3m was to be dubbed "Iron Annie" by the Allies of WWII. (1) Ju 52/3m g4e (1Z+AF) of Stab IV/KGzbV 1 (Kampfgeschwader zur besonderen Verwendung, or Battle Group for Special Duties) which participated in Balkan/Cretan

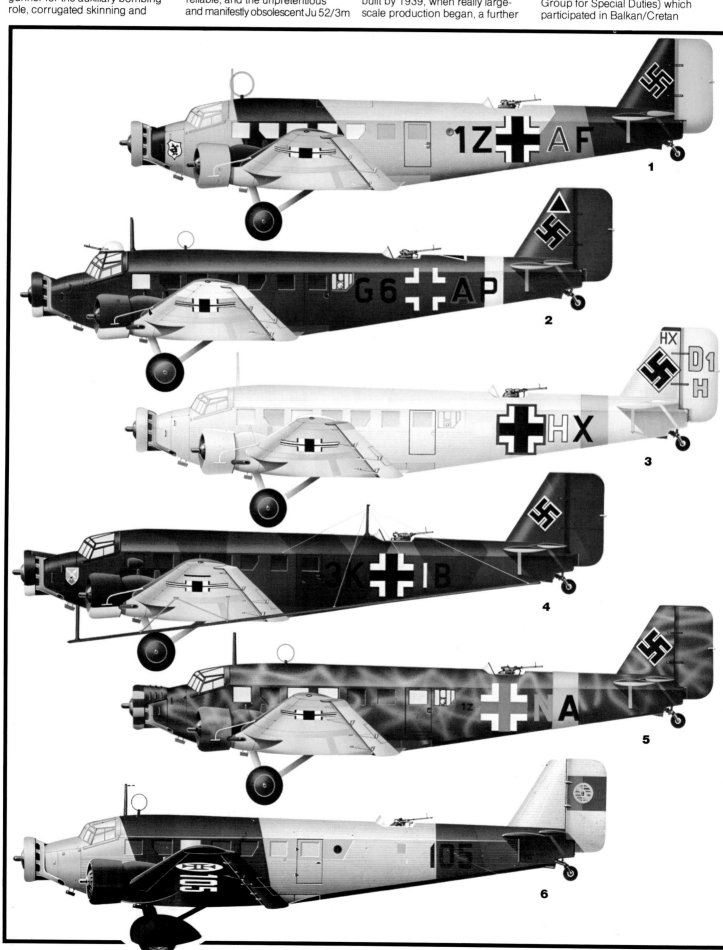

campaigns of April–May 1941. Note yellow areas signifying theatre of operations. (**1a**) Top planview of 1Z+AF. (**2**) Ju 52/3m g6e (G6+AP) of 2./KGrzbV 102 in the Mediterranean area under KGzbV "N" (Naples), 1942. (**3**) Ju 52/3m g6e (G6+AP) of IV/KGzbV 1 (1Z+HX) on Stalingrad Front, winter 1942-43. Note D1H tactical coding on rudder and white water-soluble paint for temporary winter finish on upper surfaces. (**4**) Ju 52/3m g6e (MS) (3K+IB) minesweeper of Stab/Minensuchgruppe, Malmi, Gulf of Finland, winter 1943-44. (**5**) Ju 52/3m g7e (1Z+NA) of Stab IV/Transportgeschwader 1 on the Courland Front, winter 1944-45. (**6**) Ju 52/3m g3e (105), Grupo de Bombardeamento Nocturno of the Portuguese Arma da Aeronáutica, circa 1938. (**7**) Ju 52/3m g4e (22·62) "Maria Magdalena" of Escuadrilla 2-E-22 "Las tres Marias", Spain, summer 1937. (**8**) Ju 52/3m g3e (22·76) of the Kampfgruppe 88, Legion Condor, Spain, late 1936. (**9**) Ju 52/3m g4e (22·59) of Grupo de Bombardeo Nocturno 1-G-22, Nationalist Arma de Aviación, spring 1938. (**10**) Ju 52/3m g4e (22·99) of the Grupo de Bombardeo Nocturno 2-G-22 of the 1ª Escuadra (1ª Brigada Hispana), Nationalist Arma de Aviación, 1938. (**10a**) Top planview of 22·99 showing German-style splinter-type segmented camouflage and St Andrew's Cross wing markings.

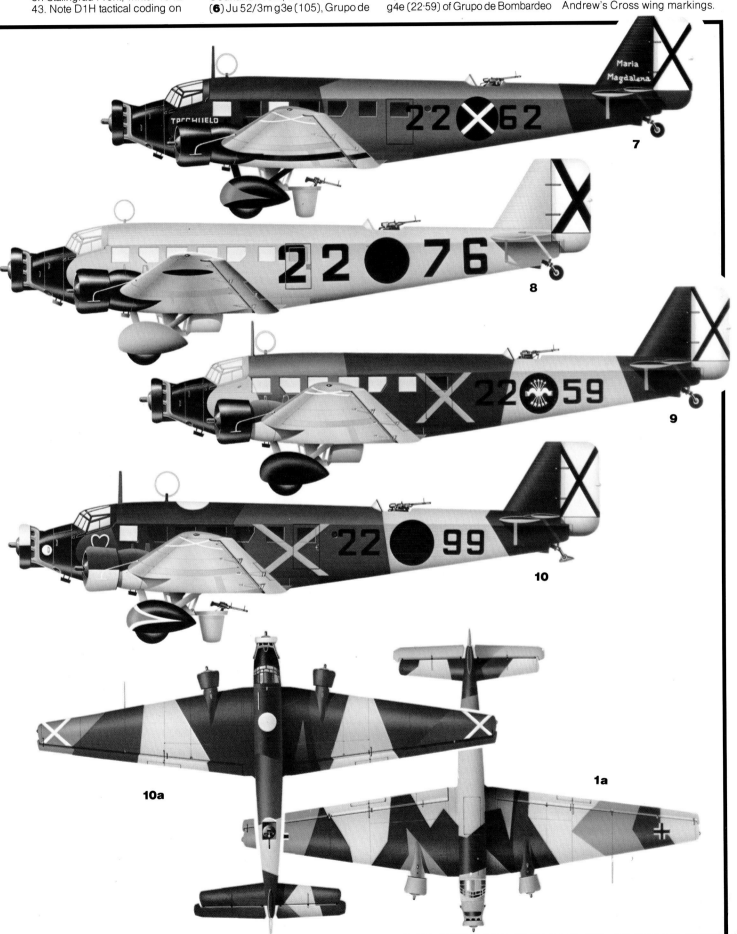

# Grumman G-5 (GE-23) (1933)

The first shipboard aircraft to combine fully-enclosed cockpits and a retractable undercarriage, the G-5 was first in a long line of Grumman carrier-based fighters operated by the US Navy to this day. Considered epoch-marking at the time of its début, when the prototype of this two-seater was found capable of out-

flying and out-performing the smaller and lighter contemporary single-seat shipboard fighters, the G-5 combined good man-euvrability, docile handling, excellent dive characteristics and exceptional sturdiness. The prototype (XFF-1) flew on 29 December 1931, and the delivery of 27 FF-1 fighters to the US

Navy began in April 1933, these being followed by a total of 33 SF-1 scouts a year later, but as a result of changes in US Navy tactical thinking, both FF-1 and SF-1 had been withdrawn from Fleet service by the end of 1936. Meanwhile, Grumman had been promoting a land-based version for export. This, the GE-23, had

features of both the FF-1 and SF-1, and was intended for the combined fighter and assault roles. Spanish Republican interest prompted arrangements for licence assembly by Canadian Car & Foundry, Grumman pro-ducing the fuselages and Brewster the wings and tail surfaces. The initial Spanish

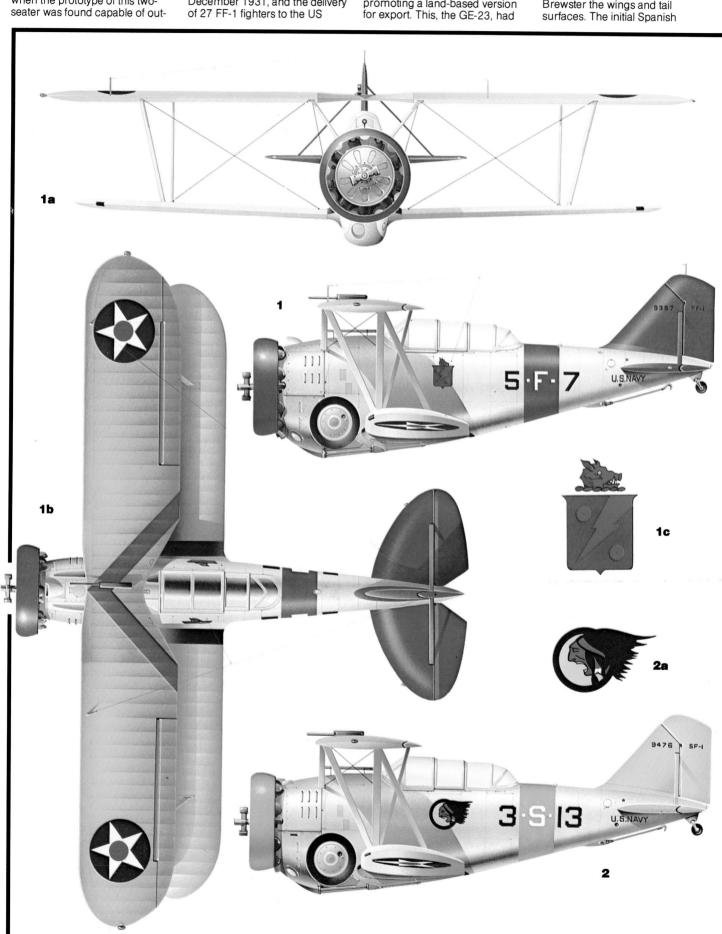

order called for 40 GE-23s, a follow-on contract calling for a further 10. In the event, only 34 were delivered to Spain, the GE-23 being named Delfin (Dolphin) in Republican service. Of the GE-23s built against Spanish contracts and not delivered, 16 were taken on charge by the RCAF and were flown as the Goblin. (**1**) FF-1 (BuAer No 9357) of the 3rd Section Leader of VF-5B "Red Rippers" aboard USS *Lexington* (indicated by blue tail surfaces) 1934-35, and (**1a**) head-on and (**1b**) topside planview of same aircraft. (**1c**) The "Boar's Head" and shield of VF-5B. (**2**) SF-1 (BuAer No 9476) of 5th Section Leader of VS-3B aboard the USS *Lexington,* 1935, and (**2a**) the "Indian Head" emblem of Scouting Three. (**3**) GE-23 Goblin (344) of No 118(F) Sqdn, RCAF, Dartmouth, Nova Scotia, 1941, and (**3a**) topside and (**3b**) underside planviews of Goblin No 344. (**4**) GE-23 supplied to the Nicaraguan government in 1938. (**5**) GE-23 Delfin of the 2ª Escuadrilla of Spanish Republican Grupo Núm 28 operating from Cardedeu-Le Garriga airfield, early summer 1938. (**5a**) Half-and-half planview of same aircraft. (**6**) GE-23 Delfin of 1ª Escuadrilla of Grupo Núm 28 and (**6a**) the "Indian Head" emblem employed by 1ª Esc.

# PZL P.11/P.24 (1933)

For a brief period in the mid-'thirties, Zygmunt Pulawski of the State-controlled P.Z.L. carried Poland to the forefront of international fighter development with his gull-winged P.11. Flown as a prototype in August 1931, it first entered service (as the P.11b) with Rumania, priority being given to export, reaching Polish service (as the P.11a) in autumn 1934. Licence manufacture took place in Rumania (P.11f), the definitive Polish model being the P.11c, and despite obsolescence it equipped the Polish fighter force (12 squadrons with 125 aircraft) when Germany invaded in September 1939. The P.24 was an export equivalent of the P.11c supplied to Greece, Bulgaria, (and licence-built by) Turkey and Rumania. As delivered from the factory, the P.11c was finished in dark olive green with pale blue wing and tailplane undersurfaces. Immediately before and during first days of WWII, a camouflage of dark forest green, meadow green and yellow-gold was applied. Rumanian P.11s and P.24s, and Bulgarian P.24s used similar schemes (the former a lighter shade of olive and the latter a dark green). (**1**) P.11b of the Rumanian Fighter Flotilla. Pipera-Bucuresti, 1935-36. (**2**) P.11c (8.39) of No 113 Sqdn, IVth Dyon of 1st Air Regi-

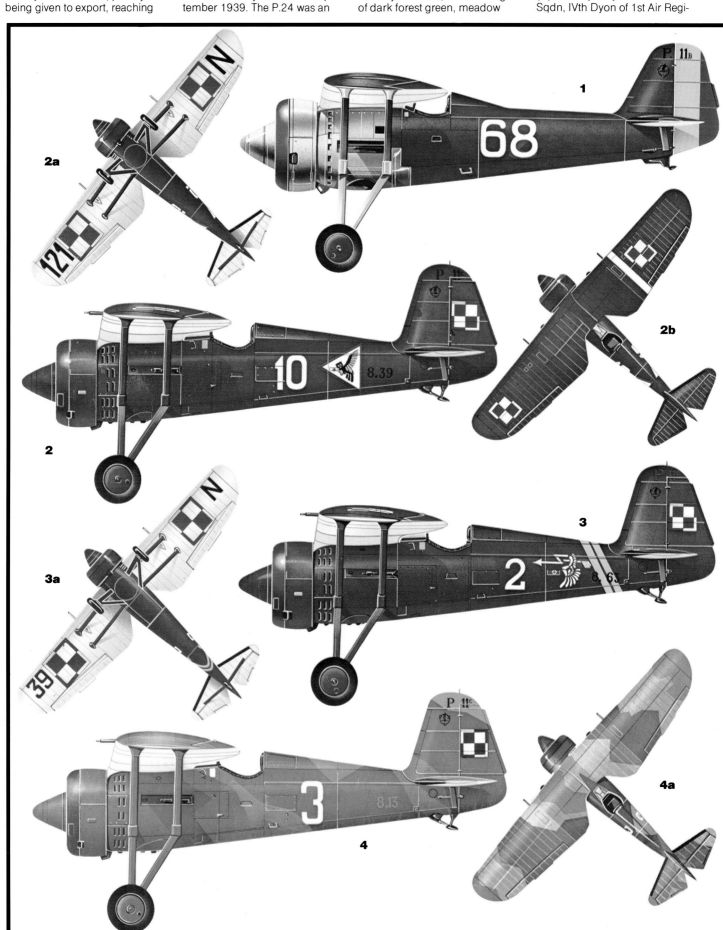

ment, Warsaw-Okecie.
(**2a**) Underside and (**2b**) upper surfaces of same aircraft, the latter showing white stripe on starboard wing signifying squadron CO's aircraft. (**2c**) The "Owl" emblem of No 113 Sqdn. (**3**) P.11c (8.63) of No 121 Sqdn, IIIrd Dyon of 2nd Air Regiment, Krakow, 1938, the diagonal rear

fuselage striping signifying squadron CO's aircraft.
(**3a**) Underside of P.11c (8.63), and (**3b**) P.Z.L. emblem appearing on tail and (**3c**) No 121 Sqdn emblem. (**4**) P.11c (8.13) in three-colour camouflage applied August-September of 1939.
(**4a**) Upper surfaces of same aircraft. (**5**) P.11f of one of the

three fighter flotillas of the Rumanian Royal Air Forces, 1937-38, this being the last of 70 licence-built aircraft. (**6**) P.24F (Delta 129) of the 22nd Fighter Sqdn, Royal Hellenic Air Force, Larissa, 1941, and (**6a**) upper surfaces of same aircraft.
(**7**) P.24C of Turkish Air Force's 4th Regiment, Kütahya, 1939.

Note scrap view of wingtip underside (**7a**). (**8**) P.24F of 1st Orliek Royal Bulgarian Air Force, Sofia/Bojourishté, late 1939.
(**8a**) Underside view of same aircraft and (**8c**) Bulgarian national insignia employed until October 1940, with enlarged detail of the rampant lion of the Bulgarian Royal House in centre of insignia.

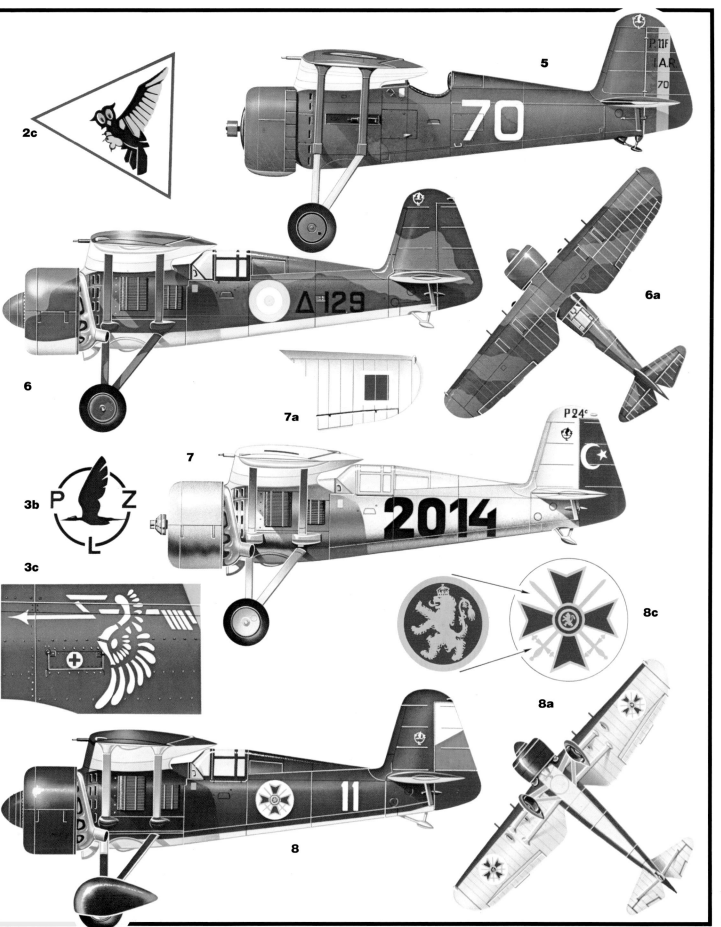

# Polikarpov I-15/I-15bis (1934)

Although thoroughly orthodox, the I-15, designed by a team led by Nikolai Polikarpov, raised Soviet fighter development to world standard. Flown in October 1933, the I-15 began to enter V-VS service late in 1934, proving itself a sturdy, agile and well-armed fighter. Committed to the Republican cause over Spain, it

was master of the He 51 (see pages 42-43), and although slower than the CR.32 (see pages 38-39) in level and dive speeds, it could out-turn and out-climb the Italian fighter. The I-15bis (alias I-152) was an extensively redesigned derivative in which the gulled wing gave place to a more orthodox cabane. This saw

service from mid-1937, making a brief appearance in Spanish skies and seeing much combat over China. It was being phased out of V-VS service when the Wehrmacht invaded the Soviet Union. I-15 and I-15bis fighters ex-factory had olive green upper and pale blue undersurfaces, but irregular patches of earth brown

were often applied at unit level early in the German-Soviet conflict, white distemper being applied as a winter camouflage. (**1**) An I-15 of an unidentified V-VS regiment in standard mid-'thirties finish with insignia in the style of the period. (**2**) I-15 flown by the CO of the 1ª Escuadrilla de Chatos (circa 1937) of the Spanish

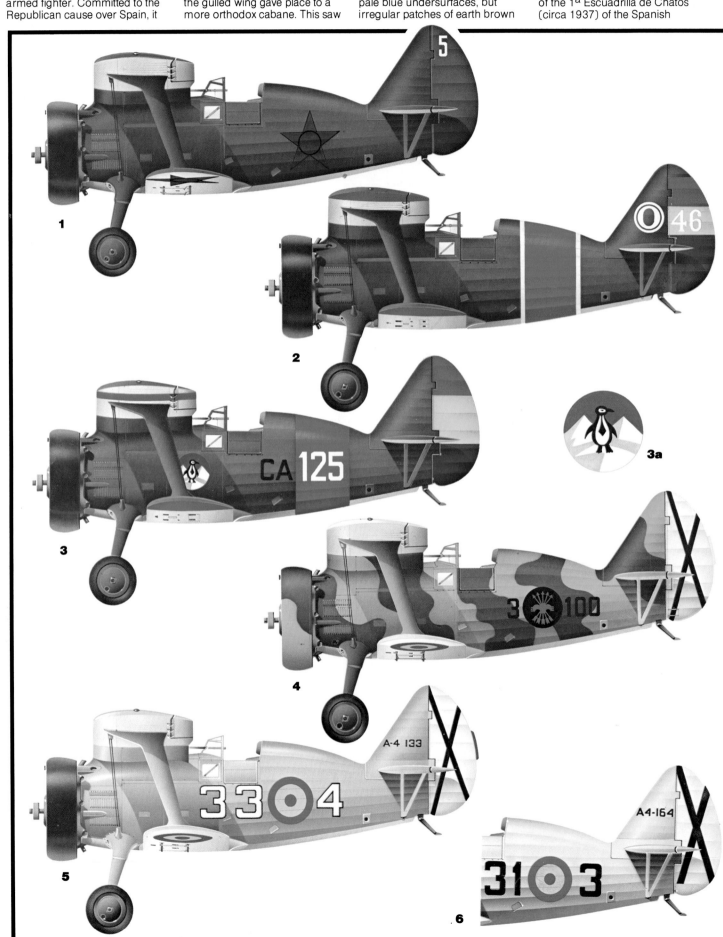

Republican Grupo de Caza núm 26. (**3**) I-15 of the 2ª Escuadrilla de Chatos at Cartagena, January 1939, and (**3a**) the "penguin" emblem of the Escuadrilla. (**4**) I-15 serving with Spain's Ejército del Aire (circa mid-'forties), possibly with the Escuela de Caza. Note "yoke-and-arrows" emblem. (**5**) I-15 of Spanish

Regimiento de Asalto 33, Valladolid-Villanubla, early 'forties. (**6**) Rear fuselage of I-15 assigned to Regimiento de Asalto 31 with non-standard overall silver dope finish and standard black cowl ring. (**7**) I-15bis of Air Force of Chinese Central Government in Nanking area, early 1938. (**8**) One of five I-15bis fighters obtained by

Finland during "Winter War" seen in finish and markings that were standardised for "Continuation War". (**9**) An I-15bis of Spanish Republican Fuerzas Aéreas at Villajuiga, January 1939. (**10**) I-15bis of Grupo 24, Regimiento de Caza Núm 23 of the Spanish Ejército del Aire at Reus, early 'forties. (**11**) I-15bis of the

Leningrad VO, V-VS, winter 1939-40, captured and delivered to the Finnish LLv 29 (as VH-10 and successively VH-1 and IH-1) in February 1940. (**12**) Rear fuselage of I-15bis (with similar overall finish) of the 70 IAP of V-VS during the "Nomonhan Incident" on the Manchkuoan-Mongolian border in the summer of 1939.

# Fiat CR.32 (1934)

With the CR.32, the fighting biplane line created by Celestino Rosatelli reached its apex. The interplane strutting arranged in the form of Warren trusses that had become virtually a hallmark of Rosatelli fighters and had first been used by the S.V.A. scout of 1917, was retained for the CR.32 which first flew on 28 April 1933. First entering Regia Aeronautica service in the summer of 1934, the CR.32 soon demonstrated that it possessed few peers in agility. It offered superlative handling, provided a good platform for its long-ranging 12,7mm guns and was outstandingly robust, being a thoroughly proven warplane when it joined combat over Spain in August 1936, as the vanguard of the Aviación de el Tercio that was contributed by Italy to the Nationalist cause. For five years the CR.32 was to provide the mainstay of the Regia Aeronautica fighter element, and production was to continue until May 1939, 1,211 being delivered of which 405 were sent to Spain. Four versions were built, the CR.32bis having an improved engine and a heavier armament, the CR.32ter and quater having improved gun sights and instrumentation, but reverting to original armament. (1) CR.32 (M.M.2830) of the 155ª squadriglia, 3º Gruppo, 6º Stormo "Diavoli Rossi" (Red Devils) at

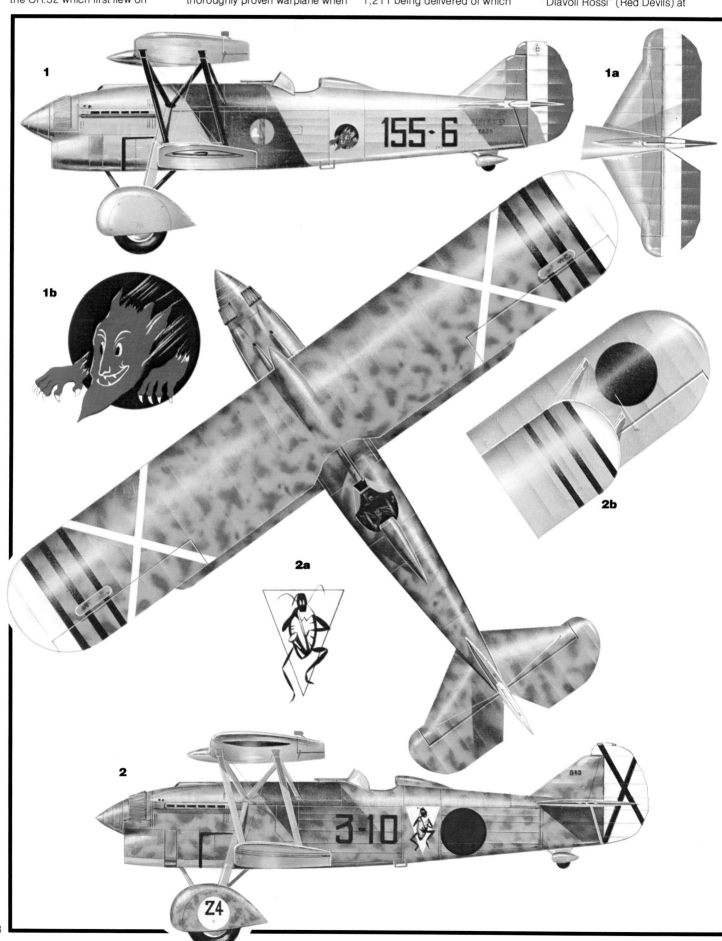

Campoformidao, Udine, early 1936. (**1a**) Tail detail showing national tricolour on horizontal surfaces (above and below), and (**1b**) the "Diavolo Rosso" emblem. (**2**) CR.32 of XVI Gruppo "La cucaracha" of Italian Aviación de el Tercio, Spain, 1937, this aircraft being flown by Sgt Tarantella. (**2a**) "La cucaracha" emblem of XVI Gruppo and topside planview of same CR.32. Note basic terracotta upper surface finish with olive green dapple. (**2b**) Detail of wing under-surfaces. (**3**) CR.32 of X Gruppo "Baleari" (101ª squadriglia), Spain, 1937, in three-segment upper surface disruptive scheme. (**4**) CR.32 (M.M.2856) of 85ª squadriglia, XVIII Gruppo, 3º Stormo, Bresso, Milan, spring 1936, and coat of arms of the House of Savoy, normally super-imposed on rudder striping, and (**4a**) emblem of XVIII Gruppo. (**5**) CR.32ter of 360ª squadriglia, 52º Stormo, Pontedera, Pisa, mid-1939. Note temperate zone olive green finish with darker green dapple. (**6**) CR.32quater (M.M. 4666) of 160ª squadriglia, 12º Gruppo, 50º Stormo, Tobruk, October 1940, with emblem of 50º Stormo, the legend reading "Mi Fanno un Baffo" (They bluff with me). (**6a**) Fasces emblem. (**7**) CR.32 of 1./1 Sqdn, 1./1 Hungarian Fighter Group at Börgönd, Veszprém, summer 1939, and emblem of the 1./1 Sqdn.

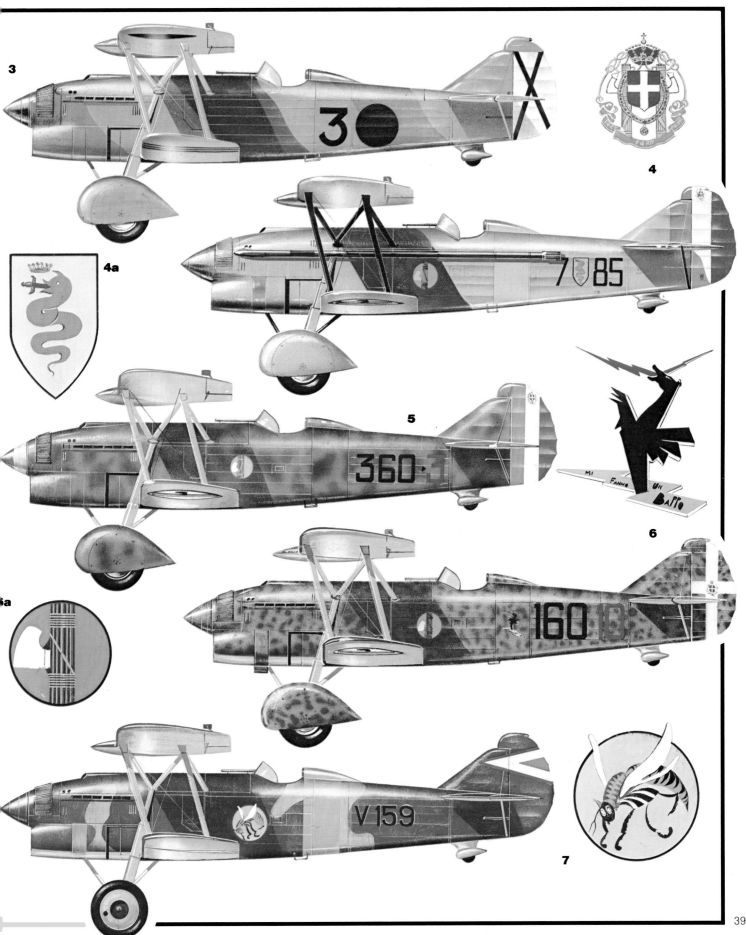

# Boeing P-26 (1934)

With its multiplicity of bracing wires, fixed undercarriage and open cockpit mated with metal construction and monoplane configuration, the P-26 represented a transitory stage in fighter evolution which was obsolescent within a year or so of service debut. First flown in prototype form on 20 March 1932, it might be said to have represented both vanguard and rearguard in the development of fighters when delivery of 136 aircraft of this type commenced in January 1934. Destined to become affectionately and unofficially known as the "Peashooter", the P-26 was responsive, manoeuvrable and sturdy, but suffered a very high landing speed for its day and a troublesome sideways rolling motion on landing whenever a wheel touched uneven ground. (1) P-26A of 94th Pursuit Sqdn, 1st Pursuit Group, Selfridge Field, Mich, 1937. Note that all aircraft of this Group featured a diagonal fuselage band painted in the squadron colour with unit emblem superimposed. (1a) "Sioux Indian Head" emblem of 94th Pursuit Sqdn. (2) P-26A (FAG 0816 ex-AAC 33-135) of the Escuadrón de Caza, Fuerza Aérea de Guatemalteca, Campo de la Aurora, Guatemala City, late 'forties. (2a) Upper surfaces of FAG 0816. (3) P-26A of 19th Pursuit Sqdn, 18th Pursuit Group,

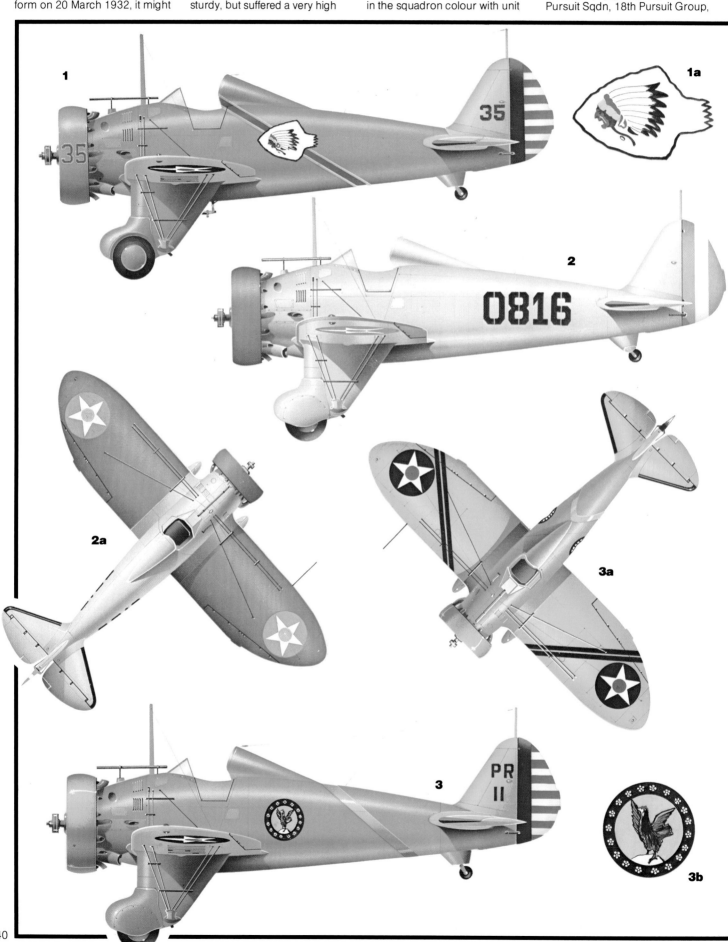

Wheeler Field, Hawaii, in 1939. Note that diagonal fuselage stripe indicated CO of flight and PR11 tail designator signified (P=) Pursuit (R=) 18th Group (11=) 11th aircraft in Group. (**3a**) Upper surfaces of PR11. (**3b**) Emblem of the 19th Pursuit Sqdn. (**4**) P-26A of 95th Pursuit Sqdn. Note that squadron number appeared on the fuselage underside. Olive drab fuselage preceded standardisation on blue. (**4a**) Emblem of 95th Pursuit Sqdn. (**5**) P-26A of CO, 20th Pursuit Group, Barksdale Field, Louisiana, 1936. Note cowl striping in Group colours (red, yellow and blue) and the Group emblem superimposed on blue lozenge.

(**5a**) The emblem of 20th Pursuit Group. (**6**) P-26A included in the inventory of 18th Pursuit Group, Wheeler Field, Hawaii, December 1941. The Group had re-equipped with P-40Bs, but P-26As remained as training and hack aircraft. (**7**) P-26A of 34th Pursuit Sqdn, 17th Pursuit Group, involved in disruptive paint scheme evaluat-ion in 1935. Note reddish-pink tone (referred to as Desert Sand) had randomly-applied areas of olive drab and neutral grey superimposed. (**8** and **8a**) P-26A of 34th Pursuit Sqdn, 17th Pursuit Group, March Field, Calif, 1934. Note aircraft and squadron numbers on the topside and under-side of fuselage, respectively.

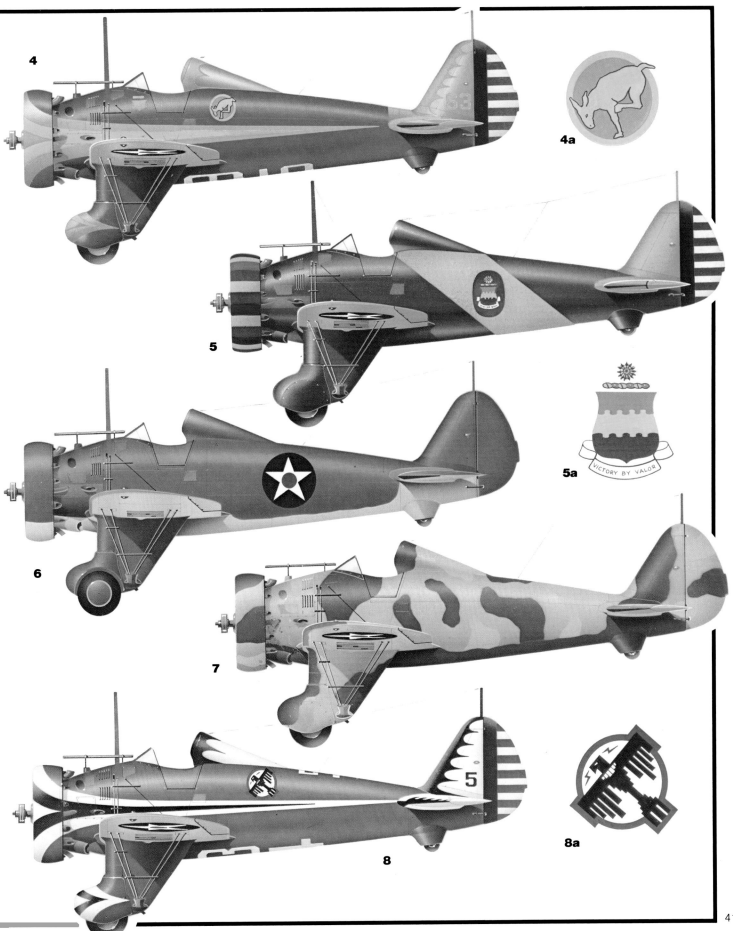

# Heinkel He 51 (1935)

The He 51 was the first single-seat fighter to be built in large numbers for the fledgeling Luftwaffe, and when sent to Spain in the summer of 1936 became the first German fighter to fire its guns in anger since World War I. Flown as a prototype in 1933, the He 51 entered service during the summer of 1935, most aircraft of this type being painted light grey or RLM grey overall, the latter subsequently being standardised. The Geschwader colour was usually used to decorate the engine cowling and, sometimes, the upper fuselage decking (eg, red for JG 132, blue for JG 233, etc). Some He 51s participating in the Spanish Civil War were painted with an irregular pattern of light grey, green and dark brown camouflage applied over all upper surfaces and adopted pale blue for the undersides. The He 51 was finally withdrawn from first-line service in the autumn of 1938, and relegated to the fighter training task. Most retained overall RLM grey finish, but a small number were repainted black-green (schwarzgrün) over upper surfaces and pale blue (hellblau) on the undersides, and the He 51 was to remain in service with the Jagdfliegerschulen throughout WWII. The He 51 was not a very outstanding warplane in the air-air role and proved manifestly

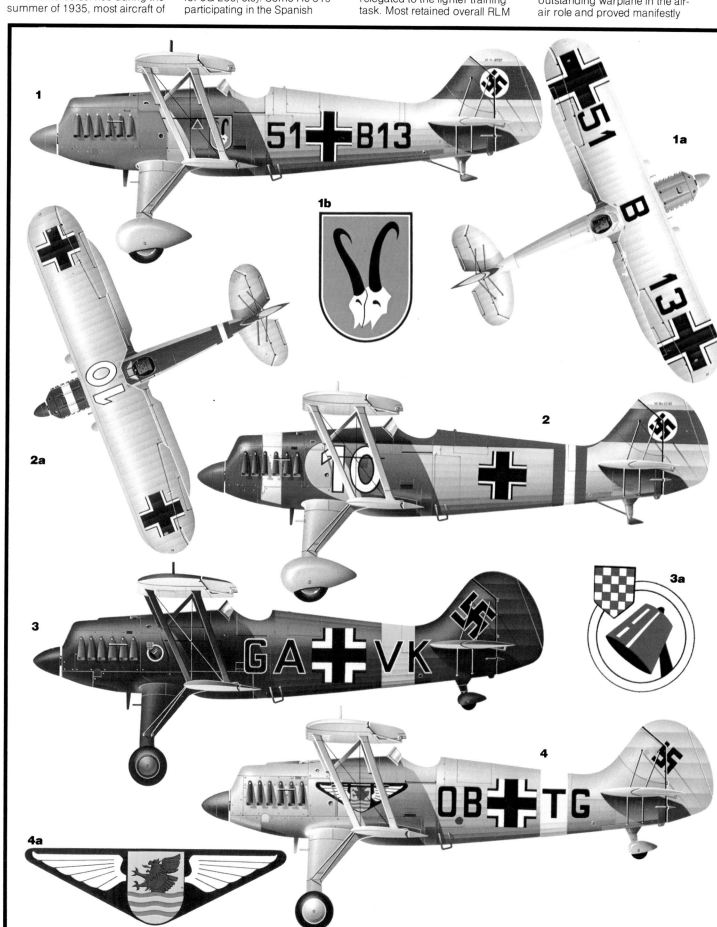

inferior to the I-15 (see page 36) by which it was opposed in Spanish skies, but it performed a useful service in close support. (**1**) He 51A-1 of 3.Staffel of Jagdgeschwader 233 at Wien-Aspern in autumn 1938, with (**1a**) upper surface planview and (**1b**) JG 233 emblem. (**2**) He 51B-1 of 2.Staffel of Jagdgeschwader 132

Richthofen at Döberitz in 1937. (**2a**) upper planview of same aircraft (**3**) He 51B serving in the fighter training role with A/B Schule 123 at Agram (Zagreb) in spring of 1942, and (**3a**) the emblem of A/B 123. (**4**) He 51B for fighter training in 1942 by A/B Schule 71 at Prossnitz (Prostějov) and (**4a**) the A/B 71

emblem. (**5**) He 51B-1 of 2.Staffel of Jagdgruppe 88, Legion Condor, spring 1937, with (**5a**) the "Zylinder Hut" emblem of 2./J88 and (below) an individual emblem applied to an example with similar overall RLM grey finish and coded 2-102. (**6**) He 51C-1 of 4.Staffel of Jagdgruppe 88 in late summer of 1938, with (**6a**) insignia of 2.102

of 3./J88, (**6b**) upper planview and wing underside surface detail, and (**6c**) the "Pikas" emblem of 4./J88 and (above) the "Cadena" (chain) emblem of Spanish Nationalist close air support Grupo de Cadena 1-G-2 carried by an He 51B-1 coded 2-107 and having similar overall finish to that of 4./J88.

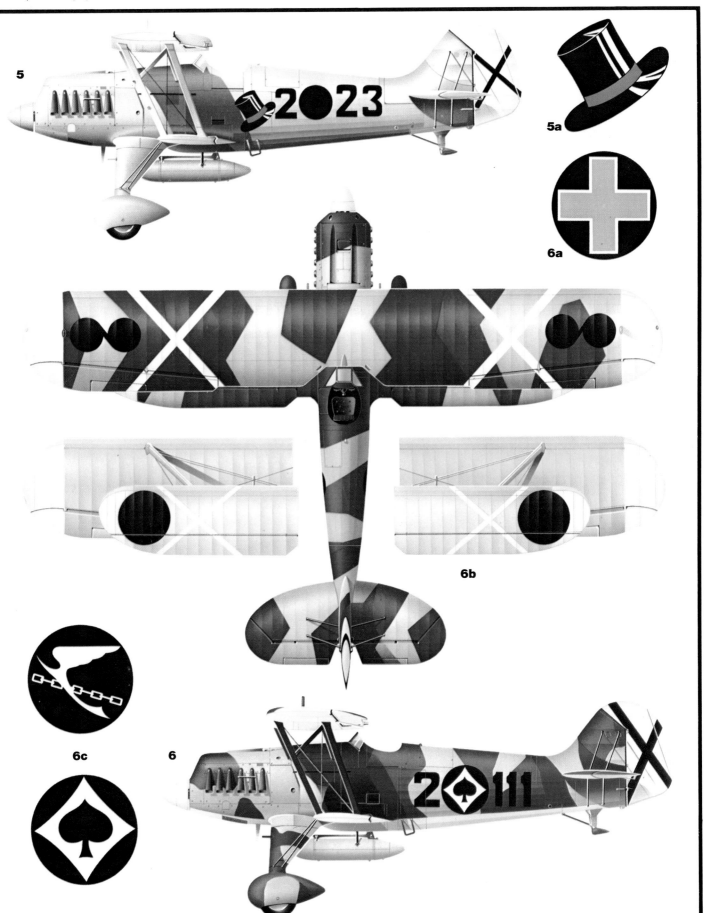

43

# Avia B.534 (1935)

Widely considered the finest fighter biplane in Continental Europe in its day, the B.534 produced by the Czechoslovak Avia concern was the ultimate production model of the B.34 flown as a prototype summer 1932. Extensively refined, the B.534 entered service in Czechoslovakia in 1935, the final production models being the Bk.534 and B.534-IV with three and four guns respectively. These were very sturdy fighters, excelling in high-speed manoeuvres and having outstanding climb and dive capabilities, and 328 of the Avia fighters were in first-line use in September 1938. With the dissolution of the Czechoslovak Republic, some 65 of these provided the equipment nucleus of the Slovak Air Force, these later being flown operationally in the Soviet Union. The remainder were taken into the Luftwaffe, 72 later being sold to Bulgaria, these being used in August 1943 to intercept USAAF B-24s en route to Ploesti. Factory finish comprised dark olive green upper surfaces and pale blue undersides, and this was largely retained by the various B.534 operators. (1) B.534-IV of Slovak Air Force at Zitomir-Kiev, Ukraine, 1941-42, with (1a) underside view of same aircraft with scrap detail of upper wing surfaces. (2) B.534-IV of 2nd Regiment, Royal Bulgarian

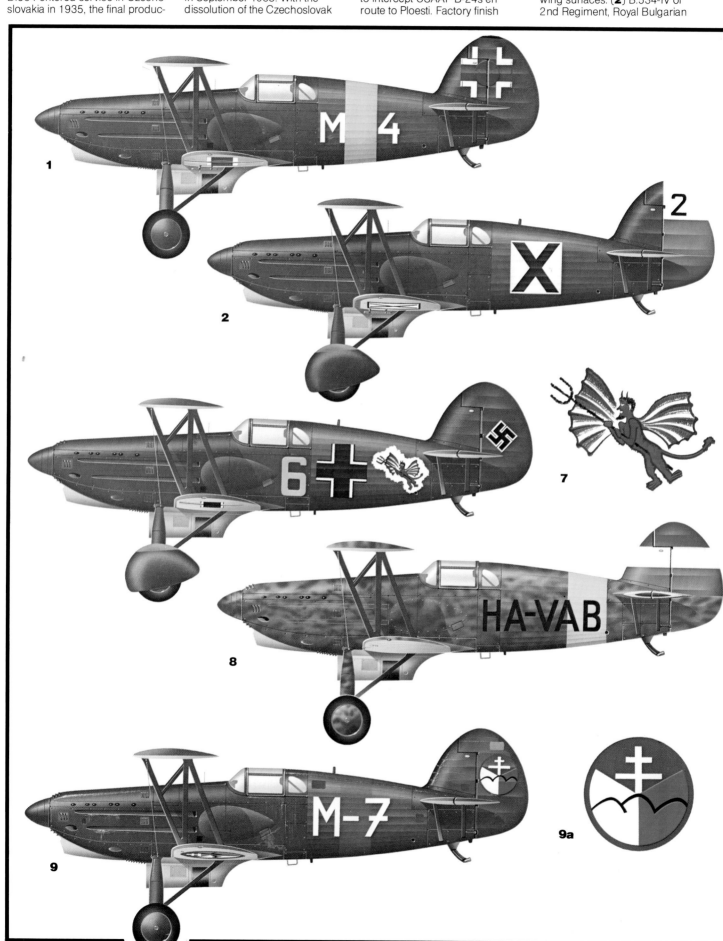

44

Air Force, 1941-42, with (**2a**) top-side planview and scrap detail of wing undersurfaces of same aircraft. (**3**) Rear fuselage of modified (360-deg vision canopy) Bk.534 of Luftwaffe serving as trainer at Olomouc-Holice, summer 1941. (**4**) Slovak Air Force Bk.534 (similarly modified) serving at Trenčin, August 1941. (**5**) B.534-IV (B.534.195) of the Czechoslovak Air Police, 1938, with enlarged detail of Avia emblem that appeared on tail fin. (**6**) Early Hungarian (left) and early Slovak (right) national insignia applied to B.534-IV. (**7**) A B.534-IV of 3.Staffel of Jagdgeschwader 71 at Eutingen near Stuttgart in November 1939, displaying crude personal emblem. This unit was redesignated as 6.Staffel of Jagdgeschwader 51 in following month and re-equipped with the Bf 109. (**8**) B.534-IV flown as towplane at Ferihegy, Hungary, with civil registration during 1941-42. Captured from the Slovak Air Force, this aircraft had previously flown in the communications role (as G-192) with the Hungarian Air Force. (**9**) A B.534-IV operated by the Slovak insurgent air arm from the "Tri Duby" (Three Oaks) airfield, near Zvolen, in September 1944, during the Slovak National Uprising. Note insurgent air arm insignia (**9a**) based on the Czechoslovak national insignia.

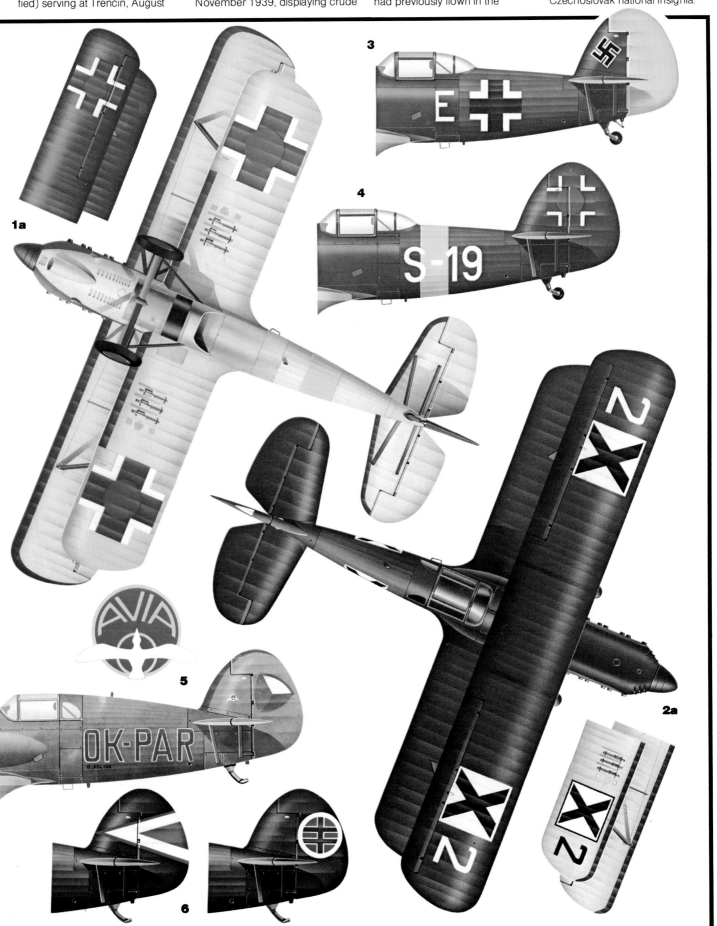

# Gloster Gauntlet (1935)

Possessing the somewhat dubious distinction of having been obsolescent by the time it first entered service, the Gauntlet was the last of the RAF's open-cockpit fighting biplanes. It was viceless, it was extremely manoeuvrable and it possessed delightful handling qualities, but its evolution had not kept pace with the accelerated tempo of fighter development elsewhere. The Gauntlet was the definitive development of the SS.18 which, designed to meet the demands of a 1927 specification (F.10/27) calling for a multi-gun fighter, had flown in January 1929. For five years the basic design was refined, until, in February 1934 (as the SS.19B), it was finally the recipient of a production order for the RAF. Named Gauntlet, it entered service in May-June 1935. For a brief period it was numerically the most important of the RAF's first-line fighters, and, in 1937, equipped 14 squadrons, but by the end of the year it had begun to give place to the very much superior but still somewhat anachronistic Gladiator. In all, 228 Gauntlets were built for the RAF. A few of these were later passed to the SAAF and to the RAAF, and others to Finland. (**1**) Gauntlet II (UV-R) of No 17 Sqdn at RAF Kenley, late 1938. The application of dark earth and dark green disruptive upper

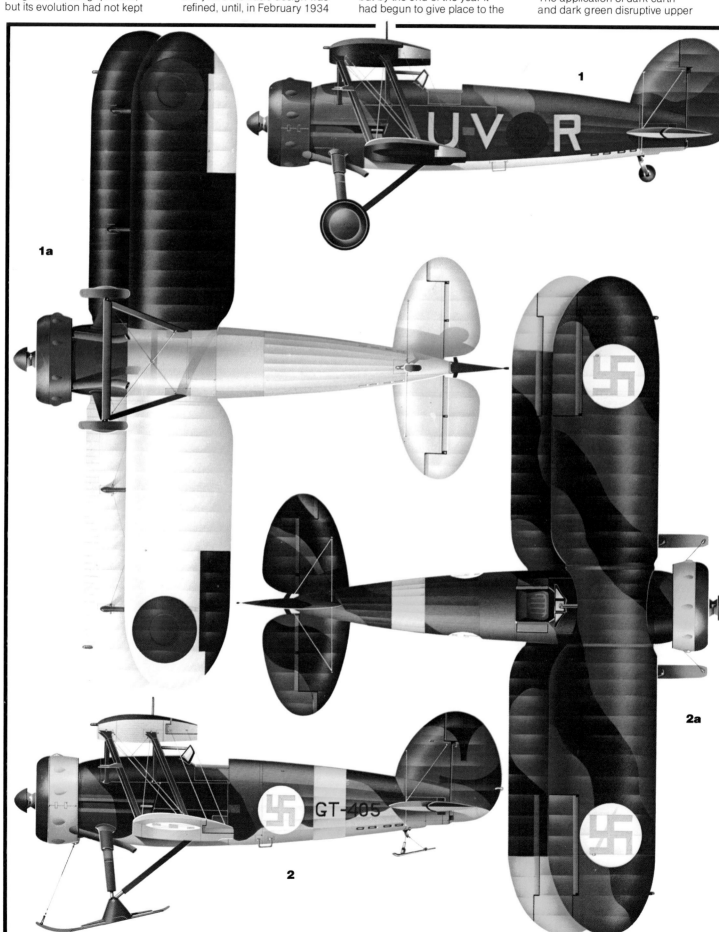

surface camouflage during autumn of that year had obscured the aircraft serial. Note Type B matt blue-and-red roundels. (**1a**) Underside planview of UV-R showing black (port) and white (starboard) undersurfaces of wing halves, remainder of underside being silver. (**2**) Gauntlet II (GT-405) serving as advanced trainer with T/LeLv 35, Finnish Ilmavoimien, in spring 1942. (**2a**) Upper surfaces of GT-405 showing standard "Continuation War" black-and-green disruptive camouflage. (**3**) A Gauntlet II (K5272) of No 111 Sqd, RAF Northolt, March 1937. Note the standardised spearhead-type frame containing squadron crest on fin. Black bar on aft fuselage (repeated across upper wing between roundels) denoted No 111 Sqdn. Black fin signified flight leader. (**4**) Gauntlet II (K7890) of No 151 Sqdn, RAF North Weald, 1937. Narrow black bar centred on broad blue bar denoted No 151 Sqdn. (**5**) Gauntlet II (K7843) of No 3 Sqdn, RAAF, Helwan, Egypt, November 1940. (**6**) Gauntlet I (J-21) of Danish Hærens Flyvertropper (Army Aviation Troops) at Vaerløse, 1937. (**7**) Danish-built Gauntlet of 1 Eskadrille, Hærens Flyvertropper at Værløse, early 1940, after application of upper surface camouflage of greenish-yellow and dark greyish-green, with light grey-blue underside.

# Polikarpov I-16 (1935)

Precursor of a new vogue in that it was the first single-seat cantilever monoplane fighter with a retractable undercarriage to achieve service, the I-16, designed by Nikolai Polikarpov, briefly carried Soviet fighter development *ahead* of the state of the art. First flown (as the TsKB-12) on 31 December 1933,

the I-16 began to reach the V-VS fighter eskadrilii (in its Type 5 form) early in 1935. With its ponderous, abbreviated nose and unique truncated fuselage, the I-16 was blooded over Spain in the service of the Republican government, but when called upon to participate in WWII, the apex of its development was long past.

Representing slightly more than 65 per cent of the entire V-VS fighter inventory when the Wehrmacht attacked the Soviet Union, the I-16 was obsolete and outclassed, but remained the most frequently encountered Soviet fighter until late 1942. A total of 7,005 I-16s was built, plus 1,639 in two-seat training form.

(**1**) I-16 Type 18 flown by Capt Boris F. Safonov of the 72 AP (Aviatsionnye Polk - Aviation Regiment) of the VVS SF (Northern Fleet Air Force), Keg-Ostrov, Murmansk, summer 1941. Safonov was an "ace" and the inscription on the portside reads "Za Stalina!" (For Stalin!). On the starboard side was painted

"Smert fashistam!" (Death to fascists!) (**1a**) Half-and-half planview of Safonov's aircraft showing both upper and lower surfaces of portside. (**2**) Scrap view of rear fuselage of I-16 Type 10 of AP of Leningrad Military District, summer 1939. (**3**) I-16 Type 24 of 4 IAP, Lake Ladoga area, winter 1940-41.

(**4**) I-16 Type 6 (IR-101) used by 3./LLv 6 (3.lentue/Lentolaivue 6, or 3rd flight of 6th Squadron) with fixed wheel undercarriage, late summer 1942. This aircraft had been captured at Suursaari on 28 March 1942. (**5**) I-16 Type 10 of 4th Fighter Wing, Chinese Central Government Air Force, Chankiakow, Shansi, winter 1937-

1938. (**6**) I-16 Type 10 "Super Mosca" (CM-225) of the 7 Escuadrilla de Moscas, Spanish Aviación Militar Republicana, autumn 1938. (**6a**) Topside plan-view of CM-225. (**7**) I-16 Type 10 flown by José Bravo Fernández as CO of 3ª Escuadrilla de Moscas. Note "Double Top" emblem of the 3ª Esc. (**7a**) Emblems of related

escuadrillas, 1ª (left) and 2ª (right). (**7b**) Scrap view of captured 3ª Esc I-16 retaining (**7c**) "Double Top" emblem. (**8**) I-16 Type 10 (CM-177) of 4ª Escuadrilla de Moscas, and (**8a**) scrap view of CM-274 showing variation in style of "Popeye" emblem of Escuadrilla. (**8b**) Alternative styles of 4ª Escuadrilla emblem.

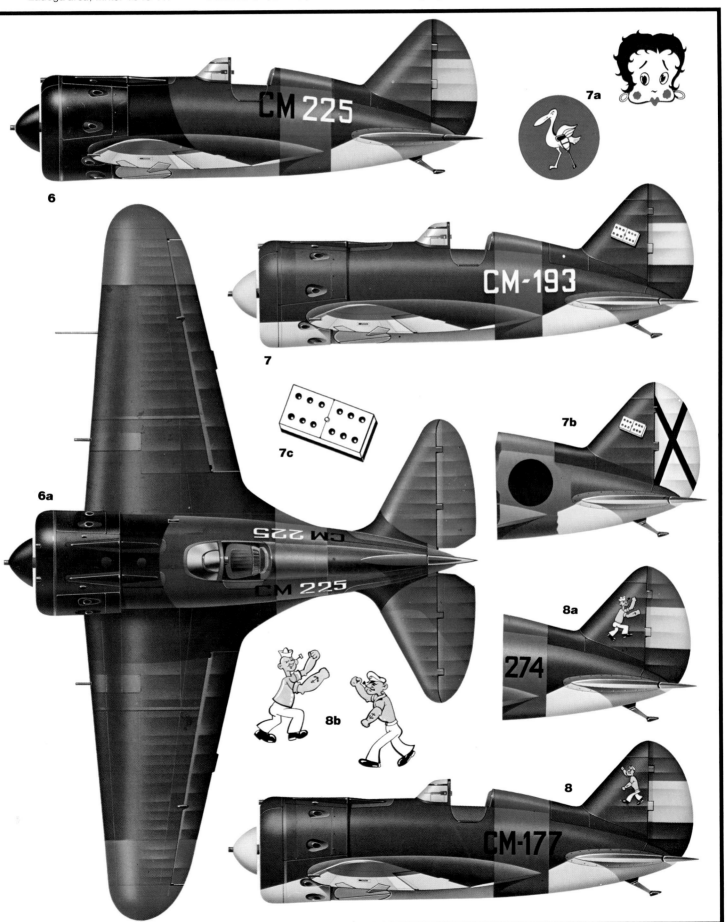

49

# SIAI (Savoia-Marchetti) S.81 (1935)

The first in a distinguished line of trimotor medium bombers that was created under the aegis of Alessandro Marchetti and evolved from the commercial S.73, the mixed-construction S.81 was already suffering a degree of technical obsolescence when it first entered service with the Regia Aeronautica. With its immense fixed and spatted undercarriage, it was hardly to be expected that performance would set new standards, and in the event it was to be rapidly overtaken by the S.79. This notwithstanding, the S.81 was to play an important part in Italian military aviation annals. First flown on 8 February 1935, it began to enter Regia Aeronautica service in the following April, seeing service before the year's end in the Ethiopian campaign. But its primary claim to fame was to result from the prominent role that it played in the Spanish Civil War in which it was to demonstrate exceptional qualities of reliability and robustness.

Production continued until March 1938, when 534 had been delivered of which 304 were on the strength of the Regia Aeronautica when Italy entered WWII, production being resumed in 1943 for the transport role (S.81/T), some 80 additional aircraft being built. (1) S.81 of XXV Gruppo (215ª squadrigilia, 25º Gruppo, 21º

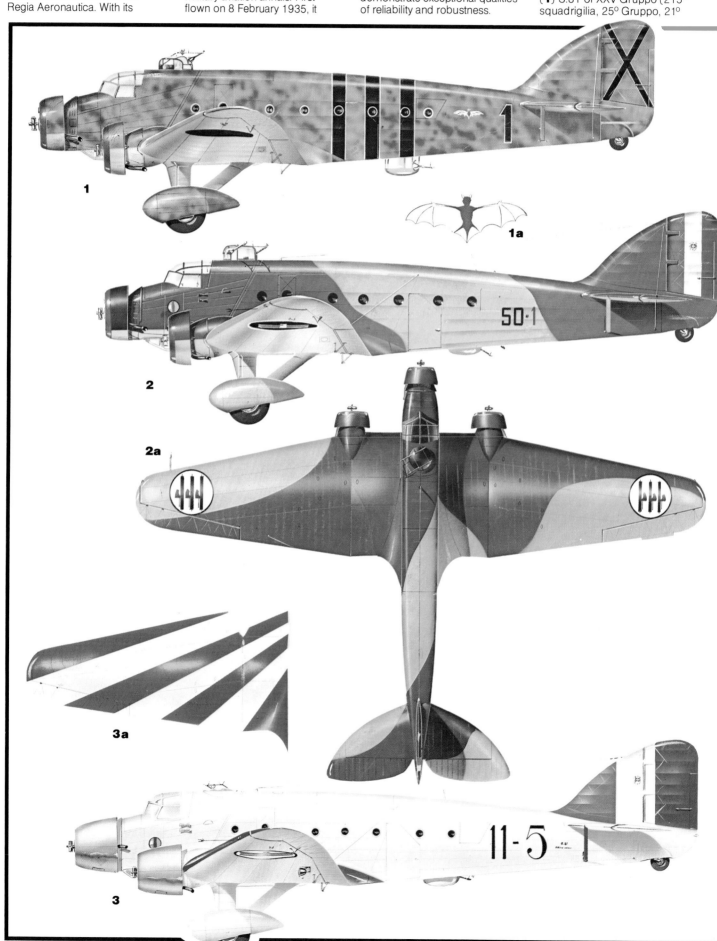

50

Stormo) "Pipistrelli" (Bats) of (Italian) Aviación de el Tercio, Talavera de la Reina, Spain, October 1936. (1a) "Pipistrello" emblem of 21º Stormo. (2) S.81 of 50ª squadriglia, 38º Gruppo, 32º Stormo, Sardinia, 1939. (2a) Topside planview of same aircraft. Note camouflage of terracotta, and dark ochre and dark green, and reversal (black to white) of the fasces emblems on the wings. (3) S.81 of 11ª squadriglia, 26º Gruppo, 9 Stormo, operating from Macelle, Ethiopia, early 1936. Note colonial cream-white overall finish and (3a) "anti-camouflage" radiating red striping on wing topside to facilitate location of aircraft in event of a forced landing. (4) S.81/S (Sanitario) aeromedical transport, Libya, 1941. (5) S.81 of the 202ª squadriglia, 40º Gruppo, 38º Stormo, operating over Albania, 1941. Note "quick identification" yellow engine cowls. (6) S.81/T (M.M.60984) 8Q+GH of 1º Gruppo Trasporto "Terracciano"/ Transportgruppe 10 (Italien) of the Aeronautica Nazionale Repubblicana, Riga, Latvia, 1944. The unit coding (8Q) in black is barely discernible against dark olive green finish. (7) S.81 of 245ª squadriglia trasporto, Krivoy Rog, Ukraine, September 1941. (8) S.81 of 600ª squadriglia, North Africa, spring 1943.

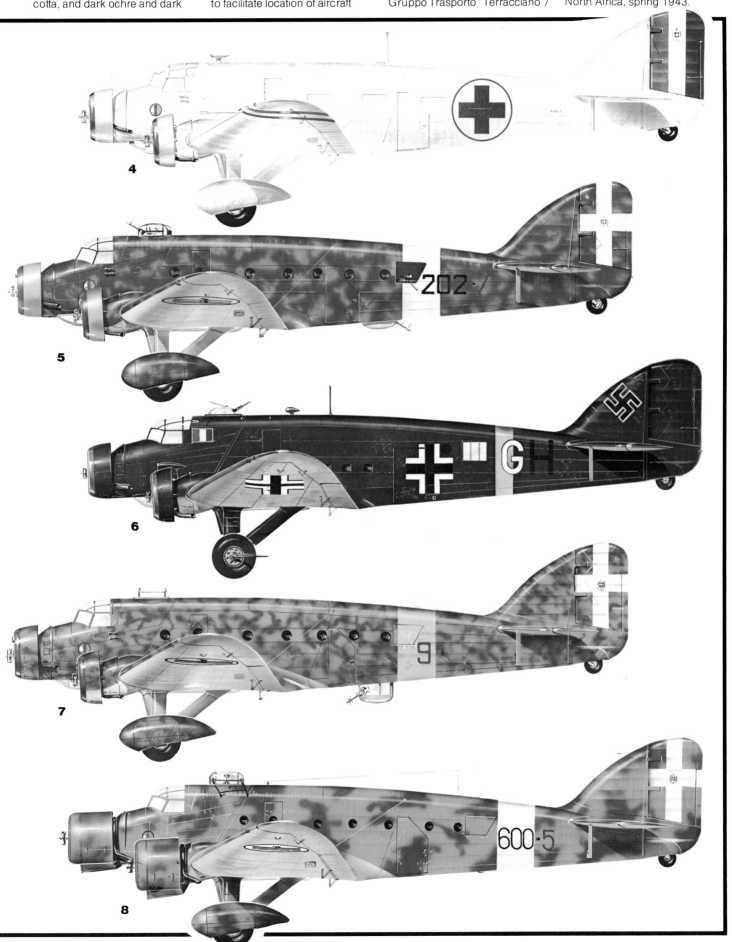

# Dewoitine D.500/510 (1935)

Representing a dramatic advance in fighter development in being a flush-riveted metal-skinned monoplane with a monocoque fuselage, the D.500 flew on 18 June 1932, entering service mid-1935, and being followed in 1936 by the similar, more heavily armed D.501 and a more powerful cannon-armed derivative, the D.510.

(1) D.500 Nº 47 of the 1ère Escadrille, Groupe de Chasse I/4 (4e Escadre was previously 42e Escadre Mixte), Reims, early in 1937. Note upper surfaces of wings and tailplane were green. "R-O" appeared beneath stbd and "46" beneath port wing. (1a) Ex-SPA-95 emblem of 1ère Esc. (2) D.501 Nº 170, Escadrille 3C3

of Marine National, Marignane. Note pale grey upper and pale blue lower surfaces. (2a) Emblem of Esc 3C3 and (2b) insignia of Marine Nationale. (3) D.510 Nº219 of 3ème Escadrille, GC II/1, Etampes, 1938. "R-2" appeared beneath stbd and "49" beneath port wing. (3a) Emblem of 3ème Esc. (4) D.510 Nº 317,

Regional Defence Esc, June 1940. Note weathered camouflage and national insignia centred on the overpainted unit emblem. (5) D.510 of 1ère, GC I/8, Marignane, with Munich crisis (September 1938) three-tone camouflage. (6) D.510C of 41st Sqdn, Chinese Central Government Air Force, Yunan-fu, autumn 1938.

1
1a
2
2a
2b
3
3a
4
5
6

# Henschel Hs 123 (1936)

A sturdy all-metal single-bay sesquiplane designed to fulfil an official requirement for a dual-role (fighter and dive bomber) aircraft, the Hs 123 flew on 1 April 1935, entering Luftwaffe service in late autumn 1936. Its configuration being considered passé, the Hs 123 saw a production life spanning but a

year, some 260 being built. Its Luftwaffe service career was to be prolonged, however, when the Hs 123 was proved outstandingly successful in the close support role. It fought in Poland, the Low Countries and France, and until autumn 1944 on the Eastern Front where it achieved some success with the Schlachtflieger.

(1) Hs 123A (52 + H37), 7.Staffel, Stukageschwader 165 "Immelmann", Fürstenfeldbruck, October 1937. (1a) Upper surfaces of 52+H37 and (1b) starboard camouflage pattern. (2) Hs 123A (L2+EN) of 5.(Schlacht)/LG 2, St Trond, Belgium, May 1940. (2a) Emblem of 5.Staffel (partly obscured by interplane strut). (3) Hs 123A

(CB+AF) of A/B Schule 71 at Prossnitz, Moravia, summer 1941. (4) Hs 123A of 4./Schlacht-geschwader 2, Russia, winter of 1942-43. (4a) "Infanterie-Sturmabzeichen" (obscured by interplane strut). (5) Hs 123A (24·4), Grupo 24, Arma de Avia-ción, Tablada, spring '39. (5a) Plan and (5b) starboard of 24·4.

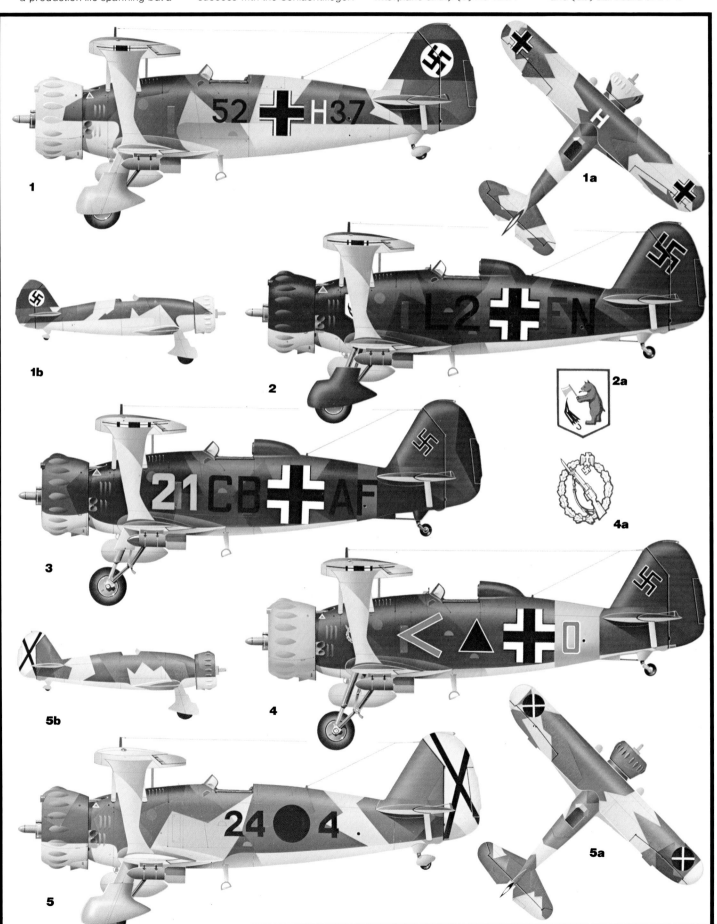

# Fairey Swordfish (1936)

The Swordfish shipboard torpedo-bomber was obsolescent when it entered service and anachronistic when Britain's Fleet Air Arm went to war. It nevertheless served throughout WWII with distinction in a variety of roles, seeing almost continuous operation and participating in a number of epic actions. Extraordinarily easy to fly, with viceless handling characteristics, the Swordfish was essentially simple and very robust. Much of its success was undoubtedly due to this lack of sophistication and the inherent sturdiness, coupled with the fact that it operated primarily in an environment in which the fighter opposition was conspicuous by its absence.

Once committed to a torpedo run it was supremely vulnerable. The true prototype of the Swordfish, the TSR II, flew on 17 April 1934, and it entered service early summer 1936, remaining in production until 1944, and first-line service until May 1945. Initially painted aluminium overall, it adopted a disruptive pattern of dark sea grey and dark green for upper surfaces and pale grey (Sky Grey) for sides and lower surfaces in 1939. The green later gave place to dark slate grey, the under surface colour was changed to pale greenish duck egg (the so-called Sky Type S) and the camouflage demarkation line was

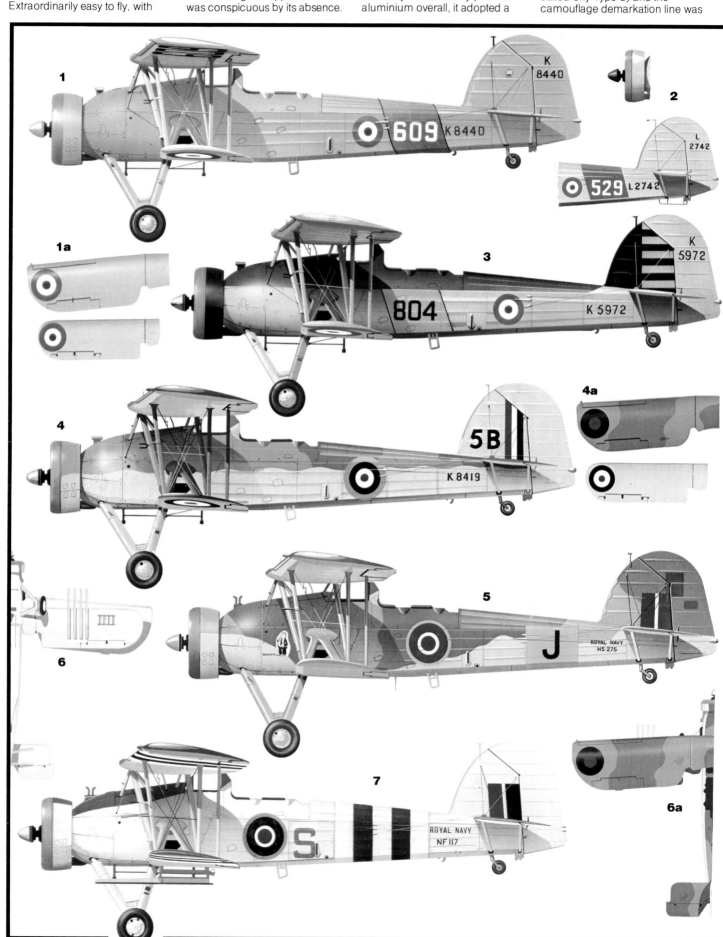

lowered. (**1**) Swordfish I (K8440) of No 822 Sqdn, HMS *Courageous,* 1939, with (**1a**) detail of the roundel positioning on upper and lower mainplanes. (**2**) Detail of similarly finished (aluminium paint overall) floatplane (Ł2742) of No 701 Catapult Flight, Gibraltar, 1938. (**3**) Swordfish I (K5972) of No 823 Sqdn, HMS *Glorious,* 1936. Note Flight CO's fin striping, black top decking and cowling ring. (**4**) Swordfish I (K8419) of No 824 Sqdn, HMS *Eagle,* 1940, and (**4a**) detail of upper (topside) and lower (under surface) mainplanes. (**5**) Swordfish II (HS275) of No 1 Naval Air Gunnery School at Yarmouth, Nova Scotia, 1943. (**6**) Under surface and (**6a**) upper surface scrap views of Swordfish II showing rocket rail position. (**7**) Swordfish II (NF117) of No 811 Sqdn, HMS *Biter.* Note the invasion striping. (**8**) Swordfish I (L2731) of No 820 Sqdn, HMS *Ark Royal,* 1939. (**9**) Swordfish I (P4210) of No 821 Sqdn, HMS *Ark Royal,* 1940. (**10**) Swordfish III (NF410) of No 119 Sqdn, RAF Coastal Command, 1945. Note the personal emblem. (**11**) Swordfish II (HS268) of No 1 Naval Air Gunnery School, Canada, 1944. Note this winterised version sometimes erroneously referred to as Mk IV. (**12**) Royal Navy Swordfish I (V4367) of Catapult Flight, HMS *Malaya,* 1940.

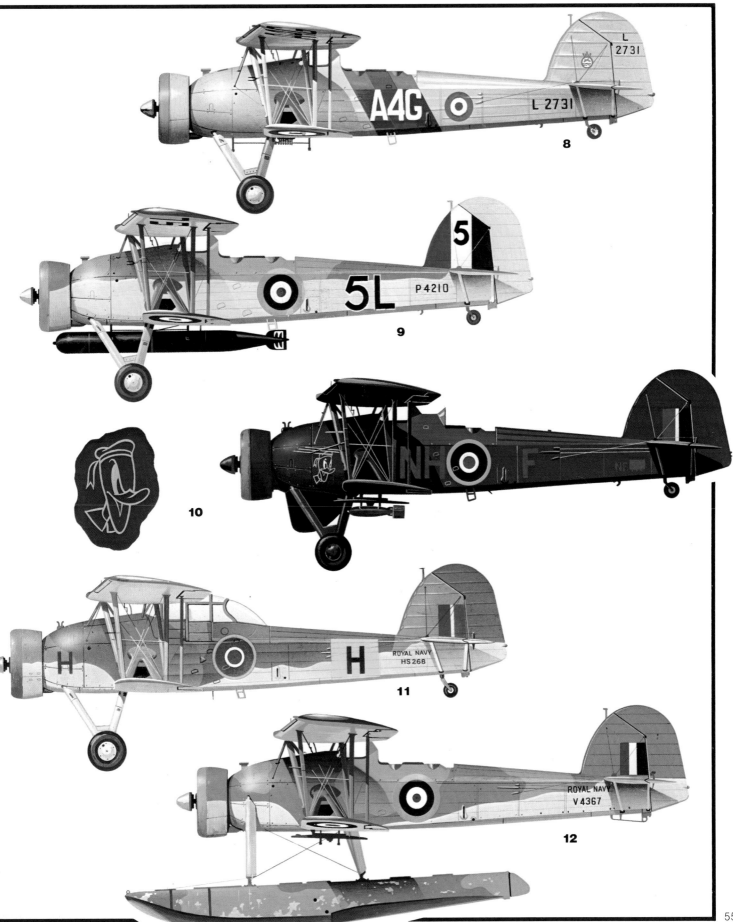

# Junkers Ju 86 (1936)

A dimorphic design in that it provided the basis for a military bomber and a commercial transport which evolved in parallel, Germany's Ju 86 was first flown on 4 November 1934 as a bomber prototype. Of comparatively advanced concept, the initial production Ju 86A-1 bomber was first issued to the Kampfgeschwader 152 Hindenburg

in the late spring of 1936. Some shortcomings in stability and range resulted in modifications leading to the Ju 86D, the most significant production model and five examples of which served operationally with the Legion Condor in Spain. Serviceability problems with the Jumo 205C Diesel engines led to replacement

by the air-cooled radial BMW 132F in the Ju 86E which provided a basis for the export Ju 86K, the licence manufacture of which was undertaken in Sweden where 16 were built. Some 390 Ju 86s (in all versions) were produced, 235 being in service with the Kampf-gruppen on 19 September 1938, but a year later only one first-

line Luftwaffe Gruppe retained the type which was subsequently relegated to training and other second-line duties. The Ju 86 remained operational with the Hungarian Air Force until 1942. (1) A Ju 86K-1 as demonstrated at Vienna-Aspern in September 1937 in Austrian markings. This was in fact a Swedish contract aircraft,

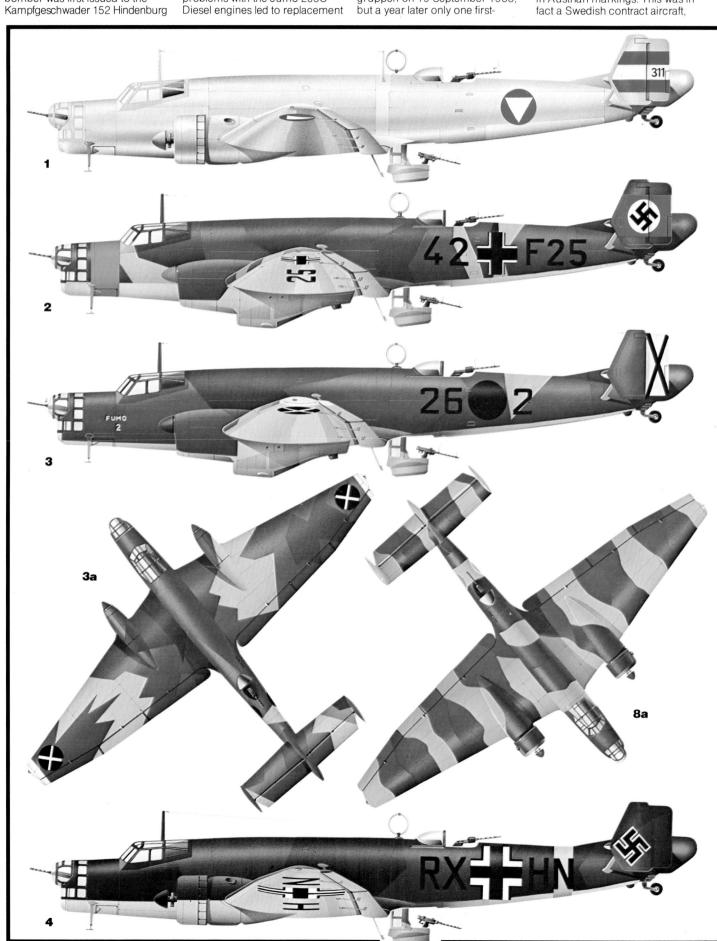

the genuine "311" not arriving at Vienna-Aspern until February 1938. This, a Ju 86E-2 ordered by the Austrian Luftstreitkräfte for Fliegerregiment 2, employed a standard Luftwaffe splinter-type finish as for 42+F25. (2) Ju 86D-1 of 5.Staffel of Kampfgeschwader 254, Eschwege, September 1937. The nose band

and spinner indicated "Blue Force" in autumn manoeuvres. (3) Ju 86D-1 "Fumo 2" of the Kampfgruppe 88, Legion Condor, Spain, late 1937, and (3a) upper planview showing the splinter-type three-colour camouflage. (4) Ju 86E-2 with a C-Schule for bomber crew training, circa 1941. (5) Ju 86K-1 (B3) of Flottilj 1

of Swedish Flygvapen, spring 1937. Note retention of German camouflage colours. (6) Ju 86K-2 of the Hungarian 1st Bomber Combat Proficiency Sqdn, summer 1939. (7) Ju 86K-2 of Hungarian 4th Bomber Regiment operating in Soviet Union in early 1942. (7a) Emblem of 3./11 Group and, subsequently, the 4/0 Sqdn.

(8) Ju 86K-13 (B 3D) of 2nd Sqdn, Flottilj 17, operating as a torpedo-bomber (T 3), Ronneby, 1944. (8a) Upper planview of the same aircraft, and (8b) "Sea eagle with mine" emblem on aircraft "M" of 2nd Sqdn. (9) Ju 86K-13 (B 3C) transport of Flottilj 11, circa 1955, and (9a) the emblem used by F 11.

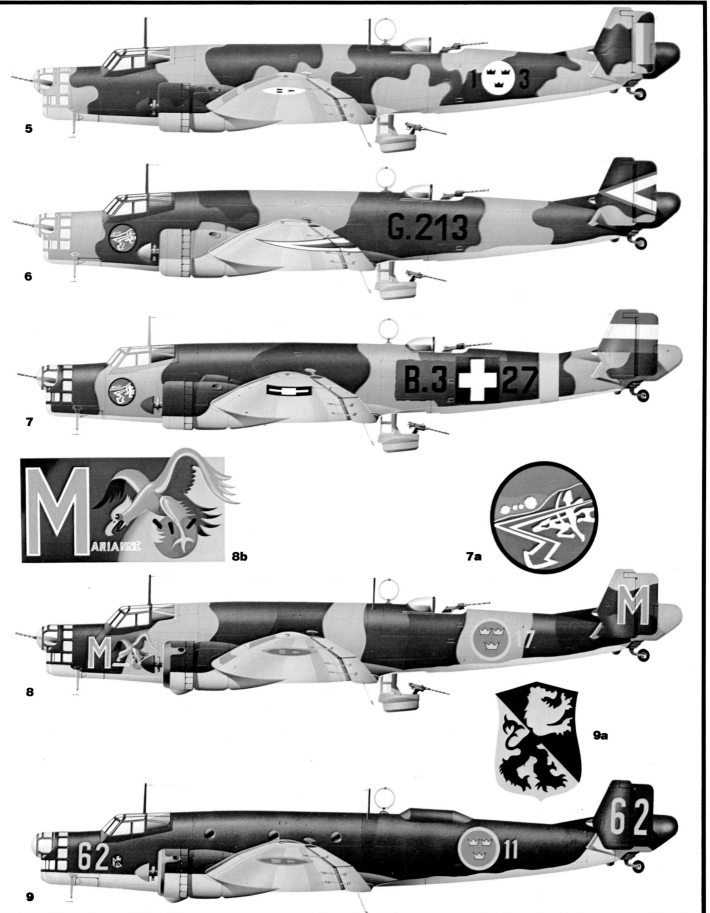

57

# SIAI (Savoia-Marchetti) SM.79 Sparviero (1936)

Undoubtedly to be numbered among the most efficacious warplanes created by the Italian aircraft industry, respected by its antagonists and lauded by its crews for its handling qualities and sturdiness, the SM.79 Sparviero (Sparrowhawk) medium bomber was, like its predecessor, the S.81 (see pages 50–51), a derivative of a commercial type, which, the SM.79P, had flown in October 1934. The prototype of the bomber version followed on 2 September 1935, and production deliveries to the squadrigli of the Regia Aeronautica commenced in October 1936. Within less than a year, the Sparviero was being employed operationally over Spain with the Aviación de el Tercio, enjoying considerable success, and by the time Italy entered WWII, this warplane equipped a total of 14 Stormi (594 aircraft of which 403 were serviceable), representing almost two-thirds of the offensive capability of the Regia Aeronautica. Employed widely for both diurnal and nocturnal bombing, it achieved its greatest fame in the role of torpedo-bomber, the exploits of the SM.79-equipped gruppi aero-siluranti becoming legendary in Italian military aviation annals. When production terminated in 1944, a total of 1,330 Sparvieri had been built in several models with various engines. Forty-five

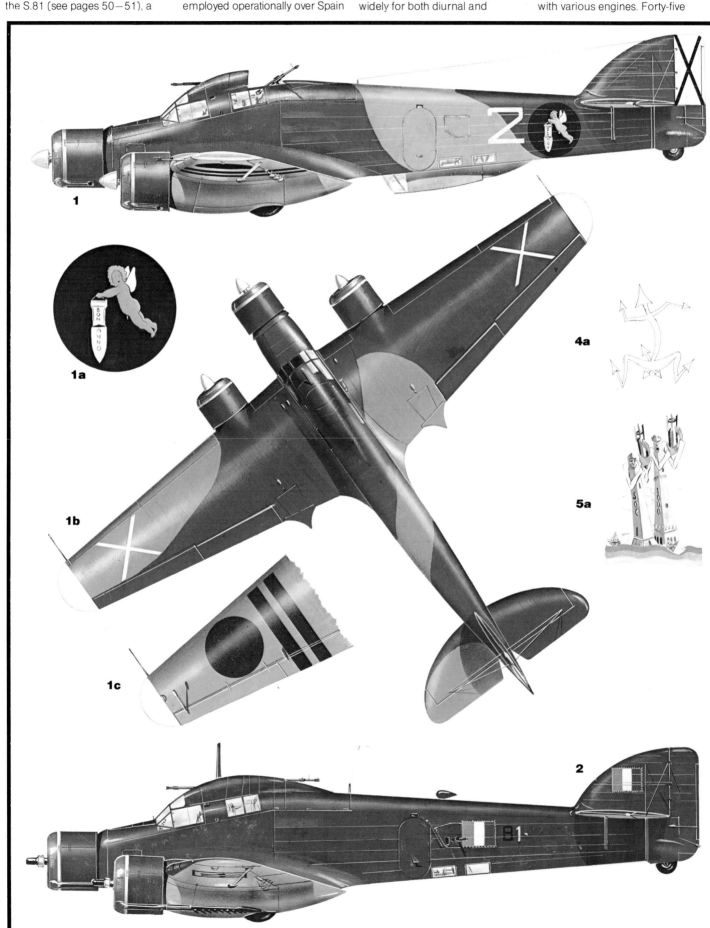

1

1a

1b

1c

2

4a

5a

58

had been supplied to the Royal Yugoslav Air Force, and a twin-engined version, the SM.79B, had achieved some export success, four being purchased by Iraq, three by Brazil and 24 by Rumania. (**1**) SM.79 of 52ª squadriglia of XXVII Gruppo "Falchi delle Baleari" (Hawks of the Baleares), 8º Stormo, (Italian) Aviación de

el Tercio, operating from Palma, Majorca, May 1938. (**1a**) Emblem of 52ª squadriglia and (**1b**) topside planview of same aircraft. Note white wingtips. (**1c**) Detail of outer wing underside. (**2**) SM.79 of the Gruppo Aerosiluranti "Buscaglia" of the Aviazione Nazionale Repubblicana, Gorizia, March 1944. (**3**) SM.79C (Corsa=

Speed) I-5 (I-BIMU) which took third place in 1937 Istres-Damascus-Paris race. (**3a**) The "Sorci Verdi" (Green Mice) emblem of the 12º Gruppo. (**4**) SM.79 of 193ª squadriglia, 87º Gruppo, 30º Stormo, Sicily, 1941. Note non-standard extension of tail cross. (**4a**) The "Electric Man" emblem of 193ª squadriglia. (**5**) SM.79 of

257ª squadriglia, 108º Gruppo, 36º Stormo, Sicily, early 1941. (**6**) SM.79 of 283ª squadriglia, 130º Gruppo Autonomo, operational in the Mediterranean in 1942 in the anti-shipping role. (**7**) One of four SM.79 aircraft operated until the mid-'fifties by the Lebanese Air Force. These were obtained in 1950 for transport use.

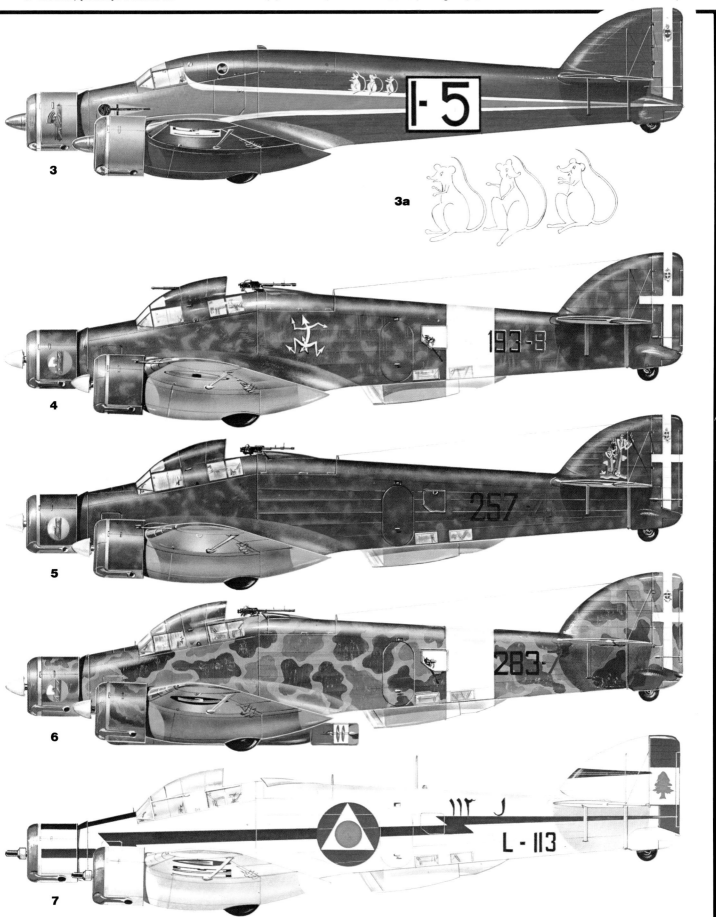

# Heinkel He 111 (1936)

An aerodynamically efficient and shapely aircraft with very good flying characteristics, the He 111 was a classic design and an outstanding warplane of the mid-'thirties. Regrettably for the Luftwaffe, it had lost some of its potency by the time it was committed to WWII. First flown as a prototype on 24 February

1935, the first series model, the He 111B-1, joined the Luftwaffe in the early winter of 1936. With the He 111P and H series, the stepped windscreen was supplanted by an unstepped, asymmetric and almost completely glazed nose which became a unique characteristic of He 111s employed during WWII. Production

of all versions exceeded 7,300 aircraft, others being built in Rumania and, post-war, in Spain. (1) He 111P-2 of Kampfgeschwader 55 based at Dreux, Chartres and Villacoublay for night sorties against UK, autumn 1940. Note KG 55 emblem (coat of arms of Giessen) and the temporary black overall finish obscuring the

swastika and fuselage coding. National marking and individual aircraft letter restricted to white outlines, and dark grey disruptive pattern superimposed crudely over upper surfaces. (2) He 111H-3 (6N+CK of 2./KGr. 100, Vannes, Brittany, winter 1940-41. Equipped with X-Gerät for pathfinder role in nocturnal

60

Blitz on UK. (**2a**) "Viking Long-boat" emblem of KGr.100. (**3**) He 111H-6 (7A+FA) of Gefechtsverband (Combat Formation) Kuhlmey, Immola, Finland, July 1944. Note that coding was of Stab LLG 2 to which aircraft was previously attached. (**4**) He 111H-6 (1H+FK) of 2./KG 26 "Löwen-Geschwader", Ottana, Sardinia, August 1943.

Note "Vestigium Leonis" emblem of KG 26. (**5**) He 111H-8/R2 of Schleppgruppe (Towing Wing) 4 based at Pskov-South, February-March 1942. Note Gruppe emblem. (**6**) He 111H-20 (5J+GH) of I/KG 4 "General Wever", supply-dropping from Dresden-Klotzsche, April 1945. (**6a**) Emblem of KG 4. (**7**) He 111H-3 of Slovakian Air

Force, Trenčin, spring 1943. (**8**) He 111H-3 (V4+AM) of II/KG 1 "Hindenburg", Montdidier, France, August 1940. (**8a**) Forward upper surfaces of V4+AM showing the temporary formation marking on starboard wing repeated from rudder. (**8b**) Emblem of 4./KG 1. (**9**) He 111H-3 of Grupul 5 of Rumanian Corpul 1 Aerian oper-

ating in Zaporozh'ye area of Ukraine, early 1943. (**9a**) The forward upper surfaces of same aircraft and (**9b**) alternative rudder striping style. (**10**) A CASA-built He 111H-16 (93-34) of Ala 94, Spanish Ejército del Aire, late 'fifties. (**10a**) Upper surfaces of 93-94 showing pre-WWII style "splinter" finish.

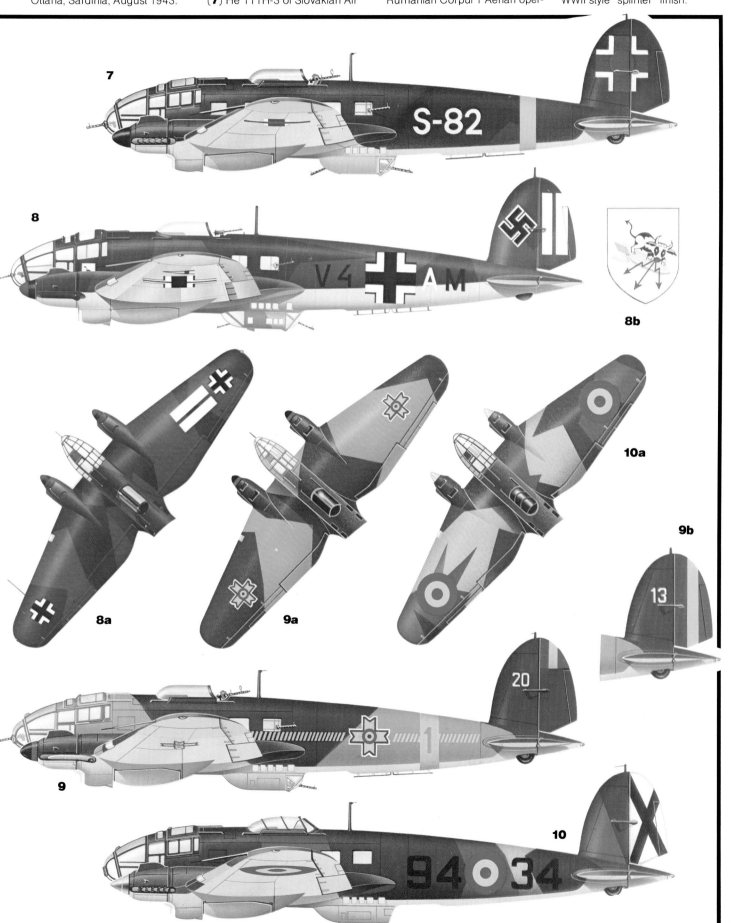

7

8

8b

8a

9a

9

10a

9b

13

20

94 34

10

# Curtiss SBC Helldiver (1937)

The SBC Helldiver brought to an end both the most colourful era in US shipboard aviation and that of the US Navy's combat biplane. Known as the Helldiver, although this was a generic name assigned to all Curtiss aircraft employed in the dive-bombing role rather than official Navy nomenclature, this carrier-based biplane

paradoxically began life as a *monoplane*. The first biplane prototype, the XSBC-2, flew on 9 December 1935, with deliveries to the US Navy of the first series model, the SBC-3, commencing in July 1937. Despite rapidly approaching obsolescence, some lingering US Navy conservatism towards shipboard aircraft led

to follow-on contracts being placed in January 1938 for a re-engined version, the SBC-4, the delivery of which did not begin until March 1939, by which time it was tacitly admitted to be obsolete. The Navy placed orders for 124 SBC-4s, production being completed in April 1940, but 50 of these were diverted for France

and replaced in 1941 with another 50. Two squadrons of SBC-4s were aboard the USS *Hornet* at the time of Pearl Harbor, and the US Marines were to keep a squadron of land-based SBC-4s until June 1943, but the Curtiss biplane was to play no active role in the conflict. Those diverted for the use of France's Aéronavale were

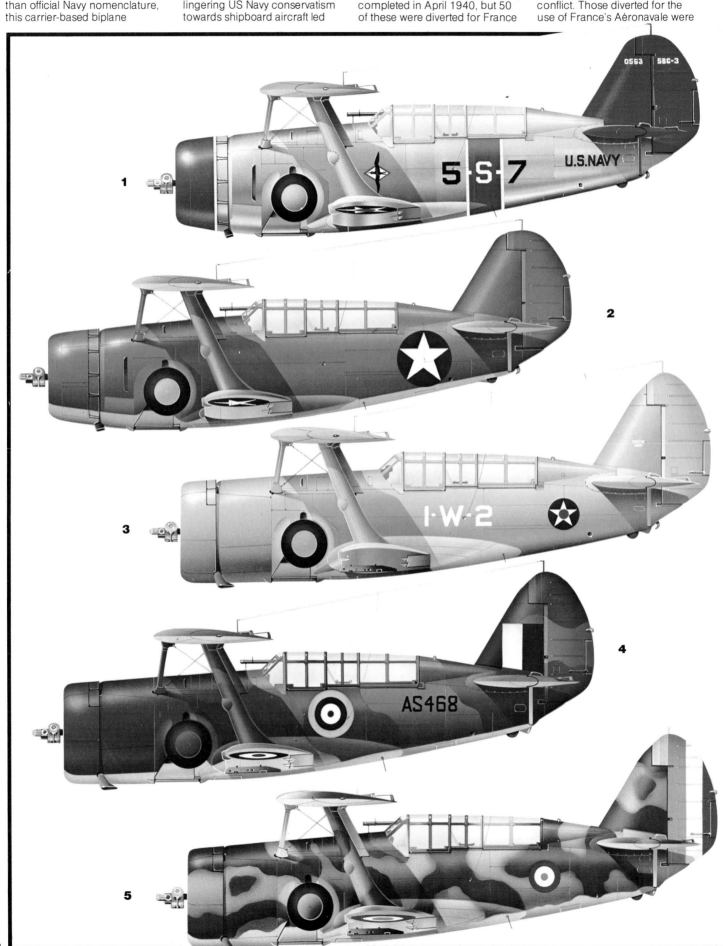

off-loaded at Martinique when the French capitulated, apart from a batch of five which reached the UK and were assigned the name Cleveland. The RAF found no use for these aircraft, which were promptly assigned the ground instructional role. (**1**) SBC-3 (BuAer No 0563) of VS-5 aboard USS *Yorktown* in 1937. Natural metal finish overall, apart from chrome yellow upper wing top and red tail surfaces, the latter signifying the *Yorktown*. The full engine cowl and fuselage band in blue signified 3rd section leader. Note the black "Man O'War Bird" emblem of Scouting Five on red-outlined horizontal white diamond. (**2**) SBC-3 in (post May) 1942 US insignia style (ie, red centre spot of star and rudder striping discarded) in reserve squadron service. All upper surfaces were by now non-specular blue-grey and under surfaces were non-specular light grey. (**3**) SBC-4 (BuAer No 1287) serving as command liaison and transport aircraft with 1st Marine Aviation Wing, San Diego.1941. In conformity with order of 30 December 1940 applying to all shipboard aircraft, a light grey overall finish was employed. (**4**) SBC-4 Cleveland I (AS468) and (**4a**) topside planview of same aircraft. (**5** and **5a**) SBC-4 in (French) Aéronavale green-and-grey and sky blue camouflage.

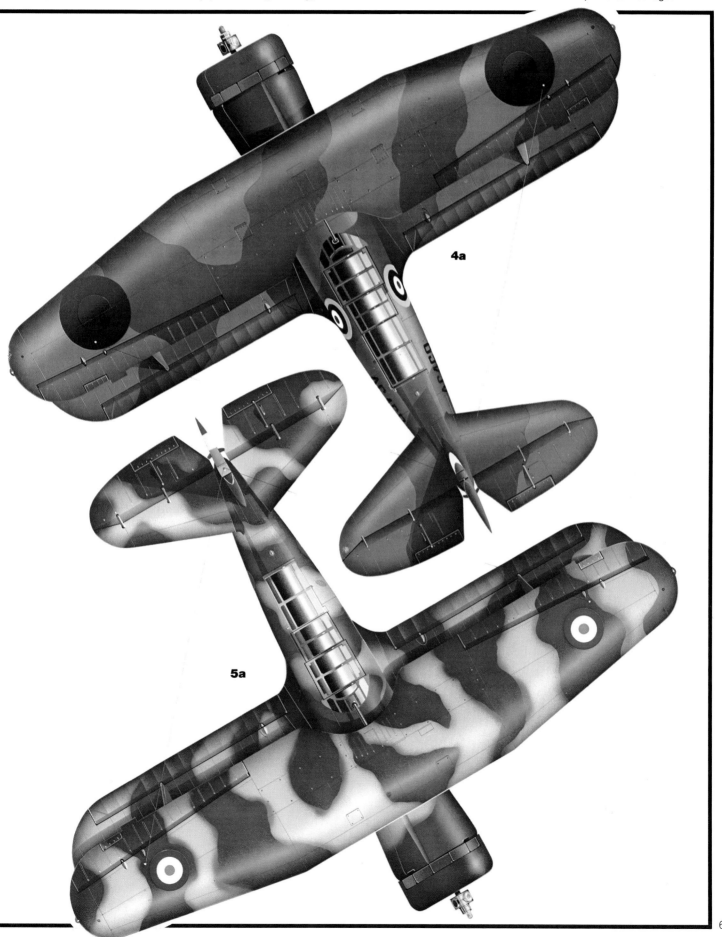

4a

5a

# Mitsubishi A5M (Claude) (1937)

Laying claim to the distinction of having been the world's first shipboard single-seat low-wing cantilever monoplane fighter to have achieved service, the A5M, or Navy Type 96 carrier-based fighter, did more than any other aircraft to raise Japanese original aeronautical design and manufacturing capability to world standard, although this fact was not immediately obvious to the West where the Japanese were still regarded as copyists. An extremely clean all-metal stressed-skin aircraft designed by Jiro Horikoshi, who was later to achieve international recognition for his Zero-Sen fighter (see page 153), the A5M was one of the most manoeuvrable fighter monoplanes ever built. Flown as a prototype on 4 February 1935, it entered service with the Imperial Navy as the A5M1 early in 1937 and, in A5M2ko form, was deployed operationally for the first time in September of that year in the Shanghai region where it established immediate ascendancy. The more powerful A5M4 appeared in the following year, but this had been largely phased out of first-line service when the Pacific War commenced, those remaining aboard carriers quickly giving place to the Zero-Sen. A total of 1,085 A5Ms of all types (excluding prototypes) was manufactured.

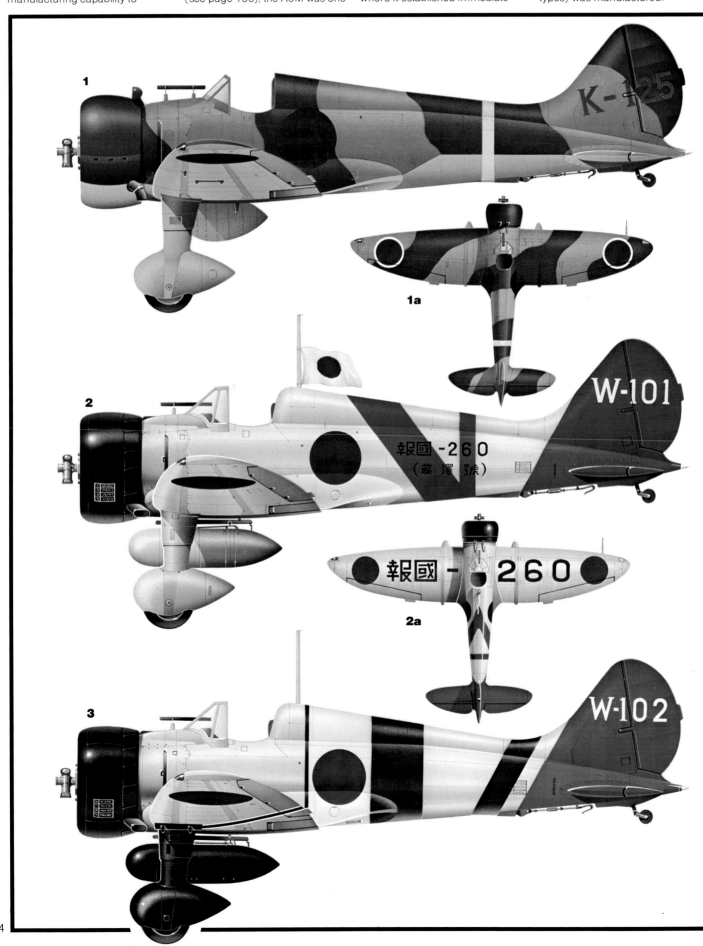

(**1**)A5M2ko flown by Lt JG Hideki Shingo assigned to the carrier *Kaga* engaged in operations off Chinese coast, mid-1938. Note use of Roman letter "k" to signify *Kaga,* this having replaced the Katakana character "ni". (**1a**) Upper surfaces of K-125. Note light tan and dark olive green disruptive pattern upper surface camouflage which was combined with mid-grey underside and adopted from late 1937. Natural metal finish was restored from mid-1938. (**2**) A5M4 flown by Lt Tamotsu Yokoyama (leader, or Buntaicho, of the carrier's fighter element) from carrier *Soryu* on East China Sea blockade duties, November 1939. *Soryu* was identified by the Roman "W", the accompanying Arabic numerals indicating the individual aircraft. (**2a**) Upper surfaces of W-101. (**3**) A5M4 flown by Naval Pilot 1st Class Matsuo Hagiri assigned to *Soryu* in summer 1939. (**4**) A5M4 aboard *Soryu* at Kasanbaru Naval Base, 1941. Note adoption of overall pale grey finish and change of carrier ID to "VII". (**4a**) Upper surfaces of VII-111. (**5**) A5M4 fighter trainer of Kasumigaura Kokutai, Omura. Kanji character "ka" and aircraft number were repeated (**5a**) beneath the wings. (**6**) A5M4 flown by Lt Motonari Suho of the 14th Kokutai, Wichow Island, China, in 1940.

# Vought SB2U (Vindicator) (1937)

The advent in service with the US Navy of the SB2U scout-bomber at the end of 1937 had signified a noteworthy advance in shipboard aircraft development, introducing to the carrier the cantilever monoplane with folding wings. Such was the pace of development, however, that it was to be outmoded well before its combat committal. The prototype, the XSB2U-1, had flown on 4 January 1936, and the first production model began to enter service in December 1937, 54 SB2U-1s being followed by 58 SB2U-2s, and 40 examples of an export version of the latter, the V-156-F, ordered for France's Aéronavale, being accepted from June 1939.

The performance of the SB2U was not to be described as vivacious, and poor aileron control adversely affected its bombing accuracy. Higher weights without any commensurate increase in power which characterised the SB2U-3 and its export equivalent, the V-156-B1, built in parallel, exacerbated the shortcomings, take-off and climb being sluggish and manoeuvrability marginal. The SB2U-3, 57 of which were produced for the US Marine Corps, was the only model named Vindicator and saw some action in the Pacific. The fifty V-156-B1s delivered to the Royal Navy were named Cheasapeake, but were considered unsuited for opera-

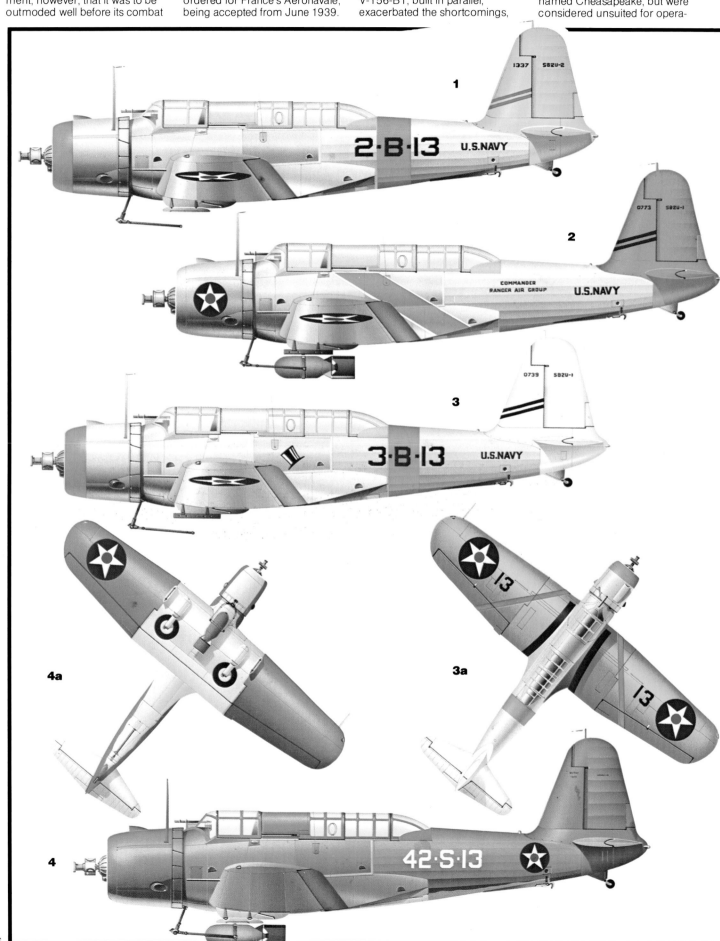

tional use. (**1**) SB2U-2 (BuAer No 1337) of 5th Section Leader of VB-2 deployed aboard USS *Lexington,* July 1939. Lemon yellow tail signified the *Lexington.* Note non-standard green inclined landing assistance stripes. (**2**) SB2U-1 (BuAer No 0773) of Commander Ranger Air Group. Note neutrality patrol star on engine cowling and green tail signifying USS *Ranger.* (**3**) SB2U-1 (BuAer No 0739) of VB-3 deployed aboard USS *Saratoga* (signified by white tail surfaces), May 1939. Note willow green cowl and band of 5th Section Leader. (**3a**) Topside plan view of same aircraft. (**4**) SB2U-2 of VS-42 aboard USS *Ranger,* and (**4a**) underside planview of same aircraft. In accordance with 13 October 1941 directive, this had non-specular blue-grey upper surfaces, this colour being extended to the undersides of the folding wing surfaces, and light grey undersurfaces. (**5**) V-156-F Nº 10 of Escadrille AB 3 at Cuers in July 1940, and (**5a**) topside planview of same aircraft. (**6**) V-156-B1 Chesapeake (AL924) of No 811 Sqdn, Royal Navy, Lee-on-Solent, Autumn 1941. (**6a**) Topside planview of AL924. (**7**) SB2U-1 of VS-41 aboard USS *Ranger,* August 1942, immediately prior to relegation to training role (**8**) V-156-F Nº 13 of Escadrille AB 1 of France's Aéronavale at Lanvéoc-Poulmic, October 1939.

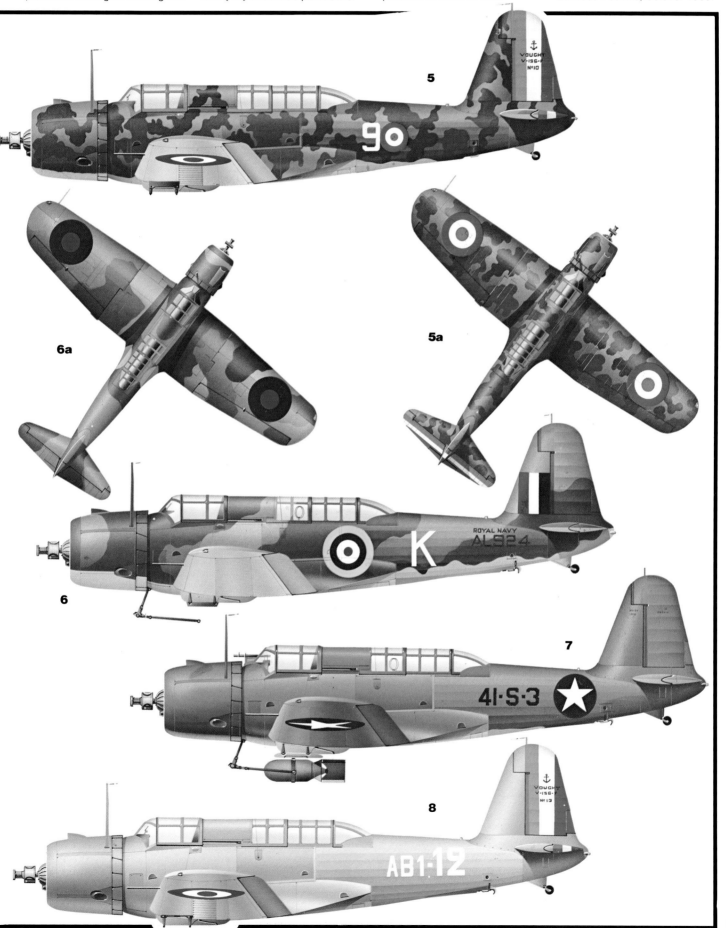

# Armstrong Whitworth Whitley (1937)

Angularly ugly, with a ponderous slab-sided fuselage and thick, broad wings, the Armstrong Whitley was aesthetically one of the least appealing of warplanes. Classed as a heavy night bomber—the term *heavy* being purely relative —it was significant in being the RAF's first bomber to offer a stressed-skin light alloy monocoque fuselage, completely turreted defensive armament and a retractable main undercarriage. A docile, matronly aeroplane, the Whitley was pleasant and easy to fly, with no serious vices, being noteworthy for its distinctive and disconcerting nose-down attitude in flight. The Whitley was first flown on 17 March 1936, and the aircraft entered RAF service the following year, in March 1937; a total of 1,812 was to have been built when production was ended in July 1943. Forming one of the mainstays of RAF Bomber Command during the first two war years, it was largely responsible for laying the foundations upon which that Command built its later auspicious achievements. (**1**) Whitley I (K7185) of No 10 Sqdn, Dishforth, Yorks, 1937, shown in the standard dark green and dark earth upper surface camouflage with black undersides and serial number in white under both port and starboard wings. (**2**) Whitley II (K7207) of No 78 Sqdn (as delivered to Airwork at Heston

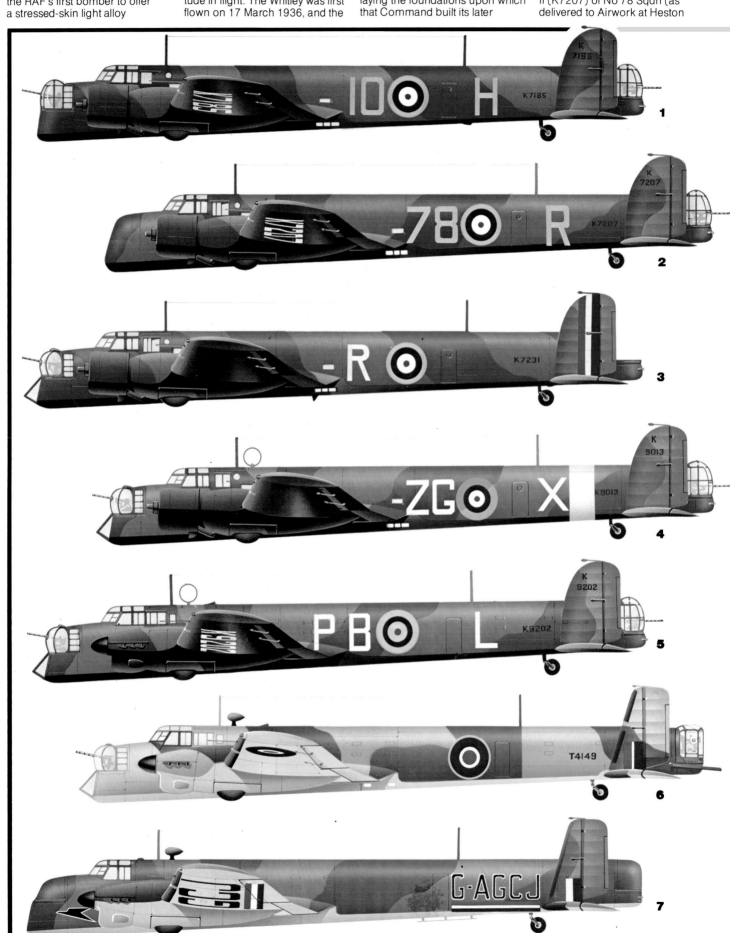

in 1937 for installation of the Frazer-Nash nose turret). (**3**) A Whitley II (K7231) modified for service at the Central Landing School, Manchester, in 1940. (**4**) A Whitley III (K9013) of No 10 Operational Training Unit, Abingdon. Note overpainting of yellow roundel outline. (**5**) A Whitley IV (K9202) of No 10 Sqdn

with the code letters adopted in 1938 (but changed to "ZA" when hostilities commenced). (**6**) A Whitley V (T4149) in day bomber finish in 1943, with a glider-towing yoke on rear fuselage. (**7**) Whitley V (BD383) as G-AGCJ of the British Overseas Airways Corporation fleet, 15 Whitleys having been used by BOAC in 1942.

(**8**) Whitley V (N1347) of No 77 Sqdn, Linton-on-Ouse, Yorks, October 1940. Note extension up fuselage sides of black finish. (**8a**) Upper surface planview and (**8b**) scrap head-on view of N1347. (**9**) Rear fuselage of Whitley V (Z6640) of No 78 Sqdn, Croft, Co Durham, late 1941. Note the overall application of black finish with

code letters and the original roundel still visible beneath new finish. (**10**) Whitley VII (Z9190) of No 502 Sqdn, one of two RAF Coastal Command squadrons to operate this type. Note dark green and ocean grey camouflage applied to the fuselage and engine nacelle upper decking and upper wing surfaces.

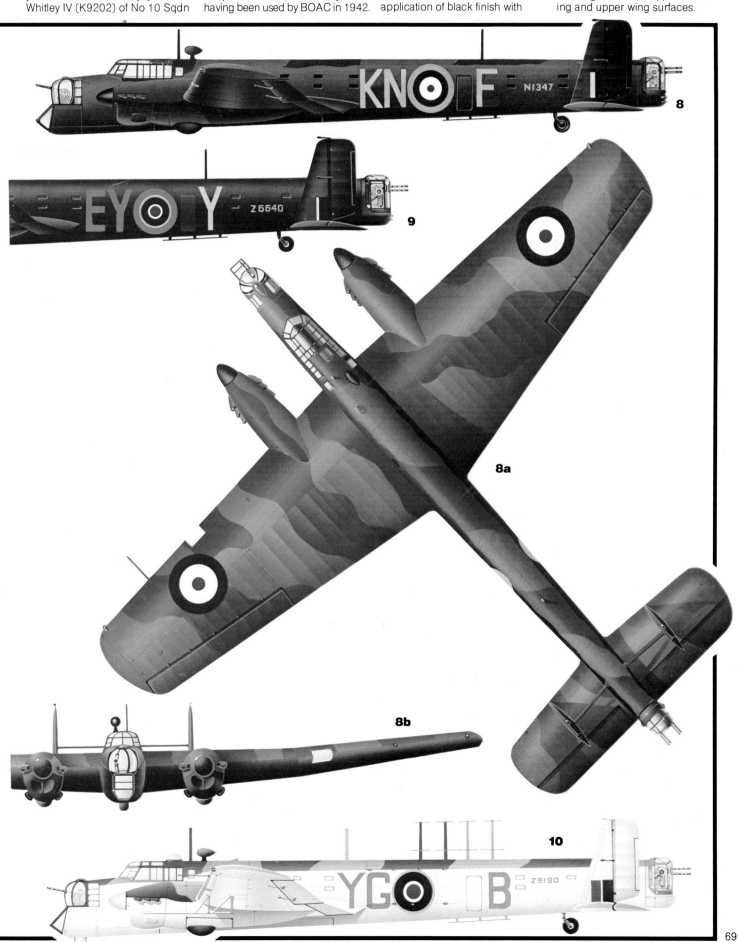

# Fairey Battle (1937)

The Battle three-seat light day bomber, conceived to fulfil a requirement formulated in 1932 and first flown on 10 March 1936, was an elegant and viceless aeroplane with amiable handling characteristics. Regrettably, the tempo of international combat aeroplane development was such that it was obsolescent by the time it first entered service in May 1937. Underpowered, slow and lacking in manoeuvrability, it was to prove highly vulnerable to both fighters and groundfire. As a key type in the RAF expansion programme, production could not be halted without unacceptable disruption, and most of the 2,184 built were relegated to training.

(**1**) Battle (K7639) of No 106 Sqdn at Abingdon, Oxon, August 1938. (**2**) Battle (953) ot SAAF, Algato, East Africa, July 1941. (**3**) Battle (T63) of 5ᵉ Escadrille, Groupe III, 3ᵉ Regiment, Belgian Aeronautique Militaire, at Evere-Bruxelles, May 1940. (**4**) Battle (B282) of the 33 Mira Vomvardismou, Royal Hellenic Air Force, October 1940. (**5**) Battle Trainer (R7365), September 1940. (**6**) Battle Trainer (1696) of No 8 Service Flying Training School, Moncton, Canada, mid-1943. (**7**) Battle Trainer (1966) of No 3 Bombing and Gunnery School, Macdonald, Canada, 1943. Note original camouflage showing through finish beneath turret.

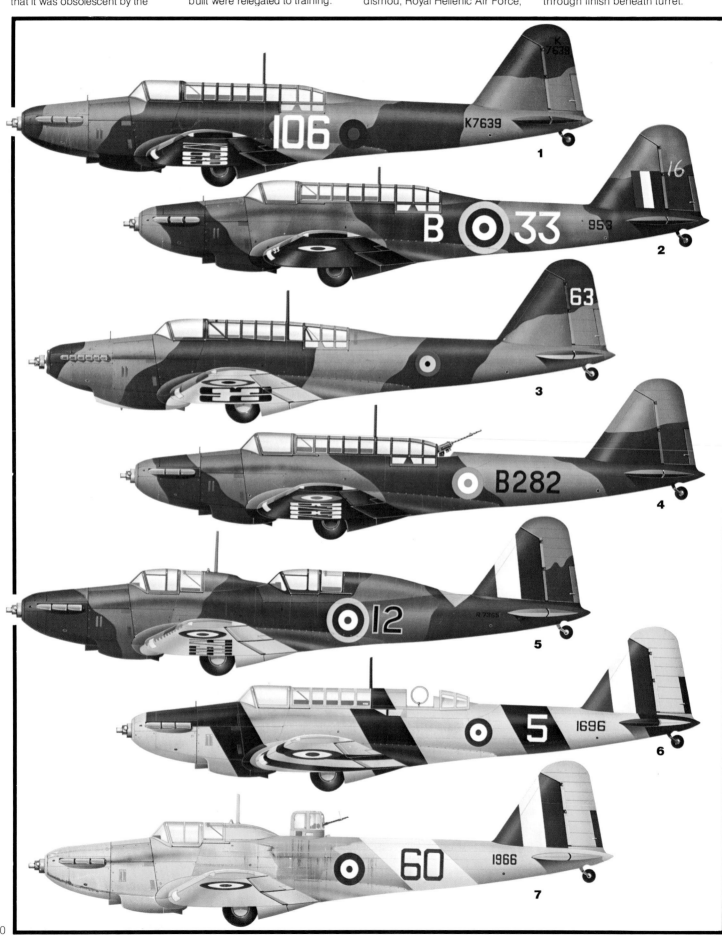

# Dornier Do 18 (1937)

When first flown early in 1935, the Do 18 set new standards in flying boat elegance. A supremely graceful machine, it was probably the most advanced water-borne aircraft conceived to that time. The military version, the Do 18D, was ordered for the equipment of the Küstenfliegergruppen, or Coastal Aviation Wings, for long-range reconnaissance, entering service spring 1937. A more powerful version with improved defensive armament, the Do 18G, appeared late in 1939, but from 1941, the Do 18Ds and Do 18Gs were progressively converted as Do 18Hs and Do 18Ns for use by the Seenotstaffeln, or air-sea rescue squadrons.

(1) Do 18D of 2./Kü.Fl.Gr.506 and Staffel emblem, spring 1939. (2) Rear hull of similarly finished Do 18D of 2./Kü.Fl.Gr.406, with Staffel emblem, at List, summer 1938. (3) Do 18D of FFS (See), summer 1939, with emblem and (3a) upper wing surfaces. (4) Do 18D of 2./Kü.Fl.Gr.906 (with emblem) at Kamp/ Pomerania, winter 1939-40 and (4a) topside planview of same boat. (5) Do 18D of 3./Kü.Fl.Gr.406 at List, Sylt, August, 1939, and (5a) emblem of 3./Kü.Fl.Gr.406. (6) Do 18G, 6.Seenotstaffel, Central Mediterranean, 1941-42, with Staffel emblem. (7) Rear hull of Do 18G of 2./Kü.Fl.Gr.106, 1940, with unit emblem.

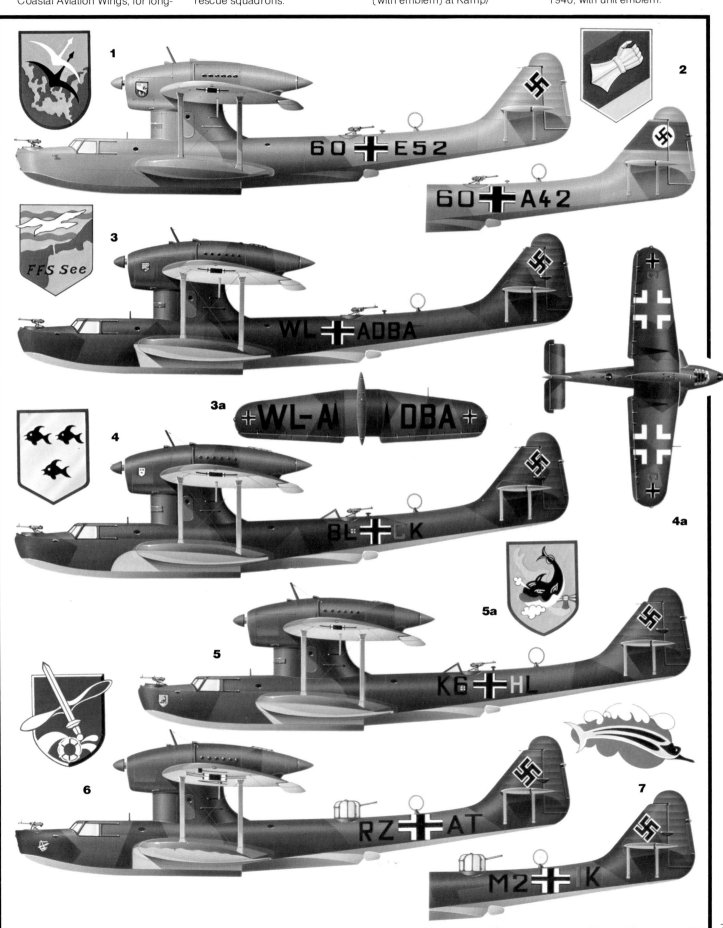

# Seversky P-35 (1937)

Subject of an extraordinarily convoluted development history, the P-35 single-seat fighter was end product of a strange series of metamorphoses undergone by a design that saw birth as a three-seat commercial twin-float amphibian! Flown as the SEV-1XP prototype late in 1935, the P-35 possessed the somewhat ephemeral claim to being the first "modern" fighter of the US services. The delivery of 77 P-35s began in May 1937, but the Seversky lacked the two most important attributes of an effective fighter: adequate performance and firepower. It was too stable for its intended role; inverted flight and outside loops were prohibited, and it tended to fall away in a spin when near its official service ceiling. However, the P-35 was popular for its undemanding and sturdy characteristics, and capacious cockpit. An improved export model, the EP-1, was ordered by Sweden, 60 being delivered and a similar number being taken over by the USAAF for use as P-35As. (1) P-35A of Lt Boyd Wagner, CO of 17th Pursuit Sqdn, Nichols Field, Luzon, Philippines, 1941. Note fuselage bands indicating CO's aircraft and "4MP" tail designator for Philippine-based 24th Group. (1a) Emblem of 17th Pursuit Sqdn. (2) P-35 flown by CO of 27th Pursuit Sqdn, 1st

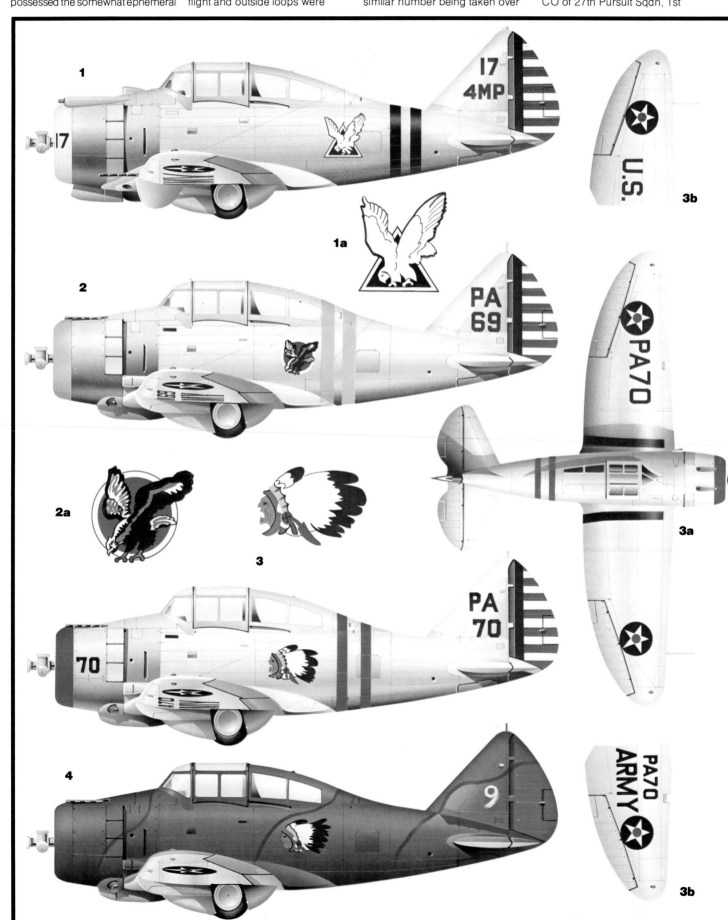

Pursuit Group, Selfridge Field, Mich, 1938-39. (**2a**) Emblem of 27th Pursuit Sqdn. (**3**) P-35 of Major H. H. George, CO of 94th Pursuit Sqdn, 1st Pursuit Group, Selfridge Field, 1938-39, and (**3a**) upper planview of same aircraft showing designator on topside of port wing, with (**3b**) scrap views of undersides of starboard and (lower) port wings. (**4**) P-35 of 94th Pursuit in temporary (soluble paint) two-tone camouflage for war games, 1939. Note the crudely applied tail number. (**5**) EP-1 (alias J 9) of Flygvapnet in initial delivery finish, early 1940. See also (**5a**) wing scrap view showing positioning of the national insignia. (**6**) EP-1 of 3rd Sqdn, Flygflottilj 8, at Barkarby, 1942-43. (**6a**) Port top surfaces of EP-1 "43" and (**6b**) "Falcon" emblem of F 8, the circular background of which was painted in the Sqdn colour (1st red, 2nd blue and 3rd yellow). (**7**) EP-1 of 1st Sqdn, F 8, in finish standard-ised in 1944. (**7a**) Starboard top surfaces of EP-1 "J" with full-chord national insignia. (**8**) EP-1 of 1st Sqdn, F 8, in "Italian-style" earth brown and green dapple applied to some aircraft, with (**8a**) scrap view of wing upper surfaces. Outer panel undersides were black to port and white to starboard.

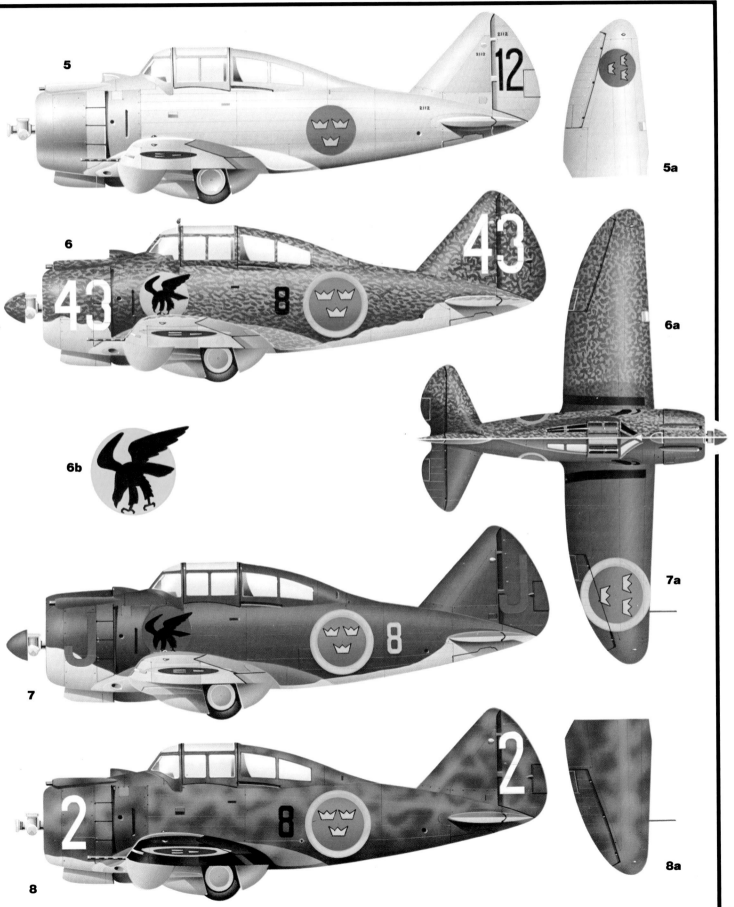

# Bristol Blenheim (1937)

Hailed as a major advance in the design of combat aircraft at its debut, being the RAF's first all-metal stressed-skin monoplane to achieve production, the Blenheim was fated never to fulfil the high hopes placed in it. Such was the pace of combat aircraft evolution immediately prior to World War II that the Blenheim was no longer a redoubtable weapon when the RAF went to war, offering inadequate performance and being woefully vulnerable to fighter attack. Flown as a prototype on 25 June 1936, it entered RAF service in its short-nosed Mk I version in March 1937, licence manufacture of this model being undertaken in Yugoslavia and Finland. It was succeeded by the long-nose Mk IV, fighter conversions of both models being used as Mks IF and IVF, and a Canadian equivalent of the Mk IV was known as the Bolingbroke. At the start of WWII, all Blenheims wore matt dark green and dark earth upper surface camouflage with black undersides, but in 1940, the RAF adopted pale blue (Sky) under sides. By mid-1941, some anti-shipping Blenheims had replaced the dark earth areas with dark sea grey, and in the Middle East a dark earth and mid-stone were used for the upper surfaces with azure blue undersides. (1) A Blenheim I (K7059) of No 90 Sqdn, Bicester, Oxon, winter 1938-39.

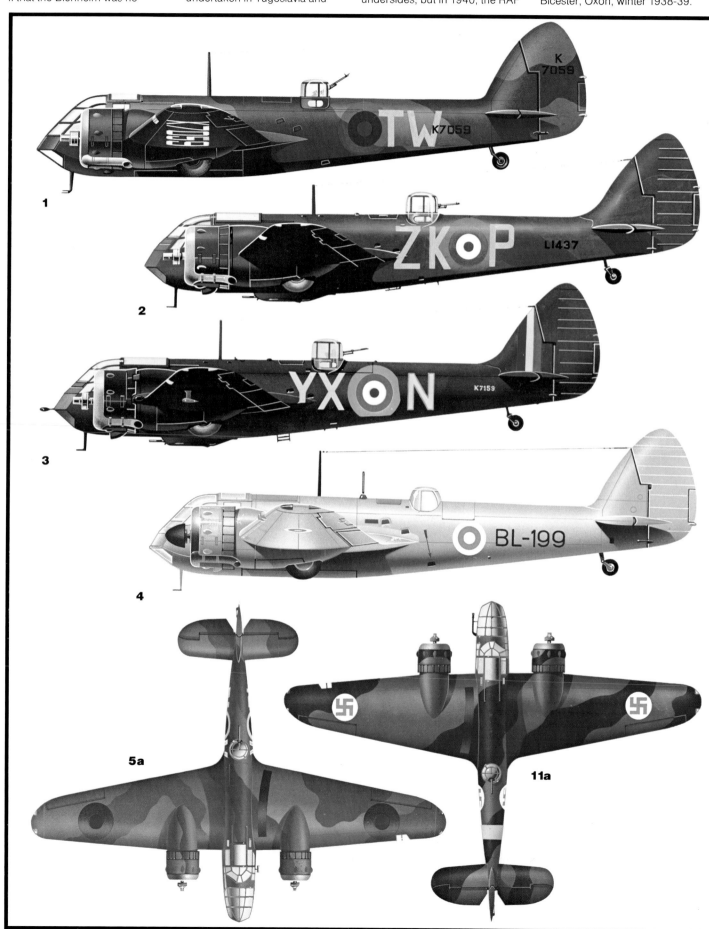

Note overpainting of yellow outer roundel ring as Munich crisis measure. (**2**) Blenheim IF (L1437) of No 25(F) Sqdn, North Weald, Essex, early 1940. (**3**) Blenheim IF of No 54 Operational Training Unit, summer 1941. Note yellow outline of aircraft letter and part overpainting of outer roundel ring. (**4**) Valmet-built Blenheim I of Ilmavoimat, Malmi, 1956, this being one of the last surviving examples. (**5**) Blenheim IV (R3612) of No 40 Sqdn, Wyton, Hunts, July 1940, and (**5a**) upper plan of same. (**6**) Blenheim IV (Z9601) of No 55 Sqdn, Fuka, Egypt, early 1942. Note blue Mediterranean camouflage scheme. (**7**) Bolingbroke IV of No 115 (BR) Sqdn, RCAF, Patricia Bay, August 1943. (**8**) Bolingbroke IV target tug of No 1 Training Command Bombing and Gunnery School, RCAF, 1944. (**9**) Blenheim IV (Z9583) of GRB 1, Free French Air Forces, Abu-Sueir, Egypt, October 1941. (**10**) Blenheim IV (T2249) of No 84 Sqdn, Aqir, Palestine, April 1941. (**11**) Ilmavoimien Blenheim IV (BL-129), LeLv 42, late 1942, with (**11a**) upper surface planview showing standard "Continuation War" black-and-green camouflage. (**11b**) "Ace of Hearts" emblem partly obscured on nose, and (**11c**) Black "Elk" emblem of LeLv 42 appearing on vertical fin. The white mission markers appeared on portside of rudder only.

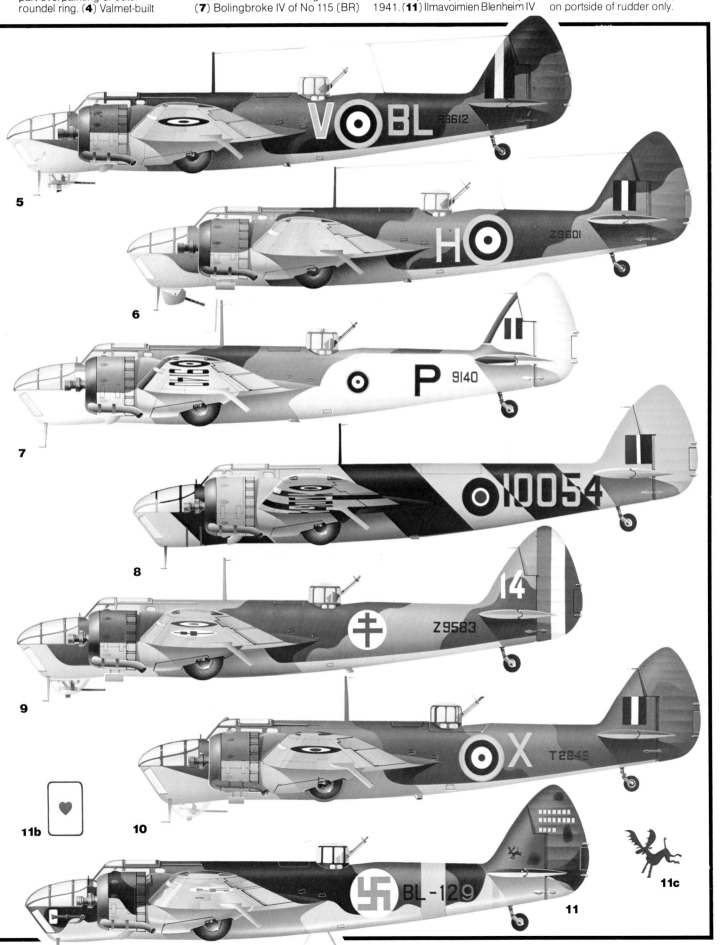

# Fiat BR.20 Cicogna (1937)

In the years immediately before World War II, the Italian aircraft industry excelled in the development of trimotor medium bombers, but rather less success attended the parallel efforts to evolve twin-engined warplanes in this category owing to a lack of adequately reliable engines of sufficient power. One twin-engined bomber was built in some numbers for the Regia Aeronautica, however, and this, the BR.20 Cicogna (Stork), equipped four Stormi Bombardamento Terrestre when Italy entered WWII, serving until the Armistice of September 1943. First flown on 10 February 1936, the BR.20 was to attain production status with quite exceptional rapidity, deliveries commencing in the following autumn and initial service being achieved early 1937. It was to have its baptism of fire over Spain in the following summer, and 72 were to be exported to Japan, but, somewhat underpowered, the BR.20 offered an inauspicious performance and poor defensive capability. Production continued until July 1943, by which time a total of 512 had been delivered. The BR.20M had more extensive duralumin skinning, a redesigned nose and structural modifications. (1) BR.20M of 56ª squadriglia of 86° Gruppo at Castelventrano, April 1942. Note overpainting of insignia for nocturnal

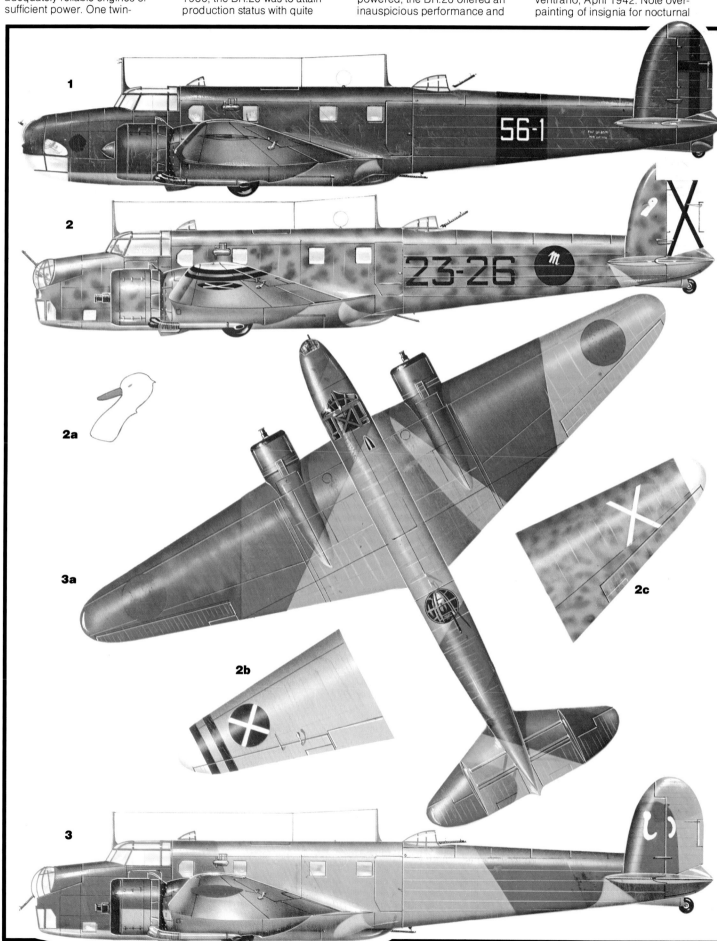

operations against Malta. (2) BR.20 of 230ª squadriglia of the XXXV Gruppo Autonomo, Italian Aviación de el Tercio, Tudela, Spain, November 1937, and (2a) emblem of 230ª squadriglia. (2b) Underside and (2c) upper wing surface detail of 230ª aircraft (3) BR.20, or Type I (Y-shiki) of 12th Sentai, 7th Hikodan, Japanese Imperial Army Air Force, operating over the Nomonhan plateau against Soviet forces, summer 1939, and (3a) topside planview of same aircraft. (4) BR.20 (M.M.21719) of 235ª squadriglia, 60º Gruppo, 41º Stormo Bombardamento Terrestre, Jesi, July 1939, and (4a) emblem of 41º Stormo. Note tricolour rudder (5) BR.20 (M.M.21718) of 65ª squadriglia, 31º Gruppo, 18º Stormo, Catania, Sicily, June 1941, and (5a) 18º Stormo emblem. (6) BR.20M of 277ª squadriglia, 116º Gruppo, 37º Stormo, operating on Greco-Albanian Front from Grottaglie, late 1940. Note high-visibility engine cowlings. (7) BR.20M (M.M.21894) of 4ª squadriglia, 11º Gruppo, 13º Stormo, attached to Corpo Aereo Italiano for operations against UK from Melsbroek, Belgium, late 1940. (7a) Emblem of 4ª squadriglia. (8) BR.20M of 1ª squadriglia, 43º Gruppo, 13º Stormo, at Bir Dufan, Libya, February 1942, and (8a) emblem of 1ª squadriglia. Note extended ventral gun.

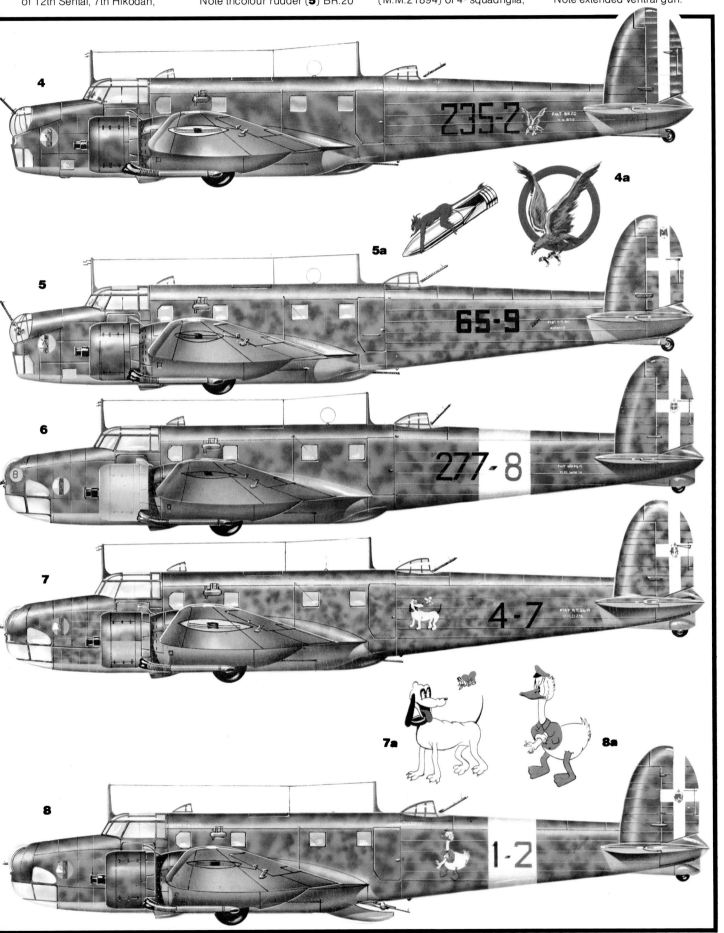

# Junkers Ju 87 (1937)

No warplane of WWII aroused more controversy than the Ju 87 dive bomber; none enjoyed greater réclame. Synonymous with the abbreviation "Stuka" from the term Sturzkampfflugzeug which was, in fact, descriptive of *all* dive bombers, the Ju 87 enjoyed an almost legendary reputation until it entered its eclipse over

the UK, reaching its nadir over the Soviet Union. Flown in the spring of 1935 and entering service in its initial Ju 87A form in 1937, the basic design was to be the subject of years of incremental development and was to be retained in production until the summer of 1944, by which time, more than 5,700 had

been manufactured. Cumbersome, poorly armed and possessing poor manoeuvrability, the Ju 87 was woefully vulnerable to fighters and was an anachronism for much of its service life. It was, however, a supremely sturdy warplane and almost certainly the most *accurate* dive bomber of WWII. From the end of 1942, it

was optimised for the schlacht-flugzeug (close support) role. (**1**) Ju 87R (S2+M2) of 7.Staffel, Stukageschwader 77, Balkans, April 1941. Note yellow cowl, wingtips and rudder signifying theatre. (**1a**) Emblem of 7./StG 77. (**2**) Ju 87B-1 (6G+JR) of 7./StG 51 (later 4./StG 1), French campaign, May-June 1940.

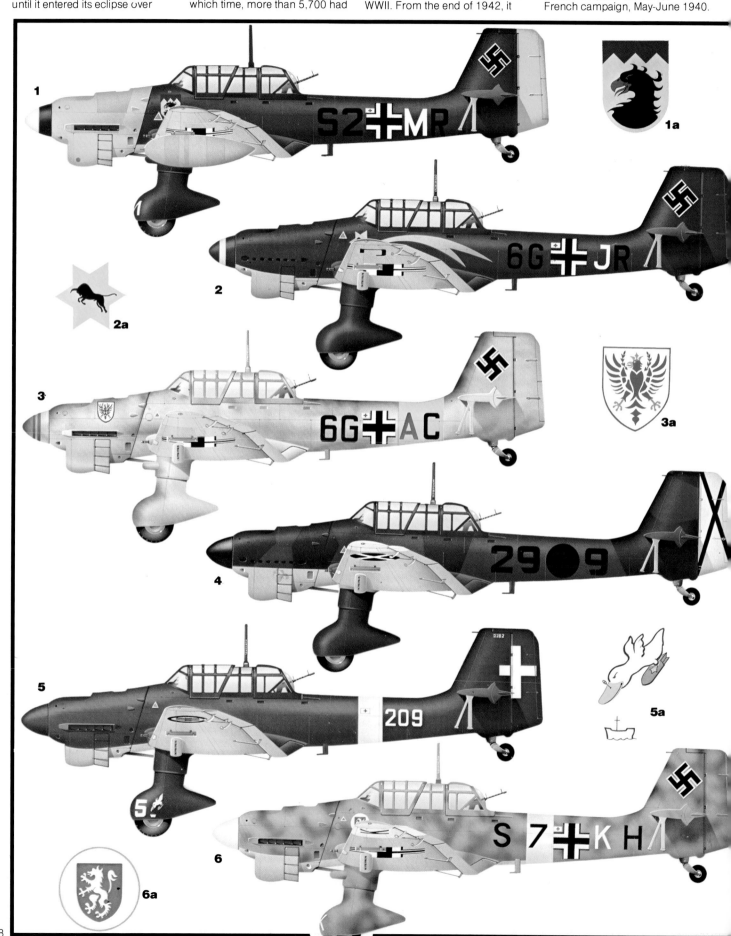

78

(**2a**) Emblem of 7./StG 51, and (**2b**) Top planview of 6G+JR. Note individual aircraft letter at wingtips. (**3**) Ju 87B-2 (6G+AC) of Stab II/StG 1 (originally) III/StG 51) on Eastern Front, late 1941. Note application of white water-soluble paint as temporary winter camouflage. (**3a**) Emblem of II/StG (retained from III/StG 51). (**4**) Ju 87B-1 (29·9) of the so-called Staffel Jolanthe, Kampfgruppe 88, Legion Condor, Spain, winter 1938-39. (**5**) Ju 87B-1 of 209ª squadriglia of 101º Gruppo autonoma, Regia Aeronautica, Gars el Arid, September 1941. (**5a**) Emblem of 209ª sqd. (**6**) Ju 87B-2/Trop (S7+KH) of 1./StG 3, North Africa in support of the Afrika Korps, early 1942. (**6a**) Emblem of I/StG 3 (ex I/StG 76) and (**6b**) topside planview of S7+KH. (**7**) Ju 87D-1/Trop (S7+KS) of 8./StG 3, Libya, mid-1942. Note non-standard dark earth and dark sand-brown disruptive camouflage on upper surfaces. (**8**) Ju 87D-3 of Dive Bomber Group 6, Rumanian 1st Air Corps, Soviet Union, summer 1943. (**9**) Ju 87G-1 of the Versuchskommando für Panzerbekampfung (Experimental Detachment for Tank Combat), April 1943. (**9a**) Emblem of Kommando. (**10**) Ju 87D-3 (B6+31) of 102./1 (Hungarian) Dive Bomber Sqdn, 1943. (**11**) Ju 87D-5 of Royal Bulgarian Air Force, summer 1944.

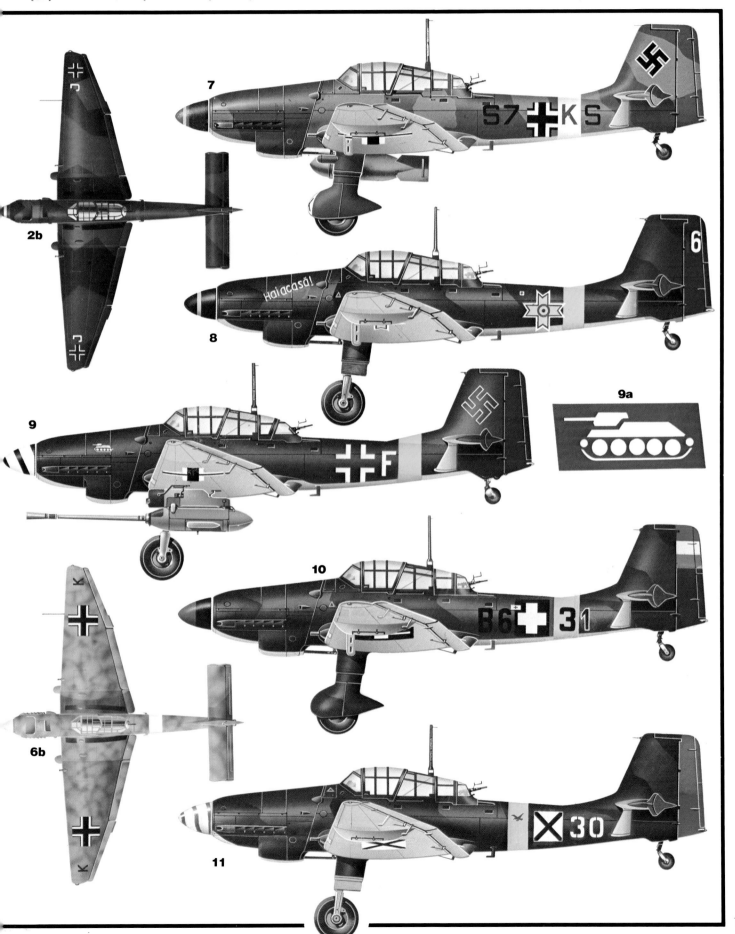

79

# Mitsubishi Type 96 Attack Bomber (G3M) (1937)

The Navy Type 96 Attack Bomber, or G3M, to become known to the Allies by the reporting name of Nell, was without doubt among the most significant warplanes ever created by the Japanese aircraft industry. Its service debut was to signify the attainment by Japanese military aviation of a level favourably comparable with

that achieved by the western air powers. The G3M was the product of the far-sightedness of Rear Admiral Isoroku Yamamoto when chief of the Technical Division of the Imperial Naval Bureau of Aeronautics, and it was to be responsible for the first trans-oceanic bombing attacks in the history of aerial warfare. The

first prototype was flown in July 1935, and the initial production version, the G3M1, entered Navy service early in 1937, a batch of 34 of these being followed by the improved G3M2 with which the first trans-oceanic bombing raid was mounted on 14 August 1937, a week after the commencement of the second Sino-Japanese conflict.

Backbone of the Imperial Navy's first-line striking force when the Pacific War began, the G3M remained in production until 1943, the parent company building 581 G3M2s and Nakajima building a further 412 G3M2s and G3M3s, the latter having higher-powered engines and more fuel capacity. (1) G3M1 of the Kisarazu Kokutai

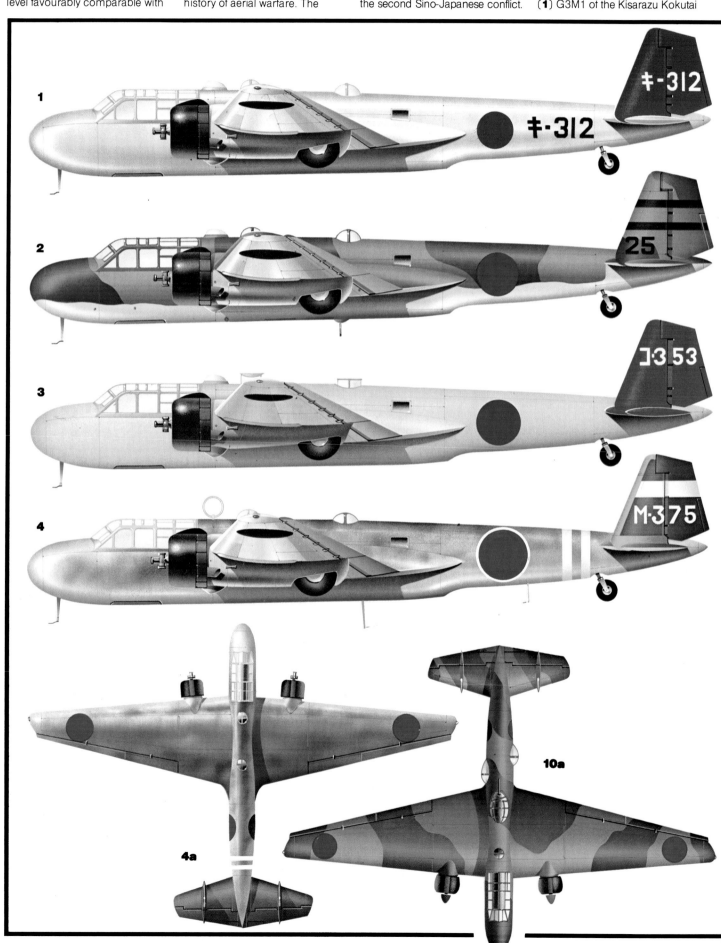

based on Kisarazu, Chiba, April 1937. This unit subsequently flew against Chinese targets from Cheju Island, Korea. (**2**) G3M1 of the same Kokutai after applications of camouflage as operated from Omura, Kyushu, mid-August 1937, for attacks on Chinese targets, including Nankin and Suchow. (**3**) G3M1 of Ominato Kokutai based at Ominato in autumn 1937. (**4**) G3M2 of the Mihoro Kokutai based at Hankow for operations over the Szechwan Province of China, April-May 1941. (**4a**) Upper surfaces of same aircraft showing irregular application of dark green over natural metal. (**5**) G3M2 of the Takao Kokutai, 23rd Koku Sentai, based at Takao, Taiwan, April 1941. (**6**) G3M2 of Genzan Kokutai operating from Saigon, Indo-China, December 1941, and participating in sinking of HMS *Prince of Wales* and HMS *Repulse*. (**7**) G3M2 of Yokosuka Kokutai assigned to Marianas in February 1944, one of last areas in which G3M saw extensive use. (**8**) G3M2 also of Yokosuka Kokutai based at Yokosuka for training, March 1944. (**9**) L3Y2 (transport conversion of G3M2) attached to the 221st (Fighter) Kokutai, mid-1944. (**10**) G3M2 of Takao Kokutai with 21st Koku Sentai operating from Hanoi, Indo-China, March 1941, and (**10a**) topside planview of the same aircraft.

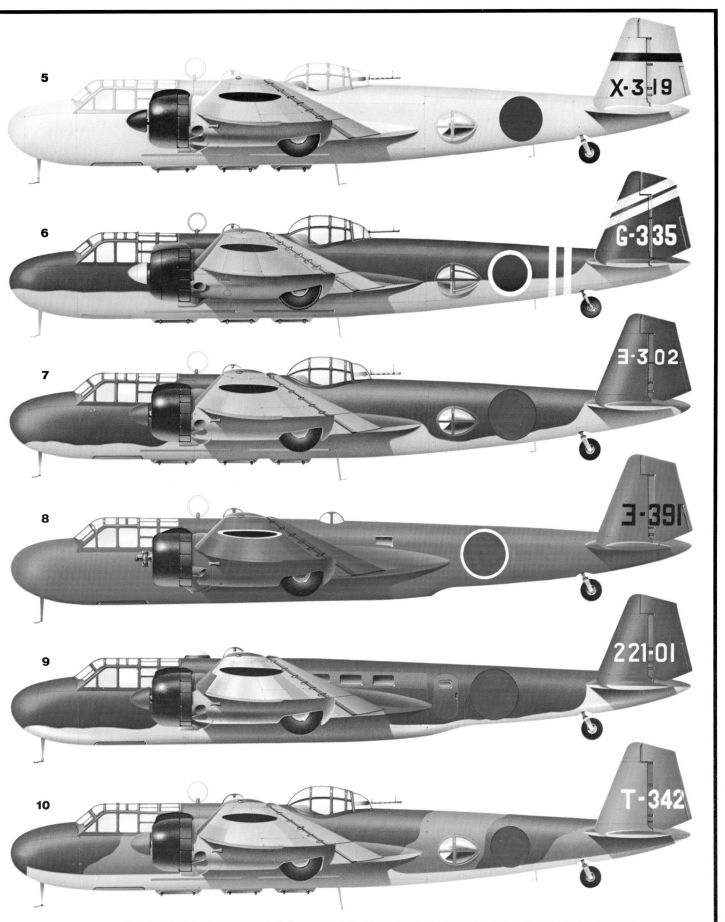

# Boeing B-17 Fortress (1937)

Numbered among the most famous bombers of all time, the B-17 Fortress represented a quantum advance in combat aircraft design when flown on 28 July 1935. Entering service (as the Y1B-17) in 1937, it was to gain the universal affection of its crews, a total of 12,677 B-17s being built. (**1**) B-17D, 14th Sqdn, 19th Bomb Group, Clark Field, Luzon, December 1941. Note retention of the tail striping and deletion of the tail designator. (**2**) B-17E (41-9023) "Yankee Doodle" of 414th Sqdn, 97th Bomb Group, Grafton Underwood, September 1942. Note medium green/earth disruptive camouflage and azure blue underside. (**3**) B-17F-40 (42-5177), 359th Sqdn, 303rd Bomb Group, Molesworth, summer 1943. Note medium green blotching on olive drab upper surfaces. (**4**) Rear fuselage of B-17G-60 (44-8398) of 602nd Sqdn, 398th Bomb Group, Nuthampstead, autumn 1944. Note "W" Group marking. The red fin, (**4a**) wingtips and (**4b**) tailplane were adopted July 1944. (**5**) B-17G-40 (42-97976) of 447th Bomb Group, Rattlesden, Norfolk, early 1945. The aircraft name "A Bit O'Lace" may be seen above reclining female figure on nose, together with evidence of 83 missions. The green fuselage bands, yellow wingtips and tail surfaces were adopted late January 1945 (this particular aircraft

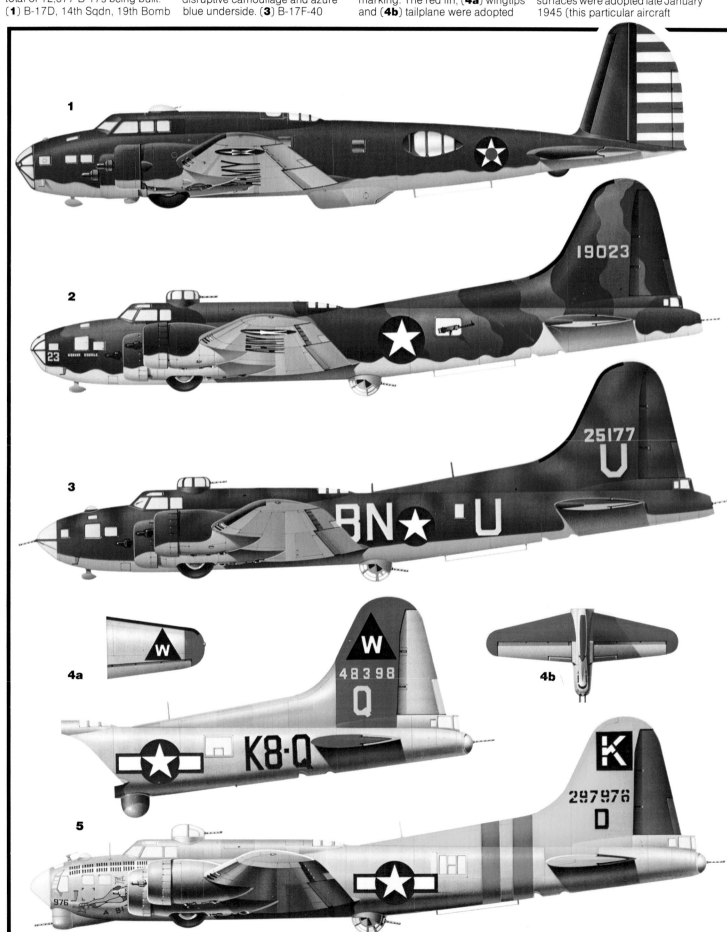

having olive drab replacement rudder). Insignia blue wing chevrons (starboard upper and port lower) applied late 1944 and retained. (**6**) Fortress IIA (FL459) of No 220 Sqdn, RAF Coastal Command, Ballykelly, in N Ireland, late 1942. (**7**) Fortress B III (KJ109) — B-17G-55 (44-8240) — of No 223 (SD) Sqdn, Oulton, in

Norfolk, on electronic jamming and intelligence duties. (**8**) Rear fuselage of B-17G-15 (42-97503), 533rd Sqdn, 381st Bomb Group, Ridgewell, in Essex, early 1945. Red fin, tailplane and wingtips adopted July 1944. (**9**) B-17F-27 (41-24585), originally "Wulf Hound", 303rd Bomb Group, Molesworth, which force-

landed in France on 12 December 1942, after attacking Rouen Sotteville marshalling yards. Subsequently flight tested at Rechlin (as DL+XC), it was employed (in the finish illustrated) for demonstrations to Jagdgruppen and, in September 1943, assigned (after repainting in night camouflage) to I Gruppe of

Kampfgeschwader 200 for clandestine operations. (**10**) B-17F-115 (42-30661), originally "Veni Vidi Vici" of 388th Bomb Group, Knettishall, which landed at Rinkaby, Sweden, on 29 February 1944. Subsequently converted (as illustrated) as a 14-passenger transport, serving with AB Aero-transport from 6 October 1944.

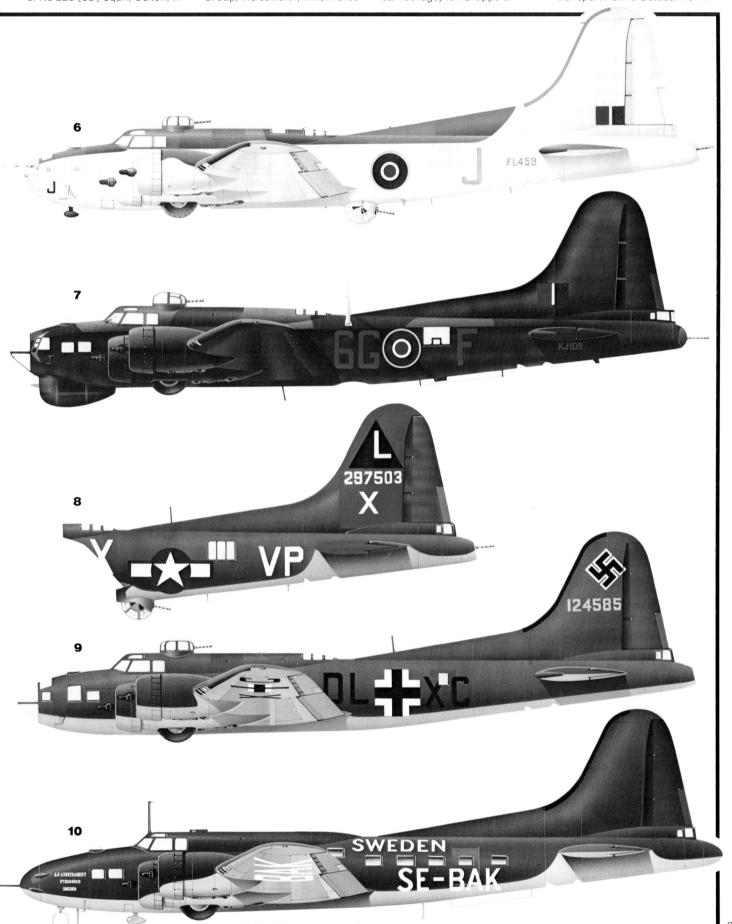

# Hawker Hurricane (1937)

The RAF's first fighter monoplane and the service's first combat aircraft capable of a level speed exceeding 300mph, the Hurricane was something of a compromise between tradition and the demands of a new era in aerial warfare. Destined to carry the bulk of the burden of Britain's defence in the most significant air conflict

ever fought, the Hurricane never achieved the truly legendary status of the numerically — so far as the Battle of Britain was concerned — less important Spitfire, which it complemented to a remarkable degree. It is to be numbered among the true immortals of aviation history's annals, nevertheless, laying

claim to versatility exceeded by few if any warplanes in WWII. It first flew on 6 November 1935, entering RAF service in December 1937, and was to prove a first rate gun platform, extremely manoeuvrable and very robust. If slower than its primary opponent, the Bf 109, it was a far superior dogfighter, and production was to

continue until September 1944, 12,780 being built in the UK, supplemented by 1,451 built in Canada. Licence manufacture was undertaken in Yugoslavia and Belgium, but, in the event, only 20 were completed in the former and three in the latter country. (1) Hurricane I (L1555), No 111 Sqdn, Northolt, 1937. Note Sqdn

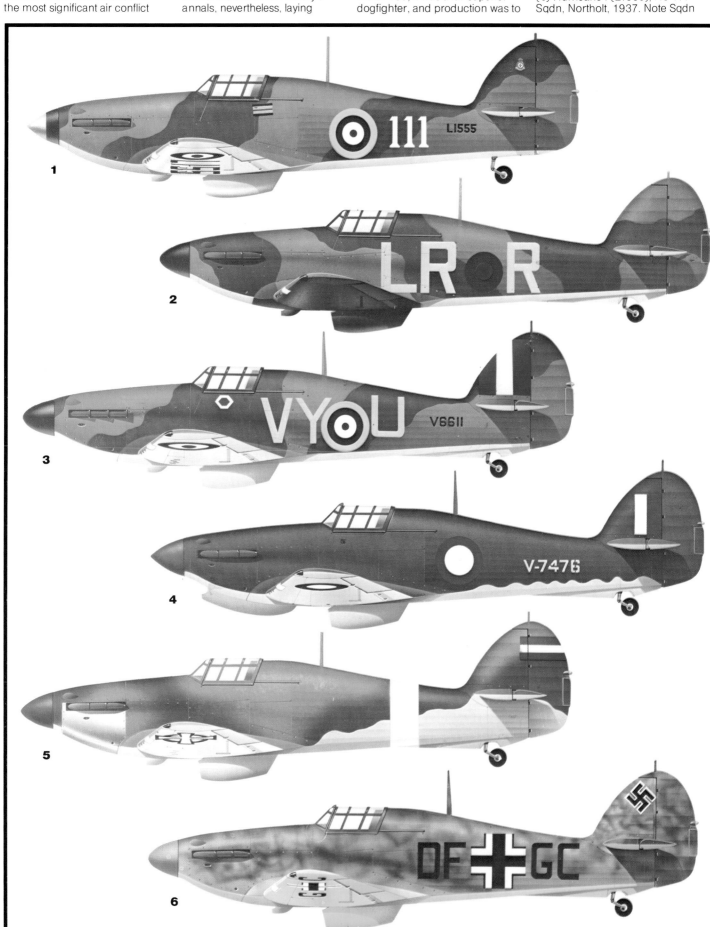

Ldr's pennant on fuselage.
(**2**) Hurricane I (L1990) of No 56 Sqdn, North Weald, 1939. Note 1938-allocated fuselage coding. (**3**) Hurricane I (V6611) of No 85 Sqdn operating from Debden and Croydon, August 1940. Note Sqdn white hexagon. (**4**) The only Hurricane operated in Australia with RAF serial (V7476) and RAAF colours. Used by Nos 2 and 3 Communications Flights. (**5**) Zmaj-built Hurricane I of Royal Yugoslav Air Force, Zemun, April 1941. (**6**) Hurricane I (original identity unknown) repainted after capture for Luftwaffe test at Magdeburg. (**7**) Hurricane IIB (Z3768) as operated by No 81 Sqdn at Vaenga, Soviet Union, autumn 1941, with British coding and V-VS identity numerals.
(**8**) Hurricane IIB (BD930) of No 73 Sqdn, Western Desert, 1942. Note unofficial version of pre-war Sqdn marking on fuselage.
(**9**) Hurricane IIB of Esquadrilha RV, Portuguese Arma de Aero-náutica, Espinho, Oporto, 1948, and (**9a**) emblem of Esquadrilha RV. (**10**) Hurricane IIC (HL603) of No 1 Sqdn, Acklington, summer 1942. Note newly-adopted day fighter finish. (**11**) Hurricane IID (BP188) of No 6 Sqdn at LG 91, Western Desert, July 1942.
(**12**) Hurricane X (BW850) with arrester hook for RN service as Sea Hurricane but retained in Canada for service with No 440 Sqdn.

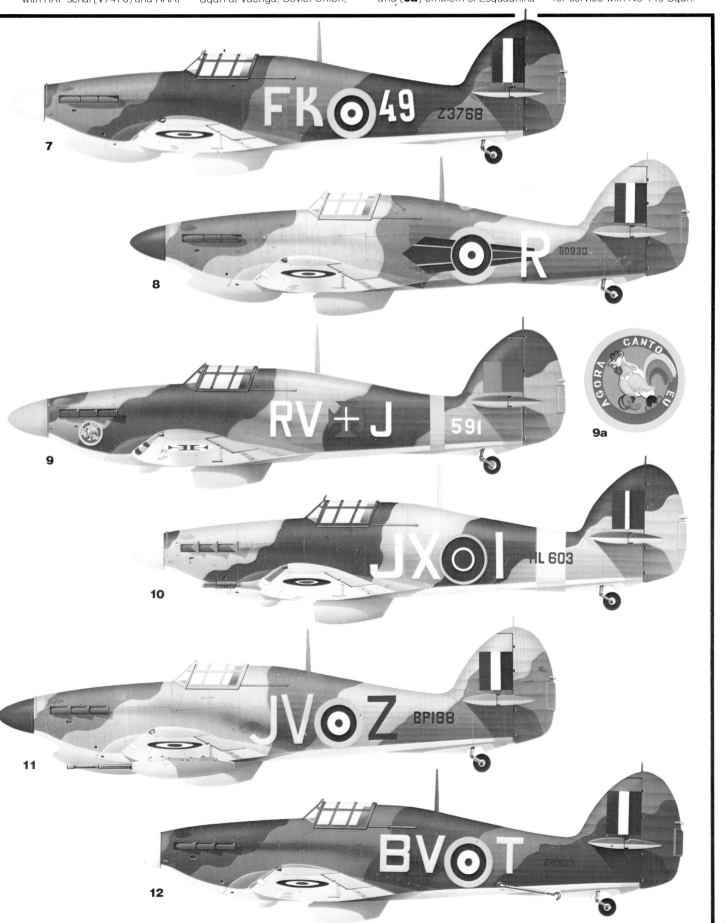

# Messerschmitt Bf 109 (1937)

Without doubt the world's most advanced single-seat fighter when first flown as a prototype in May 1935, the Bf109 entered Luftwaffe service in its initial Jumo-engined form early in 1937. The Jumo 210 was retained for the Bf 109B, C and D models, but it was the mating of Daimler-Benz DB 601 with the airframe as the Bf 109E that truly carried the Messerschmitt to the fore of international fighter development. Remaining in production until early 1942, this model was to prove master of the Spitfire in the vertical plane and in level speed, but it lacked the agility possessed by the British fighter. (**1**) Bf 109B of 6. Staffel of Jagdgeschwader 132 "Richthofen" at Jüterbog-Damm, autumn 1937. Black bar indicated II Gruppe. (**1a**) JG 132 emblem (later JG 2). (**2**) Bf 109B of Luftwaffe Schule (indicated by "S") of Luftkreiskommando (Local Air Command) II (indicated by "2"), Berlin, early 1939. (**3**) Bf 109C of 10. (Nacht)/JG 77 interim night-fighting Staffel, Aalborg, July 1940. (**3a**) Early form Nachtjäger emblem. (**4**) Bf 109D of Jagdfliegerschule 1, Werneuchen, in 1940. Note ejector-type exhaust. (**4a**) Emblem of JFS 1. (**5**) Bf 109C-2 of 1./JG 137, Bernburg, in summer 1938. (**5a**) The "Bernburger Hunter" emblem of 1./JG 137 (later 1./ZG 2). (**6**) Bf 109D of

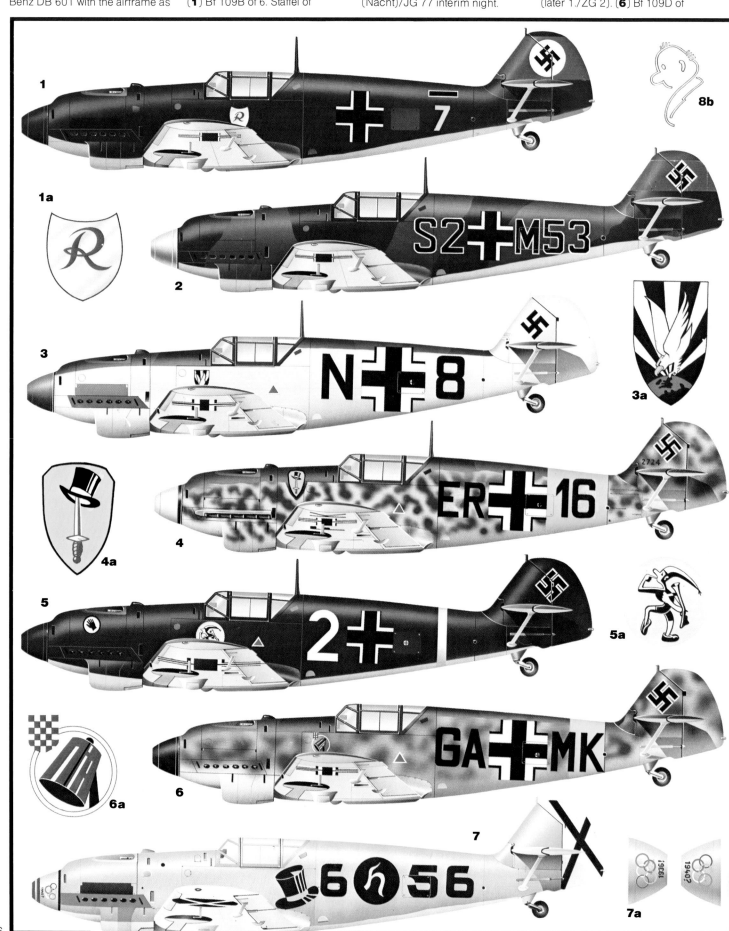

Flugzeugführerschule A/B 123 (kroat.) at Agram, Zagreb, March 1942. (**6a**) Emblem of A/B 123. (**7**) Bf 109D of Hptm Gotthard Handrick, Gruppenkommandeur, J88, Legion Condor, Calamocha, Spain, February 1938. Note the "Zylinder Hut" (Top Hat) emblem of 2./J88. (**7a**) Olympic ring-decorated spinner of Handrick's

Bf 109D. (**8**) Bf 109E-4B of Ltn Steindl, Geschwader-Adjutant (see fuselage symbol) JG 54 "Grünherz", Leningrad area of the Eastern Front, spring 1942. (**8a**) Vienna-Aspern Coat of Arms used as II/JG 54 emblem, and (**8b**) personal emblem of Steindl. (**9**) Bf 109E-1 of IV/JG 132 (later I/JG 77), Werneuchen, in

early 1939. (**9a**) "Wanderzirkus Jahnke" emblem of IV/JG 132. (**10**) Bf 109E-3 of Hpt Henschel, Gruppenkommandeur, II/JG 77, Aalborg, Norway, in July 1940. (**10a**) II/JG 77 emblem. (**11**) Bf 109E-7B of II Gruppe, Schlacht-geschwader 1, Stalingrad area, winter 1942-43. (**11a**) Infanterie-Sturmabzeichen. (**12**) Bf109E-1,

II/JG 26 "Schlageter", Düsseldorf, August 1939. White soluble paint was applied to the tail for exercise. (**12a**) JG 26 emblem. (**13**) Bf 109E-3, 9./JG 26, at Caffiers, France, August 1940. (**13a**) 9./JG 26 emblem. (**14**) Bf 109E-1 of III/JG 52, Hopstädten, August 1940. (**14a**) "Winterfield'-scher Wolf" III/JG 52 emblem.

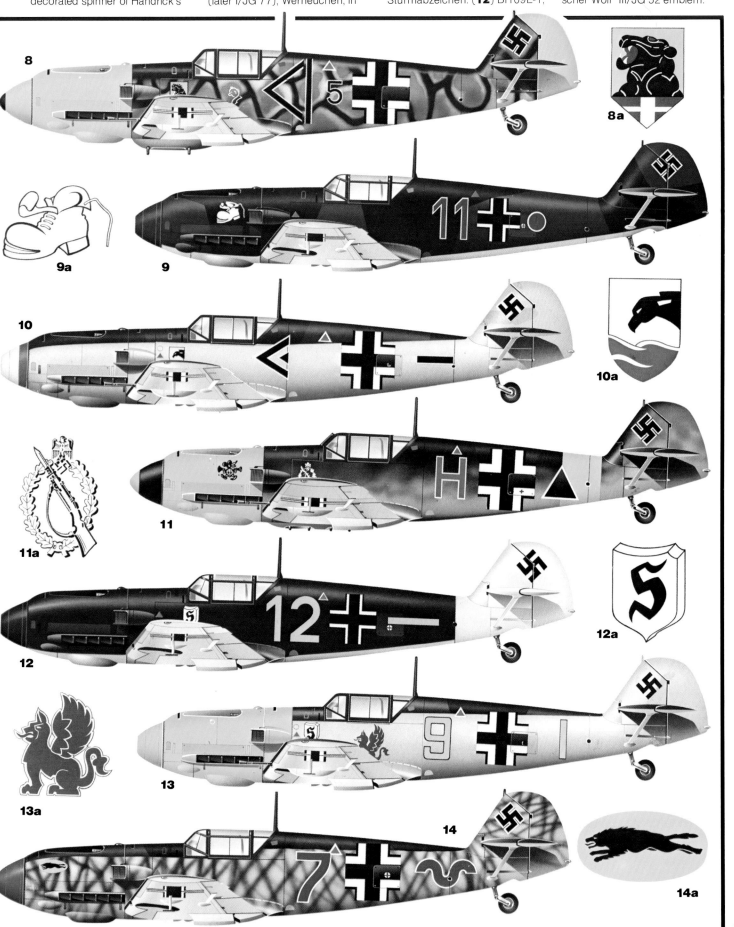

8

8a

9a

9

10

10a

11a

11

12

12a

13a

13

14

7

14a

87

# Messerschmitt Bf 109 (continued)

Characterised by a more powerful engine, the Bf 109G carried development of the Messerschmitt fighter to its zenith. While the higher weight and power loadings adversely affected handling and manoeuvrability, performance was greatly enhanced, a process which was carried still further by the definitive model, the Bf 109K.

(1) Bf 109-2 of 4./JG 54 "Grünherz", Siverskaya, northern sector of Eastern Front, summer 1942. Note Vienna-Aspern Coat of Arms ahead of the windscreen (see page 87), horizontal bar signifying II Gruppe on rear fuselage and the field-applied camouflage. (2) Bf 109G-2/Trop of II/JG 51 "Molders" at Casa Zeppera, Sard-

inia, in summer 1943. (2a) The Jagdgeschwader "Molders" emblem and (2b) that of II Gruppe. (3) Bf 109G-10/U4 of kroat. Jagdstaffel, Eichwalde, November 1944, while operating under Jagdfliegerführer Ostpreussen. Note the taller wooden fin-and-rudder assembly. (4) Bf 109G-5/U2 (MT-422 Werk-Nr 411 938)

of HLeLv 31, Finnish Ilmavoimien, Utti, 1948. (5) Bf 109G-14/U2 of Hungarian 101 Fighter Group, South Germany, April 1945. Note non-standard spinner and the FuG 16ZY antenna. (6) Bf 109K-4 of I/JG 27, Rheine, December 1944. Note "Defence of Reich" band. (7) Bf 109K-4 of II/JG 77 at Bönninghardt, December 1944.

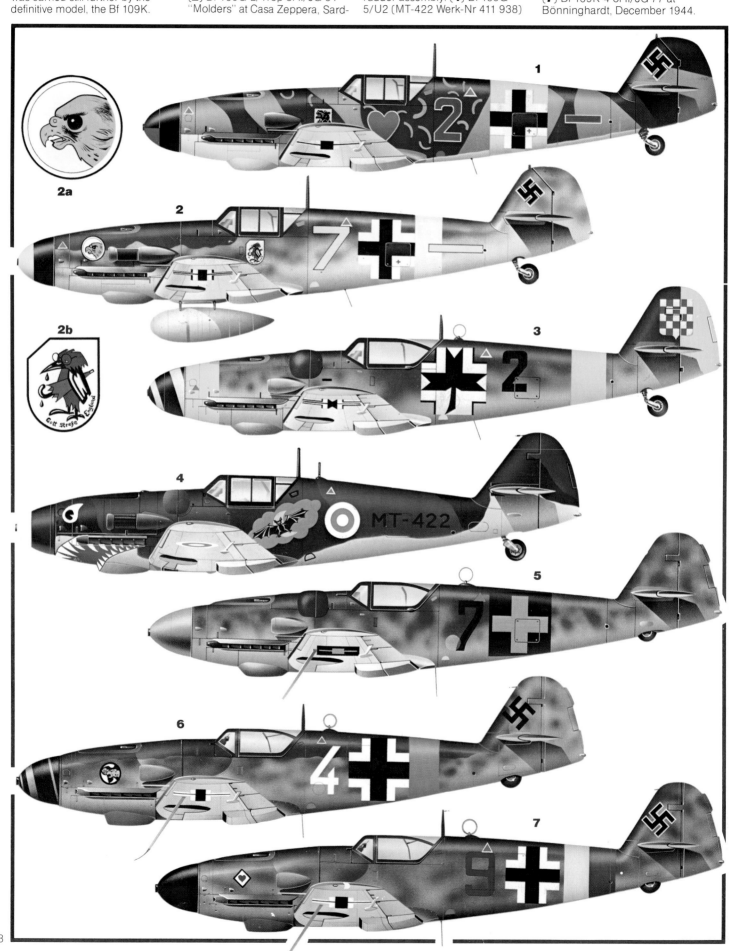

# Nakajima Ki.27 (1938)

Lightly constructed and lightly armed, the Ki.27 (or Type 97 Fighter) was almost certainly the most agile combat monoplane ever produced in quantity. Supremely successful from its operational debut over China in April 1938, the Ki.27 was conceptually outdated by the time that the Pacific conflict began.

First flown on 15 October 1936, a total of 3,396 was produced. (**1**) Ki.27-Otsu of Chutai leader, 10th Direct Command Chutai, Manchuria, 1938. (**2**) Ki.27-Otsu of Lt Col Toshio Katoh, CO of 1st Sentai, Kagamigahara, June 1939. (**3**) Ki.27-Otsu of 4th Chutai, 11th Sentai, the "Red-legged Hawks", operating over the Khalkhin River, Mongolian-Manchurian border, during the "Nomonhan Incident", summer 1939. Note "Lightning Flash" Sentai insignia in Chutai colour. (**4**) Ki.27-Otsu of 2nd Chutai, 24th Sentai, flown by Sgt Goro Nishihara during "Nomonhan Incident". The horizontal striping (in Chutai colour) signified the numbers two and four, the katakana character on the rudder being an individual marking. (**5**) Ki.27-Otsu of 1st Chutai, 50th Sentai, Burma, early 1942. (**6**) Ki.27-Otsu of 3rd Chutai, 246th Sentai, based at Kakogawa for defence of Osaka-Kobe area, early 1943. Note the traditional Japanese pine tree emblem on tail.

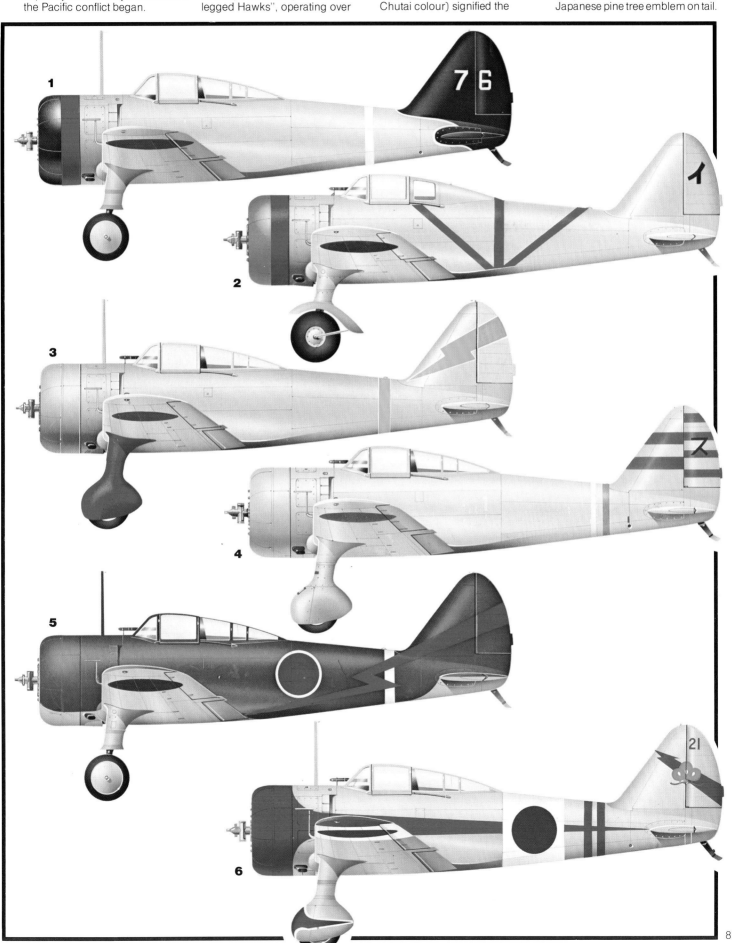

# Curtiss Model 75 (1938)

Conceived in 1934, and designed under the aegis of Don A. Berlin, the Model 75 was to enjoy very considerable export success as the Hawk 75A, more than 750 being sold abroad. Deliveries against an order for 210 for the US Army Air Corps began in the spring of 1938 as the P-36A, the final 30 being completed as

P-36Cs with wing armament. The principal foreign recipient was France's Armée de l'Air which began to receive Hawk 75A-1s in February 1939. France ordered 335 Twin Wasp- and 285 Cyclone-engined examples, the majority of the latter being diverted to the RAF as Mohawk IVs. The Curtiss fighter possessed light,

beautifully harmonised controls, good handling characteristics and was sturdy but, while more manoeuvrable than the Bf 109E, its principal opponent over France, it was out-climbed and out-dived by the German fighter, and much slower. (**1**) P-36A of 79th Pursuit Sqdn, 20th Pursuit Group, Moffett Field, Calif,

November 1939. Note tail designator indicating 21st aircraft of 20th Pursuit (PT). (**1a**) Emblem of 79th Pursuit Sqdn. (**2**) P-36C in olive drab and neutral grey, early 1942. Note the tail designator restricted to aircraft number (within Group), and last four digits of serial number (38-191). (**3**) Hawk 75A-5 of the

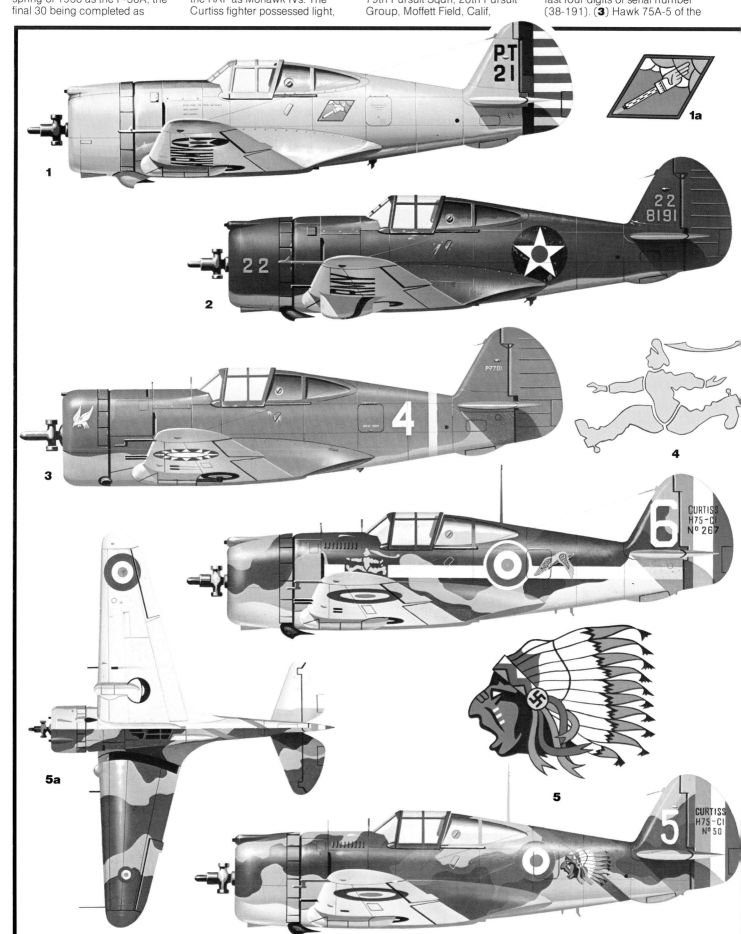

Nationalist Chinese Air Force, Kunming, 1942. (**4**) Hawk 75A-3 of 2nd Escadrille, GC I/5, Armée de l'Air, Casablanca, Morocco, summer 1941. Note that the "Charognard" (stylised eagle) emblem of this escadrille is accompanied by "Petit Poucet" emblem (enlarged above tail) of 2nd Escadrille, GC II/4, which was disbanded June 1940. (**5**) Hawk 75A1 of 1st Esc, GC II/5, winter 1939-40, with the "Lafayette" (Sioux Indian Head) emblem, and (**5a**) upper and lower surfaces of the same aircraft. (**6**) Hawk 75A-3 of 2nd Escadrille of GC II/5, Casablanca, Morocco, summer, 1941, with (**6a**) "Stork" unit emblem. Note deletion of green component of camouflage. (**7**) Hawk 75A-3 of 2nd Escadrille of GC I/4, Dakar, Senegal, in summer of 1942. Note so-called "Vichy" identification striping and introduction of sand brown to camouflage. (**7a**) Upper and lower surfaces of same aircraft, and (**7b**) "Gypaete Egyptien" (stylised vulture) unit emblem. (**8**) Hawk 75A-8 of Norwegian flying training centre, Island Airport, Toronto, 1941. (**9**) Hawk 75A-7 flown by Col Boxman of 1.Vliegtuigafdeling, KNIL Luchtvaartafdeling, Madioen, Netherlands East Indies, December 1941. (**10**) Hawk 75A-3 of Finnish LeLv 32, Suulajärvi, September 1941.

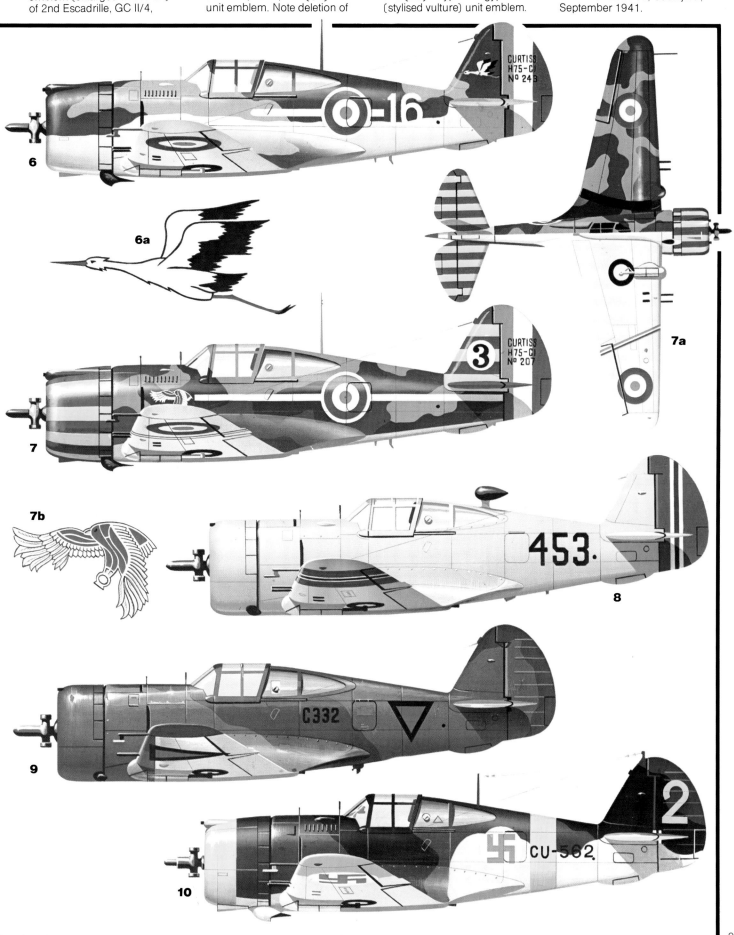

# Dornier Do 24 (1938)

Through most of the 'twenties and throughout the 'thirties, Dornier gained much acclaim for a series of robust and efficient flying boats characterised by inherently stable broadbeam hulls and sponsons. The last of these to be built in quantity was the Dornier Do 24 trimotor flying boat bearing a close family resemblance to the twin-engined Do 18 (see page 71). Designed to meet a Dutch Navy maritime reconnaissance-bomber requirement, it was to be adopted in World War II by the Luftwaffe for the air-sea rescue role in which it excelled as a result of its outstanding rough-water capability. First flown on 3 July 1937, the Do 24 was licence-built in Holland and France, 195 being built in the former country and 48 in the latter, a further 12 having been previously built under Dutch contract by Dornier's Swiss subsidiary. The Do 24 first entered service with the Dutch Navy in 1938, and the last were withdrawn from Spanish service in the late 'sixties—a span of 30 years! (**1**) Do 24T-1 (CD+UT) of the 3. Staffel of Seenotgruppe (Air-Sea Rescue Wing) operating under Seenotbereichskommando (SBK) III from Boulogne-Wimereux, summer 1941. Note "Gull and Lifebelt" emblem of the 3./Seenotgruppe (**2**) Do 24T-1 (CM+IV) of the 8.

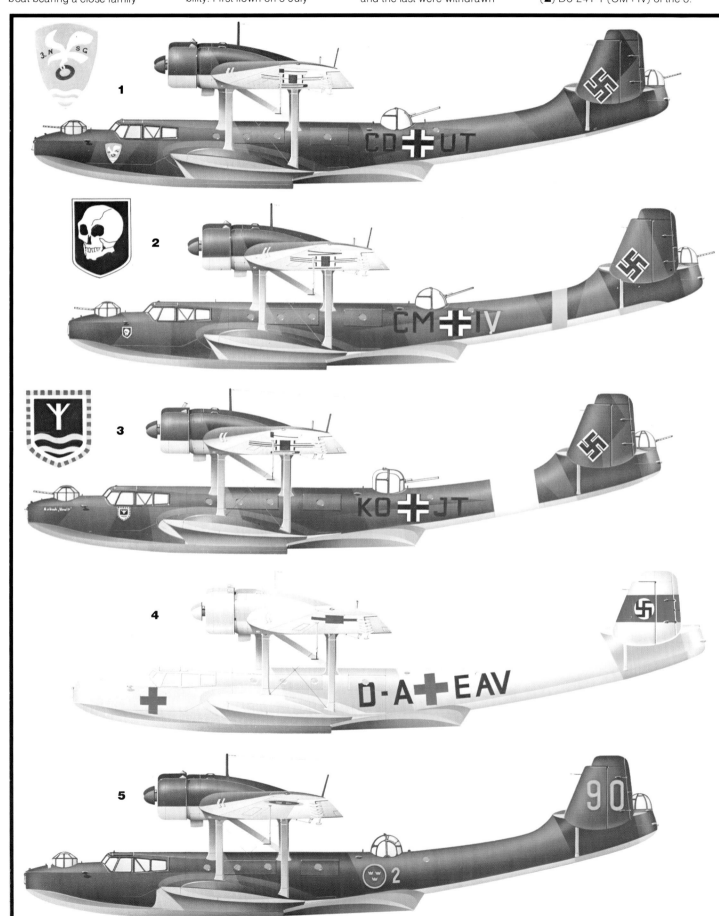

Seenotstaffel, SBK XII, Black Sea area, 1942. Note non-standard use of colour for fourth letter of radio call-sign and "Skull" emblem of Staffel. (**3**) Do 24T-2 (KO+JT) of the 7. Seenotstaffel, SBK XI, Aegean, 1942 (subsequently to SBK XII in Black Sea minus white wingtip and rear hull theatre markings). Note name "Asbach Uralt" on bow and the Staffel emblem. (**4**) The Do 24T-1 (D-AEAV) operated by the Reichsdienst (State Service) on aeromedical duties. Note civil registration and presentation of swastika. (**5**) Do 24T-1 operated as Tp 24 by Flottilj 2, Swedish Flygvapen from Hägernäs, 1945-50. (Originally CM+RY of the Seenotgruppe 81, which alighted at Hällevik on 31 October 1944). (**6**) Do 24K-2 (X-17) of Dutch Marine Luchtvaartdienst (Naval Air Service), Surabaya, Java, in summer 1939. (**7**) Do 24K-2 (A49-4) ex-MLD serving with No 41 Sqdn, RAAF, in the transport role, 1942-43. (**8**) Do 24T-2 of Escadrille 30S (former Flottille 9F Tr), French Aéronavale, ASR role from St Mandrier, 1946. Note emblem of Esc 30S. (**9**) Do 24T-3 as operated by Spain's Ejército del Aire for ASR from Pollensa, Majorca, early 'fifties. (**10**) Do 24T-2 (ex-Aéronavale), Ejército del Aire, Pollensa, in the early 'sixties. Note the SAR service emblem (bow) and unit emblem.

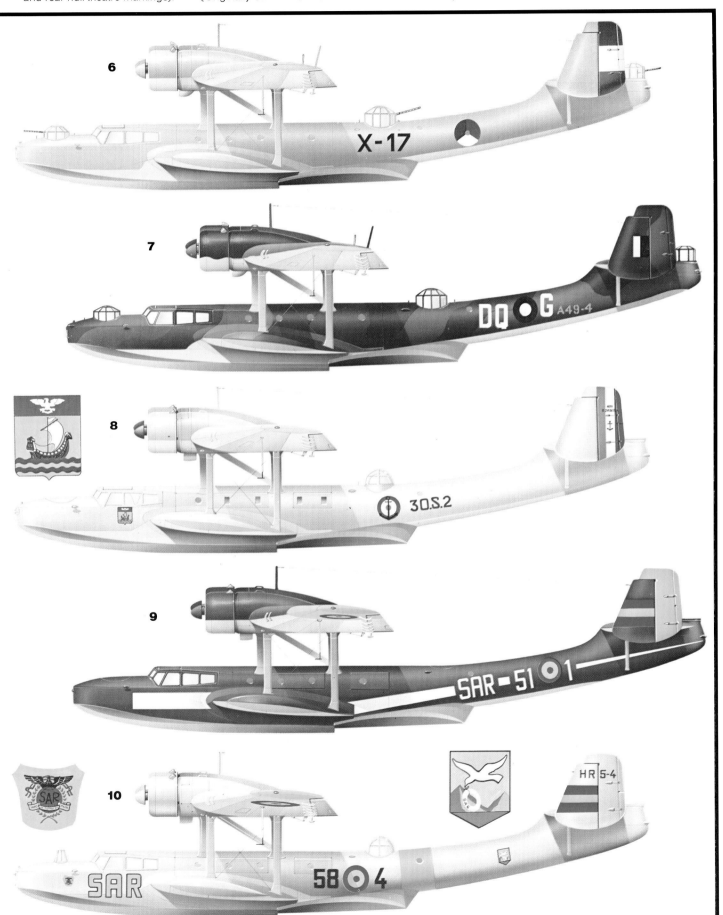

# Supermarine Spitfire (1938)

More than a supremely successful fighter, the Spitfire was the material symbol of final victory to the British. A ballerina-like aeroplane with immense aesthetic appeal, the Spitfire was the distillation of years of experience with Schneider Trophy racing seaplanes; aircraft that endowed it with a distinguished pedigree.

First flown on 5 March 1936, it began to enter service in July 1938, and a total of 20,351 had been built for the RAF by the time production was finally completed in October 1947. (**1**) Spitfire I (K9794) newly fitted with the curved canopy subsequently standardised, and flown by Sqdn Ldr Henry Cozens,

CO of No 19 Sqdn at Duxford, October 1938. (**2**) Sole Spitfire I supplied to the Armée de l'Air, late 1938; believed to have been captured by the Wehrmacht at Orleans in the summer of 1940. (**3**) Spitfire IA (371) of the Esquadrilha XZ, Arma da Aeronáutica Militar, Tancos, Portugal, 1943. (**4**) Spitfire IIA

(P7666) of Sqdn Ldr D O Finlay, CO of No 41 Sqdn, Hornchurch, in December 1940. This was an Observer Corps presentation aircraft. Note use of so-called Sky (Camotint or pale greenish-blue) for the underside, coding rear fuselage band and spinner. (**5**) Spitfire IIB (P8342) of No 306 (Polish) Sqdn, Northolt, in

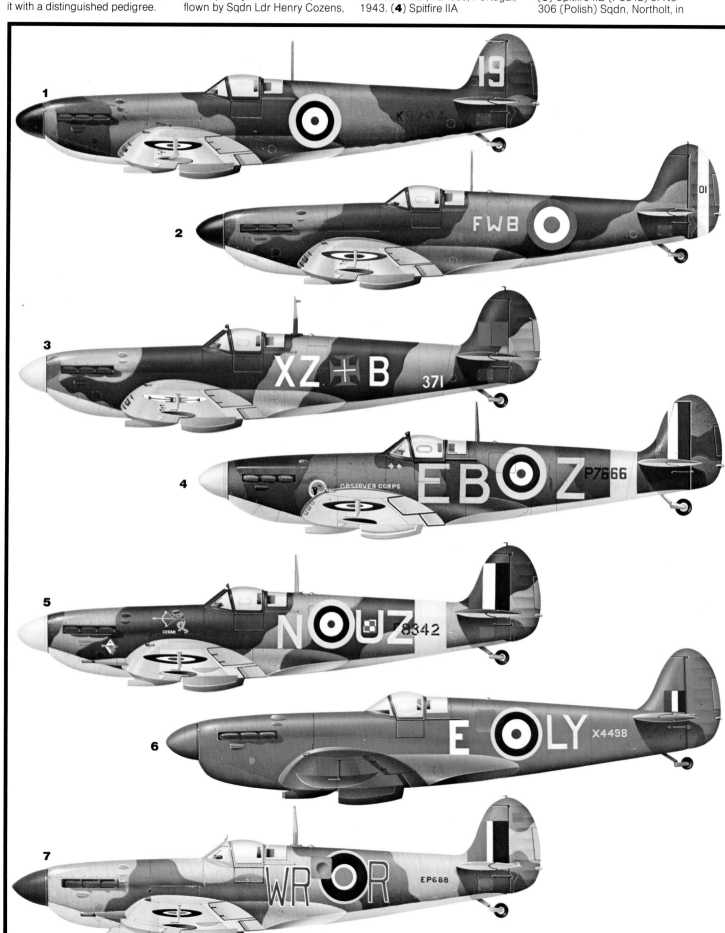

August 1941. Note emblem of the Polish "Torunski" unit on lower front cowling. (**6**) Spitfire PR Type F (X4498)—later PR Mk VI —of No 3 Photo Recce Unit, RAF Oakington, July 1941. (**7**) Spitfire VB (EP688), No 40 Sqdn, SAAF, Italy, August 1943. Note Aboukir tropical filter, oblique camera in fuselage and orange component of the South African markings. (**8**) Spitfire VC (LZ846) of No 54 Sqdn, RAF, based at Darwin for defence of northern Australia, 1943, as part of 1 Fighter Wing. (**9**) Spitfire VIII (A58-615) of No 457 (Australian) Sqdn, 1 Fighter Wing, Livingstone, in 1943. (**10**) Spitfire VIII of Lt L P Molland, CO of 308th Sqdn, 31st Fighter Group, USAAF, Italy, 1944, with (**10a**) personal emblem. (**11**) Spitfire IXC (MJ238), No 73 Sqdn, Hal Far, Malta, 1945. Note distinctive unit marking carried throughout most of World War II. (**12**) Spitfire IXE (ex-Czecho-slovak) of Heyl Ha'Avir, the Israeli Defence Force/Air Force, circa early 1950s. (**13**) Spitfire IXE used as personal aircraft by Ezer Weizman (third CO of No 101 Sqdn, Israel's premier fighter unit) and airworthy until 1976. Note alignment with groundline of the "Star of David" insignia. (**13a**) The Heyl Ha'Avir crest. (**14**) Spitfire IX two-seat conversion undertaken by the 1 Aircraft Depot, Leningrad, in 1945.

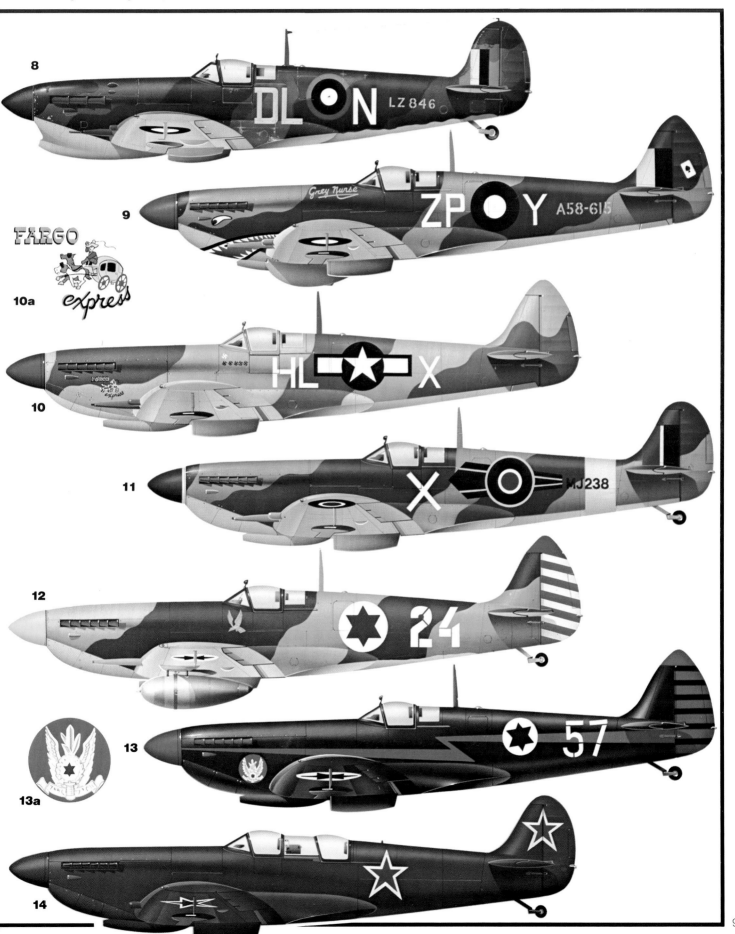

# Supermarine Spitfire (continued)

(**1**) Spitfire VII (MD111) of No 131 Sqdn in high-altitude day fighter finish (introduced June 1943) of Medium Sea Grey upper surfaces and PRU Blue under surfaces. Note the Sky Grey code lettering and Type B roundel, and undersized invasion stripes. (**2**) Spitfire PR X (MD194) as it was operated by Nos 541 and 542 squadrons, Benson, Oxon, 1945. Note special pink finish used for some photo-reconnaissance Spitfires. (**3**) Spitfire PR XI (PA892) of the 7th Photo Group, USAAF, Mount Farm, Oxon, 1943-44. Note natural metal finish. (**4**) Spitfire XIV (RB159) of Sqdn Ldr R A Newbury, CO of No 610 Sqdn operating anti-"Diver" patrols from Lympne, September 1944. (**5**) Spitfire FR 18 (TZ214) of No 32 Sqdn, Ein Shemer, in the Suez Canal Zone, 1947-48. Note "Hunting Horn" emblem of squadron beneath windscreen and port for oblique camera aft of cockpit. (**6**) Spitfire PR 19 (PM660) of No 2 Sqdn, Fürsten-feldbrück. West Germany, circa 1948. Note so-called PRU Blue finish overall and red coding. (**7**) Spitfire 21 (LA224) of No 91 Sqdn, Ludham, Norfolk, spring 1945. No 91 was the only squadron to employ this Spitfire variant operationally before the end of hostilities, flying armed reconnaissance over NW Europe and anti-shipping missions.

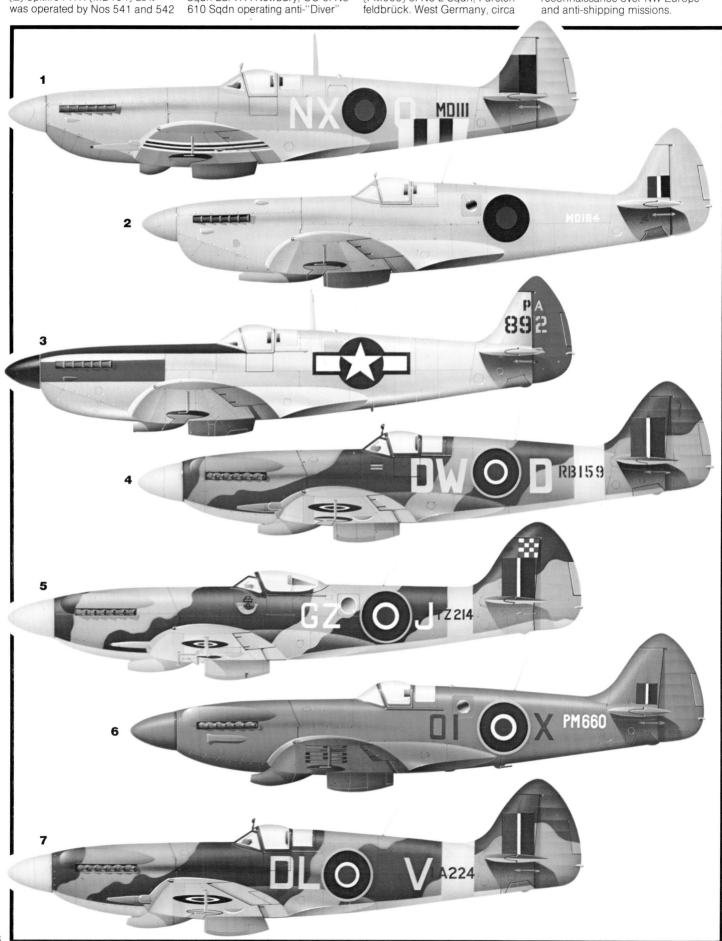

# Vickers Wellington (1938)

Utilising an ingenious fail-safe geodetic structure covered by fabric at a time when metal stressed skinning had become the accepted formula for the modern bomber, the Wellington was, from some aspects, an anachronism when it first flew on 15 June 1936. Geodetics yielded high strength for comparatively low weight,

however, and thus the ability to absorb fantastic battle damage yet stay airborne. Characterised by an unusual amount of structural flexing in turbulence, and accompanied by erratic wandering of the control column, the Wellington established a brilliant battle record. The 11,461st and last was delivered October 1945.

(**1**) Wellington I (L4235) of No 38 Sqdn, Marham, Norfolk, summer 1939. (**2**) Wellington IA (L7779), No 37 Sqdn, Feltwell, Norfolk, April 1940. (**3**) Wellington III (X3763), No 425 (Alouette) Sqdn, an RCAF-manned unit in No 4 Grp, Dishforth, in September 1942. (**4**) Wellington X (HZ950), No 99 (Madras Presidency) Sqdn operat-

ing in Burma during the Imphal crisis, June-July 1944. (**5**) Wellington XIII (MF639), No 415 (Canadian) Sqdn, operating within No 16 Group, Bircham Newton, early 1944. Note ASV Mk II radar aerials. (**6**) Wellington XIV of No 304 (Polish) Sqdn, Chivenor, late 1944. Note ASV Mk III nose radome and ventral Leigh Light.

# Morane-Saulnier M.S.406 (1938)

An inelegant and decidedly under-powered fighter monoplane, with armament and equipment leaving much to be desired, the M.S. 406 represented a synthesis of previous fighter experience translated into low-wing cantilever monoplane terms and retaining classic tubular metal construction with fabric skinning. First

flown (as the M.S.405) on 8 August 1935, it entered Armée de l' Air service late 1938, and some 1,080 were built. The M.S.406 proved inferior to the Bf 109E on all counts apart from turning circle. It was licence-built in Switzerland as the D-3800 and D-3801, and some were re-engined in Finland (with Klimov's M-105)

as Mörkö (Werewolf) Moraanis. (1) M.S.406 (No704) of 1e Esc, GC I/2, Nimes, July 1940, with (1a) upper surfaces of the same aircraft showing green, dark earth and blue-grey camouflage. (1b) The (SPA 3) "Cicogne" of the 1e Esc. (2) D-3801 of a Überwachungsstaffel (Surveillance squadron) of the Swiss

Fliegertruppe, 1944. (3) M.S. 406 (No775), Escadron de Entrainement, Toulouse, 1941, and (3a) upper surfaces of same aircraft. Note sienna, dark earth and dark green camouflage. (4) Mörkö-Moraani (MSv-657) of HLeLv 21, Finnish Ilmavoimien, Rissala, 1946. Note "Continuation War" camouflage scheme.

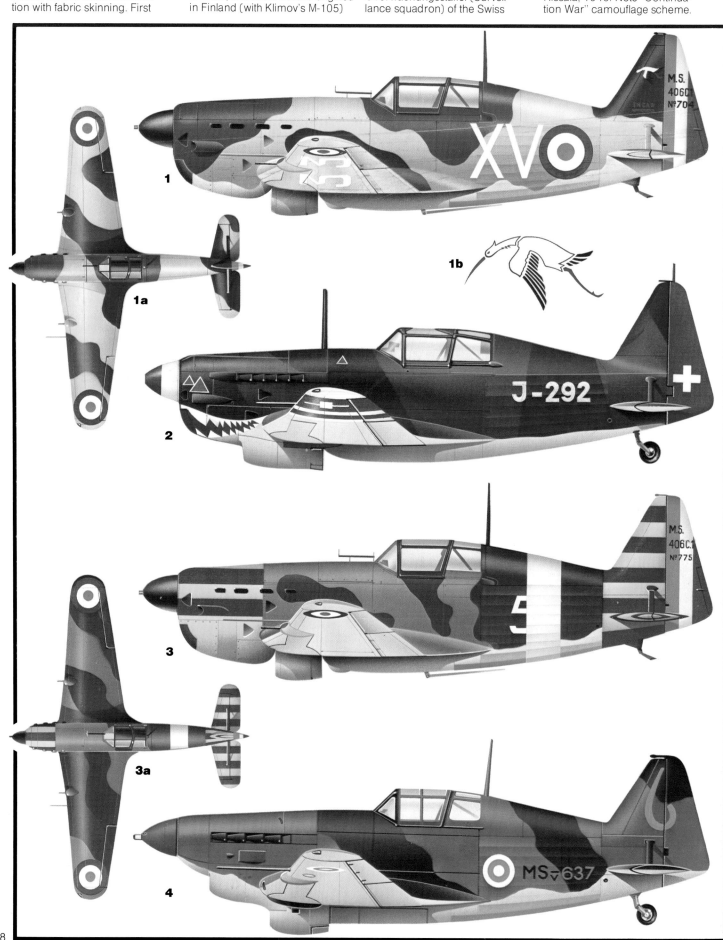

# Fiat G.50 Freccia (1938)

The first Italian all-metal low-wing cantilever monoplane single seat fighter, the G.50 Freccia (Arrow) flew on 26 February 1937, entering Regia Aeronautica service in the following year, production totalling 778 aircraft. The G.50 was rather underpowered and inadequately armed, but it was sturdy and very manoeuvrable.

(1) G.50 (M.M.3580) of 1º Gruppo Sperimentale of Italian Aviación de el Tercio, Escalona, Spain, March 1939. (1a) Half-and-half planview of M.M.3580 depicting starboard upper and lower surfaces. (1b) "Asso di Bastoni" emblem of 23º Gruppo of Regia Aeronautica. (2) G.50 (M.M.3582) of Grupo Núm 27, Regimiento Mixto de Africa, Spanish EdA, Melilla, Morocco, March 1940. (2a) Falangist "Yoke and Arrows" emblem. (2b) "Greyhound" emblem of Grupo Núm 27. (3) G.50bis (M.M.4744), Scuola Caccia IIº Periodo, Regia Aeronautica, in the summer of 1942. Note white wing bands signifying training role. (4) G.50bis of 20º Gruppo,

51º Stormo, operating as component of 56º Stormo Caccia Terrestre of Corpo Aereo Italiano, based at Ursel, Belgium, October 1940 to April 1941. (4a) "Gatto Nero" (Black Cat) emblem of 51º Stormo. (4b) Coats of Arms of House of Savoy. (5) G.50 (M.M.3599) flown by Sen Lt Kalkkinen as FA-17 of 2/LeLv 26 at Malmi, July 1942.

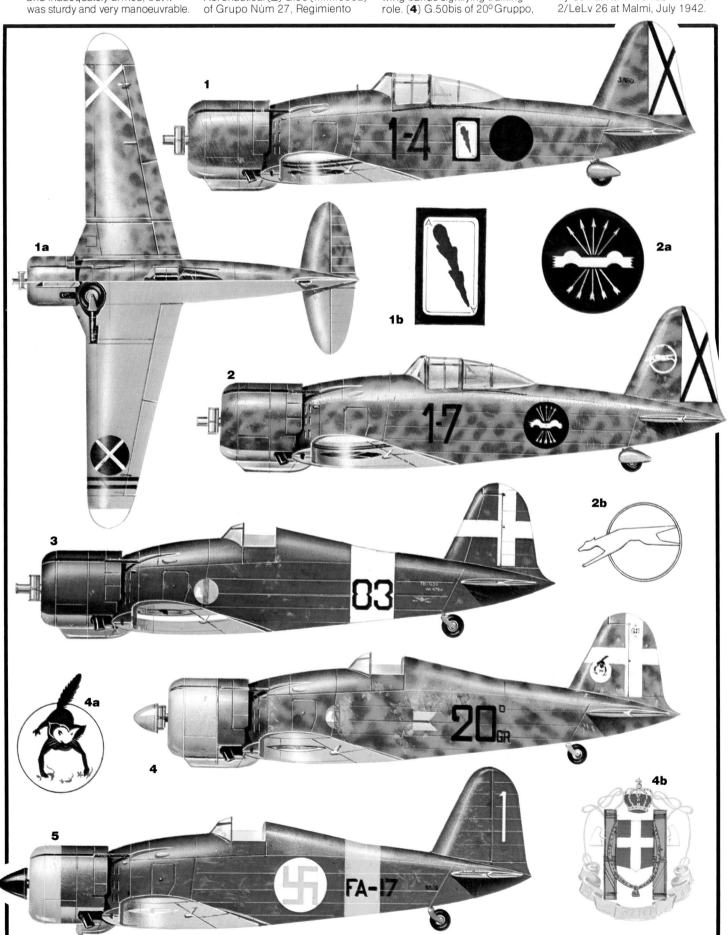

# Lockheed Hudson (1938)

First US-built aircraft to see RAF operational service in WWII, the Hudson was one of the rare examples of a successful military type being evolved from an existing commercial aircraft (ie, Lockheed 14 Super Electra). It was developed expressly to meet British coastal recce-bomber requirements and ordered for the RAF in June 1938 on the basis of a mock-up fuselage. The Hudson first flew on 10 December 1938, and just over 2,000 Hudsons were subsequently to be delivered to the RAF, the RAAF and the RNZAF, some repossessed by the US government serving with the US Army (as the A-29) and US Navy (as the PBO-1). (**1**) A-29 (41-23325), a repossessed RAF Hudson III (BW454), engaged on West Coast anti-submarine patrol from Portland, Oregon, April 1942. Note retention of RAF temperate land scheme. (**2**) Hudson III (NZ2083) of No 2 (GR) Sqdn, RNZAF, Nelson, New Zealand, in 1942. (**3**) Hudson V (AM579), No 48 Sqdn, RAF Coastal Command, Stornoway, Outer Hebrides, late 1941. (**4**) Hudson VI (FK689) with matt white vertical and gloss white undersurfaces as adopted by Coastal Command from August 1941. Note the dark green and ocean grey upper surfaces. (**5**) Hudson III (V9158) of No 279 Sqdn, Sturgate, 1942, engaged in air-sea rescue duties with ventrally-mounted airborne lifeboat.

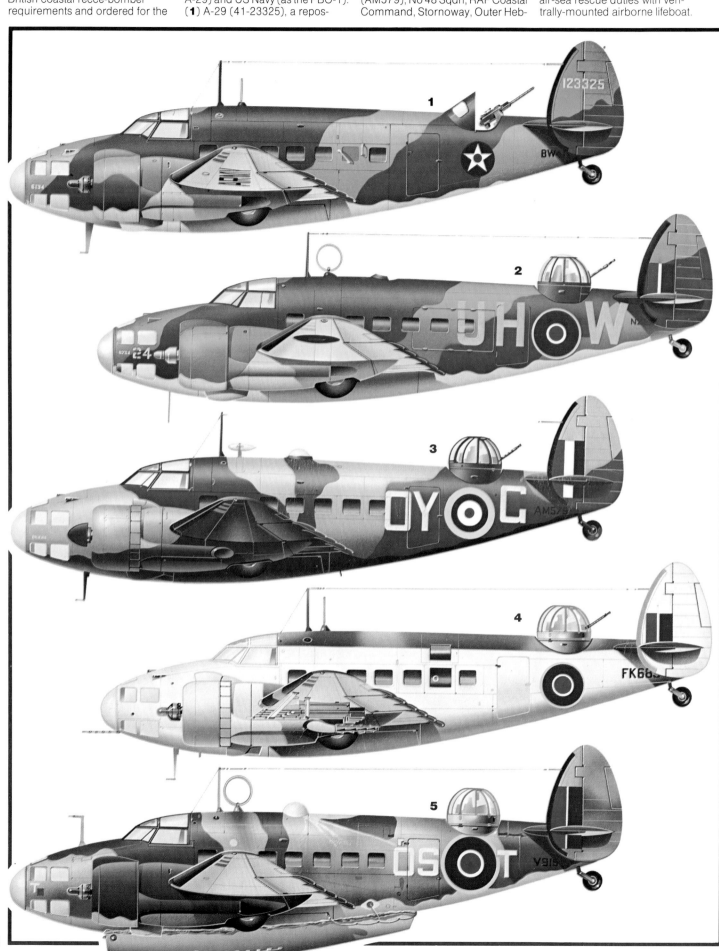

# Handley Page Hampden (1939)

Of unique design, with its deep but narrow fuselage pod and slender tailboom, the Hampden offered near perfect handling characteristics and almost fighter-like manoeuvrability, but its cramped accommodation led to crew fatigue and its defensive firepower was totally inadequate. Flown on 21 June 1936, it entered RAF service in autumn 1938, a total (including the Dagger-engined Hereford version) of 1,584 being produced. (**1**) Hampden I (P1320) of No 106 Sqdn, Finningley, Yorks, April 1940. Note overpainting of the yellow roundel outline and non-standard coding style. (**2**) Hampden TB I (X3015) (note deepened weapons bay for torpedo) of a Scottish-based OTU in 1942. (**3**) Hampden I (AE202) of No 44 (Rhodesia) Sqdn, Waddington, Lincs, September 1941. (**4**) Hampden TB I (AN172) of No 489 Sqdn, RNZAF, Leuchars, Fife, autumn 1942. (**5**) Hampden TB I, V-VS SF (Northern Fleet Air Force) at Vaenga, near Murmansk, October 1942, after transfer to Soviet Union by No 455 (RAAF) Sqdn. (**6**) Sole Hampden supplied to Sweden as operated by Flottilj 11 from Nyköping as P 5 in 1941. Delivered to Sweden on 22 September 1938, it was sold to SAAB in November 1945, and (as SE-APB) served as an electronic test-bed, surviving until November 1947.

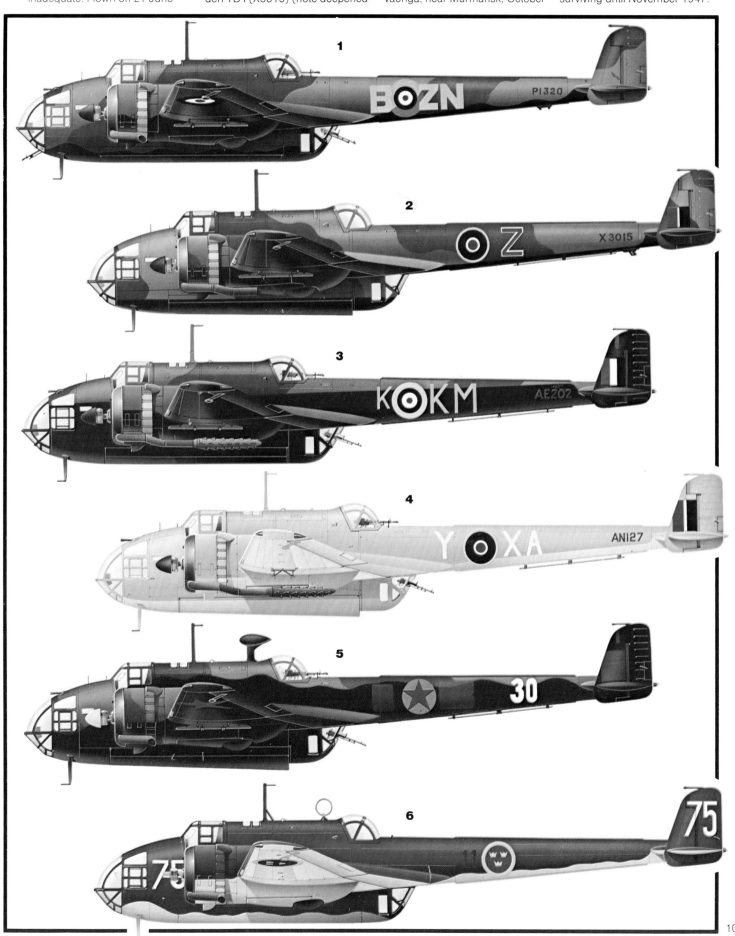

# Polikarpov I-153 (I-15ter) (1939)

Difficulties experienced in 1937 over Spain by Soviet pilots in combating the Fiat CR.32 biplane (see pages 38-39) when flying the I-16 monoplane (see pages 48-49) convinced the Soviet Union that there was still a place in the first-line inventory of the modern air arm for fighters of biplane configuration. Aleksei

Shcherbakov, one of Nikolai Polikarpov's team leaders, was, accordingly, assigned the task of developing a more advanced fighter based on the I-15bis (see page 37). Retaining the basic structure of the earlier fighter, Shcherbakov discarded the cabane for a gulled arrangement of the wing, added manually retractable

main undercarriage members, and as the I-153 (alias I-15ter), prototypes completed acceptance tests autumn 1938. Deliveries began late spring 1939, priority being assigned to forces fighting the Japanese over the Nomonhan plateau, but it was quickly manifest that the reasoning behind I-153 development had been

unsound; the fighter biplane was obsolete. Two factories had begun full-scale production, however, and as these could not re-tool, there was no recourse but to continue building I-153s, and during an 18-month production life, no fewer than 3,437 were built. Ninety-three were supplied to China early 1940, and when the

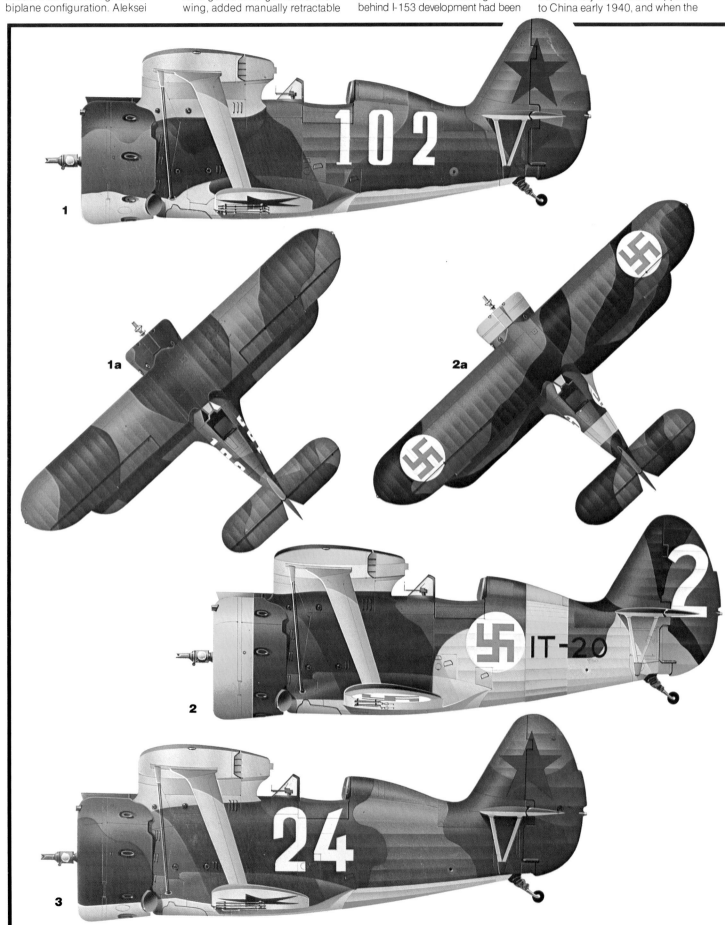

Wehrmacht attacked the Soviet Union, almost one in two V-VS fighter regiments were flying the I-153. It was totally outclassed by the Bf 109E, although presented difficulties if flown by an experienced pilot as a result of its exceptional agility. (**1**) I-153 of the 71 IAP attached to Baltic Fleet and flown by Major Biskun, an eskadril CO, from Lavansaari, Gulf of Finland, August 1942. (**1a**) Upper planview of same aircraft (**2**) I-153 (IT-20) captured by Finns at Sommarö (see 4), October 1941, and delivered to 3/LeLv 6 of Ilmavoimat in July 1942. (**2a**) Upper planview of same aircraft. (**3**) I-153 of the 71 IAP flown by Capt Solovyov at Suomenlahti in 1942. (**4**) I-153 forced down on 3 October 1941 at Sommarö and impressed by Ilmavoimat (see 2) as IT-20. Note dilapidated finish. (**5**) I-153 in temporary winter finish of unidentified IAP forced down on Eastern Front 1941-42. (**6**) I-153 captured on Eastern Front and subsequently transferred to Ilmavoimat, December 1942. It was subsequently assigned to 1/LeLv 30 in April 1943 as IT-31. Luftwaffe coding indicates staff flight of I/Luftlandegeschwader 1 by which presumably flown before transfer. (**7**) I-153 (P-7271), 27th Sqdn, Nationalist Chinese Air Force, Kunming, 1942.

# Fiat CR.42 Falco (1939)

Italy's CR.42 Falco (Falcon) had, together with the Soviet I-153, the distinction of being the last single-seat fighter biplane introduced into service. Flown as a prototype on 23 May 1938, it entered service in May of the following year. Proving a superbly manoeuvrable warplane, it had the misfortune to be born into a scene dominated by monoplanes. Despite conceptual obsolescence, its production continued into 1943, reaching a total of 1,781. (**1**) CR.42 of 97ª squadriglia, 9º Gruppo, 4º Stormo, Benina, Libya, 1940. (**1a**) "Cavallino Rampante" emblem (left) of 4º Stormo, and (right) emblem of the 97ª sqd. (**2**) CR.42 of 162ª sqd. 161º Gruppo, in markings of the Aegean theatre, on Isle of Scarpanto, April-May 1941. (**2a**) "Fasces" emblem (left) on fuselage and (right) 162ª sqd emblem, the Venetian dialect legend reading "Beware, I will scratch you!" (**3**) Rear fuselage scrap view depicting alternative (to **5**) presentation of 377ª sqd emblem, full unit coding and the overall black night fighting finish of some aircraft. (**4**) CR.42 of the Cmdte (note pennant) of 83ª Sqd, 18º Gruppo, 3º Stormo, Libya, in early 1941. Note the three-colour camouflage remaining as used in Belgium the previous autumn. The dark band was overpainted white stripe (used to signify Cmdte in

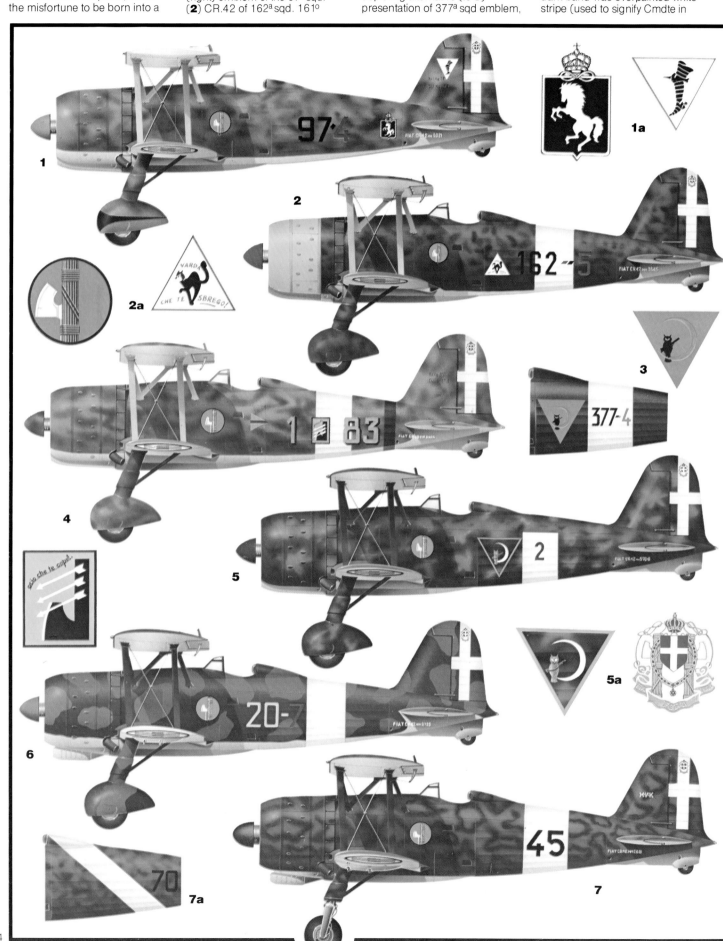

Belgium). Note 180 °Gruppo emblem. (**5**) CR.42 of 377ª sqd autonoma, Palermo-Boccadifalco, Sicily, summer 1942. (**5a**) 377ª sqd emblem (left), with (right) coat of arms of House of Savoy. (**6**) CR.42 of 20ª sqd, 46º Gruppo Assalto, 15º Stormo, September-November 1942 on the El Alamein front. (**7**) CR.42 of auxiliary

assault group, Ravenna area, 1942. (**7a**) Scrap view of 70ª sqd CR.42, Tirana, Albania, 1942, showing Cmdte fuselage stripe (practice discontinued in following December). (**8**) CR.42 of Sezione Autonoma Colleg-amenti, Rome-Centocelle, winter 1945-6. (**8a**) Subsequent CR.42 trainer finish (overall silver),

late '40s. (**9**) CR.42 of the 2. Staffel, Nachtschlachtgruppe 9, Rimini area, early 1944. (**10**) CR.42 of 4ème Escadrille, IIème Groupe de Chasse, 2ème Regiment, Aéronautique Militaire Belge, at Nivelles, May 1940. (**11**) CR.42 of 1./4 Sqdn, 1/II Group, 1st Fighter Regt, Royal Hungarian Air Force, Budapest, 1941, and

(**11a**) the 1./4 Sqdn "St George" emblem. (**11b**) Alternative 1/II Group CR.42 finish. (**12**) CR.42 of 1./3 Sqdn, 1/II Group with Soviet Union, late 1941. Note "Ace of Hearts" emblem of 1./3 Sqdn. (**13**) CR.42 (J 11) of 3 Division of Flygflottilj 9, at Säve, Gothenburg, Sweden, late 1942.

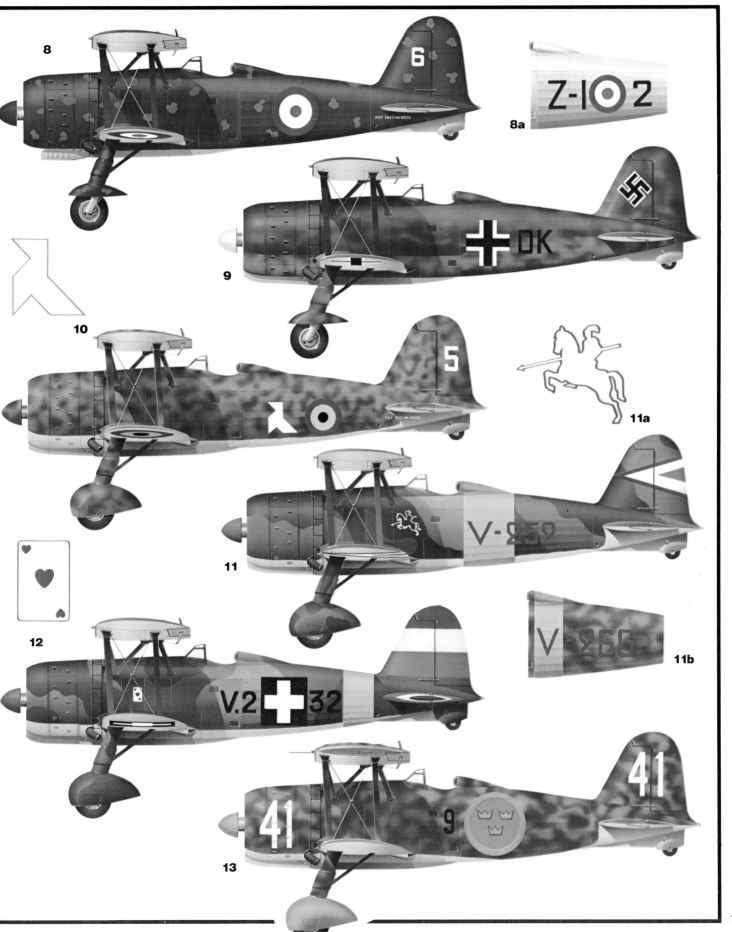

# Messerschmitt Bf 110 (1939)

A supremely elegant warplane for which a formidable reputation had been assiduously fostered by German propagandists, the Bf 110 proved an abysmal failure when it was committed to the "Battle of Britain". But the Messerschmitt twin was not the indifferent warplane that the debacle in British skies in 1940 suggested. The near disastrous mauling that the Bf 110 received from the more nimble single-engined opposition was the result of inadequate understanding of the limitations of its strategic fighter concept and incorrect deployment as a consequence. Once these limitations were appreciated, the Bf 110 was to serve throughout the remainder of WWII with some distinction in a variety of diurnal and nocturnal roles—a thoroughly tractable aircraft with pleasant handling characteristics, a very good performance and considerable agility for its size and twin-engined configuration. First flown on 12 May 1936, the Bf 110 began to enter service early in 1939, and it was to remain in production until March 1945, by which time approximately 6,050 of all versions had been built. Its basic design proved amenable to power plant changes and to the application of equipment and armament far beyond anything envisaged when it was conceived.

1

1a

3a

1a

1b

1c

106

(**1**) Bf 110C-4/B (G9+IN) of 5./ZG 1, Caucasus, October 1942. Known as the Wespen (Wasp) Geschwader, the aircraft of this unit bore an elaborate "Wasp" design (**1a**) on the fuselage nose. The II Gruppe, of which 5.Staffel was a part, was formed in 1942 by the re-designation of SKG 210 whose aircraft had also borne the "Wasp" design, its nucleus being provided by 1.Staffel of the original ZG 1. (**1b**) Half-and-half plan and (**1c**) head-on views of G9+IN. Note unusual combination of the splinter and dapple patterns on wing upper surfaces. (**2**) Bf 110G-2 of 5./ZG 76 at Grosenhain, winter 1943-44. (**3**) Bf 110C-2 (A2+AH) of I/ZG 52 operating from Charleville, France, June 1940. (**3a**) Emblem of I Gruppe of ZG 52. (**4**) Bf 110G-2 (3J + YW) of 12./NJG 3, Stavanger, Norway, spring 1945. (**5**) Bf 110G-4 (D5+DS) of 8./NJG 3. Note "Shark's Mouth" decoration inherited from original Haifischgruppe (II/ZG 76). (**5a**) "Englandblitz" emblem of the Luftwaffe night fighting arm carried beneath windscreen of D5+DS. (**6**) Bf 110G-4 (3C+BR) of 7./NJG 4, North-West Germany, 1943-44. (**7**) Bf 110D-3 (M8+GM) of 4./ZG 76 flying in support of insurgent Iraqi forces from Raschid, Iraq, May 1941. Note crudely overpainted rear fuselage and temporary Iraqi insignia.

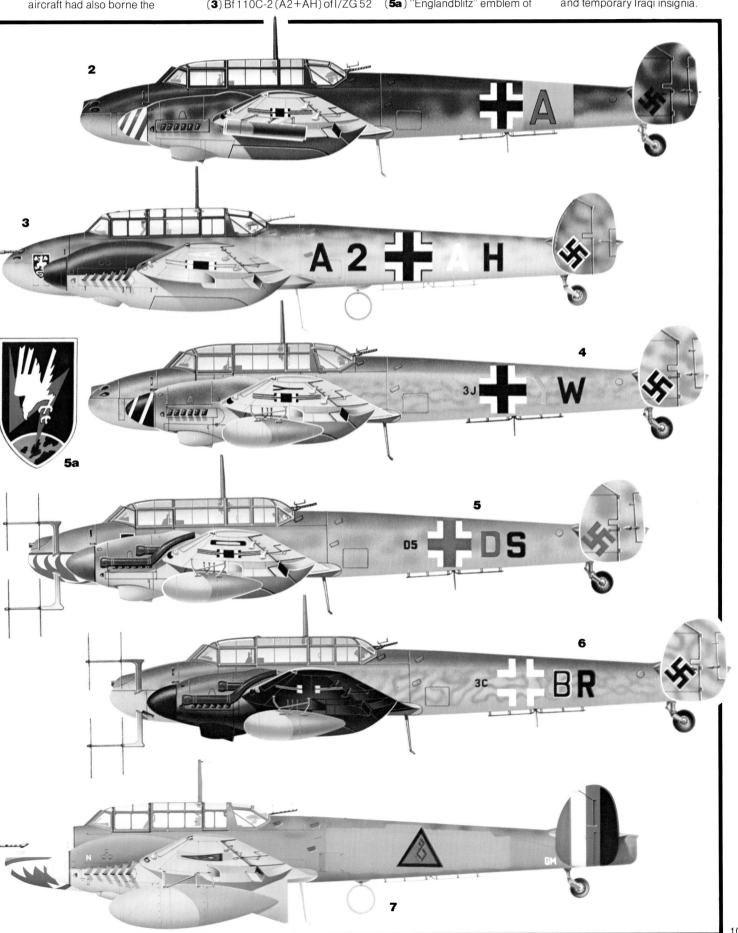

# Junkers Ju 88 (1939)

Perhaps exemplifying the German philosophy of adapting a sound basic airframe for a multitude of tasks, the Ju 88 was arguably the most versatile warplane of WWII; it was certainly the outstanding Luftwaffe bomber, long-range heavy fighter and night fighter. The Ju 88's startlingly broad repertoire included anti-shipping strike

and torpedo attack, tank busting and reconnaissance; it was a pilot's aeroplane first and last. Flown as a prototype on 21 December 1936, it entered Luftwaffe service in bomber form in August 1939. By the time production finally terminated in 1945, a total of 14,676 Ju 88s of all versions had been completed.

(1) Ju 88A-1 (9K+GL) of I Gruppe, Kampfgeschwader 51 "Edelweiss", based at Melun-Villaroche, in autumn 1940. Note the temporary black undersides and overpainted insignia for night blitz on UK. (1a) "Edelweiss" emblem of KG 51. (2) Ju 88A-4 (B3+FL) of I/KG 54 "Totenkopf", Bergamo, Italy, September 1943. Note so-called

"Wellenmuster" camouflage over standard Mediterranean two-tone scheme for anti-invasion tasks over Sicily/Salerno beachheads. (2a) "Totenkopf" emblem of KG 54 applied immediately aft of nose transparencies. (3) Ju 88A-4 (ex-Luftwaffe) serving with Groupe de Bombardement I/31 "Aunis", with the Forces Françaises de

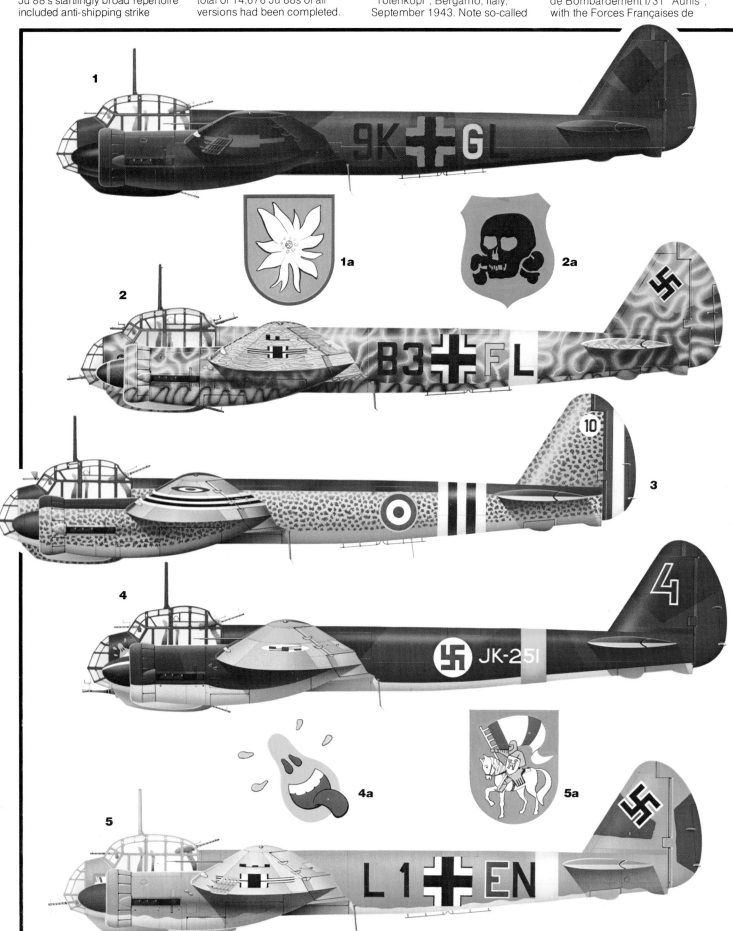

l'Atlantique, Bordeaux-Mérignac, March 1945. (**4**) Ju 88A-4/R (JK-251) of 1. lentue (flight), Lentolaivue 44 (1./LeLv 44) of Finnish Ilmavoimien, Onttola, summer 1943. (**4a**) The emblem of 1./LeLv 44. (**5**) Ju 88A-10 (L1+EN) of II Gruppe, Lehr-geschwader 1 (II/LG 1), at Heraklion, Crete, October 1942.

Note that this aircraft was engaged on Mediterranean anti-shipping operations but retained desert finish from earlier North African service. (**5a**) Emblem of II/LG 1. (**6**) Ju 88A-14 (Q1+JC) believed to be of Stab II Gruppe/Zerstörergeschwader 1, Mamaia, Rumania, April 1944. (**6a**) Scrap view showing "Skeletal Hand"

emblem as also carried by Bf 110s of I Gruppe. (**7**) Ju 88C-6 (F1+XM) of Zerstörerstaffel 4./KG 76, Taganrog, Ukraine, late 1942. Note painted simulation of nose transparencies to confuse opposition. (**7a**) Emblem of 4.(Z)/KG 76. (**8**) Ju 88S-1 (Z6+DL) of I/KG 66, Dedelsdorf, winter 1944-45, for individual

Y-Gerät radio-beam sorties. Note small coding on tail fin. (**9**) A Ju 88G-6b (9W+CL) of I/NJG 101, Ingolstadt, late 1944. Note replacement rudder and "Schräge musik" oblique gun installation. (**10**) Ju 88G-7a (2Z+AW) of IV/NJG 6, Schwäbisch Hall, winter 1944-45. Note painting of the vertical tail to resemble Ju 88C.

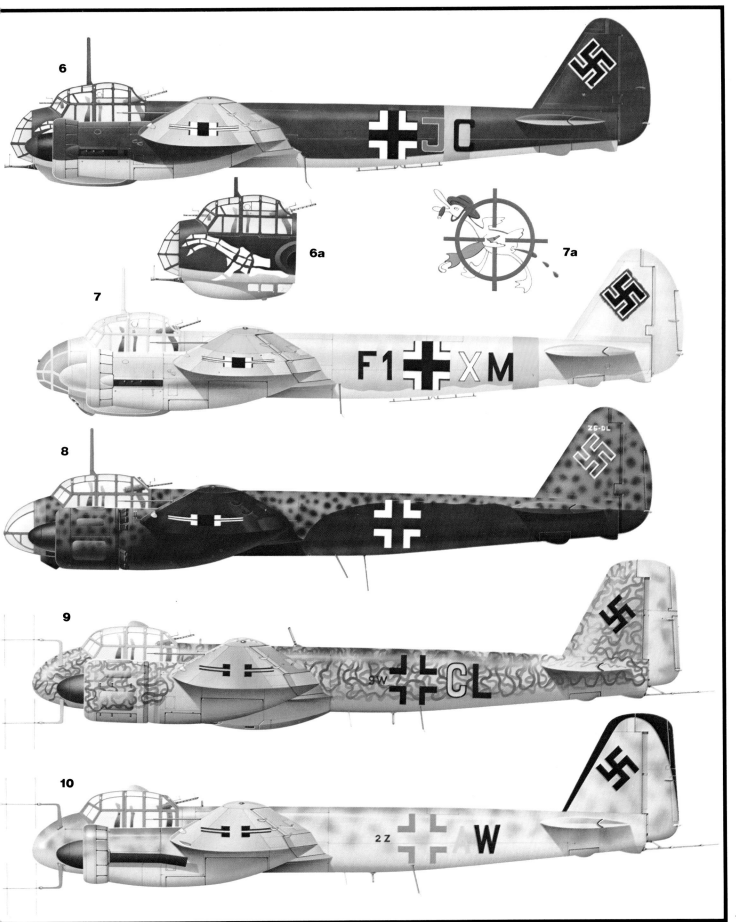

# Dornier Do 17Z/215 (1939)

A derivative of the original Dornier Do 17 "Flying Pencil" with a new forward fuselage, the Do 17Z entered Luftwaffe service early 1939, an export version differing essentially in engine type being designated Do 215 and, in the event, also seeing Luftwaffe service. Although essentially medium bombers, they also appeared in night fighter form as the Do 17Z-7 and Z-10, and Do 215B-5. (1) Do 17Z-2 (5K+FD) of Stab III Gruppe, Kampfgeschwader 3, based at Heiligenbeil, East Prussia, in September 1939. (2) Do 17Z-2 (5K+HU) of 10.(kroat.)/KG 3 deployed on Central Sector of the Eastern Front, December 1941. (2a) Emblem of Croatian Ustachi volunteers. (3) Do 17Z-2 (U5+BH) of I/KG 2, Tatoi, Greece, in May 1941. (3a) Emblem of 1.Staffel/KG 2. (4) Do 17Z-3 of PLeLv 43 (formerly PLeLv 44) photographic flight, Finnish Ilmavoimien, at Malmi, July 1948. (4a) Unofficial emblem of PLeLv 43 photo flight and (4b) PLeLv 43 "Bison" emblem. (5) Do 17Z-10 Kauz (R4+LK) of I/NJG 2, Gilze-Rijen, in October 1940 for nocturnal intrusion missions over UK. (5a) Emblem of Nachtjagd-Division. (6) Do 215B-5 Kauz III (R4+DC) of Stab II/NJG 2 based at Leeuwarden, in the summer of 1942, and flown by Hpt Helmut Lent, Gruppenkommandeur. Note the ventral MG FF cannon pack and Lichtenstein radar array.

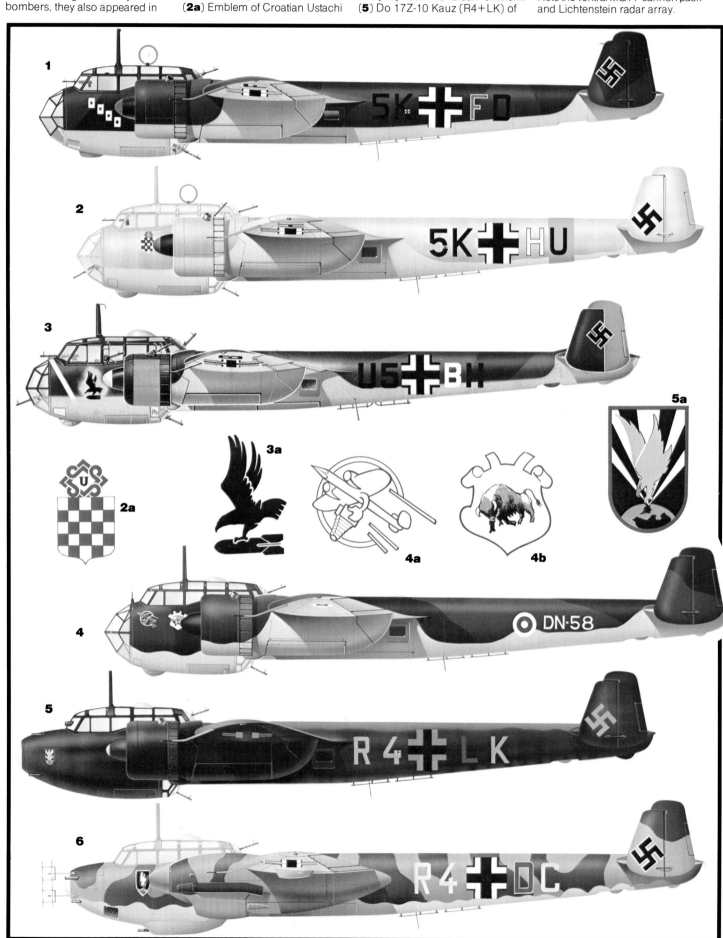

# Bristol Beaufighter (1940)

An outstanding example of improvisation in being essentially an adaptation of the Beaufort torpedo-bomber, the Beaufighter was to be numbered among WWII's most versatile warplanes. Displaying a measure of handling precocity, it was nevertheless a formidable aircraft, first seeing service in the nocturnal intercept role

—it was the only RAF aircraft capable of carrying the AI Mk IV radar without sacrificing either endurance or firepower. Flown on 3 July 1939, it first entered RAF service in August 1940, and by 21 September 1945, when the 5,562nd and last Beaufighter was completed, it had fulfilled many tasks, among its most successful

being the anti-shipping strike role. (**1**) Beaufighter Mk IF (R2059) of No 25 Sqdn, North Weald, late summer 1940. (**2**) Beaufighter Mk IC (T4767) of No 252 Sqdn, RAF Coastal Command, Edcu, Egypt, mid-1942. Note Middle East dark earth and mid stone camouflage. (**3**) Beaufighter Mk VIF (KV912) of 416th Night Fighter Sqdn,

USAAF, Corsica, 1943-44. (**4**) A Beaufighter TF Mk X (NE237) of No 455 Sqdn, RAAF, based in UK, late 1944. (**5**) Beaufighter Mk X of Escuadrilha 8, Portuguese Fôrças Aéreas du Armada, Portela de Sacavem, 1945. (**6**) A Beaufighter TF Mk X, Cuerpo de Aviacion Militar, Trujillo AB, San Isidoro, Dominican Republic, 1948.

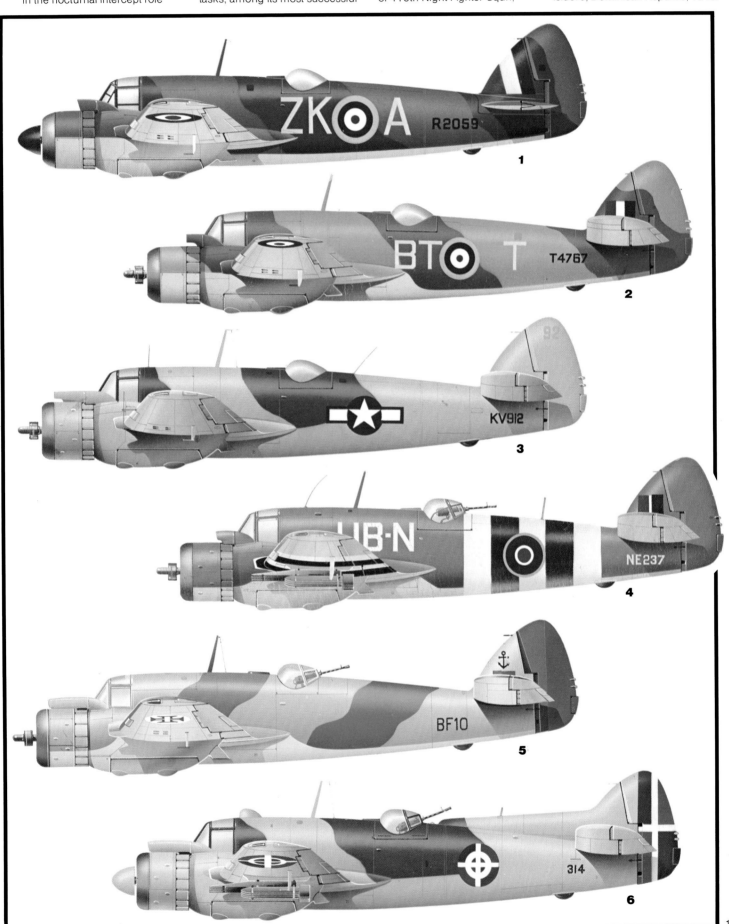

1

2

3

4

5

6

# Reggiane Re.2000 (and Re.2001) (1940)

Without doubt the most modern Italian fighter of its era, the Re.2000 introduced the Italian aircraft industry to the latest US technology. Aerodynamically and structurally advanced, it embodied integral wing fuel tanks which, at the time, were considered revolutionary. The Re.2000 first flew on 24 May

1939, but only 27 were to enter Regia Aeronautica service, 130 being built for export to the Hungarian and Swedish air forces, service with the former commencing in summer 1940. Hungarian licence manufacture totalled 191. The Re.2001 Ariete (Ram) I was an adaptation for a liquid-cooled engine with first flight in

July 1940, and 237 were built. (1) Prototype Re.2000 (M.M.408) as originally flown at Reggio, and (2) in definitive form. Note the irregular pattern of yellow ochre sprayed on dark olive green base (adopted in 1940). (2a) Upper and lower starboard surfaces of M.M.408. Note the reversed style (ie, white on

black) of the underwing fasces. (3) Re.2000 Serie IIIª (M.M. 8284) of 1ª squadriglia, Aviazione Ausiliaria per la Regia Marina, Sarzana (La Spezia), 1942. (3a) "Duck" emblem of Aviazione Ausiliaria. (3b) Coat of Arms of the House of Savoy. (4) Re.2000 (V.412) Héja I of 1./1 Szazad (Sqdn), 1./I Osztaly (Group) of

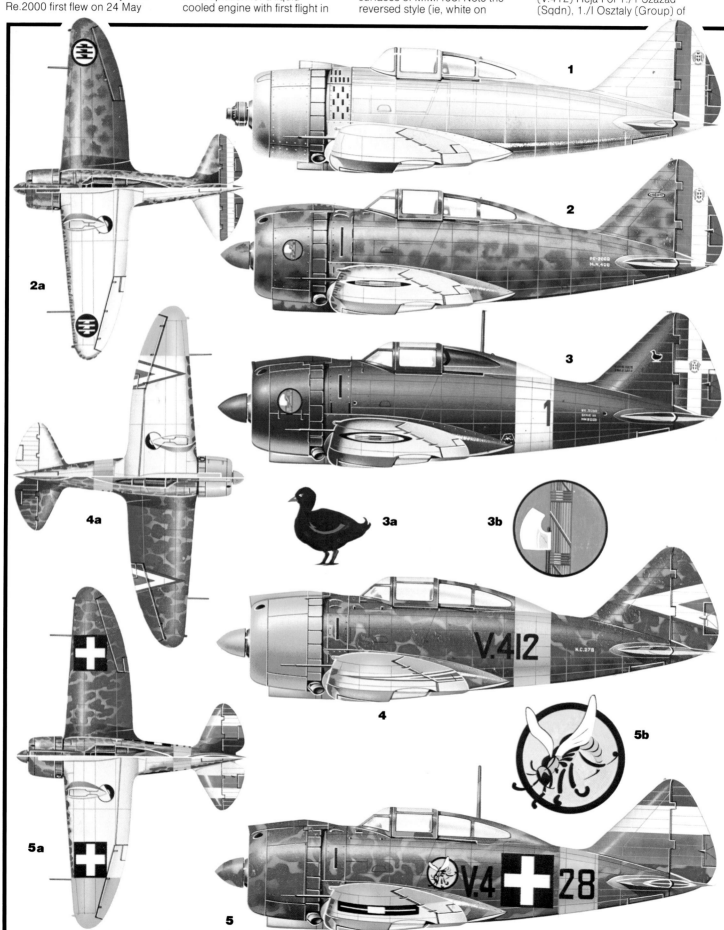

1.Vadász Ezred (Fighter Regt) of the Royal Hungarian Air Force, Szolnok, summer 1941. Note the yellow cowl, wingtips and aft fuselage band serving as theatre ID markings, and "wedge"-type national insignia (autumn 1938 until late 1941). (**4a**) Half-and-half planview of V.412. (**5**) Re. 2000 Héja I (V.428) of 1./1 Szazad, Independent Fighter Group (Önálló Vadász Ostály) of Air Brigade attached to 2nd Hungarian Army, Soviet Union, summer 1942. (**5a**) Planview of V.428. (**5b**) "Wasp" emblem of 1./1 Szazad. (**6**) Re.2000 (J 20) of 1st division, Flygflottilj 10, Ängelholm, Sweden, early 1945, and (**6a**) half-and-half planview of same aircraft. (**7**) MAVAG-built Re.2000 Héja II (V.613), home defence, Ferihegy, spring 1943. Note Hungarian national insignia adopted from late 1941. (**8**) Scrapview of Re.2000 of F 10 showing (**8a**) "Ghost" emblem of 1st division. (**9**) Re.2001 of 362ª squadriglia, 22° Gruppo "Spauracchio" 52° Stormo, at Capodichino, May 1943. (**9a**) Emblem of 22° Gruppo. (**10**) Re.2001, 150ª squadriglia, 2° Gruppo "Golletto", 6° Stormo, Pantellaria, August 1942. (**10a**) Emblem of 2° Gruppo. (**11**) Re.2001, 82ª squadriglia, 21° Gruppo, 51° Stormo, Italian Co-Belligerent Air Force, Puglia, late 1943, and (**11a**) topside of same aircraft.

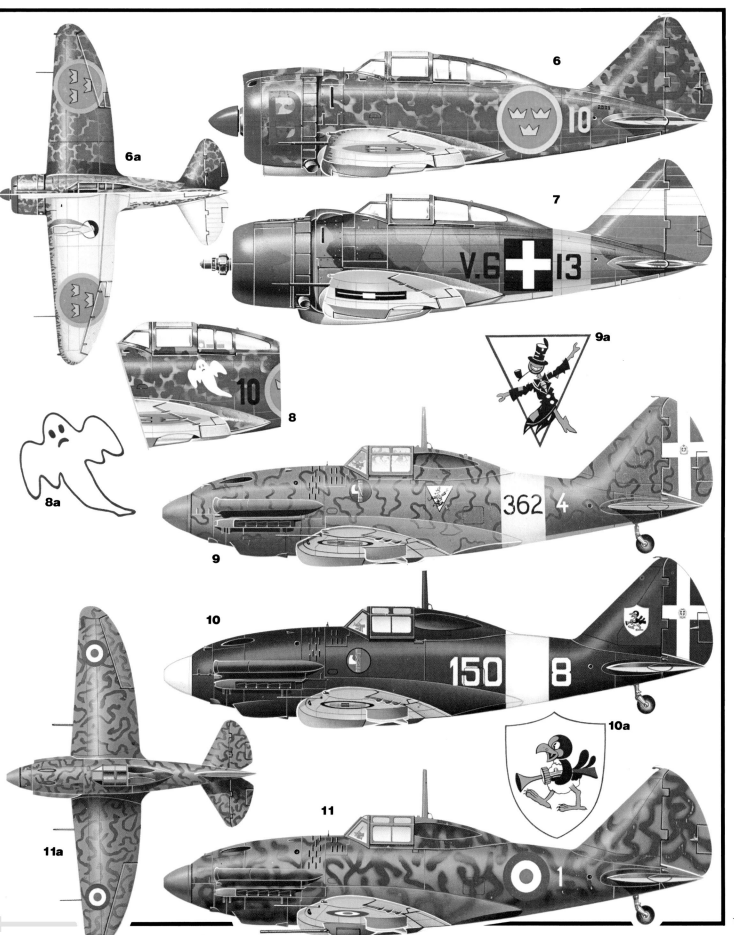

# Douglas SBD Dauntless (1940)

The principal shipboard US Navy dive bomber throughout the war in the Pacific, and the only US aircraft to participate in all five naval engagements fought exclusively between carriers, the Dauntless was an underpowered and painfully slow aircraft. It was short on range and woefully vulnerable to fighters, but its handling was innocuous and it was responsive; it was dependable and sturdy, but, most important, it was an *accurate* dive bomber. The prototype (XBT-2) first flew on 22 April 1938, and deliveries of the initial model, the SBD-1, began in September 1940. Armament and fuel capacity were increased with the SBD-2, self-sealing fuel tanks and some armour were added with the SBD-3, while an upgraded electrical system characterised the SBD-4, the SBD-5 and -6 having progressively more engine power. A total of 5,321 SBD dive bombers was built, including 953 for the USAAF as the A-24, these entering service from June 1941, and seeing limited action in the Pacific. (**1**) SBD-1 of VMSB-232 (ex-VMB-2) of US Marine Corps Air Group 21 based at Ewa, Oahu (Hawaii) in December 1941, at the time of Pearl Harbour. Note overall light grey finish as per directive of 30 December 1940. (**2**) SBD-3 of VS-41 aboard USS *Ranger* during Operation "Torch"

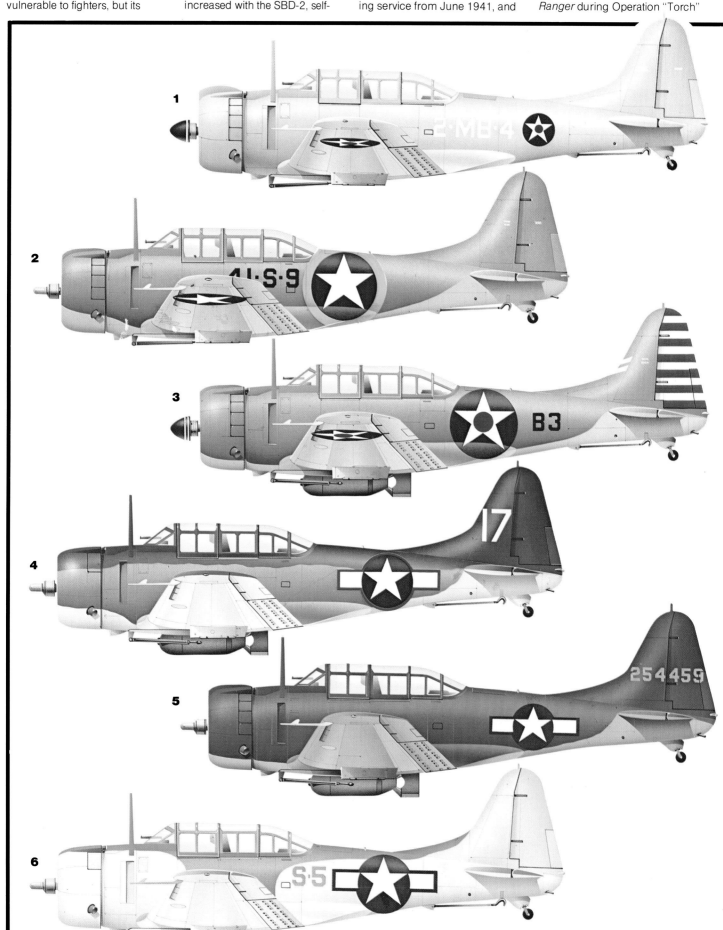

in November 1942. The outline of national insignia (applied by hand and ragged) was carried by all US Navy aircraft participating in operations against French North Africa. (**3**) SBD-3 of VSB-6 on the USS *Enterprise* in February 1942, and (**3a**) topside view of same aircraft showing the assymetric insignia. (**4**) SBD-4

of VMSB-243 of the 1st Marine Air Wing operating from Munda, New Georgia, August 1943. White bar was added to national insignia and red outline adopted in accordance with 28 June 1943 directive. (**5**) A-24B (42-54459) of 312th Bomb Group (Dive), USAAF, Makin Is, Gilbert Islands in December 1943. (**6**) SBD-5 of VMS-3, US

Marine Corps, in the Caribbean, May 1944. Note dark gull grey and white scheme adopted for Atlantic Theatre early 1944. (**7**) SBD-5 (BuAer No 36897) of RNZAF (NZ5049) based at Piva, Bougainville Is, April 1944. (**8**) A-24B (42-54543) of French Groupe de Chasse-Bombardement (GCB) 1/18 "Vendee" flying from Vannes,

France, in November 1944, with (**8a**) unit emblem and (**8b**) starboard topside showing striping. (**9**) SBD-5 of Flottille 4FB, French Aéronavale, Cognac, January 1945, with (**9a**) unit emblem and (**9b**) port topside. (**10**) SBD-5 of Escuadron Aéreo de Pelea 200, Fuerza Aérea Mexicana at Pie de la Cuesta. 1946.

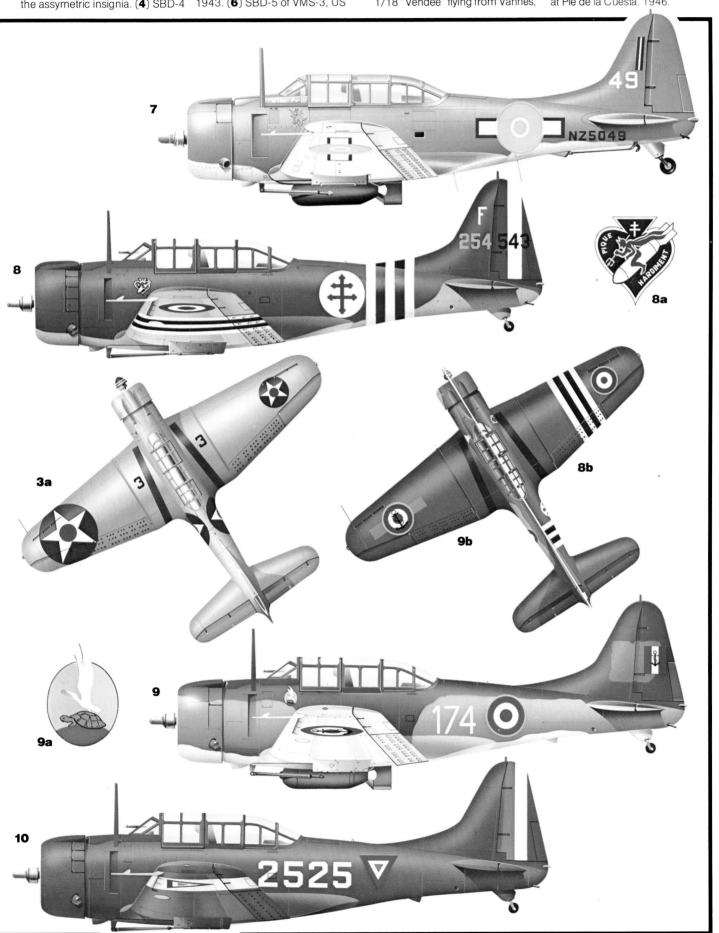

# Dewoitine D.520 (1940)

An aerodynamically refined and structurally robust fighter, the French D.520 could not compete with the opposing Bf 109E in terms of level speed, but it enjoyed a marked edge over the German fighter in manoeuvrability and it it possessed excellent diving characteristics. The D.520's principal shortcomings were a lack of damping in yaw, over-sensitivity to turbulence and any abrupt use of the throttle, and a tendency to ground loop, but it acquitted itself well in the desperate fighting in French skies in the summer of 1940. The first of three D.520 prototypes flew on 2 October 1938, but when the devastating Wehrmacht assault on France began 19 months later, only one Armée de l'Air Groupe with the D.520 was ready for combat. By the time of the 1940 Armistice, 437 had been completed, production being resumed in Vichy France, a further 478 D.520s being built prior to and subsequent to the German occupation of the so-called "Unoccupied France".

(1) D.520 N° 277 of Adj-Chef Pierre LeGloan of the 5ème Esc, Groupe de Chasse III/6, Armée de l'Air de l'Armistice, Rayak, Syria, June 1941. Note diagonal tricolour fuselage band denoting the pilot's "ace" status, the sienna, green and light grey upper surfaces and yellow rear fuselage and tail surfaces (the

116

red striping of the Vichy identification markings remaining to be applied). (**1a**) "African Mask" emblem of 5ème Esc. (**2**) D.520 Nº 245 of 3ème Esc, GC II/7, Gabès, Tunisia, in autumn 1942. Note unusual application of the striping on nose and "Cicogne" emblem of 3ème Esc. (**3**) D.520 Nº 190 of 6ème Esc, GC III/6,

Rayak, in June 1941. Note the definitive Vichy striping on nose, rear fuselage and tail. (**3a**) "Stage Mask" emblem of 6ème Esc, and (**3b**) half-and-half planview of same aircraft. (**4**) D.520 Nº 48 of GC I/3 at Cannes-Mandelieu, April-May 1940. (**4a**) Half-and-half planview of same aircraft. Note the primarily

green and khaki disruptive camouflage. (**5**) D.520 Nº 827 of Groupe de Chasse Doret, Toulouse-Blagnac, in September 1944. (**6**) D.520 Nº 31 of Escadrille de Chasse, SNCASE factory, Toulouse, June 1940. (**7**) D.520 of the Jagdgeschwader 101, a Jagdfliegerschule unit at Pau-Nord, March 1944. (**8**) D.520 of Jagd-

geschwader 105, Chartres, May 1944. (**9**) D.520 of 3rd Sqdn, 6th Fighter Orliak (bulg.III/JG 6) of Royal Bulgarian Air Force at Bojourishté, February 1944. (**10**) D.520 Nº 510 of 164ª squadriglia, 161º Gruppo Autonomo Caccia, Regia Aeronautica, at Reggio Calabria, Southern Italy, in May 1943.

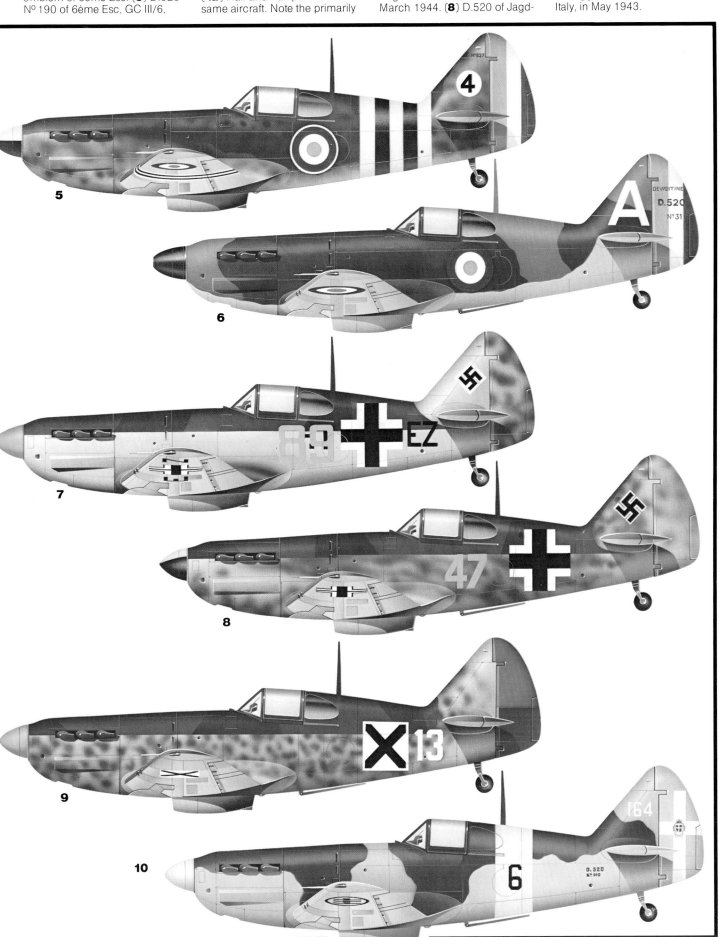

117

# Brewster F2A (Buffalo) (1940)

Possessing the distinction of being the first of the US Navy's shipboard fighter monoplanes, the Brewster fighter achieved a measure of notoriety for its mostly disastrous combat assays. In fairness, it offered good control response and pleasant flying characteristics, but its power-to-weight ratio was poor

and it was usually flown by comparatively inexperienced pilots under conditions of much superior enemy air power giving little margin for success. The prototype, the XF2A-1 (Model 239) flew in December 1937, and 54 were ordered by the US Navy as F2A-1s, 43 of these being relinquished in favour of the

Finnish Air Force which was to prove that the Brewster did possess at least some of the qualities required for success. These aircraft were replaced by 43 of the improved F2A-2 which was offered for export without carrier equipment as the B-339, with contracts placed by Belgium (40), the UK (170) and the Netherlands

East Indies (72), the last-mentioned order later being supplemented by one for 20 B-439 aircraft. In RAF service the B-339 was named Buffalo. The US Navy ordered 108 improved F2A-3s and these fought in the Battle of Midway, but, significantly outclassed by the opposition, saw no further US active use.

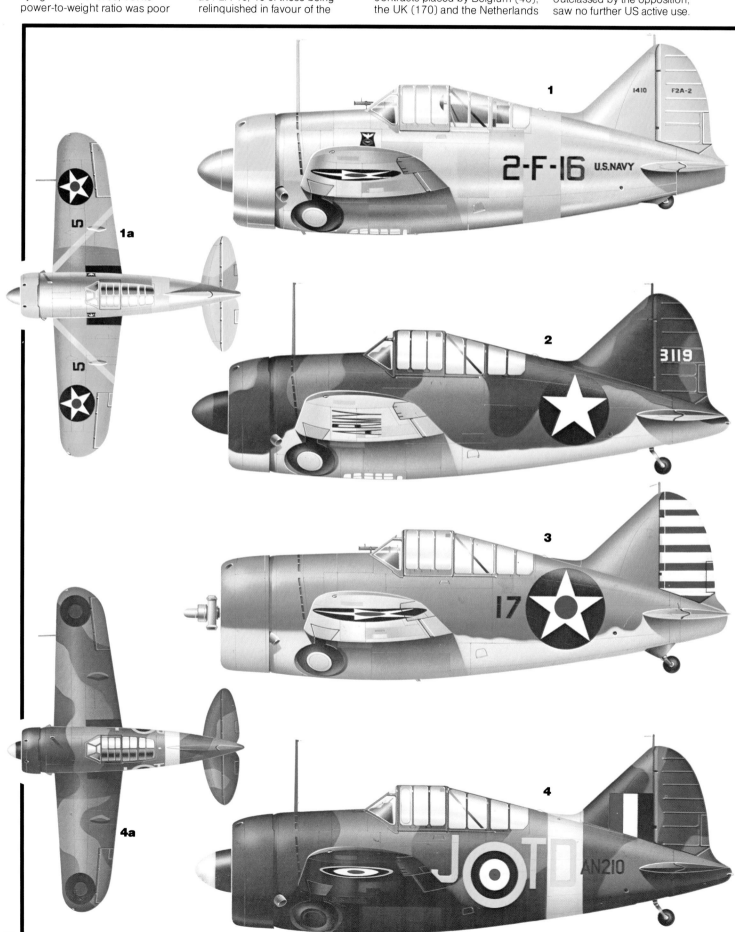

(**1**) F2A-2 (BuAer No 1410) of VF-2 "Flying Chiefs", aboard USS *Lexington,* March 1941, and (**1a**) upper surfaces of 2-F-16. Note glossy chrome yellow upper wing surfaces, 6th Section lemon yellow fuselage band and cowl, and lemon yellow tail denoting *Lexington.* (**1b**) Emblem of VF-2. (**2**) B-439 in USAAF insignia as used briefly in Australia, mid-1942. (**3**) F2A-3 of VMF-221, US Marine Corps, Ewa, Hawaii, mid-1942, in non-specular blue-grey and light grey. Note red-and-white rudder striping dispensed with from 15 May 1942. (**4**) B-339 Buffalo (AN210) of No 453 Sqdn, RAAF, Sembawang, Singapore, November 1941. (**4a**) Topside of AN210. (**5**) B-339D of 1 Afdeling, Vliegtuiggroep V. ML-KNIL (Royal Netherlands Indies Army Air Corps), Semplak, Java, summer 1941. (**6**) B-339D of ML-KNIL combined unit at Andir, Bandung, March 1942. Note Dutch national markings adopted February 1942. (**7**) Buffalo (W8153) of No 21 Sqdn, RAAF, in Dutch national markings as captured at Andir by Japanese. (**8**) B-239 (BW-354) of Sgt. H. Lampi of 2.lentue (flight), Lentolaivue (Sqdn) 24, Finnish Ilmavoimien, Tiiksjärvi, September 1942. (**8a**) Topside of BW-354. (**8b**) "Lynx" emblem (left) adopted by LLv 24 and (right) "Elk" emblem of 2.lentue/ LLv 24 (which appeared on tail).

# Grumman F4F Wildcat (1940)

When the Wildcat entered service it represented what was probably the best compromise achieved to that time between aeronautical and nautical demands in a shipboard fighter. It was a corpulent and aesthetically unappealing little warplane, and it lacked something of the speed performance of shore-based contemporary fighters. However it offered a very good climb rate, an excellent patrol range, superb ditching characteristics and, perhaps most important, the sturdiness necessary for intensive carrier operations. First flown (as the XF4F-2) on 2 September 1939, the Wildcat was ordered by the US Navy as the F4F-3 in August of that year, simultaneous production being undertaken of a model for export. The latter entered British service as the Martlet from September 1940, the F4F-3 first entering US Navy service in the following December. From March 1944, the name Martlet was discarded by the FAA in favour of the US Navy's name of Wildcat.

Eastern Motors was responsible for manufacture of more than half of the Wildcats built, producing 4,777 of the grand total of 7,815 as the FM-1 and FM-2, the production programme finally terminating in 1945. The outstanding deck behaviour of the Wildcat permitted extensive use from small escort carriers.

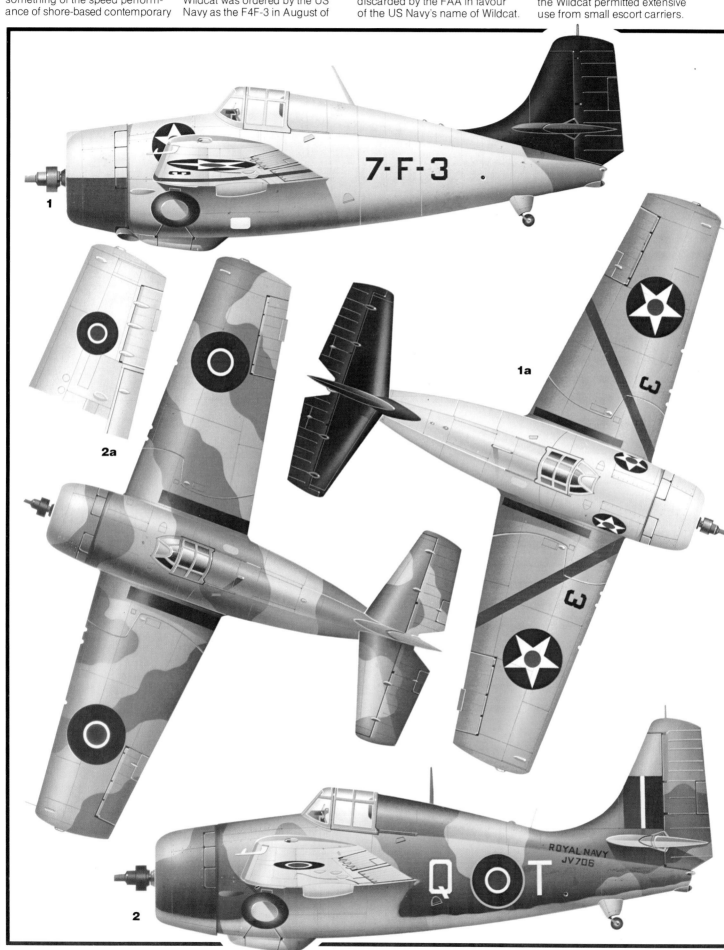

(**1**) F4F-3 of VF-7 aboard the USS *Wasp*, December 1940. Note the basic non-camouflage scheme of gloss light grey with gloss chrome yellow upper wing surface (see **1a**) authorised October 1940, and national insignia on forward fuselage in accordance with the March 1940 directive for types participating in the Neutrality Patrol. Black tail signified the *Wasp* and lower half of cowling in Royal Red indicated third aircraft of 1st Section of VF-7. (**1b**) Scrap view of underside of wing. (**2**) Wildcat VI (JV706) of No 835 Sqdn, Fleet Air Arm, in August 1944, HMS *Nairana*. Note two-tone grey finish standardised late in the war by Royal Navy. (**2a**) Upper surfaces and wing scrap view of JV706. (**3**) F4F-4 of VGF-29, USS *Santee* during Operation "Torch" (signified by yellow insignia surround) in November 1942. Note non-specular blue-grey and light grey finish. (**4**) Martlet II (AJ108) of No 888 Sqdn, HMS *Formidable*, with US markings for participation in Operation "Torch". (**5**) F4F-4 of VF-41 aboard USS *Ranger*, early 1942. From 15 May the rudder striping and the red disc in the centre of the national insignia were erased. (**5a**) The emblem of VF-41. (**6**) An FM-1 aboard USS *Block Island*, 1944. Note semi-gloss sea blue and insignia white overall finish.

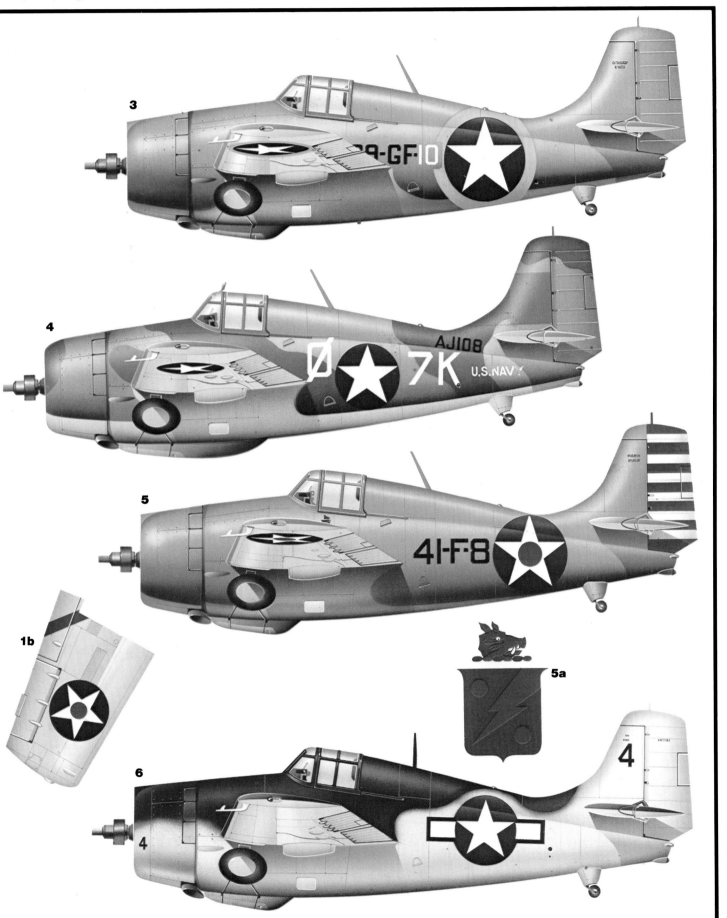

# Blohm und Voss BV 138 (1940)

Arguably the most inelegant of WWII's flying boats, the BV 138 was caustically known to its crews as der Fliegende Holzschuh — the Flying Clog! Conceived as an ocean-going reconnaissance aircraft and first flown (as the Ha 138 VI) on 15 July 1937, the BV 138 survived a catalogue of teething troubles to achieve a

reasonable standard of effectiveness in service, although its handling remained somewhat short of pleasant. A total of 276 production examples was completed. (1) BV 138C-1 (7R+RL) of 3.Staffel/See-Aufklärungsgruppe 125, Mamaia, Constanza, Rumania, in April 1943. (1a) Emblem of 3./SAGr 125. (1b) Upper surfaces of

7R+RL. (2) BV 138C-1 of 1.(F)/SAGr 131, Varna, Bulgaria, May 1944. Note crudely greyed-over white areas of markings for dawn-and-dusk convoy duties over western Black Sea coast. (2a) Emblem of 1.(F)/SAGr 131. (3) BV 138C-1 (K6+BK) of 2./Kü. Fl.Gr (Küstenfliegergruppe) 406, northern Norway, March 1942. (3a) Emblem

of 3./Kü.Fl.Gr.406. (4) BV 138C-1/U1 of 1.(F)/SAGr 130 operating in Trondheim area, northern Norway, April 1944. Note temporary winter camouflage. (4a) Emblem of 1.(F)/SAGr 130. (5) BV 138 MS (EB+UA), 6/MSGr 1, Grossenbrode, for Baltic mine-clearance tasks, 1944-45. (5a) Upper surfaces of EB+UA. Note mine-degaussing ring.

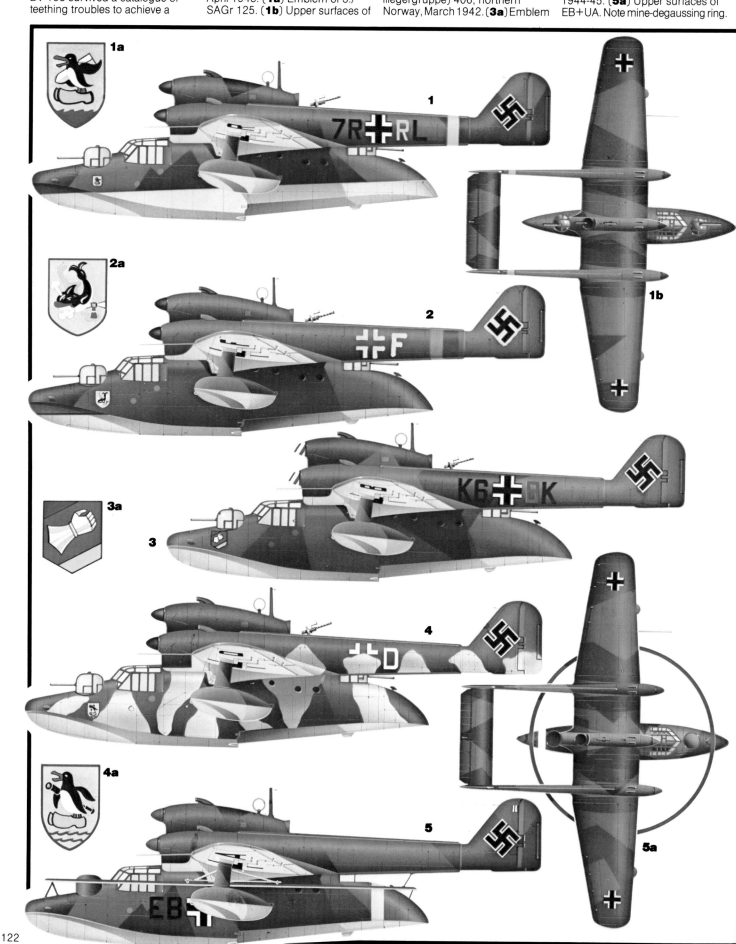

# Breguet Br 693 (1940)

A sturdy, manoeuvrable combat aircraft, the Bre 693 two-seat assault-bomber achieved service status shortly before commencement of the Wehrmacht assault on France. Evolved from the Bre 690, a three-seat fighter flown on 23 March 1938, it saw limited service, 254 being built, plus 50 with US engines as Bre 695s.

(1) Bre 691 Nº 5 as delivered to Orléans-Bricy, October 1939, for service trials by the 1e Escadrille of the 54e Escadre. (2) Bre 693 Nº 1013 of the 4e Escadrille, Groupe de Bombardement d'Assaut (GBA) II/54, Roye, May 1940. (2a) The SAL 259 emblem of GBA II/54. (3) Bre 693 of GBA I/54, Montdidier, May 1940, lost in an attack on German armour in the Tongeren area. (3a) Emblem of GBA I/54. (4) Bre 693 of 2e Esc, GBA I/51, Armée de l'Air de l'Armistice, Lézignan, mid-1942. (4a) Upper surfaces of same aircraft showing Vichy ID striping. (4b) Emblem of 2e Esc, GBA I/51. (5) Bre 693 Nº 34, Villacoublay, April 1940. (6) Bre 693 (ex-GBA I/51), Orange, March 1943, after transfer to Regia Aeronautica. Note Italian markings (see also 6a) with incorrect application of fasces (facing same direction both port and starboard) and retention of the red of the French roundel. (7) Bre 695 of 1e Esc, GBA I/51, Lézignan, 1942, and (7a) emblem of 1e Esc, GBA I/51.

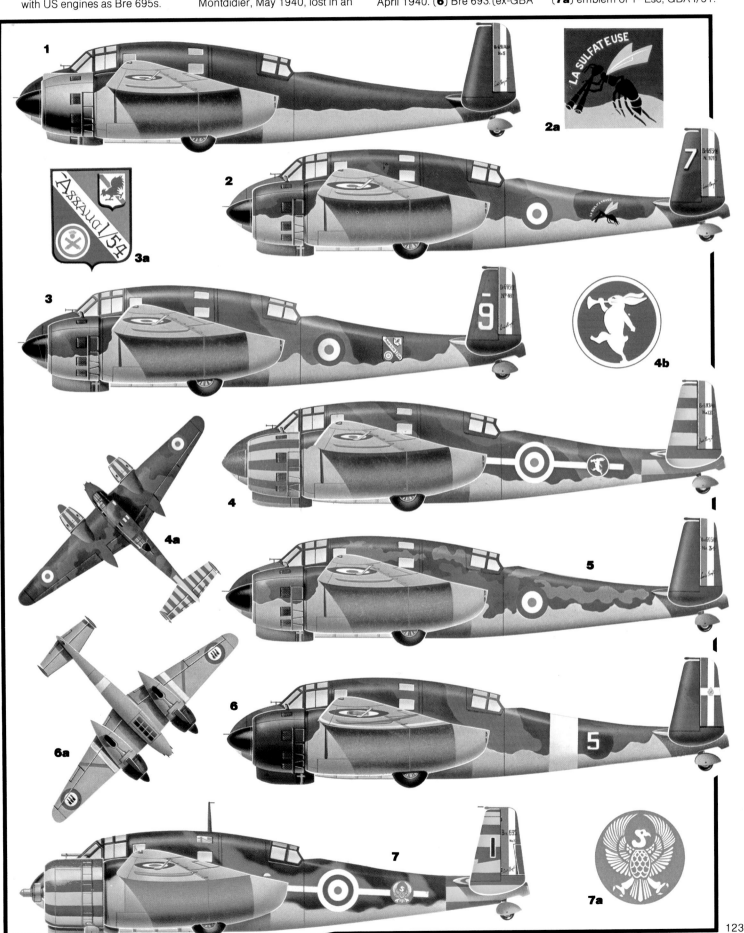

# Curtiss Hawk 81A (Tomahawk) (1940)

A straightforward extrapolation of Hawk 75A (see pages 90-91) design experience, the basis of its inception being substitution of liquid-cooled for air-cooled engine, the Hawk 81A provided the first series P-40s of the USAAF and the Tomahawk of the RAF. While retaining the outstanding handling of its pre-cursor, it lacked performance at altitude and was thus invariably inferior to the fighters by which it was opposed. It did manage to establish a reputation for sturdiness, however. The prototype (XP-40) flew on 14 October 1938 as a conversion of the 10th P-36A, and as the P-40 it saw US service from May 1940, the P-40B and C introducing modifications which enhanced combat worthiness; 524 were delivered to the US Army Air Force. A total of 1,280 was supplied to the RAF as Tomahawk Is, IIAs and IIBs (Hawk 81A-1s, -2s and -3s), and 100 were supplied to China for use by the American Volunteer Group formed during 1941.

(1) Tomahawk IIA (AH925) with standard dark green and dark earth temperate scheme, and unusual combination of azure and black undersides with Sky fuselage band and spinner, in mid-1940. (1a) Underside of AH925 showing black port wing. (2) Tomahawk IIB (AX900) in non-standard finish, Yeovil, Somerset, 1941.

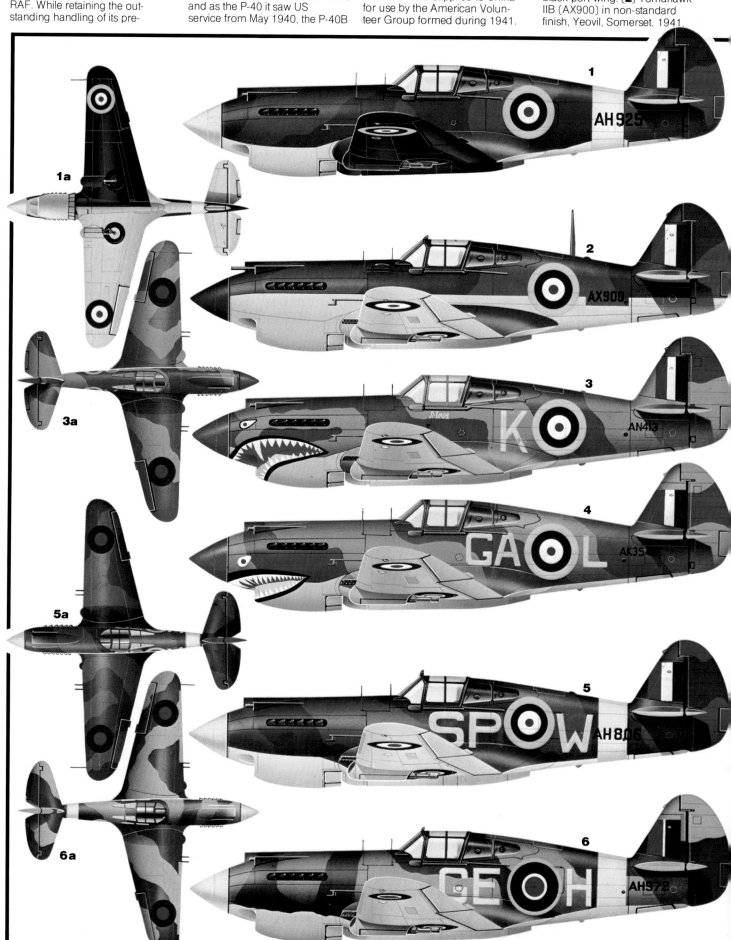

124

(**3**) Tomahawk IIB (AN413), No 112 Sqdn, Sidi Haneish, autumn 1941. (**3a**) Upper surfaces of AN413 showing dark earth and mid stone Middle East camouflage. (**4**) Tomahawk IIB (AK354) of No 112 Sqdn, Sidi Haneish, October 1941, showing sqdn code letters "GA" and variation of Shark's Mouth decoration. (**5**) Tomahawk IB (AH806) of No 400 (Canadian) Sqdn, Odiham, spring 1942, and (**5a**) upper surfaces of AH806. (**6**) Tomahawk IIA (AH972) of No 349 (Belgian) Sqdn, Ikeja, West Africa, February 1943, and (**6a**) the upper surfaces of AH972. (**7**) P-40 of 55th Sqdn, 20th Pursuit Group, Marsh Field, California, 1941. Designator repeated in yellow on upper port wing surface. (**7a**) Scrap view of the underside of the same aircraft. (**8**) P-40C of 39th Sqdn, 31st Pursuit Group, Selfridge Field, Mich, 1941. (**9**) Tomahawk IIB of 154 IAP, Red Banner Baltic Fleet Air Force, Leningrad area, 1942. (**10**) Hawk 81A-2 (P-8168) flown by Charles Older, 3rd Sqdn "Hell's Angels", AVG, Kunming, China, spring 1942. (**10a**) The upper surfaces of P-8168. (**10b**) Emblem of AVG, and (**10c**) one of several versions of "Hell's Angels" emblem. (**11**) Hawk 81A-2 (P-8138) flown by Henry Geselbracht, 2nd Sqdn, AVG, Toungoo, February 1942. (**11a**) "Panda Bear" emblem. (**12**) Turkish Tomahawk IIB, 1942.

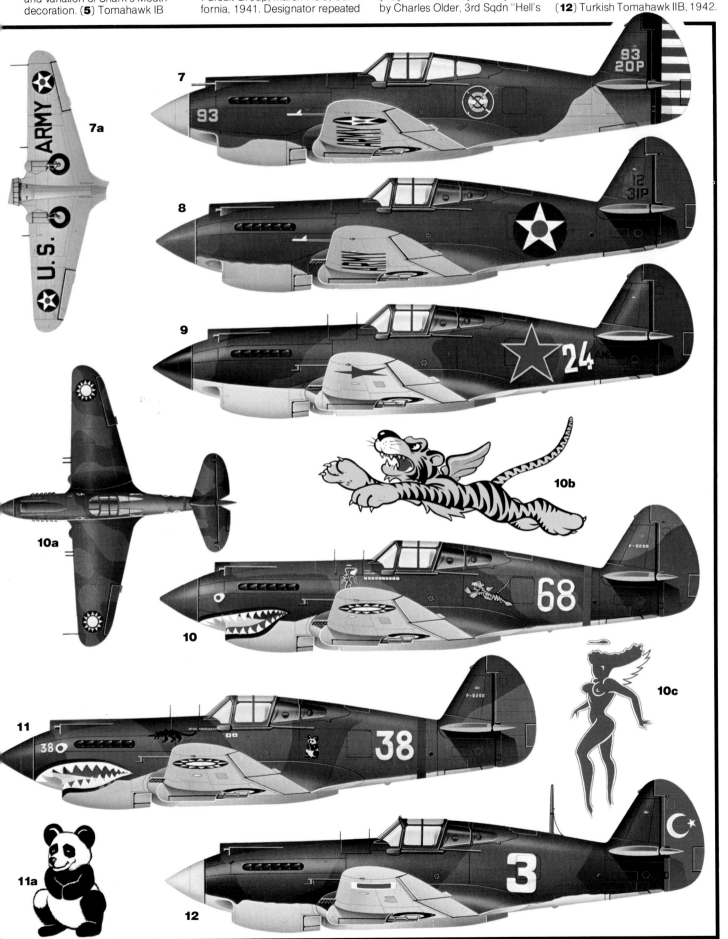

# Handley Page Halifax (1940)

Conceived initially as a twin-engined medium bomber and built eventually as a four-engined "heavy", the Halifax first flew on 25 October 1939, and began to reach RAF squadrons barely more than a year later. Unlike the Lancaster, by which it was to be joined within a further year and with which it was to share the major burden of RAF Bomber Command's prolonged night offensive over Germany, the Halifax was not an unqualified success from the outset. Its early career was marred by many accidents, which, temporarily inexplicable, were eventually traced to rudder overbalance. It was underpowered as a result of weight increases subsequent to the design being frozen, which, together with unexpectedly high drag, resulted in serious performance degradation, and operational attrition was initially alarming. Persistent improvement and judicious innovation, however, gradually overcame the most worrying of its vicissitudes, and four out of every 10 heavy bombers built in the UK during WWII were to be Halifaxes. When the last Halifax was delivered in November 1946, a grand total of 6,176 aircraft of this type had been produced. (**1**) Halifax 1 Srs 1 (L9530), No 76 Sqdn, Middleton St George, August 1941. Note the unofficial "crest" of pilot (P/O Christopher

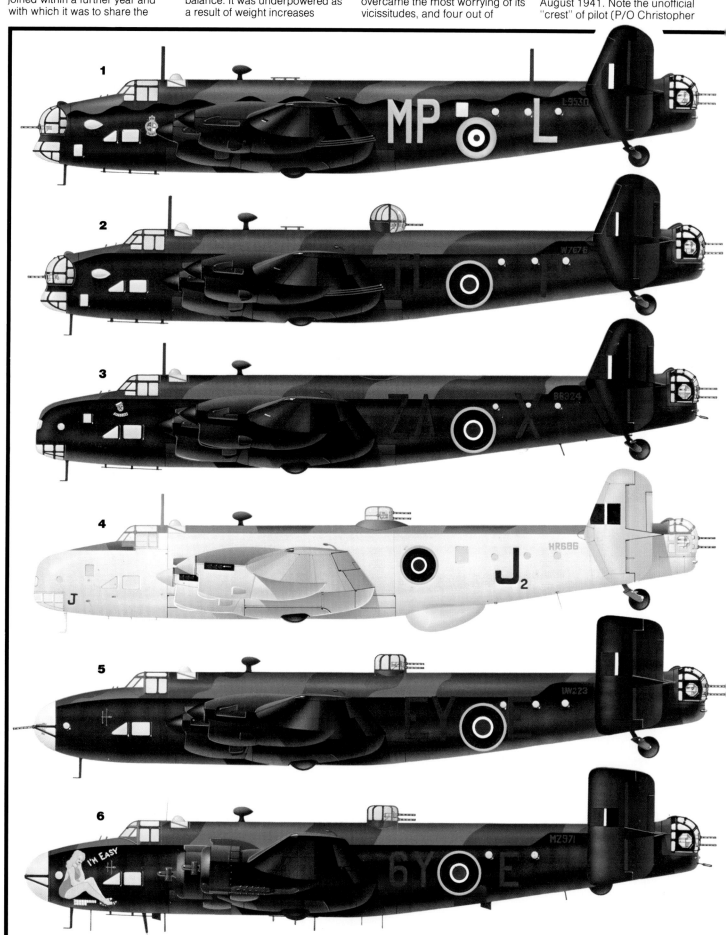

Cheshire). (**2**) Halifax B II Srs 1 (W7676), No 35 (Madras Presidency) Sqdn, Linton-on-Ouse, Yorks, May 1942. (**3**) Halifax B II Srs 1 (Special) (BB324), No 10 Sqdn, Melbourne, Yorks, April 1943. (**4**) Halifax GR II Srs 1 (Special), No 502 Sqdn, Holmsley South, mid-1943, on Atlantic and Biscay area patrol. (**5**) Halifax

B II Srs 1A (LW223), No 78 Sqdn, Breighton, Yorks, September 1943. (**6**) Halifax B III (MZ971), No 171 (SD) Sqdn on ''Mandrel'' (radio countermeasures) sorties in No 100 Group, North Creake, 1945. (**7**) Halifax B III (MZ287), No 466 Sqdn, RAAF, Driffield, Yorks, 1944, as component of No 4 Group. Note tail markings applied to No

4 Group Halifaxes in 1944 (see also Nos 8, 10 and 12). (**8**) Halifax B VI (RG590) of No 346 (Guyenne) Sqdn, a Free French unit operating from Elvington, 1944. (**9**) Halifax Met V Srs 1A (LL296) of No 518 Sqdn on meteorological recce sorties from Tiree, Inner Hebrides, 1944. (**10**) Halifax B VI (PP163), No

158 Sqdn, Lissett, Yorks, 1944. (**11**) Halifax B III (PN369) of No 1341 Flight, Digri, India, May 1945, equipped to monitor enemy radar transmissions. (**12**) Halifax B III (PN451/G) of No 462 (SD) Sqdn, RAAF, flying with ''Airborne Cigar'' for radio transmission jamming from Foulsham, Norfolk, early 1945.

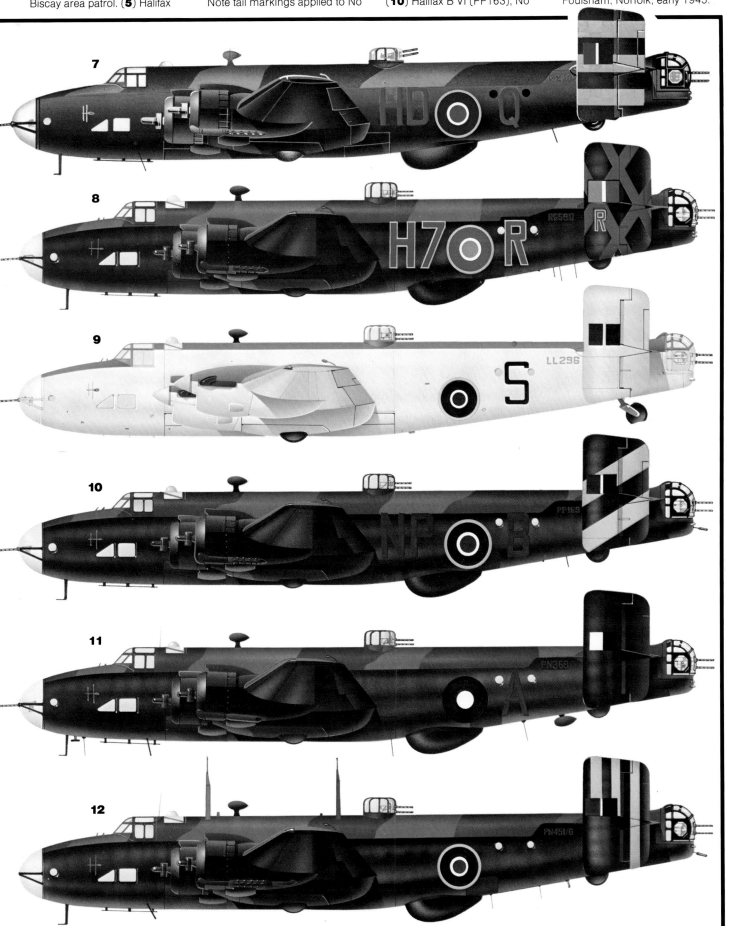

# Douglas DB-7 (A-20) (1940)

Both dependable and versatile, and among the most pleasant of WWII's combat aircraft to fly, the DB-7 first flew on 17 August 1939 as a derivative of the 1938 Model 7B. It entered service with the Armée de l'Air in 1940, and with the USAAF as the A-20 in 1941. Known as the Boston to the RAF, the DB-7 was built in

very substantial numbers, 7,385 having been delivered when the last was completed in September 1944, almost half for the USSR. (**1**) DB-7B-3 (Nº 24) of Groupe de Bombardement I/19 (ex-II/19), Armée de l'Air de l'Armistice, Blida, Algeria, Autumn 1940. (**1a**) Wing camouflage pattern of Nº 24 in dark green, light earth

and blue-grey. The undersurfaces were light blue-grey. (**2**) DB-7 Havoc I (BD112) of No 32 Sqdn, Ford, Sussex, England, April 1941. (**2a**) Upper wing surfaces of BD112. Note badly flaking matt black night finish. (**3**) Boston II (AL296), No 107 Sqdn, Great Massingham, Norfolk, March 1942. (**3a**) Upper wing surfaces of

AL296, and (**3b**) personal emblem of pilot. (**4**) Boston IIIA (AL877) of No 24 Sqdn, South African Air Force, Souk-el-Khemis, Tunisia, April 1943. Note standard desert finish of dark earth and mid stone with azure blue undersurfaces. (**4a**) Upper wing surfaces of AL877. (**5**) Boston IIIA (BZ357)

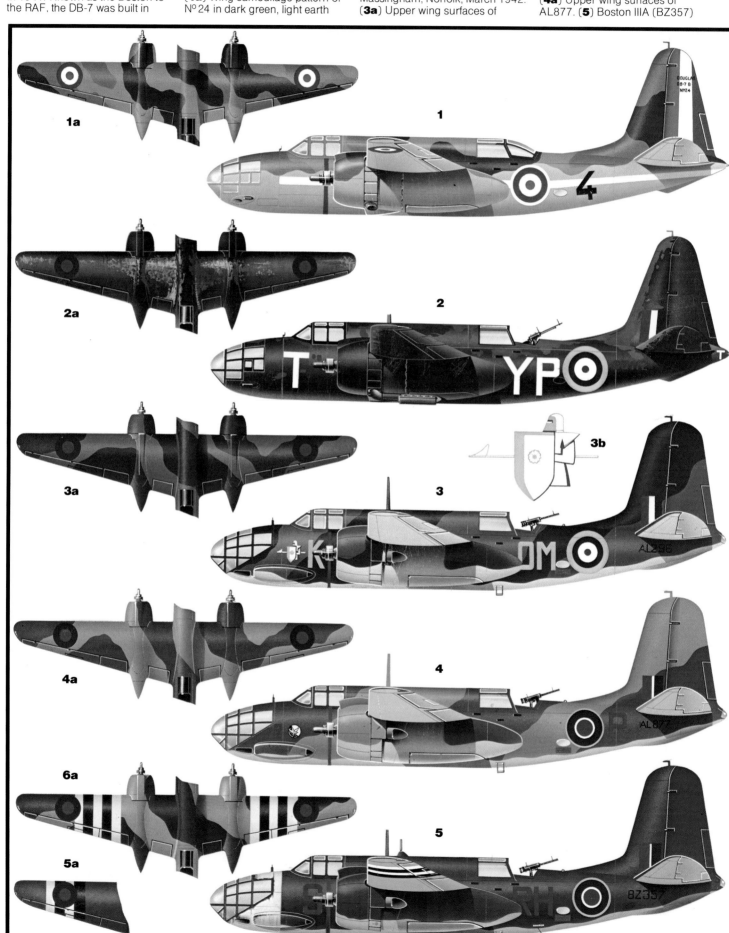

of No 88 (Hong Kong) Sqdn, at Hartford Bridge, Hants, June 1944. Note USAAF olive drab and grey finish with white soluble paint on nose section. (**5a**) Top surface detail of BZ357 showing non-standard width four-band invasion striping. (**6**) Boston IIIA (BZ261) of No 342 "Lorraine" Sqdn, Hartford Bridge in June 1944. Note overpainting of invasion striping on upper fuselage. (**6a**) Upper wing surfaces of BZ261. (**6b**) Free French "Cross of Lorraine" emblem. (**6c**) Coat of Arms of Lorraine. (**7**) A-20B (41-3241) of 47th Bomb Group, Souk-el-Arba, Tunisia, May 1943. Note Desert Sand upper surfaces, commonly known as "desert pink" owing to effect of sunlight on paint's pigmentation. (**8**) A-20B (41-3134), 84th Bomb Sqdn, 47th Bomb Group, Mediouna, Morocco, December 1942. (**9**) Boston III (A28-15) of No 22 Sqdn, RAAF, Vivigani Strip, Goodenough Is, March 1943. (**9a**) Personal emblem carried on port side. (**9b**) Upper wing surfaces of A28-15, and (**9c**) emblem carried below the cockpit on starboard side. (**10**) A-20B of Northern Fleet Air Force (VVS SF), Arctic Front, winter 1943-44. (**11**) A-20B of Black Sea Fleet Air Force (VVS ChF), spring 1944. Note Soviet dorsal turret. (**11a**) Unit emblem of Black Sea and Wild Goose.

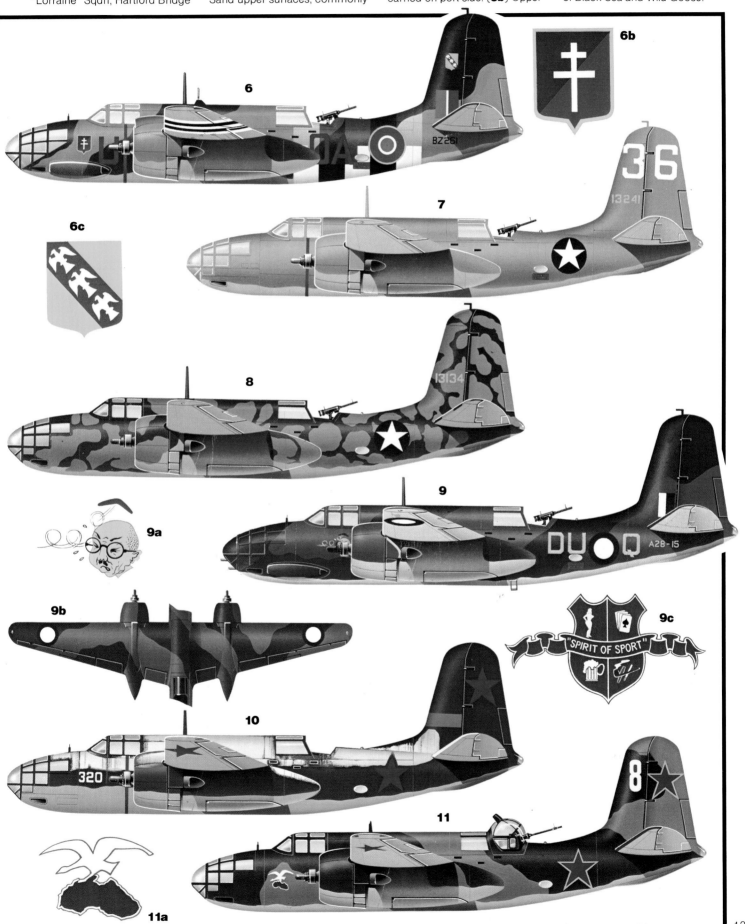

129

# Short Stirling (1940)

The RAF's first four-engined bomber monoplane, the angularly ugly Stirling was noteworthy for its disproportionately short wingspan resulting from the demand that it must fit existing hangars. Flown as a prototype on 14 May 1939, its service debut in 1940 marked a watershed in RAF strategic offensive capability. Agile for its size, the Stirling suffered somewhat poor climb and altitude performance, and by early 1944 was being relegated to glider-tug and transport roles. Many Mk III bombers were in fact converted to Mk IVs for this purpose; the last 162 of 1,910 Stirlings were built as Mk V transports.

(1) Stirling I Srs I (N6003) of No 7 Sqdn, RAF Oakington, early 1941. (2) Stirling I Srs 2 (W7455) of No 149 Sqdn, RAF Mildenhall, early 1942. Note extension of the black finish. (3) Stirling I Srs I (N3705) of No 7 Sqdn after repainting for evaluation by E-Stelle Rechlin. Note tarpaulin covering damaged nose. (4) Stirling I Srs 2 (EF369) of No 7 Sqdn operating with Pathfinder Force (8 Group) from Oakington, summer 1943. (5) Stirling IV of No 620 Sqdn, D-Day landings and Arnhem assault as glider-tug and transport. (6) Stirling V (PJ887) of No 196 Sqdn serving in the transport role, in early 1945.

# Mitsubishi G4M (Betty) (1941)

The corpulent but aesthetically pleasing G4M, or Navy Type 1 Attack Bomber, was numerically the most important Imperial Navy shore-based bomber of WWII. It was large but very light as it lacked any protection for crew, engines or fuel, becoming known as the "Flying Lighter" owing to its proclivity for flaming when attacked by fighters. Flown on 23 October 1939, the G4M was built throughout the war, 2,444 being delivered to the Navy. (**1**) G4M1 of Takao Kokutai (later redesignated 753rd Kokutai) at Rabaul, October 1942. Note light application of dark green dapple to natural metal fuselage skin, this being intensified on upper wing and tail surfaces. (**2**) G4M1 of 705th Kokutai, Rabaul, 1943. Note omission of yellow wing leading edge ID strip and the superimposition of Hinomaru on square white field. (**3**) G4M1 of 761st Kokutai, Kanoya, 1943. The Katakana symbols identified the unit and the first digit of tail number indicated the role. Note dark green finish extended to all surfaces. (**4**) G4M3 of the Yokosuka Kokutai, Atsugi, in September 1945. The Kana "Yo" signified Kokutai. (**5**) G4M2a of Air Technical Arsenal (Koku Gijitsu Sho) indicated by Kana "Ko". The "G4-33" indicated 33rd G4M development aircraft, orange finish indicating research.

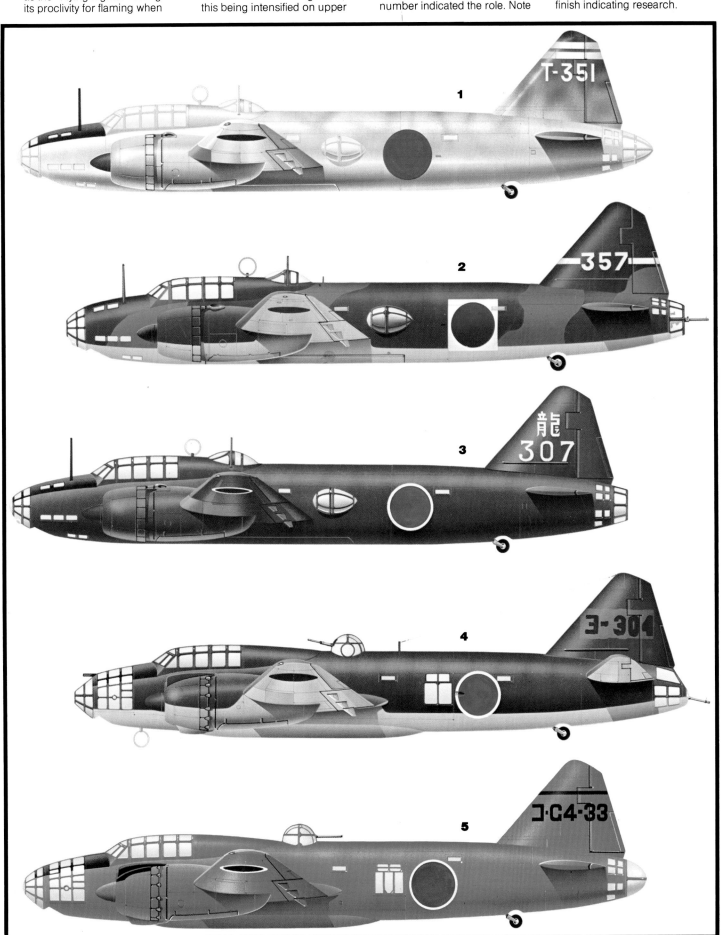

# Mikoyan-Gurevich MiG-3 (1941)

Small, heavy and very fast, the MiG-3 was the first of the new single-seat fighters evolving in the Soviet Union immediately prior to WWII to achieve service. Optimised for the high-altitude intercept mission, it suffered poor longitudinal stability and spinning characteristics, its control response was sluggish and it was taxing to fly. The design was primarily the work of Artem Mikoyan and Mikhail Gurevich, with development being initiated under the aegis of the doyen of Soviet fighter design team leaders, Nikolai Polikarpov, and the first of three prototype aircraft flew on 5 April 1940. Production was commenced as the MiG-1, but poor handling and an unacceptably short endurance led to changes which, introduced with the 101st aircraft off the line, were accompanied by a change in designation to MiG-3, no fewer than 3,322 having been built by the time the last left the assembly line in spring 1942. The MiG-3 was at a distinct disadvantage in fighter-versus-fighter combat as this mostly took place at altitudes much lower than those for which this Soviet fighter had been designed. The disruptive upper surface camouflage of dark earth and medium green standard during the first year of the conflict gave place in 1942 to an overall

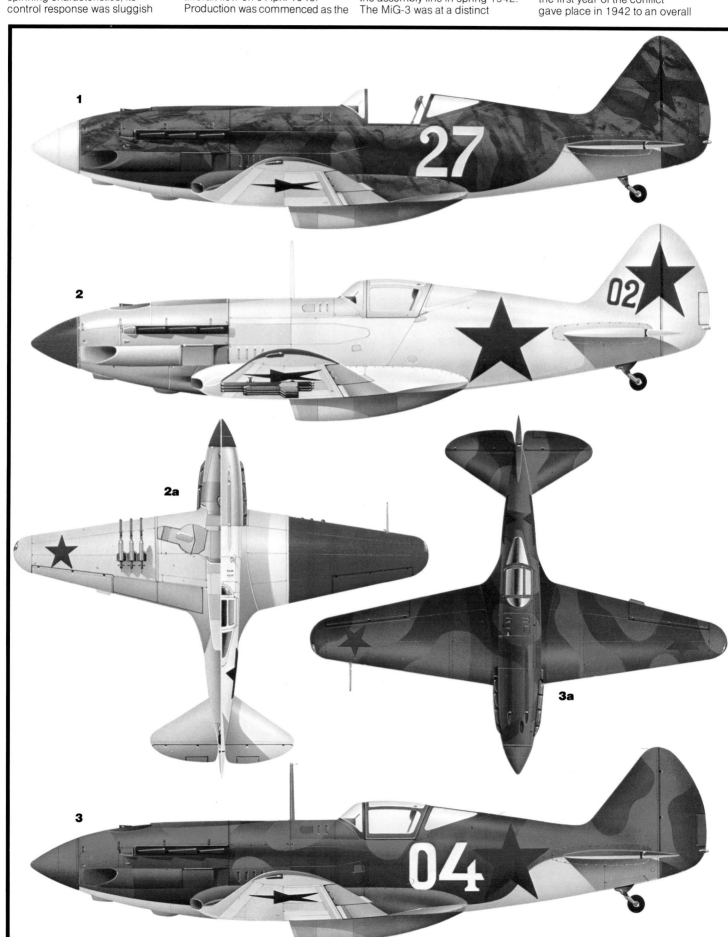

olive green upper surface finish and various temporary washable finishes were also applied.
(**1**) MiG-3 of 7 IAP (Fighter Aviation Regiment) of PVO (Air Defence), Leningrad, July 1941. Note camouflage crudely applied in the field and omission of cockpit canopy. (**2**) MiG-3 of 12 GvIAP (Guards Fighter Aviation Regiment) of 6 IAK (Fighter Air Corps), Moscow Air Defence Zone, in the winter 1941-42. Note natural metal engine cowl, (**2a**) high-visibility outer wing panel upper surfaces and (**2b**) a manufacturing number on the starboard side of cowling only. (**3**) MiG-3 of Capt S. N. Polyakov, 7 IAP, VVS KBF (Red Banner Baltic Fleet Air Force), on the Leningrad Front, in summer 1941. Note early temperate camouflage. (**4**) MiG-3 of 16 GvIAP flown by Aleksandr I. Pokryshkin, 1942. Note three "kill" stars beneath windscreen and olive green upper surface finish. (**5**) MiG-3 of 6 IAK, Moscow Air Defence Zone, flown by A. V. Shlopov, early 1942. Legend under cockpit reads "Za Stalina!" (For Stalin!). Note added UB machine guns under wings. (**5a**) Detail of wing outer panel upper surface (Shlopov's aircraft). (**6**) MiG-3 of 7 IAP, VVS KBF, 1944. (**7**) MiG-3 of 34 IAP, 6 IAK, Moscow, winter 1941-42. Note, again, the widely-used "Za Stalina" legend on the fuselage.

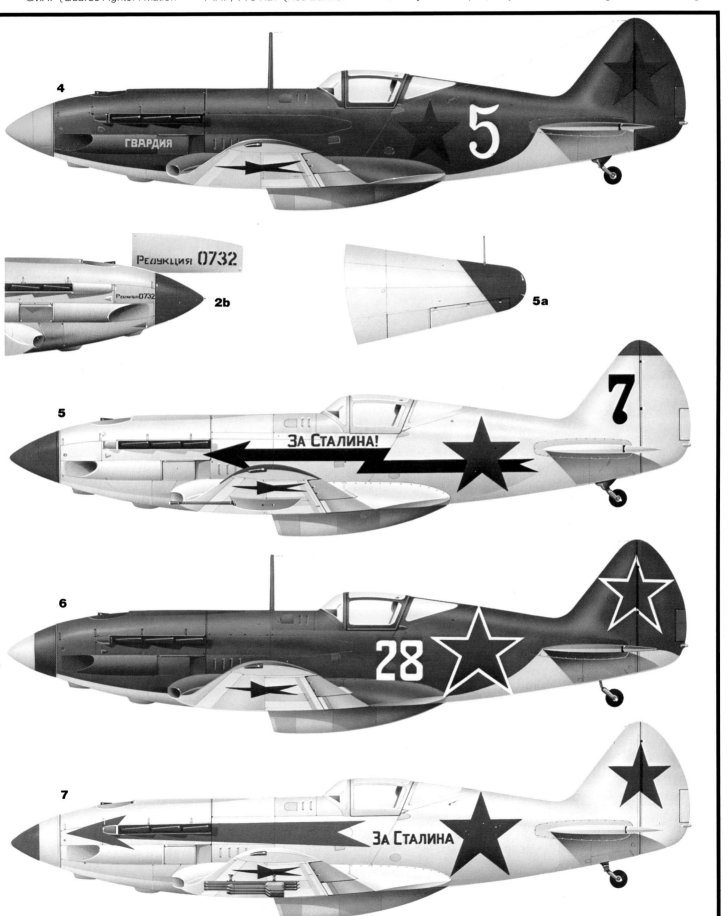

**4**

ГВАРДИЯ
5

Редукция 0732
**2b**

**5a**

**5**
За Сталина!
7

**6**
28

**7**
За Сталина

# Consolidated B-24 Liberator (1941)

Inevitably, the B-24 Liberator invites comparison with the B-17 Fortress by which it was overshadowed in fame if not in achievement, and with which it shared the strategic bombing role in the USAAF for most of WWII. The B-24 lacked the nicety of handling that endeared the B-17 to its pilots; its controls

were heavy and it was precocious in even mild turbulence. It was also inferior in altitude performance, but it offered an appreciably better range and a marginally higher speed performance. The B-24 also possessed a more commodious fuselage, rendering it amenable to a wider variety of tasks than came within the

repertoire of the B-17. Flown on 29 December 1939, it was to be built in larger numbers than any other single US aircraft type during WWII, the extraordinary total of 18,482 (excluding the rather different PB4Y-2 and RY-3 derivatives) being delivered, of which the RAF received 1,889. (**1**) LB-30B Liberator (40-2369)

requisitioned from RAF contract and utilised as transport, based at Bolling Field, October 1941. The RAF-specified night bomber finish was retained, the US flags (on top of centre fuselage and on each side of nose) serving as neutrality identification. The painted-out RAF roundel (applied at factory) is just discernible.

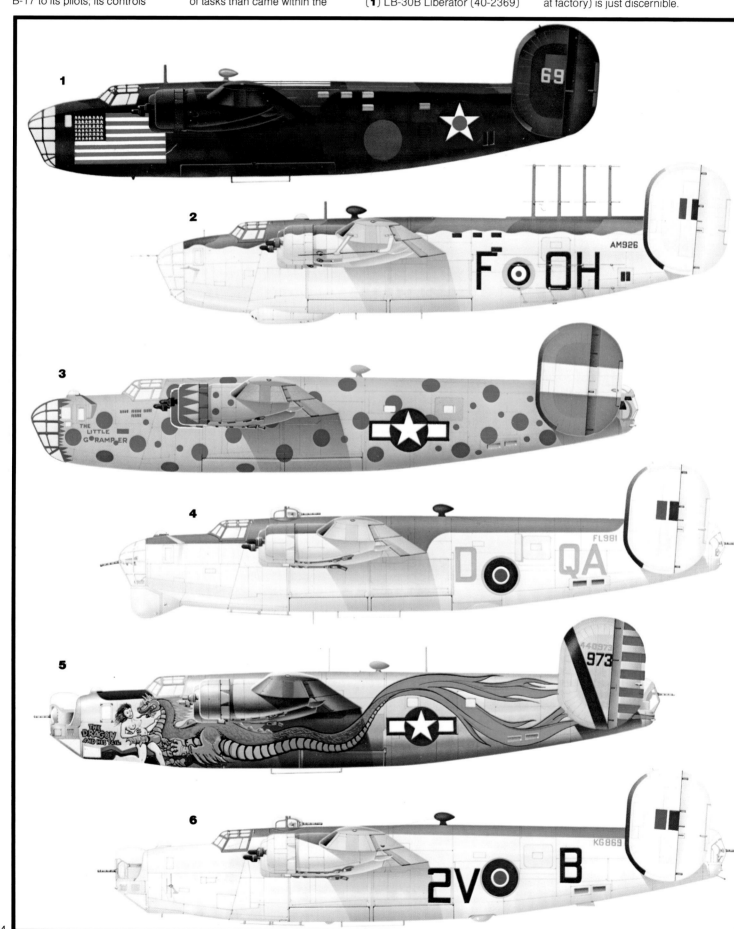

(2) Liberator GR I (AM926) of No 120 Sqdn, RAF Coastal Command, Aldergrove, N Ireland, late 1942, with extra dark sea grey and dark slate grey upper surfaces. Note ASV Mk II aerials and four-cannon ventral pack. (3) B-24D-90 (42-40722) "Little Gramper" assembly ship of the 491st Bomb Group, North Pickenham, autumn 1944. (4) Liberator GR V (FL981) of No 224 Sqdn, November 1942. (5) B-24J-190 (44-40973) "The Dragon and his Tail", 43rd Bomb Group, Ie Shima, 1945. (6) Liberator GR VI (KG869) of No 547 Sqdn, Leuchars, Fife, late 1944. (7) PB4Y-1 of Patrol Bomber Sqdn VPB-110, US Navy, Devon, winter 1944. Note non-specular sea blue top surfaces, intermediate blue vertical surfaces and insignia white underside. (7a) Topside of the same aircraft. (8) Liberator B VI (TS520) of No 223 Sqdn, No 100 Group, Oulton, Norfolk, August 1944. (8a) Topside of TS520. (9) B-24D-1 (41-23659) "Blonde Bomber II" of 98th Bomb Group, USAAF, based at Benghazi, Libya, inadvertently landed at Pachino, Sicily, 20 February 1943, after attacking Naples. (9a) Individual aircraft name on starboard side of nose, and (9b) individual emblem appearing on the portside. This aircraft is illustrated after the application of Regia Aeronautica insignia for flight test and evaluation in Italy.

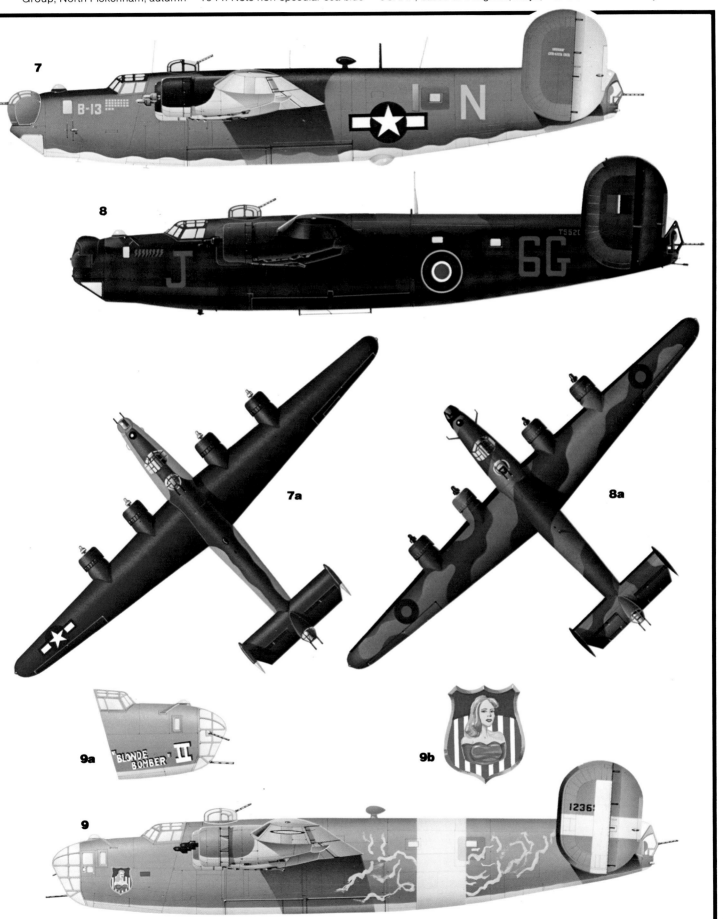

# Lockheed P-38 Lightning (1941)

Viewed as radical at the time of its debut, the P-38 Lightning was certainly innovatory in the features that it combined. The first fighter in the world with a tricycle undercarriage, it was the first fighter of twin-boom configuration adopted by the USAAF, the service's first twin-engined single-seater fighter and the first squadron fighter with turbo-superchargers. If slightly slower and somewhat less man-oeuvrable than its single-engine contemporaries, the P-51 Mustang and P-47 Thunderbolt, it mated an excellent combat radius with the safety factor offered by two engines. Initial models suffered inadequate engine cooling and compressibility effects proved troublesome, problems that were not to be finally resolved until the advent of the P-38J model, but the Lightning was to serve with distinction on every battle-front over which the USAAF was engaged in WWII. First flown on 27 January 1939, the Lightning began to enter USAAF service as the P-38D in late summer 1941, and was to prove amenable for a wide variety of tasks, including that of photo-reconnaissance (F-4 and F-5). A total of 9,923 had been delivered when production ended in August 1945. If outclassed in air-to-air combat against more nimble single-seats, the P-38 nevertheless accounted for more

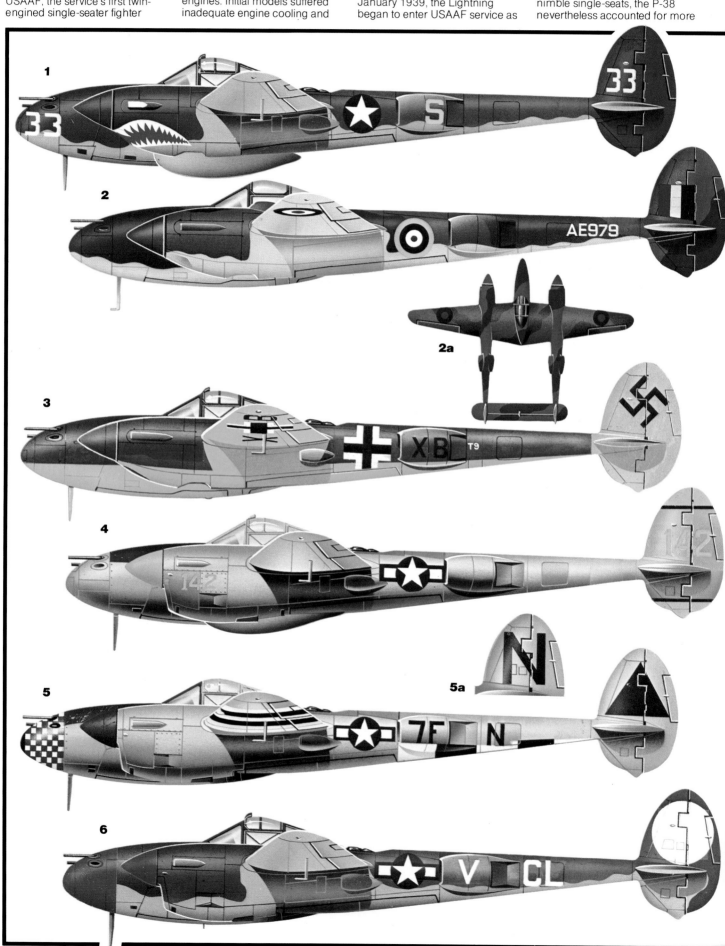

136

Japanese aircraft destroyed than did any other Allied fighter. (1) P-38F-5 of 347th Fighter Group (New Caledonia) on detachment to 13th AAF, Guadalcanal, February 1943. (2) L-322-61 Lightning I (AE979) evaluated in spring 1942 at RAF Boscombe Down. (2a) Top planview of AE979. (3) P-38E (T9+XB), Sonderkommando Rosarius for demonstrations to Luftwaffe units, 1943-44. (4) P-38J of 432nd Fighter Sqdn, 475th Fighter Group, New Guinea, winter 1943. (5) P-38J of 401st Fighter Sqdn, 370th Fighter Group, Florennes, Belgium, in November 1944. (5a) Aircraft letter on the inboard face of vertical tail. (6) P-38J of 338th Fighter Sqdn, 55th Fighter Group, Nuthampstead, UK, spring 1944. (7) P-38J-5 (42-67298) of 79th Fighter Sqdn, 20th Fighter Group, Kingscliffe, UK, spring 1944. (8) P-38L-5 of Fuerza Aérea Hondureña, Tocontin AB, Honduras, 1948. (9) P-38L (M.M. 4386) of 4º Stormo, Aeronautica Militare Italiana, Capodichino, 1946. (9a) "Cavallino Rampante" emblem of 4º Stormo. (10) F-5E (44-24082) of Nationalist Air Force, China, summer 1945. (11) F-5B-1 (42-68213) of Groupe de Reconnaissance 2/33, Armée de l'Air, Bastia-Borgho, Corsica, July 1944. (12) F-5G (44-25953) of GR 2/3, Colmar, spring 1945. Note 3e Esc "Double-headed Axe"

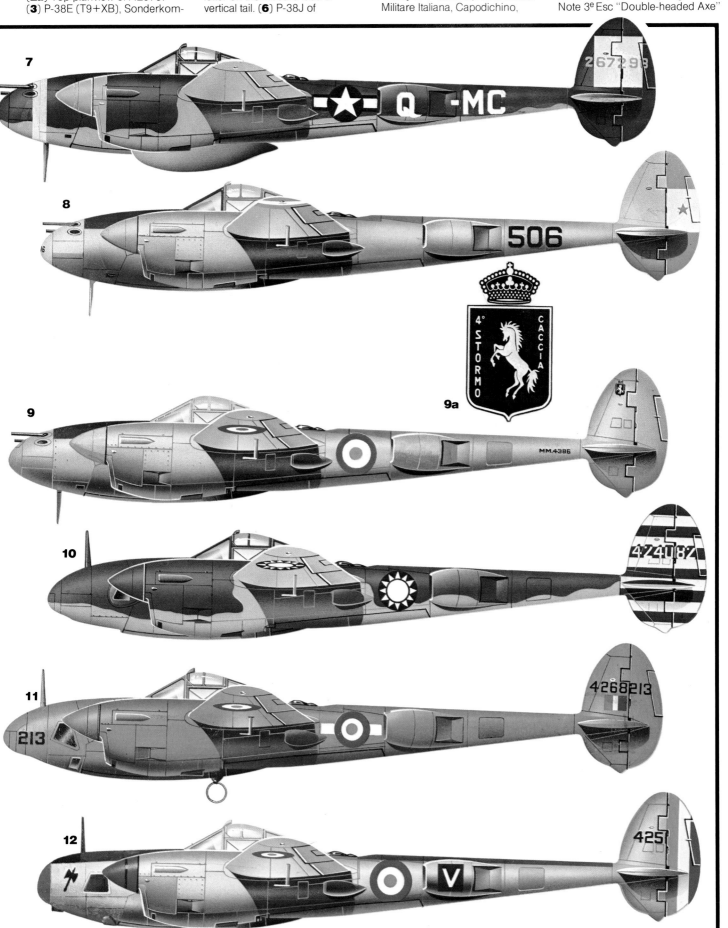

137

# North American B-25 Mitchell (1941)

Operationally efficient, docile and amenable to adaptation for a variety of roles, the Mitchell offered extremely good handling characteristics and excellent all-round performance. If it had never attacked another objective after its memorable attack on Japanese targets following a launching at sea from the flight deck of the USS *Hornet,* it would still have found a place among the ranks of the truly historic combat aircraft of all time. Flown as a prototype in January 1939, the Mitchell was to be built in larger numbers than any other US twin-engined bomber, a total of 9,816 being accepted by the USAAF, although many were destined for Allied air forces, the USAAF Mitchell inventory peaking at 2,656. Engaged on every World War II battlefront, the B-25 established an unrivalled reputation. (**1**) B-25A of 34th Bomb Sqdn, 17th Bomb Group, at Pendleton, Oregon, in September 1941. Tail designator showing Group and aircraft number within Group was deleted a few months later. Blue cowl ring identified sqdn, and "Thunderbird" emblem (see page 41) appeared on the forward fuselage. (**2**) B-25C-10 (42-32304) of 487th Bomb Sqdn, 340th Bomb Group, Catania, Sicily, in September 1943. Note the RAF style fin flash, and Desert Sand upper and Sky Blue undersides.

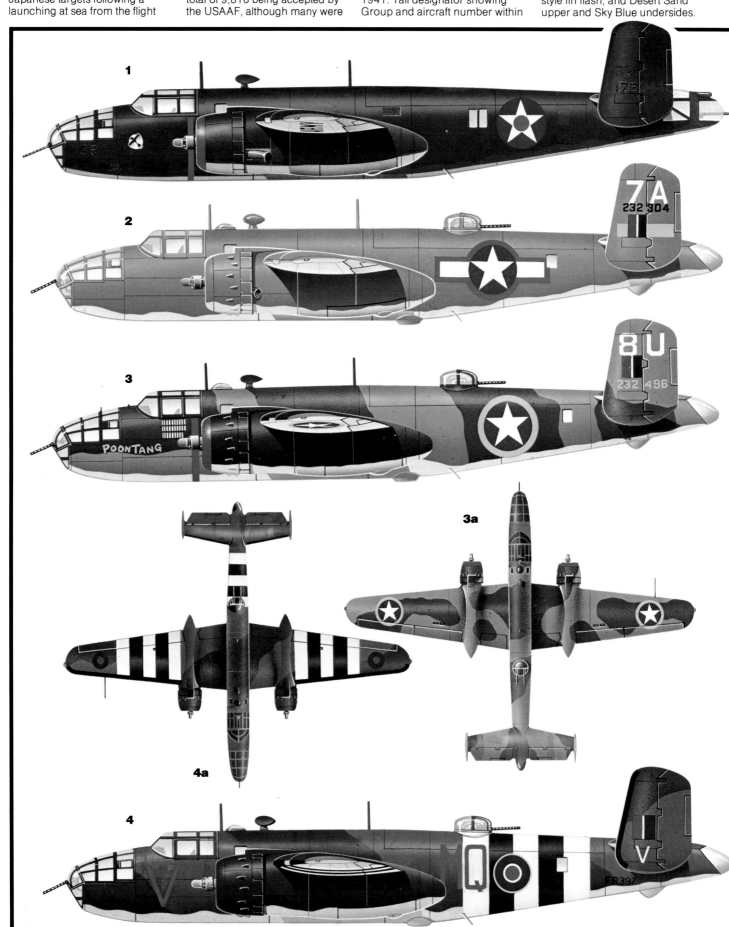

Desert Sand was commonly known as "desert pink" as the yellow pigment faded after prolonged exposure to sunlight, resulting in a pronounced pinkish shade. (**3**) B-25C-15 (42-32496) of 488th Bomb Sqdn, 340th Bomb Group, at Sfax, Tunisia, April 1943. Note disruptive pattern of olive drab applied over the original Desert Sand finish and yellow surround to insignia applied to USAAF in the Middle East until June 1942. (**3a**) Upper surfaces of the same aircraft. (**4**) Mitchell II (FR397) of No 226 Sqdn, RAF, operating from Gilze Rijen, Holland, in June 1944. Note the black-and-white invasion striping. (**4a**) Upper surfaces of the same aircraft. (**5**) Mitchell II (FR197) of No 320 (Neth) Sqdn, Dunsfold, Surrey, England, in April 1944. (**6**) B-25C-20 (42-64514) of 81st Bomb Sqdn, 12th Bomb Group, at Gerbini, Sicily, August 1943. (**7**) B-25J of 498th Bomb Sqdn "Falcons", 345th Bomb Group, San Marcelino, Luzon, Philippines, April 1945. (**8**) B-25J-32 of 499th Bomb Sqdn "Bats Outa Hell", 345th Bomb Group, Ie Shima, July 1945. (**9**) B-25J of No 18 Sqdn, Netherlands East Indies Air Force, Bachelor Field, Darwin, Autumn 1944, with an enlarged representation of Sqdn emblem. (**10**) B-25J (A47-25) of No 2 Sqdn RAAF, North-West Australia, in the spring of 1945.

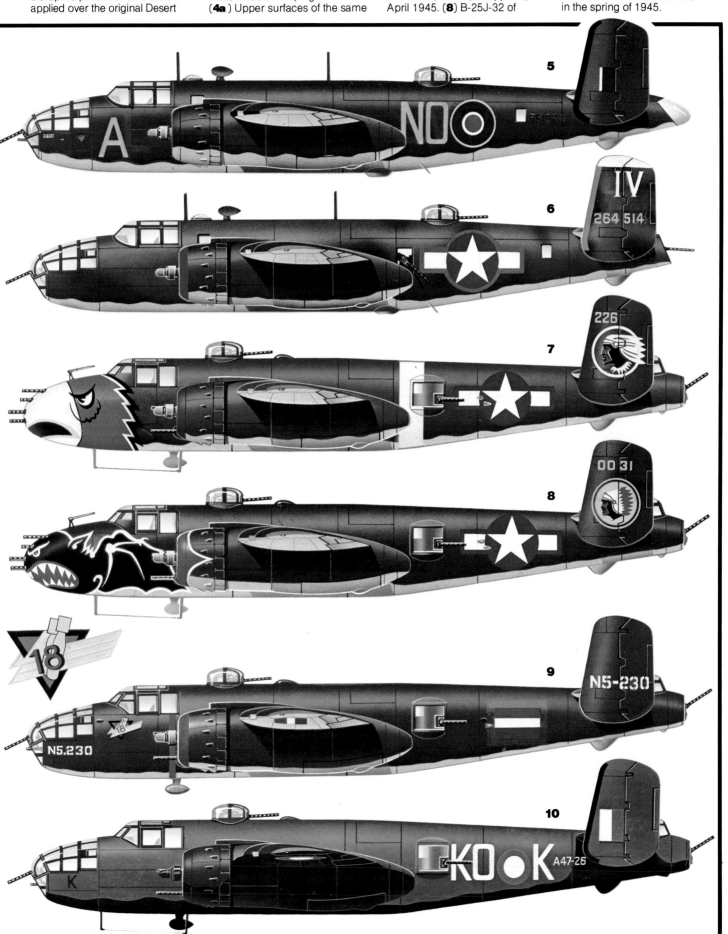

# Nakajima Ki.49 Donryu (Helen) (1941)

Created as a heavy bomber able to operate without fighter protection by combining speed with defensive armament, armour and self-sealing fuel tanks, the Ki.49 Donryu (Storm Dragon) first flew in August 1939, and entered service in autumn 1941, more than 800 being built. In the event, it was underpowered and proved to lack the speed necessary to evade interception successfully. (1) Ki.49-I of Hamamatsu Army Flying School, late 1943. The tail marking was a stylised representation of the Kanji characters identifying the school. (2) Ki.49-II-Ko of 3rd Chutai, 62nd Sentai, operating over Burma, Dutch East Indies and New Guinea, Jan-Oct 1944. (3) Ki.49-II-Ko of 3rd Chutai, 61st Sentai, the tail symbol in the Chutai colour being an abstract representation of the Arabic numerals "61". (4) Ki.49-II-Ko of 1st Chutai, 7th Sentai, 1943, the sentai emblem representing Mount Fuji. Note the disruptive snake-weave camouflage in dark green on natural metal. (5) Ki.49-II-Ko of 3rd Chutai, 95th Sentai, North-East China, March-September 1944. Inclined stripe aft of white combat stripe was painted in the Chutai colour. Note the field-applied "palm frond" camouflage. (6) Ki.49-I with segment-type camouflage, China, early 1944.

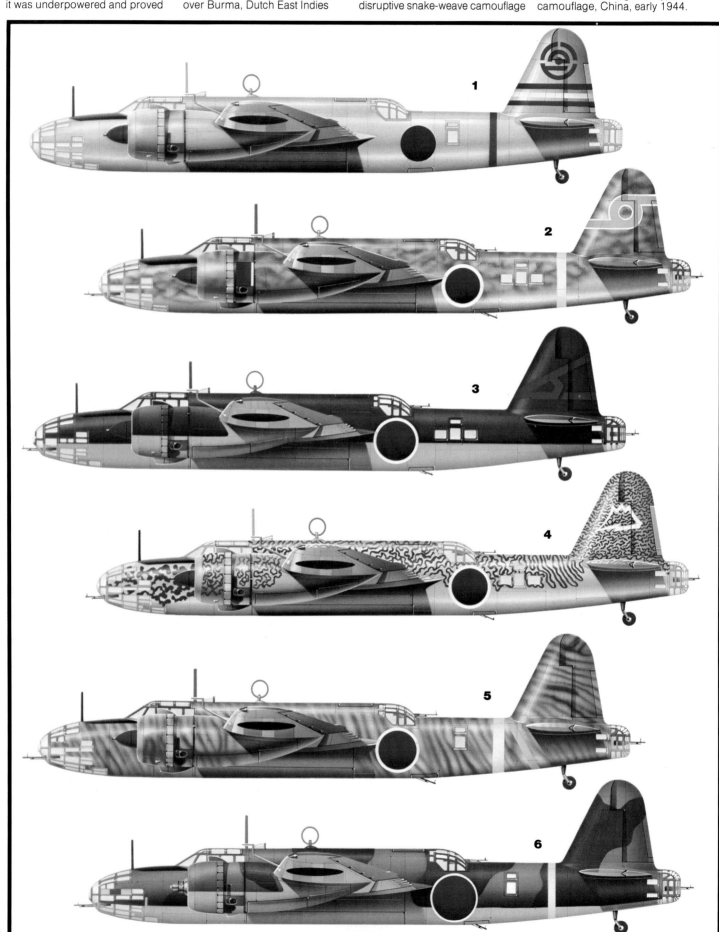

# Martin B-26 Marauder (1941)

When flown on 25 November 1940, the Marauder established totally new standards in both aerodynamic cleanliness and speed for aircraft in its category. Viewed as a quantum advance in medium bomber design when it entered service in 1941, it demanded a high standard of pilot training but offered a level of operational immunity unapproached by any contemporary. Marauder production totalled 5,157 aircraft.

(1) Marauder IA (FK375) of No 14 Sqdn, RAF, Fayid, Egypt, late 1942, operating in the torpedo-bombing role. This aircraft was named "Dominion Revenge".

(2) B-26B-55 (42-96152) of 598th Sqdn, 397th Bomb Group, at Dreux, France, September 1944. Diagonal yellow tail stripe signified the 397th BG. Note part erasure of invasion striping leaving grey primer undercoat. (3) B-26B-40 (42-43304) of 444th Sqdn, 320th Bomb Group, Decimomannu, Sardinia, 1944. Note original aircraft letter beneath olive drab finish. (4) B-26G-1 (43-34133), 456th Sqdn, 323rd Bomb Group, Laon/Athies, France, winter 1944-45. Note semi-gloss black for nocturnal use over the Ardennes. (5) B-26G-25 (44-68119) of 585th Sqdn, 394th Bomb Group, Cambrai/Niergnives, France, in November 1944. (6) B-26G-25 (44-68165) of GB I/32 "Bourgogne", Armée de l'Air, St Dizier, 1945.

# Focke-Wulf Fw 190 (1941)

A compact, well proportioned machine, the Fw 190 came, at the time of its operational debut, as close to perfection by the standards of the day as any fighter could. Possessing superlative control harmony, and being both a good dogfighter and a good gun platform, it could out-perform the contemporary Spitfire on

every count apart from turning circle. Its manoeuvre margins were limited by harsh stalling characteristics. However, it was to establish a broad operational repertoire, and in its basic BMW 801 radial-engined form it was also to be produced in versions optimised for the close air support (Fw 190F) and the

fighter-bomber (Fw 190G) roles. First flown on 1 June 1939, the Fw 190 entered service in its initial Fw 190A-1 form in the summer of 1941. A total 16,724 Fw 190s of all types was delivered by the end of 1944, and a further 2,700 or so thereafter. (**1**) Fw 190A-5/U8 of I Gruppe of Schnellkampfgeschwader (SKG) 10

at Poix, France, summer 1943, in temporary matt black finish for dawn/dusk Jabo attacks on UK. (**2**) Fw 190A-3 of Ergänzungs-jagdgeschwader (EJG) 1 (Replacement Fighter Group) at Bad Aibling, May 1945, this early model serving as a fighter-trainer. Note the late style of the insignia. (**3**) Fw 190A-5 of

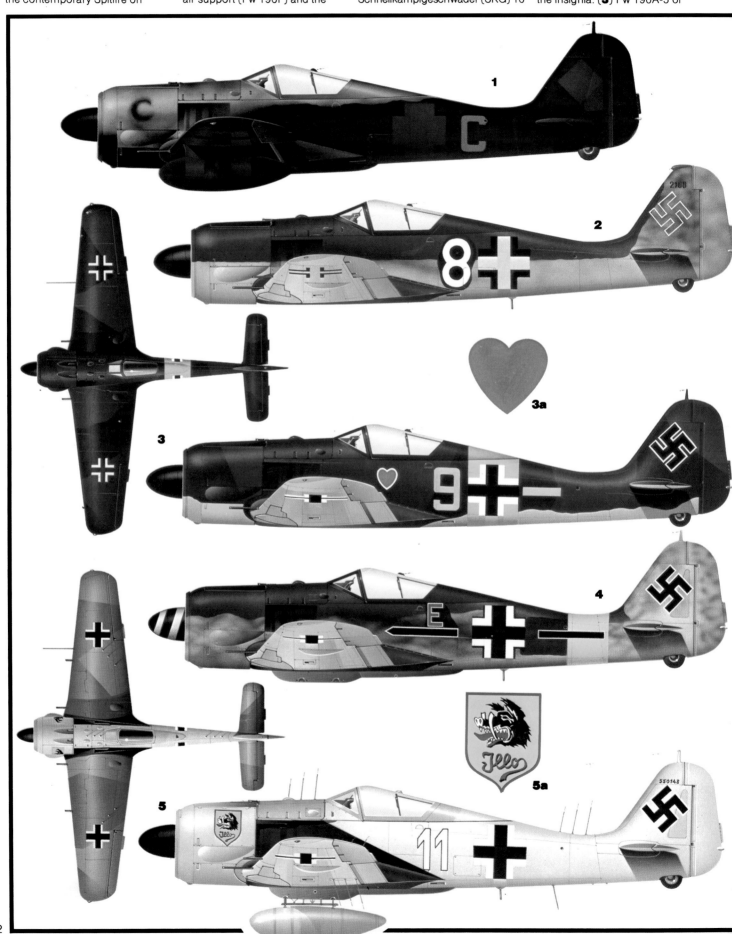

II Gruppe of Jagdgeschwader 54 "Grünherz", at Petseri, Estonia, spring 1944. Note two-tone green upper surface finish in planview and yellow theatre markings. (3a) "Grünherz" emblem of JG 54. (4) Fw 190A-4/U3 of the Gefechtsverband (or Battle Formation) Druschel (II/Sch.G.1) operating in Kursk Salient, summer 1943. Note combination of fighter arm staff markings and individual aircraft letter. (5) Fw 190A-6/R11 of 1.Staffel, Nachtjagdgruppe 10, Werneuchen, summer 1944. Note two-tone grey camouflage on upper wing and Neptun radar arrays (5a) The "Wilde Sau" (Wild Boar) emblem incorporating nickname "Illo" of pilot (Oblt Krause). (6) Fw 190A-8 of Stab/JG 2 "Richthofen" at Merzhausen, in December 1944. (7) Fw 190A-8 of III/JG 11 at Gross-Ostheim, December 1944. Note yellow "Defence of Reich" band with superimposed III Gruppe symbol. (8) Fw 190A-8 of I/JG 6 at Delmenhorst, winter 1944-45, with the red-white-red "Defence of Reich" band. (9) Fw 190A-8 of II/JG 4 at Babenhausen in the winter 1944-45, and the JG 4 emblem. (10) Fw 190A-8 of I/JG 1 at Twenthe, Netherlands, in December, 1944. Note red "Defence of Reich" band. (11) Fw 190F-8 of Schlachtgeschwader 4 at Köln-Wahn and Köln-Ostheim for "Bodenplatte", 1 January 1945.

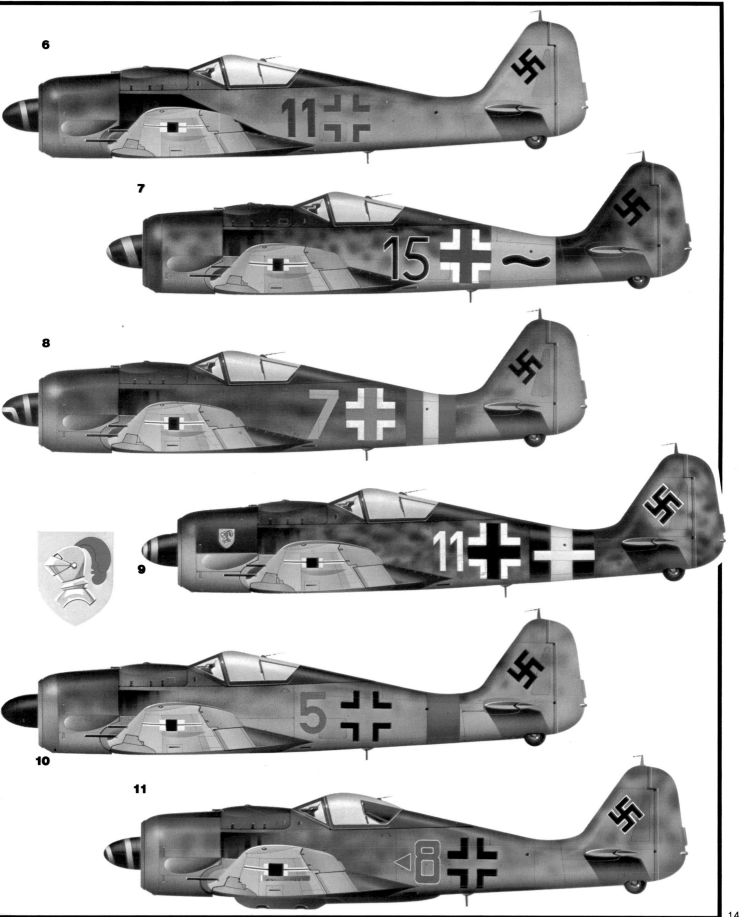

# Focke-Wulf Fw 190 (1941) (continued)

The Langnasen-Dora, or Dora-9, the principal derivative of the basic radial-engined Fw 190 fitted with a liquid-cooled inline engine, joined combat in October 1944, restoring for a brief period the capability of the Jagdflieger so equipped to at least parity with Allied units flying the most recently committed types. It was claimed to be more than a match for the vaunted P-51D Mustang. (1) Fw 190D-9 of 1.Staffel of Jagdgruppe 10 at Redlin, a satellite of Parchim, February 1945. Note the dark green and bright medium green upper surface camouflage with mottle extending to pale grey undersurfaces. (2) Fw 190D-9 (Werk-Nr 210 079) of 10./JG 54 which crash-landed at Wemmel, Belgium, 1 January 1945. Note irregular spraying of medium green over sharply-defined demarkation line to grey sides. (3) Fw 190D-9 of II/JG 26 "Schlageter", Nordhorn, near Osnabrück, January 1945. (4) Fw 190D-9 of Stab/JG 4 at Babenhausen, early 1945. Note black-white-black "Defence of Reich" band signifying JG 4. (5) Fw 190D-9 of III/JG2 "Richthofen", Altenstadt, December 1944. Note blue-grey finish with dark grey dapple. (6) Fw 190D-9 captured at Marienburg, East Prussia, and serving with an IAP of the Red Banner Baltic Fleet Air Force in the spring of 1945.

# Nakajima Ki-44 Shoki (Tojo) (1941)

The result of radical rethinking on the part of the Japanese Army, the Ki.44 Shoki (Devil-Queller) symbolized disenchantment with what had been an almost pathological belief in manoeuvrability before all else in fighter design. Placing emphasis on speed and dive-and-climb capabilities, the Ki.44 first flew in August 1940, and entered service in *pre-production* form in autumn 1941. If lacking the agility of other Japanese fighters, the Ki.44 was very fast and an excellent gun platform. A total 1,225 was built. (**1**) Ki.44-I-Hei of Instructors' Chutai, Akeno Air Training Division, 1944. Note the irregular green blotching over natural metal. (**2**) Ki.44-II-Otsu of 23rd Sentai, home island defence (as indicated by white panel), 1944. Note abstract rendering of unit number as Sentai tail marking. (**3**) Ki.44-II-Otsu of Captain Hideaki Inayama, 2nd Chutai, 87th Sentai, Eastern Defence Sector, Japan, early 1945. Note unusual black upper surfaces. (**4**) Ki.44-II-Otsu of Shinten (Sky Shadow) air superiority unit of 47th Sentai, Narimasu, Tokyo, summer 1944. (**5**) Ki.44-II-Otsu of Maj Togo Saito, CO of 85th Sentai, Canton, China, in summer 1944. (**6**) Pre-series Ki.44 of Capt Yauhiko Kuroe, leader of 3rd Hotai, 47th Independent Chutai, Malaya, January 1942.

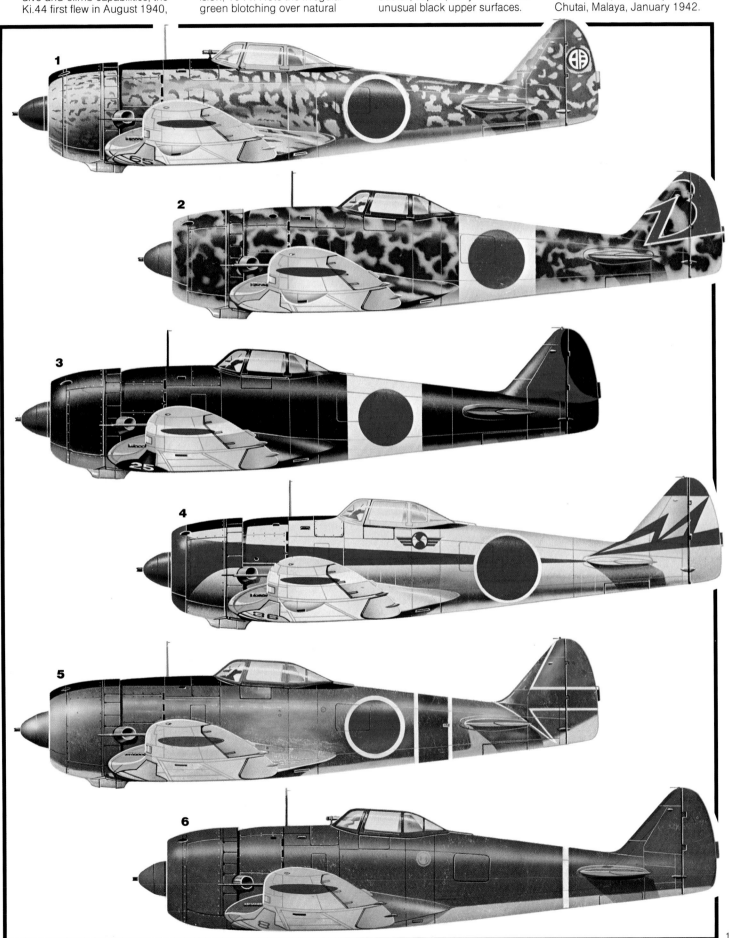

# Lavochkin-Gorbunov-Gudkov LaGG-3 (1941)

Although wooden construction for fighter aircraft was already considered passé by the early 'thirties, it was resurrected in the Soviet Union at the beginning of the 'forties for the LaGG-3, albeit wood impregnated with plastic and thus possessing special strength and fire-resistant qualities. Conceived as a so-called frontal fighter—a general-purpose tactical fighter for low- to medium-altitude operation—the LaGG-3 first flew (as the I-22) on 30 March 1940, entering service in the spring of 1941. Regrettably, however, it proved overweight and under-powered; an unforgiving aircraft, prone to developing an unherald-ed and vicious spin from a steep banking turn, nosing up during a landing approach and stalling at the least provocation. Furthermore, it possessed a weak under-carriage and lacked firepower. But the exigencies of the times dictated continued production, despite these shortcomings, and LaGG-3 output averaged 12.7 air-craft daily during the second half of 1941, a grand total of 6,528 having been built when production was terminated in the late summer of 1942. Additional airframes were adapted for a radial engined version, the La-5 . (**1**) LaGG-3 of 6 IAK (Fighter Air Corps), Moscow Air Defence (PVO) zone, summer 1942. Note the legend

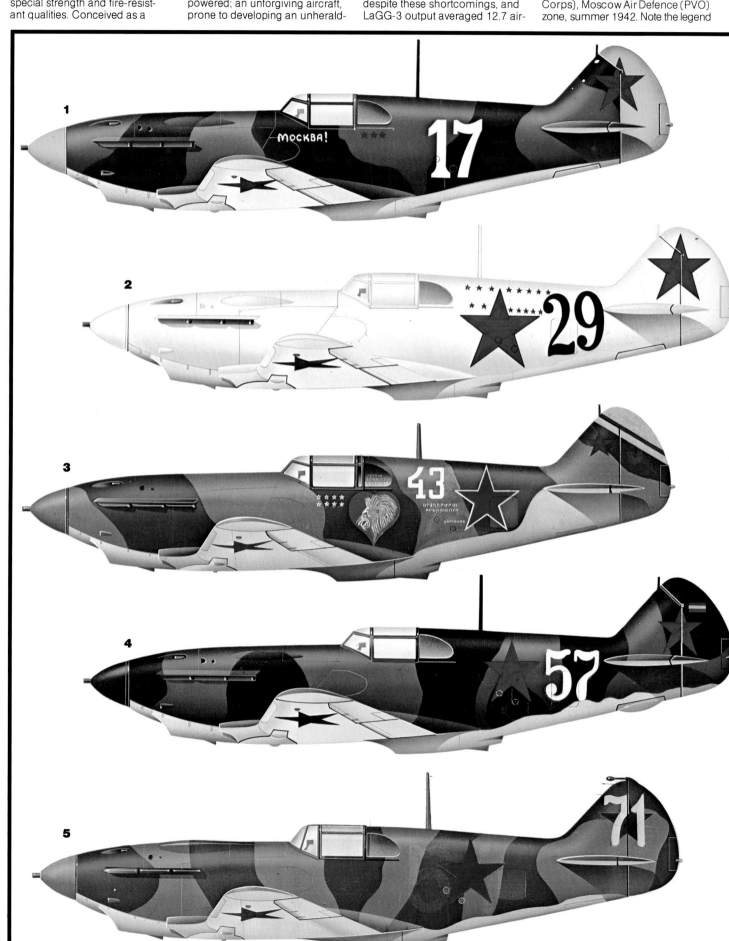

"Moskva!" (Moscow!) beneath the windscreen, and black-and-green camouflage resulting from the use of paint stocks held for tractors previously built by the factory in which this aircraft was manufactured. (**2**) LaGG-3 as flown by Capt (later Col) Gerasim A Grigoryev as deputy CO of 178 IAP of the 6 IAK, Moscow, winter 1942-43. Note 15 "victory" stars on rear fuselage and temporary winter finish of white soluble paint. (**3**) LaGG-3 flown by Yuri Shchipov of the 9 IAP, V-VS ChF (Black Sea Fleet Air Force), May 1944. Note Shchipov's personal "Lion's Head" emblem and the eight "victory" stars beneath cockpit sill. (**4**) LaGG-3 (c/n 3121357) captured by Finns after a forced landing at Ala-Sedoksa on 14 September 1942. This aircraft was subsequently repaired and placed in service by Ilmavoimat as LG-3, serving successively with LeLV 32 and HLeLv 11. (**5**) LaGG-3 (c/n 070171) of an IAP of the V-VS KBF (Red Banner Baltic Fleet Air Force) shot down over Finland on 6 March 1942. A thick layer of polish had been applied to smooth the exterior of this aircraft, the upper surfaces of which are shown below (**5a**), together with scrap views (**5b**) of underside of starboard wingtip and tailplane, and (**5c**) forward and centre fuse-lage. (**5d**) Head-on view of 070171.

5a

5b

5c

5d

# Nakajima Ki.43 Hayabusa (Oscar) (1941)

Representing an attempt to translate the lightly constructed, lightly loaded and lightly armed fighter biplane into terms of the monoplane, the Japanese Hayabusa (Peregrine Falcon) flew in December 1938 and was obsolescent by the time it entered Imperial Army service mid-1941. It was supremely manoeuvrable, but its fundamental components did not permit major increases in power or armament, or the introduction of protection for pilot or fuel. Nevertheless, 5,919 were built. (1) Ki.43-I-Hei of HQ Chutai, 64th Sentai, Chiengmai, Northern Thailand, March 1942. Note the red-brown and olive green camouflage applied locally, natural metal being retained for undersurfaces. The Sentai arrow-type symbol (blue indicating the HQ Chutai) was repeated on upper wing surfaces of some aircraft. (2) Ki.43-I-Hei of 1st Chutai, 50th Sentai, Tokorozawa, in June 1942. Note lack of outline of Hinomaru (so-called "Sun's Red Disc" national emblem). (3) Ki. 43-II-Ko of Manchukuo Army Air Corps, Mukden (Shenyang), 1944. Inscription on fuselage noted the donar (in this case a petrol company). (3a) National insignia of Manchukuo (alias Manchuria). (4) Ki.43-II-Otsu of 3rd Chutai, 25th Sentai, Hankow, in China, January 1944. Note stripe ahead of Hinomaru in Chutai colour

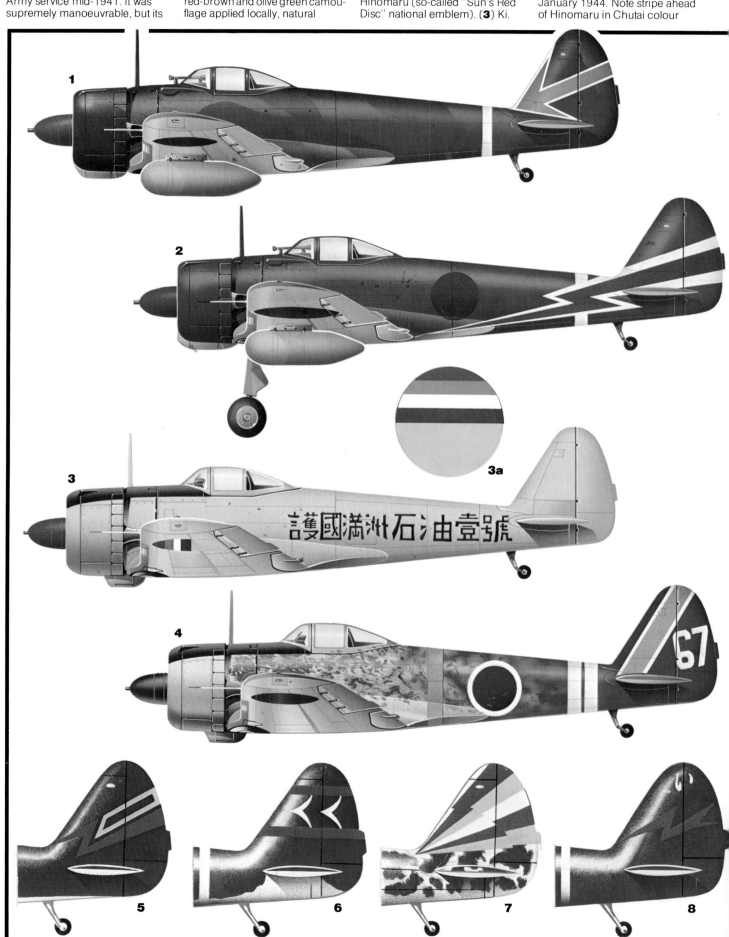

護國滿洲石油壹號

(yellow) and extensive wearing of olive green upper surface finish. (**5**) Tail of Ki.43-II of 3rd Chutai, 20th Sentai, Formosa 1944-45. Sentai symbol was an abstract rendering of "20" and painted in same colours for all Chutais. Note the dark blue upper surface finish. (**6**) Tail of Ki. 43-I-Hei of 2nd Chutai, 77th

Sentai. The seagull motif on the tail (which was applied in many forms – see **9**) appeared between bands of Chutai colour. (**7**) Tail of Ki.43-I-Hei of 11th Sentai, Netherlands East Indies, 1942. (**8**) Tail of Ki.43-II of 2nd Chutai, 59th Sentai, Manchuria, 1943. Kana characters above the "lightning flash" were pilot's

initials. (**9**) Ki.43-II-Otsu of HQ Chutai, 77th Sentai, Burma, 1943-44. Diagonal fuselage band indicated the Chutai leader. (**9a**) Upper surfaces of the same aircraft. Note camouflage scheme of dark green blotches on olive green base and the chrome-yellow wing leading-edge ID striping. (**10**) Tail of Ki.43-II of HQ

Chutai, 64th Sentai (showing the colour shade and style variation to **1**). (**11**) Tail of Ki.43-II of 13th Fighter-Attack Sentai, New Guinea, 1943-44. (**12**) Tail of Ki.43-III-Ko of 48th Sentai, China, 1945. (**13**) Tail of Ki.43-II of HQ Chutai, 13th Sentai, 1944. (**14**) Ki.43-II-Kai of GC 1/7, Phnom-Penh, Cambodia, 1945.

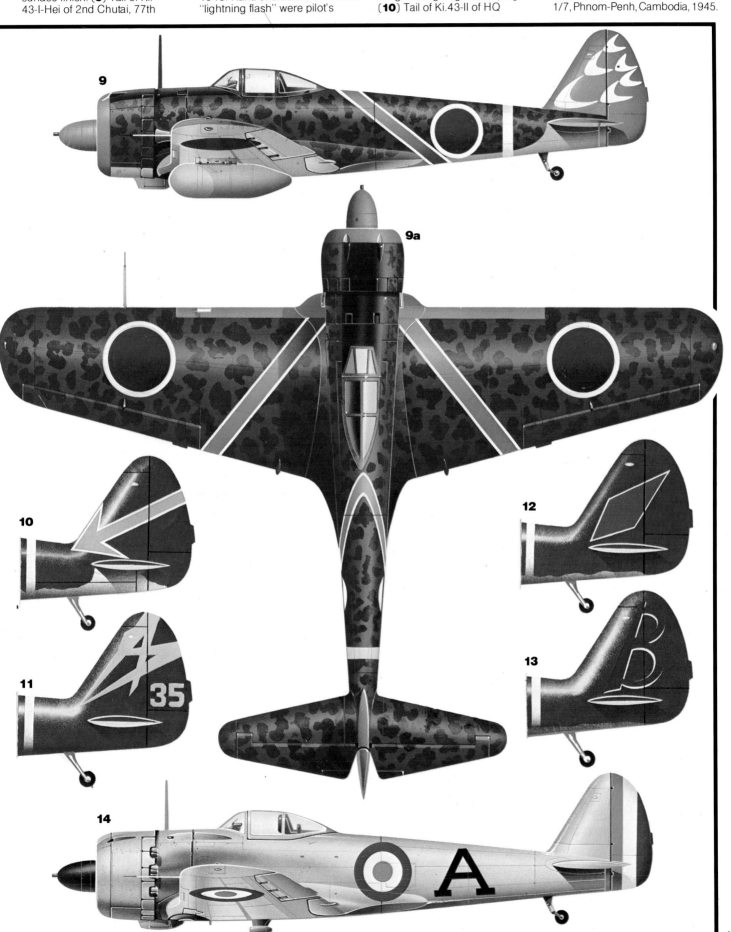

# Yakovlev Yak-1 (1941)

The first combat aircraft from the design bureau headed by A. S. Yakovlev, the Yak-1 provided the basis for a family of low-to-medium altitude fighters *par excellence;* an outstanding example of incremental design involving a fundamental airframe leading to a series of combat aircraft providing in excess of 58 per cent of fighters built in the Soviet Union during 1941-45. Rudimentarily equipped, lacking refinements common to western contemporaries, the Yak-1 was simple to build and to maintain in the field, and ideally suited to the combat scenario to which it was committed. First flown as the I-26 in March 1940, it began to re-equip the IAPs in spring 1941 as the Yak-1, the improved Yak-1M entering service in the next year, their virtues being good stability under all conditions and outstanding controllability at high attack angles. A total of 8,721 Yak-1 and -1M fighters was built. (**1**) Yak-1 of an IAP (Fighter Aviation Regiment) operating over the Central Sector, in winter 1941-42. Note the temporary winter finish provided by soluble paint. (**2**) Yak-1 of Snr Lt M. D. Baranov, 183 IAP, summer 1942. Inscription "Death to Fascists" crudely applied aft of 27 "kill" stars. Note black-and-green camouflage stemmed originally from use of available

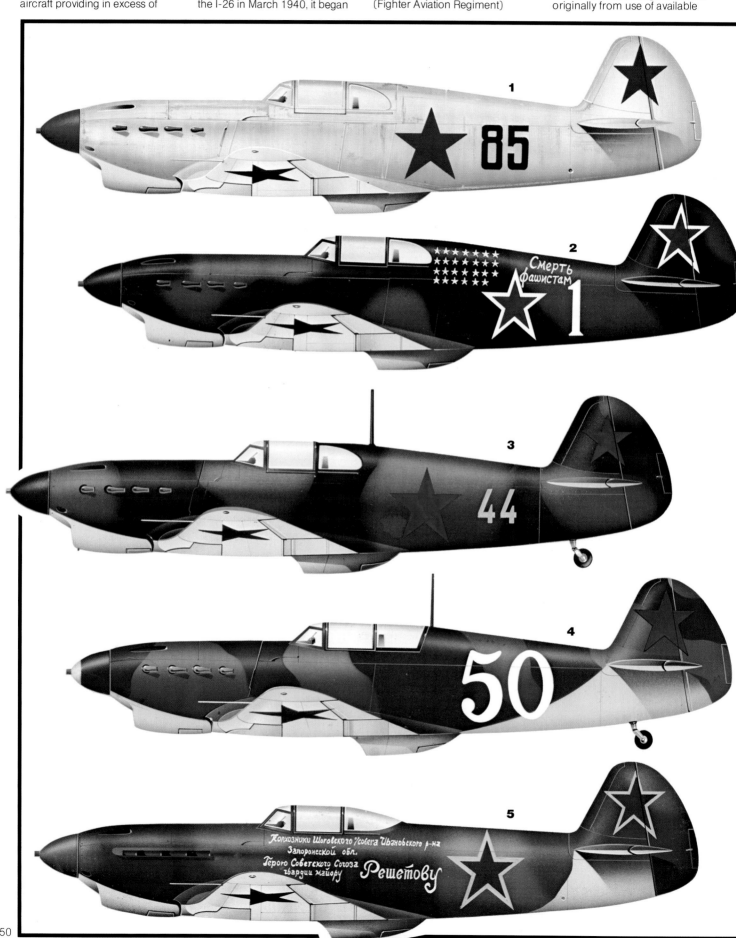

tractor paints. (**3**) Yak-1 flown by Lilya Litvak, 73 IAP, the most successful Soviet female pilot. (**4**) Yak-1 flown by Lt Col A. E. Golubov, 18 IAP, Khationki, spring 1943. (**5**) Yak-1M flown by Aleksei M. Reshetov, summer 1942. The legend reads "Collective workers of Shatovskovo village soviet, Ivanovskovo District, Zaparozhskoy Oblast, [to] HSU Guards Major Reshetov". (**6**) Yak-1M of an IAP operating in the Ukraine, in summer 1942, the inscription reading "The railway workers of Rtishchevcko". (**7**) Yak-1M flown by B. N. Yevemen, the inscription reading, "To the pilot of the Stalingrad Front Guards Major comrade Yevemen. From the collective farm workers of Collective Farm 'Stakhanov', comrade F. P. Golovatov. (**8**) Yak-1M flown by Sergei Lugansky, the inscription indicating that the aircraft had been presented to HSU Lugansky by the Youth and Young Communists of Alma Ata. Lugansky had, at the time, a score of 32 "kills", a fact recorded within the laurel wreath. (**9**) Yak-1M of the 1ère escadrille of the Normandie Niémen regiment. Note tricolour spinner and cockade beneath windscreen. (**10**) Yak-1M of the 1st "Warszawa" Fighter Regiment, operating in the Warsaw area, late autumn 1944. Note Polish insignia beneath windscreen.

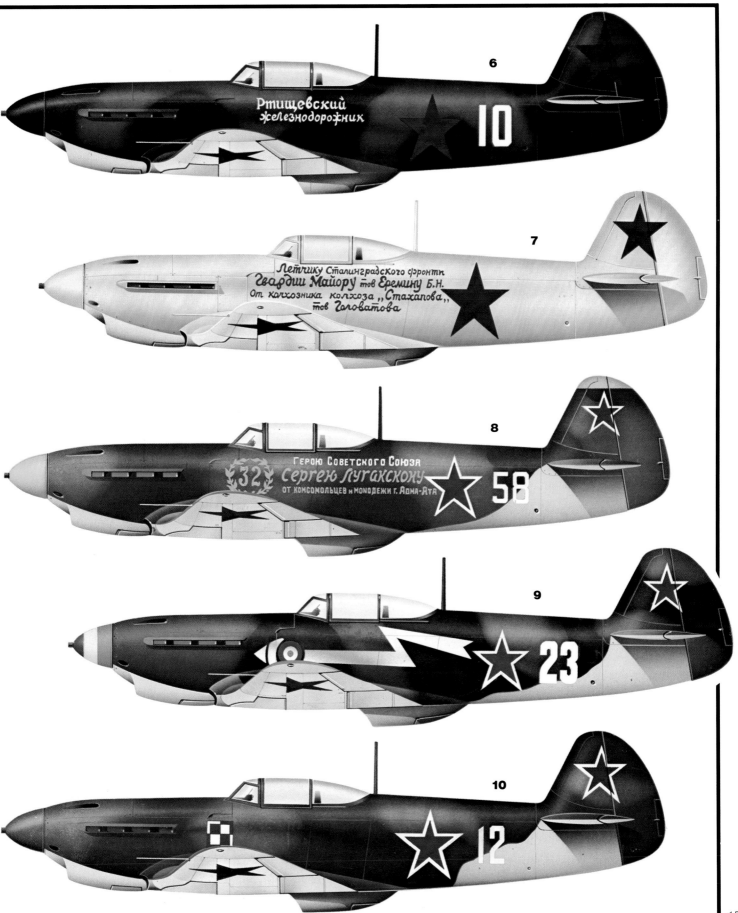

# Curtiss Hawk 87A Warhawk (1941)

Despite retention by the USAAF of the P-40 series designation for the Hawk 87A, this was a very different fighter from the preceding Hawk 81A (see pages 124-5). The thrust line of the engine was raised, the fuselage recontoured and reduced in cross section, and numerous other changes made. Flown on 22 May 1941, it was faster at altitude and more combat-worthy than the Hawk 81A, but suffered inferior take-off performance, climb and manoeuvrability. To be dubbed Warhawk by the USAAF and Kittyhawk by the RAF and Allied air forces, it proved to be a mediocre combat aircraft, but was nevertheless retained in production until the end of November 1944, more than 11,800 being built. (**1**) Kittyhawk III (FR241) of No 112 Sqdn, No 239 Wing, RAF, Cutella, Italy, 1944. (**2**) P-40E Warhawk of 11th Sqdn, 343rd Fighter Group, Aleutians, 1942. (**3**) Kittyhawk I (AK578) flown by Flg Off Neville Duke, No 112 Sqdn, at LG 91, south of Alexandria, September 1942. Note white coding and the early style of roundel. (**4**) Kittyhawk IV (FX561), No 112 Sqdn, Cutella, Italy, early 1944. (**5**) P-40L-5 Warhawk of Lt Col G H Austin, HQ Flight, 325th Fighter Group, Tunisia, 1943. Black and yellow check standardised for tail of Group aircraft from July 1943.

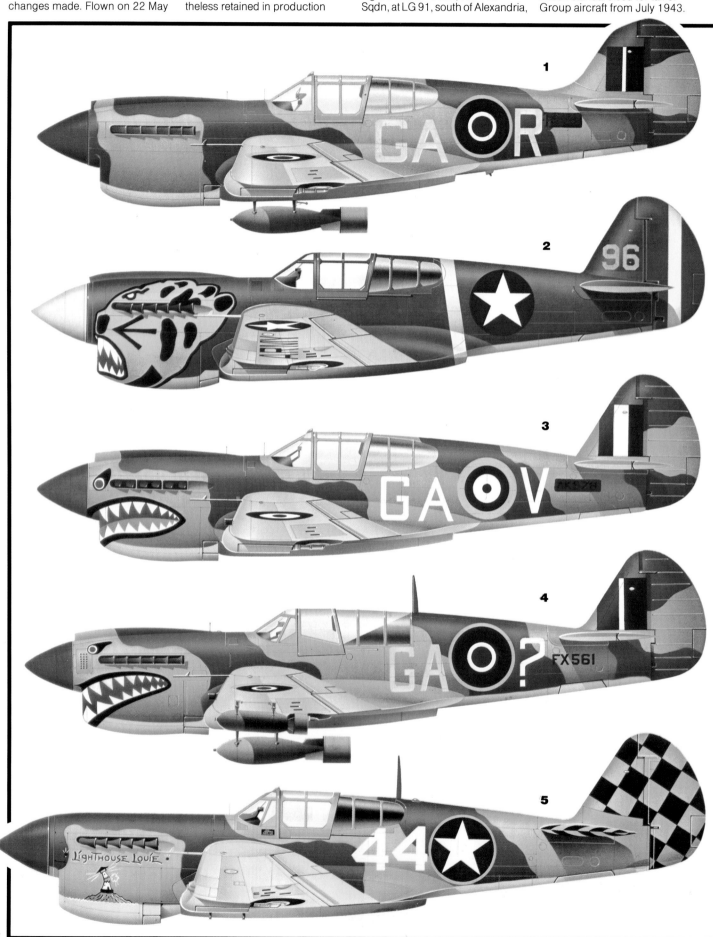

# Mitsubishi A6M (Zeke) (1941)

The A6M Reisen (Zero Fighter) was unique among WWII combat aircraft in creating a myth. The Allies credited the Reisen with almost mystical powers of man-oeuvre, fostering a myth of Japanese aerial invincibility. Everything to the Japanese that the Spitfire was to the British, the Reisen was a lightly con-structed but extraordinarily capable fighter first flown on 1 April 1939, series aircraft entering service early in 1941. Excluding float-equipped and training versions, a total of 10,449 Reisens was manufactured. (**1**) A6M2 of fighter complement of carrier *Hiryu* (signified by tail coding "BII") during attack on Pearl Harbor, December 1941. Cobalt blue tail band indicated flight leader and twin fuselage bands signified second carrier in 2nd Carrier Division (1st Air Fleet). (**2**) A6M2 of 6th Kokutai, Rabaul, New Britain, November 1942. Note mid-green dapple over basic sky grey finish. (**3**) A6M2 of 402nd Chutai, 341st Kokutai, Clark Field, Manila, winter 1944. (**4**) A6M2, 12th Combined Kokutai, Hankow region China, winter 1940-41. Note that this was a pre-series Reisen. (**5**) A6M3 of 251st Kokutai (signi-fied by the "U1"), Home Islands, November 1942. (**6**) A6M5 of Genzan Kokutai, Wonsan, North Korea, for training, winter 1944.

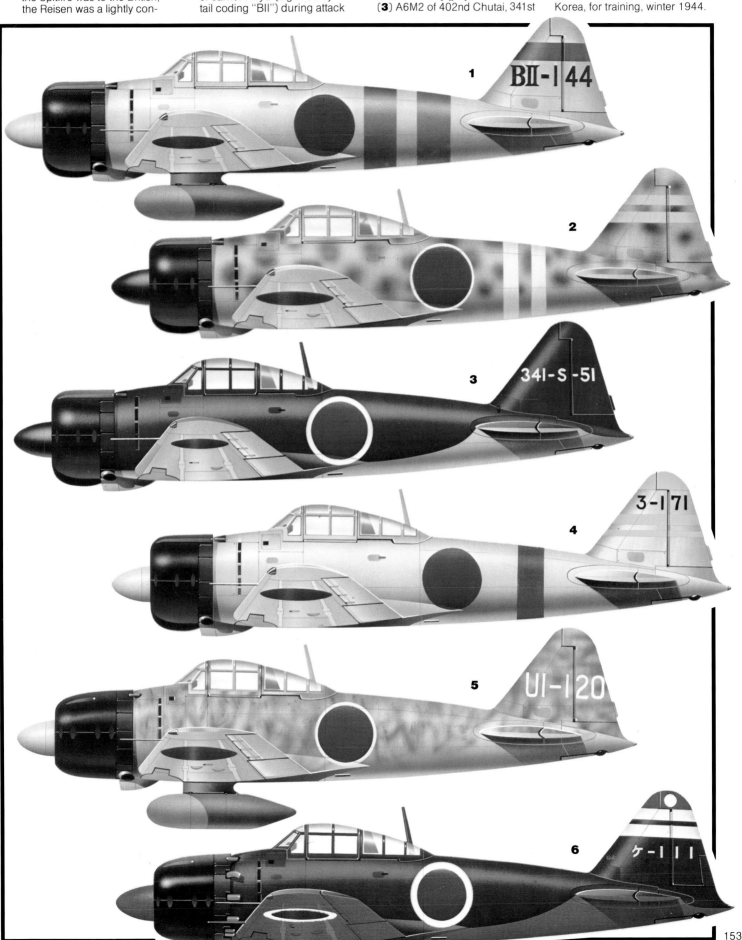

# De Havilland Mosquito (1941)

The Mosquito was without doubt one of the most outstandingly successful WWII products of the British aircraft industry. It was conceived along lines that were in direct contradiction to then-prevailing official views and it was apparently retrogressive in using wood in the day and age of all-metal stressed-skin structures. But it captured popular imagination from the moment its first sorties became known and its sensational wartime exploits continued to sustain enthusiasm to a greater degree than those of any other combat aircraft. Envisaged initially as an unarmed high-speed bomber, this extraordinary aircraft was to offer prodigious versatility; indeed, the Mosquito was to excel in all its multifarious roles. Flown on 15 May 1941, it entered RAF service in both bomber and recce versions before the year's end, a fighter version following early in 1942. A grand total of 7,781 was built and 6,710 delivered during WWII.

(**1**) Mosquito NF II (W4082) of No 157 Sqdn, Castle Camps, mid-1942. Note "Lamp Black" RDM 2A matt non-reflective Special Night Finish, Type A.1 roundel and red coding letters (adopted November 1940). (**2**) Mosquito NF II (DZ230) of No 23 Sqdn, Bradwell Bay, late 1942. Note so-called Smooth Night black underside, Dark

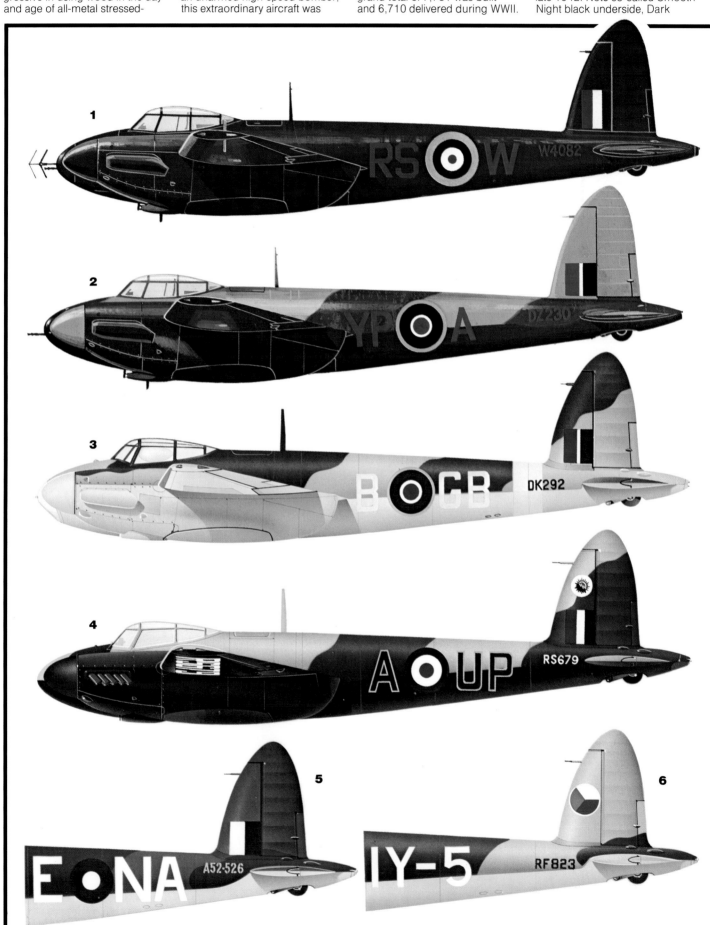

154

Green and Ocean Grey disruptive pattern on upper surfaces and Type C.1 roundel. (**3**) Mosquito B IV Srs 2 (DK292), No 105 Sqdn, Horsham St Faith, Norfolk, late 1942. Note Medium Sea Grey under surfaces with Sky fuselage band, spinners and coding. (**4**) Mosquito FB VI (RS679), No 4 Sqdn, Celle, late in 1949. (**4a**) Emblem of No. 4 Sqdn, RAF, and (**4b**) upper surfaces of RS679. (5) Rear fuselage of Mosquito FB VI (A52-526), No 1 Sqdn, RAAF, Labuan, North Borneo, mid-1945. (**6**) Rear fuselage of Mosquito FB VI (RF823) of Czechoslovak Air Force, 1949. Note the retention of original RAF finish. (**7**) Mosquito B IX (LR508) of No 105 Sqdn, Marham, Norfolk, March 1944, equipped with "Oboe" for Pathfinder missions. Note extension of the black Smooth Night finish up vertical tail. (**8**) Mosquito B XVI (ML963) of No 371 Sqdn, Oakington, Cambs, late in 1944. (**9**) Mosquito PR XVI (NS519) of 653rd Bomb Sqdn (Light), USAAF, Watton, Norfolk, for weather recce and visual coverage of target strikes. Note PRU Blue overall finish and the letter on tail fin identifying squadron. (**9a**) Under surfaces of NS519 showing invasion striping. (**10**) Mosquito NF XIX (MM650) of No 157 Sqdn, Swannington, Norfolk, late 1944, which was used for intruder missions over Luftwaffe night fighter airfields.

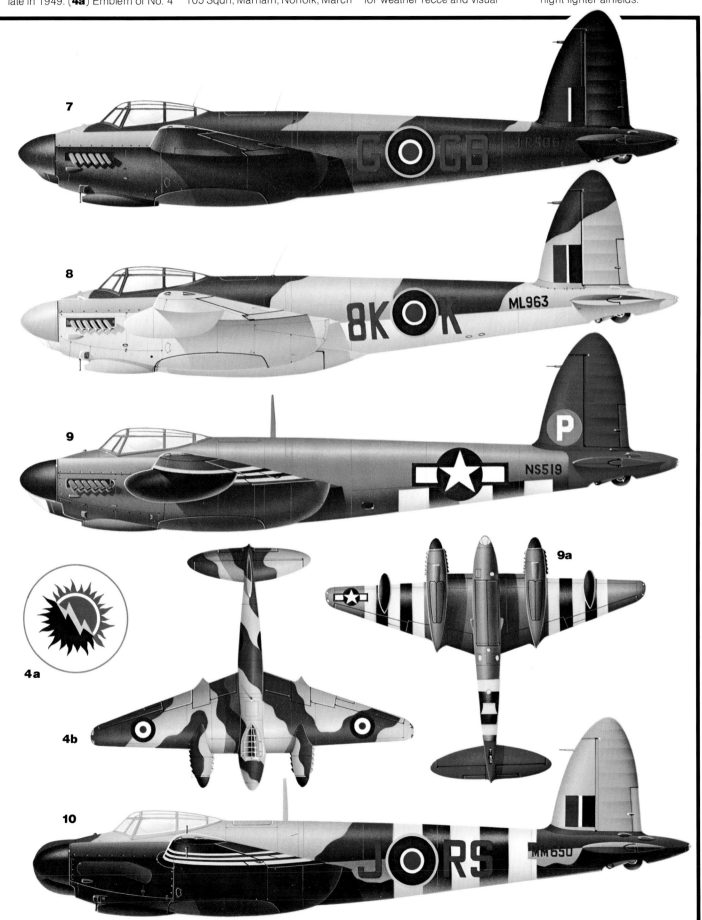

# North American Mustang (1942)

Eventually to emerge as arguably the best all-round single-seat piston-engined fighter of any of WWII's combatants, the Mustang largely owed its existence to fortuity—it was conceived in response to the urgent needs of the RAF rather than any USAAF requirement. Occupying only seven months from design

initiation to flight on 26 October 1940, it underwent phenomenally rapid genealogical processes. Its poor altitude performance with its original Allison engine (with which it saw USAAF service as the P-51 and P-51A, and for the attack role, A-36A, and RAF service as the Mustang I, IA and II) was rectified by mating with

the Merlin, and more than 15,000 Mustangs (the majority being the Merlin-engined P-51B, C, D, et seq, and RAF Mustang III and IV) in total were to be manufactured. (1) A-36A (42-84071) of the 27th Fighter-Bomber Group, Corsica, in July 1944. Note the original application of 190 mission symbols and the positioning of the serial

number on the rear fuselage. (1a) Detail of mission symbols. (2) P-51A-10 (43-6199) of Col Philip Cochrane, CO of 1st Air Commando Group, Hailakandi, India, March 1944. Note diagonal white ID striping applied over serial. (3) F-6A (one of four borrowed from USAAF) operated by No 225 Sqdn, RAF, from Souk el

Khemis, Tunisian campaign, April 1943. Note the dark earth and mid-stone camouflage with azure blue undersurfaces. (**4**) Mustang I (AG522), No 613 Sqdn, Ringway, Manchester, 1942, flying Tac-R "Rhubarbs". (**4a**) Personal Panda Bear emblem carried on starboard side of AG522 cowling (as indicated). (**5**) P-51D (ex-Swedish) as flown by Capt Atkes of Israel Defence Force/Air Force during 1956 Arab-Israeli conflict and shot down near Sharm el-Sheikh. Note the newly-adopted slate blue and tan upper surfaces, and the black-edged yellow ID bands around wings and rear fuselage. (**6**) P-51D of Air Force of the People's Liberation Army, China, in 1951. (**7**) P-51B-5 (43-6913) "Shangri-la" of Capt Don S. Gentile, 336th Fighter Sqdn, 4th FG, Debden, in March 1944. (**7a**) 334th Sqdn emblem, this being another component of 4th FG. (**8**) P-51B-10 (42-106447) "Shoo Shoo Baby" of 364th FS, 357th FG, Leiston, spring 1944. (**9**) P-51B "Dorothy-II", 318th FS, 325th, FG, Italy, late 1944. (**9a**) Group checkerboard tail markings. (**10**) P-51B-15 (42-106942) of 374th FS, 361st FG, Bottisham, June 1944. (**10a**). The invasion striping as applied to 42-106942. (**11**) Mustang IIIB (FB223) of No 316 (Polish) Sqdn, Coltishall, June 1944. (**12**) Mustang III (FZ190), No 19 Sqdn, Ford, summer 1944.

# Vultee V-72 Vengeance (1942)

Inspired by the Junkers Ju 87 "Stuka", the V-72 dive bomber was ordered "off the drawing board" by the British Purchasing Commission in 1940, the first example flying in July 1941. Named Vengeance by the RAF, it began to enter British service late in 1942, by which time the RAF was thoroughly disenchanted with the dive bomber concept, and in the event the V-72 was to see operational service only in SE Asia. Some British contract aircraft were taken over by the USAAF, and others were built, primarily for Lend-Lease supply, with the USAAF designations A-31 and A-35. The grand total of V-72s built being 1,931.

(1) V-72 (built as Vengeance II AF829 for RAF) requisitioned by USAAF and used as an air gunnery trainer in 1942. Note retention of the RAF camouflage and serial. (2) Vengeance II (AN836) of No 45 Sqdn, RAF, India, late 1943. Note Far East style national insignia (adopted June 1943) and the "Saint" personal emblem on forward fuselage. (3) Vengeance I (A27-9) of No 7 Operational Training Unit, RAAF, in November 1944, after modifications for its use as target tug. (4) A-35B (41-31589) used by USAAF in UK as station "hack" during 1944. (5) A-35B of GB I/32, Free French Air Force. The type was used briefly in North Africa in 1943.

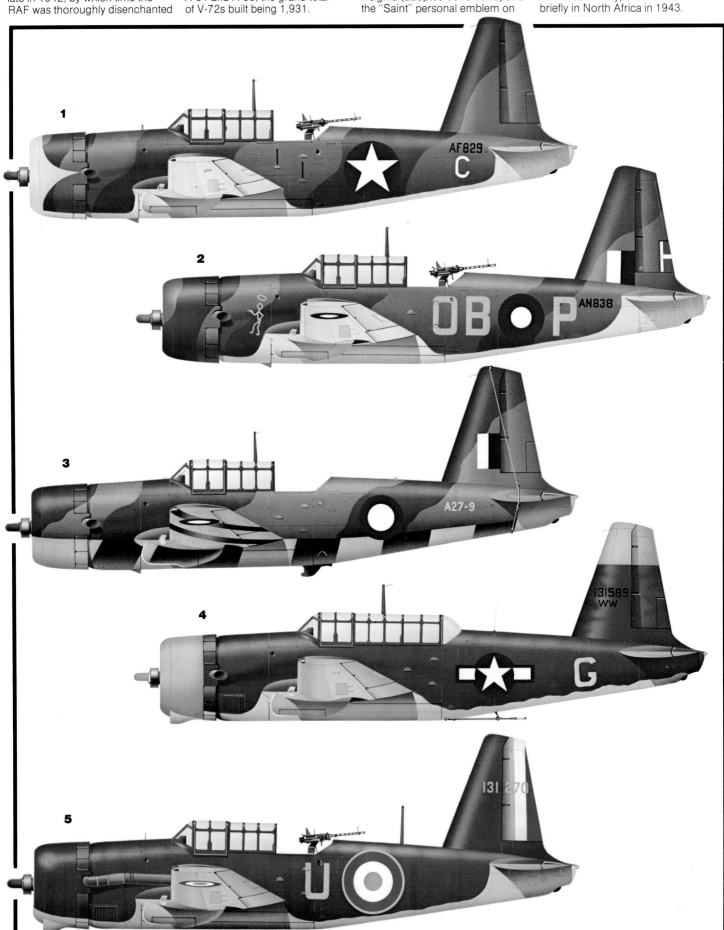

# Lavochkin La-5 (1942)

An adaptation of the LaGG-3 (see pages 146-7) to take a radial engine, the La-5 first flew in March 1942, and entered service before year's end. Possessing exemplary handling characteristics, the La-5 was austerely equipped and unsophisticated but enjoyed considerable success, a total of 9,920 being produced.

(**1**) La-5 of 523 IAP, 303 IAD (Fighter Aviation Division, or Istrebitel'naya Aviatsiya Divisiya), winter 1943-44. Note black and green camouflage that originated with the use of available tractor paints. (**2**) La-5FN of HSU Vladimir I Popkov, 5 GvIAP (Gvardeiski or Guards IAP). (**3**) La-5FN flown by HSU Ivan Kozhedub while with 240 IAP, April-June 1944. Kozhedub was the top-scoring Soviet "ace", his aircraft bearing the starboard inscription (**3a**) "From collective farm worker Konev, Vasily Viktorovich", with (**3b**) "Hero of the Soviet Union Lt Col Konev N" to port. (**4**) La-5FN presented by Mongolian People's Republic, as indicated (**4a**) by the inscription beneath cockpit. (**5**) La-5FN flown by Ladislav Valousek of the 1 Czechoslovak IAP, at Proskurov, Ukraine, in September 1944. (**5a**) Stylised cyrillic "FN" which appeared on cowling to indicate engine variant. (**6**) La-5FN of Czech Operational TU at Malacky, Slovakia, 1945-6.

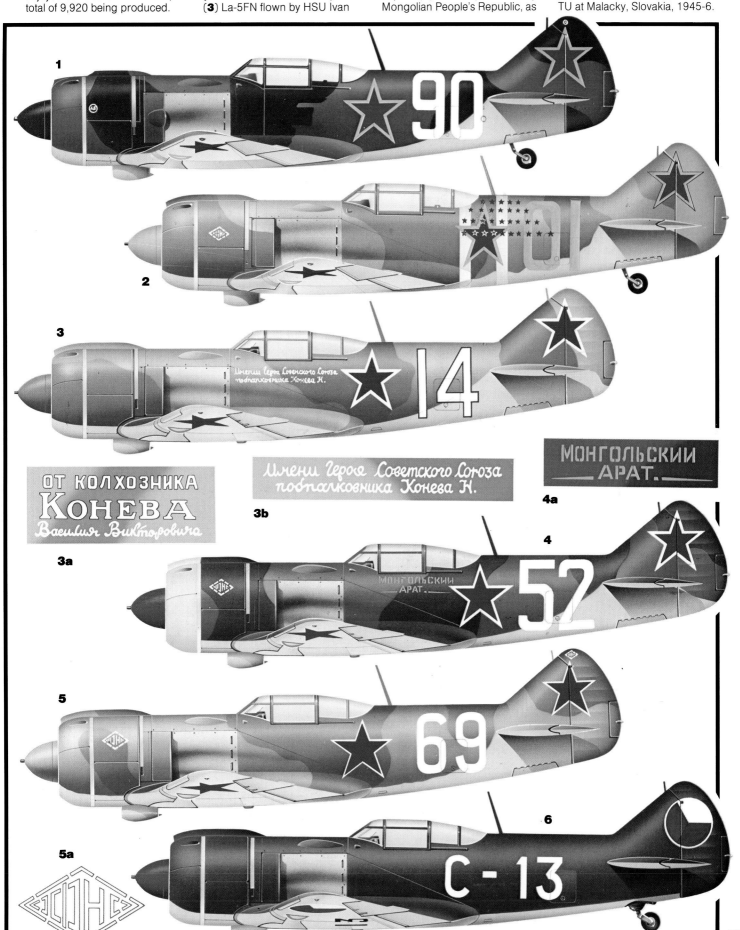

# Republic P-47 Thunderbolt (1942)

The largest and heaviest single-seat fighter ever built at the time of its service debut, the massive P-47 Thunderbolt dwarfed all preceding warplanes in its category, its sheer size prompting bestowal of the unofficial appellation of "Juggernaut"—soon to be shortened to "Jug" and widely adopted as the P-47's

colloquial name. First flown in prototype form (XP-47B) on 6 May 1941, the Thunderbolt entered service late in 1942. When it joined operations over Europe in April of the following year, it was found incapable of matching the climb rates and manoeuvrability of opposing Luftwaffe fighters. But what it lacked in

agility it compensated for with a formidable dive capability, good altitude performance, and the ability to absorb and survive punishment. Once its pilots learned to take advantage of its intrinsic characteristics, the Thunderbolt began to build an enviable operational record. The grand total of all P-47s

built came to 15,683 aircraft, the sub-type produced in largest numbers being the P-47D of which no fewer than 12,602 were built. (**1**) P-47D-20 (43-25429) of the 19th Fighter Sqdn, 218th Fighter Grp, Saipan, Marianas, July 1944. (**2** and **2a**) P-47D of 86th Fighter Sqdn, 79th Fighter Grp, Fano, Italy, in February 1945. (**3**) P-47D-25

(42-26459) of 352nd Fighter Sqdn, 353rd Fighter Grp, Raydon, Suffolk, England, July 1944. (**3a**) Upper surfaces of -26459. (**4**) P-47D-30 Thunderbolt II (HD247) of No 79 Sqdn, RAF, at Wangjing, Burma, November 1944. Note non-standard SE Asia insignia of medium and dark blue, and theatre striping. (**4a**) Upper surfaces of HD247.

(**5**) P-47D-25 (42-26756) of the Brazilian 1º Gruppo de Caça at Tarquinia, Italy, November 1944. Note the yellow (bomb) mission markers appearing on portside only. (**5a**) The Gruppo emblem. (**6**) P-47M-1 (44-21118) of 63rd Fighter Sqdn, 56th Fighter Grp, Boxted, Essex, spring 1945. Note the non-standard upper surfaces

of medium and dark blue-grey. (**7**) P-47D-30 (44-33240) of 366th Fighter Sqdn, 358th Fighter Grp, Toul, France, in winter 1944. (**8**) P-47D-30 (44-33373) of 512th Fighter Sqdn, 406th Fighter Grp, Nordholz, summer 1945. (**9**) P-47D (ex-358th Fighter Sqdn) used by Sonderkommando (Special Detachment) of the Aufklärungsstaffel

(Reconnaissance Sqdn) 103, Orly, spring 1944. Note retention of original pilot's personal emblem. (**10**) A captured P-47D used by the 2.Staffel of Versuchsverband (Experimental Formation) Oberbefehlshaber (Commander-in-Chief) der Luftwaffe operating from Hustedt for familiarisation purposes in September 1944.

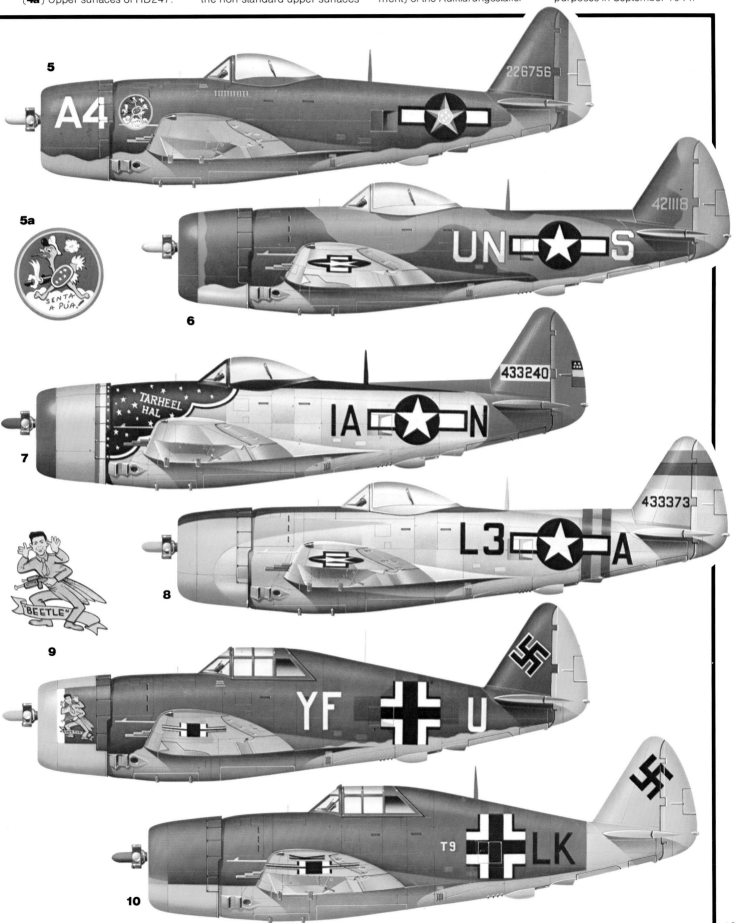

# Kawasaki Ki.61 Hien (Tony) (1942)

Retaining in some measure the agility traditionally associated with Japanese fighters and mating this with most of the better characteristics that had, prior to its debut, been exclusive to Western fighters, the Ki.61 Hien (Swallow) was therefore radical insofar as the Imperial Army Air Service was concerned.

The service's first fighter with a liquid-cooled engine for many years and the first providing pilot and fuel protection, the Hien did much to dispel belief held in the West that Japanese combat aircraft were "lightweights", incapable of taking punishment and surviving. First flown in December 1941, the Hien proved capable of mastering most Allied fighters that it met until opposed by such potent foes as America's Mustang and Hellcat. A total of 1,380 Ki.61-I Hiens had been built when production phased out in July 1944 to give place to the Ki.61-II. However, barely more than 60 of the later model were to reach the Sentais.

(1) Ki.61-I-KAI-Hei of the 1st Chutai, 244th Sentai, at Chofu, Tokyo, 1944-45. The Sentai marking (in the Chutai colour) was a stylised rendering of the arabic "244". The upper surfaces (see 1a) featured a dark green mottle on a light grey-green base. Note chrome yellow "combat identification stripe" on wing

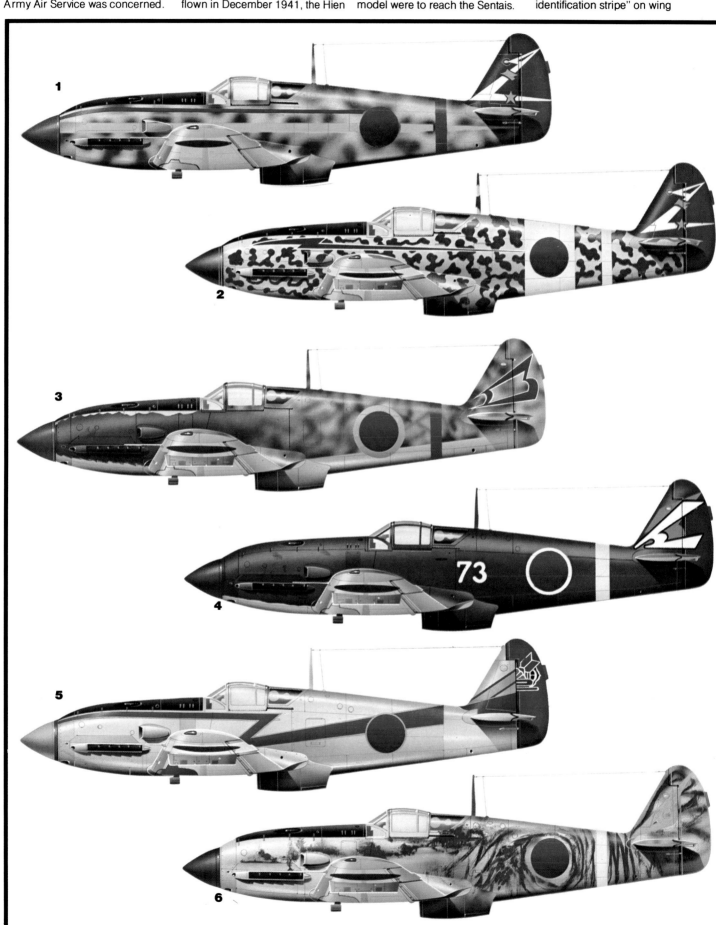

and (**1b**) aircraft number on the mainwheel fairing plates.
(**2**) Ki. 61-I-KAI-Hei of the HQ Chutai, 244th Sentai, Chofu, Tokyo, winter 1944-45. The fuselage and wing (**2a** and **2b**) Hinomarus are superimposed on white bands signifying "Defence of the Homeland", and the upper surface camouflage consists of irregular dark green blotches applied to the natural metal base. (**3**) Ki.61-I-KAI-Hei of the 23rd Independent Chutai, Yontan, Okinawa, April 1945. The Chutai emblem is a stylised rendition of "23" and the upper surfaces display a dark green snake-weave of varying intensity over the natural metal. Note the unusual chrome yellow outline of the Hinomaru and erosion of paint beneath the anti-dazzle panel and along the lower cowling line. (**4**) Ki.61-I-KAI-Hei of the 1st Chutai, 55th Sentai, at Chofu, Tokyo, winter 1944-45. Note that this aircraft was formerly with the 53rd Sentai, hence overpaint of tail insignia. (**5**) Ki.61-I-Otsu of the 3rd Chutai, 59th Sentai, at Ashiya, Japan, in August 1945. Note the replacement rear fuselage and rudder with montage of insignia. (**6**) Ki.61-I-KAI-Hei of 3rd Chutai, 19th Sentai, Okinawa, 1944-45. Note field-applied palm frond camouflage and stylised "19" tail insignia in 3rd Chutai colour (yellow).

# Vought F4U Corsair (1942)

Unique in performance and, by virtue of its reverse-gulled wing, appearance also, the Corsair commenced prototype flight trials on 29 May 1940, heralding a quantum advance in shipboard fighter capability. Regrettably, some of the problems apparent during these trials had still not been resolved

when the series model flew on 25 June 1942. An incipient landing bounce and an almost unheralded torque stall in landing configuration were compounded by some directional instability after touchdown; a lack of shipboard finesse that excluded Corsairs from US Navy carrier decks until summer 1944. The US Marine Corps

began combat missions with the Corsair from land bases, however, in February 1943, and once its pilots had learned to take full advantage of its significantly superior level and dive speeds, the Corsair enjoyed enviable combat success and a long production career which did not end until December 1952, by when

7,829 were built (1) F4U-2 night fighter of USMC Sqdn VMF(N)-532, Roi Island, Kwajalein Atoll, 1944. Note non-specular finish of sea blue, intermediate blue and gull grey, the folding wing sections being intermediate blue. (2) Corsair I (JT172) of No 1835 Sqdn, Royal Navy, Brunswick, NS, late 1943. Note Ocean Grey and

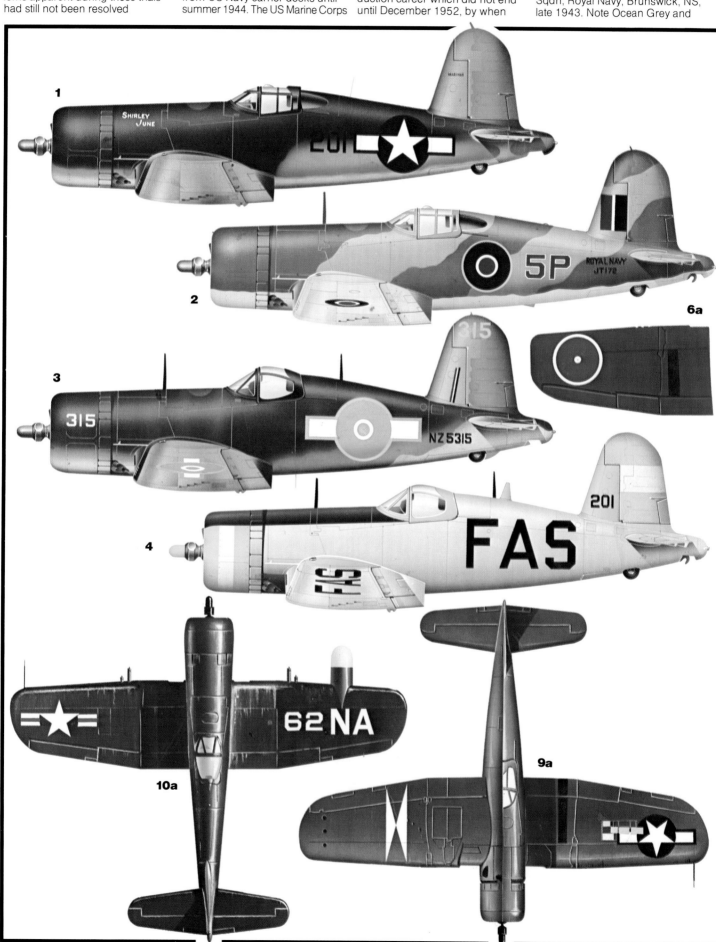

Dark Slate Grey upper surface camouflage and Sky undersides. (**3**) F4U-1A (NZ5315), No 17 Sqdn, RNZAF, Guadalcanal, August 1944. (**4**) F4U-4 of Fuerza Aérea Salvadorena, San Miguel, El Salvador, 1958. (**5**) Corsair IV (KD345) of No 1850 Sqdn, Royal Navy, HMS *Vengeance,* August 1945. Note retention of US Navy high- gloss sea blue overall finish. (**5a**) Aircraft number was usually repeated on mainwheel leg flap. (**6**) Corsair IV (KD681) also of No 1850 Sqdn, early 1945. Note "U7" coding and the differing presentation of roundel, a further variation being seen (**6a**) on upper wing surfaces of this aircraft. (**7**) F4U-4C of USN Reserve, NAS Glenview, signified by "V" of tail coding and orange band denoting reserve status, 1948. (**8**) F4U-7 (BuAer No 133703) of Flottille 12F, French Aéronavale, 1954. (**9**) F4U-1D from USS *Essex,* April 1945. The carrier marking (CV-9) on the vertical tail was repeated above starboard and below port wing (see **9a**). Note "washed-out" shade of aircraft finish due to prolonged exposure to elements. (**10**) F4U-5NL winterized night fighter of Navy Composite Sqdn VC-35 aboard USS *Antietam,* 1951. (**10a**) Carrier code and aircraft number were repeated below the port and above the starboard outer wing panels.

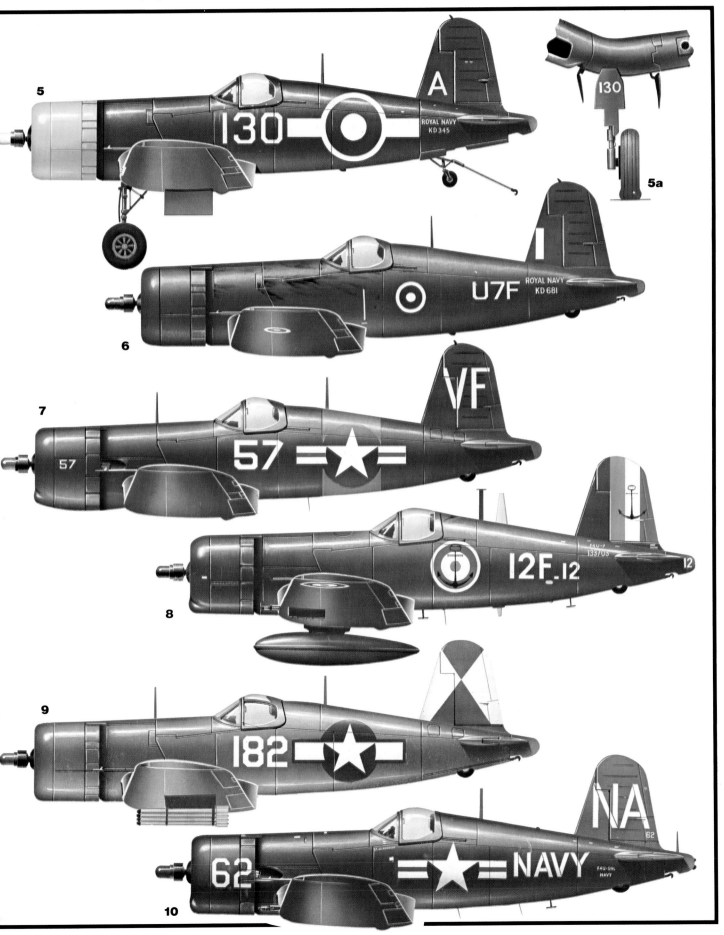

# Avro Lancaster (1942)

Of all the RAF's bombers, none achieved greater acclaim than did the Lancaster. Born of a compromise and derived from the design of a medium bomber, it emerged as probably the most successful heavy bomber of WWII. First flown on 9 January 1941, it entered service at the beginning of 1942, with 7,374 having been built when the last example was delivered in February of 1946. (**1**) Lancaster B I (RA542) of No 463 Sqdn, RAAF, at Waddington, Lincs, spring 1945. This aircraft was lost to night fighters during the last Lancaster night attack of WWII, against an oil refinery at Vallö (Tonsberg) in Norway on 25/26 April 1945. Note yellow outlining of coding, a standard practice in No 5 Group, and repetition of individual letter on the tail. (**2**) Lancaster B I (HK793) of No 149 (East India) Sqdn, Methwold, Norfolk, early 1945. Note deepened bomb bay and yellow fin bars denoting G-H radar-equipped flight leader in No 3 Group. (**3**) Lancaster GR Mk 3 (RF325), School of Maritime Reconnaissance, St Mawgan, Cornwall, 1956, and withdrawn in October of that year as the last serving RAF Lancaster. (**4**) The rear fuselage of Lancaster B III (PB410), No 97 Sqdn, Coningsby, Lincs, early 1945. Note repetition of coding (**4a**) on upper tailplane surfaces.

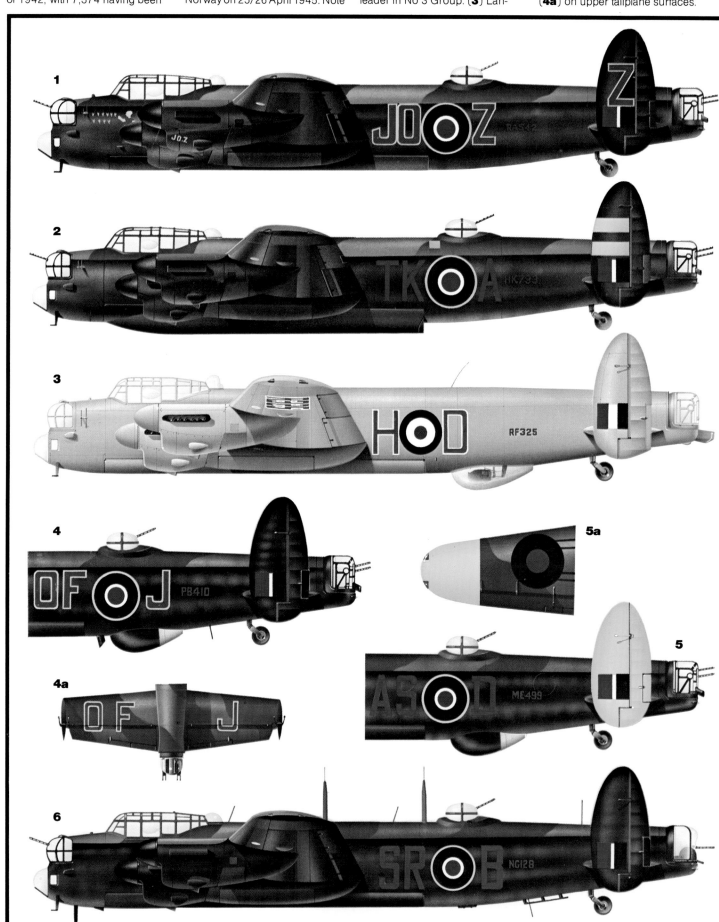

(**5**) Rear fuselage of Lancaster B III (ME499), No 166 Sqdn, Kirmington, Lincs. The yellow vertical tail and (**5a**) wingtip were a No 1 Group experiment for improving formation visibility. (**6**) Lancaster B I (NG128) of No 101 Sqdn, Ludford Magna, Lincs, 1944, carrying "Airborne Cigar" (ABC) jamming equipment (as denoted by aerials). (**7**) Lancaster B 1(FE), ex-RAF (PA342) of Flottille 24F, French Aéronavale, late 1953. (**8**) Lancaster B III (ED912/G), No 617 Sqdn, Coningsby, Lincs, May 1943. This was specially-modified aircraft for "Upkeep" dam-busting mine and flown in 17 May 1943 attack on Möhne, Eder and Sorpe dams. (**9**) Lancaster B I (Special) (PD133), No 617 Sqdn, Woodhall Spa, Lincs, early 1945, with "Grand Slam" bomb suspended beneath the fuselage. (**10**) Lancaster B VI (ND673), No 635 Sqdn, a component of Pathfinder Force (No 8 Group), Downham Market, Norfolk, late 1944. Note that the nose and dorsal turrets have been deleted, and tail fin is striped. (**11**) Lancaster B VII (NX750) of No 9 Sqdn, Salbani, India, early 1946. Note typical "Tiger Force" finish of aircraft. (**12**) Lancaster B X (KB861) of No 431 (Iroquois) Sqdn, RCAF, at Croft, Co Durham, early 1945, as a component of No 6 (RCAF) Group. This aircraft was Victory-built.

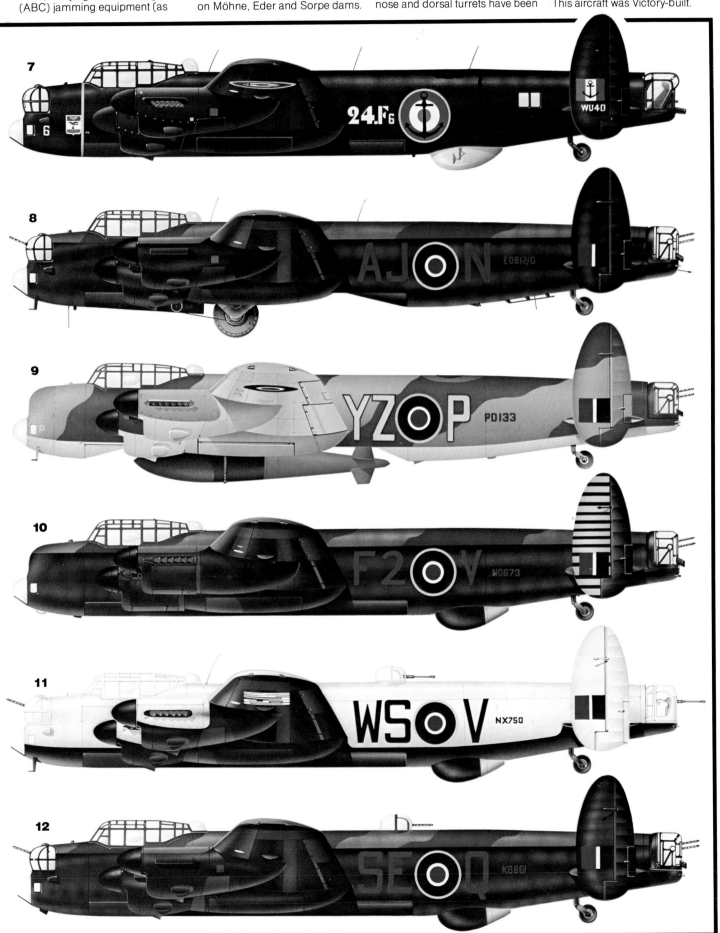

167

# Northrop P-61 Black Widow (1944)

The only Allied fighter designed from the outset for the nocturnal role to achieve service in WWII, the P-61 Black Widow was as big as a medium bomber, but despite its size it was both docile and manoeuvrable. First flown on 26 May 1942, the P-61 pioneered the use of spoilers in place of conventional ailerons, permitting the use of near full-span flaps which broadened the speed range and permitted operation from small airfields. The P-61 entered service mid-1944, a total of 706 being manufactured. (**1**) P-61A-1 (42-5528) "Jap-Batty" of the 6th Night Fighter Sqdn, East Field, Saipan, Marianas, in summer 1944. (**1a**) The personal emblem carried by 42-5528. (**2**) P-61A-5 (42-5536) "Husslin Hussey" of 422nd NFS, Scorton, Yorks, summer 1944. (**2a**) Half-and-half planview showing port top and underside of 42-5536. (**3**) P-61B-15 (42-39713) "Lady in the Dark", 548th NFS, Ie Shima, Ryukyu Is, China Sea, August 1945. (**3a**) Emblem of 548th NFS. Note non-reflective matt black overall finish. (**4**) P-61B-1 (42-39468) "Moonlight Serenade" of 550th NFS, Tacloban, Leyte, Philippines, June 1945. Note the squadron tail striping. (**5**) P-61A-5 (42-4464) "Jukin Judy" of 422nd NFS, Scorton. Note late-1944 high-gloss overall black definitive finish.

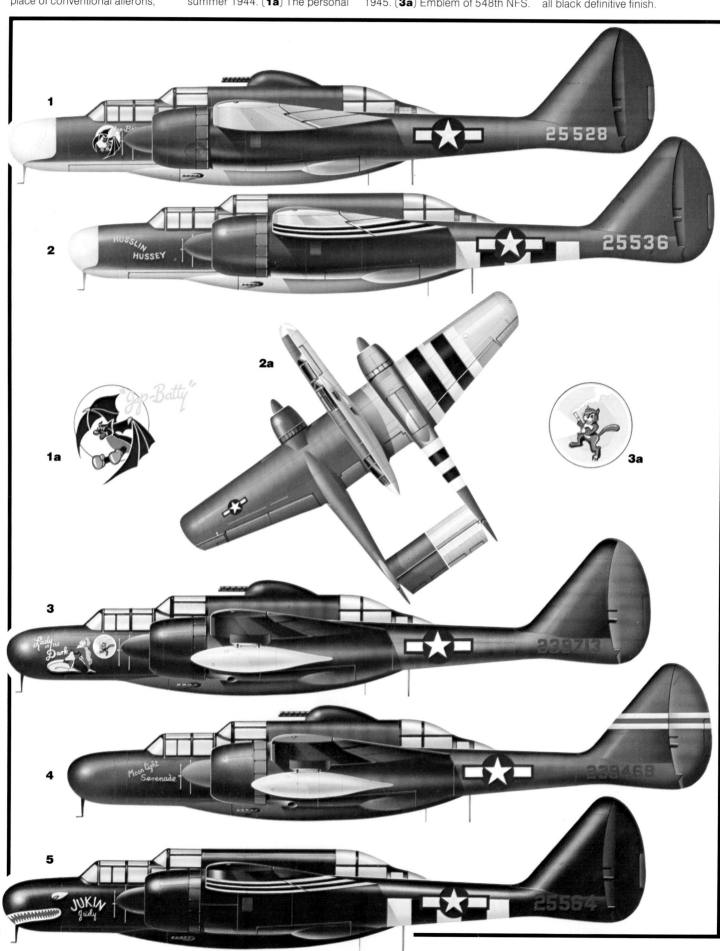

# Nakajima Ki.84 Hayate (Frank) (1944)

By consensus the most formidable fighter fielded by the Japanese Army, the Ki.84 Hayate (Gale) possessed respectable firepower, outstanding manoeuvrability and an ability to withstand battle damage to an extent previously unknown in Japanese fighters. Its handling and control characteristics were superior to those of its Western contemporaries, and it could out-climb and out-manoeuvre the US fighters by which it was opposed, turning inside them with ease. First flown in April 1943, the Hayate entered service in March 1944, and production of this outstanding and supremely agile warplane was to total 3,470 aircraft.

(1) Ki.84-I-Ko, HQ Chutai, 29th Sentai, Formosa, 1945. Note the natural metal finish widely-used in closing stage of the Pacific conflict, and the Sentai emblem, a stylised breaking wave. (2) Ki.84-I-Ko, 1st Chutai, 73rd Sentai, Philippines, in December 1944. (3) Ki.84-I-Ko of 183rd Shimbu-tai (Special Attack Group) at Tatebayashi, Japan, August 1945. Note irregular application of medium green dappling on fuselage. (4) Ki.84-I-Ko, 1st Chutai, 102nd Sentai, Kyushu, April 1945. (5) Ki.84-I-Ko, 1st Chutai, 47th Sentai, Narumatsu, Japan, August 1945. The white panel signified "Home Defence". (6) Ki.84-I-Ko of 58th Shimbu-tai, August 1944.

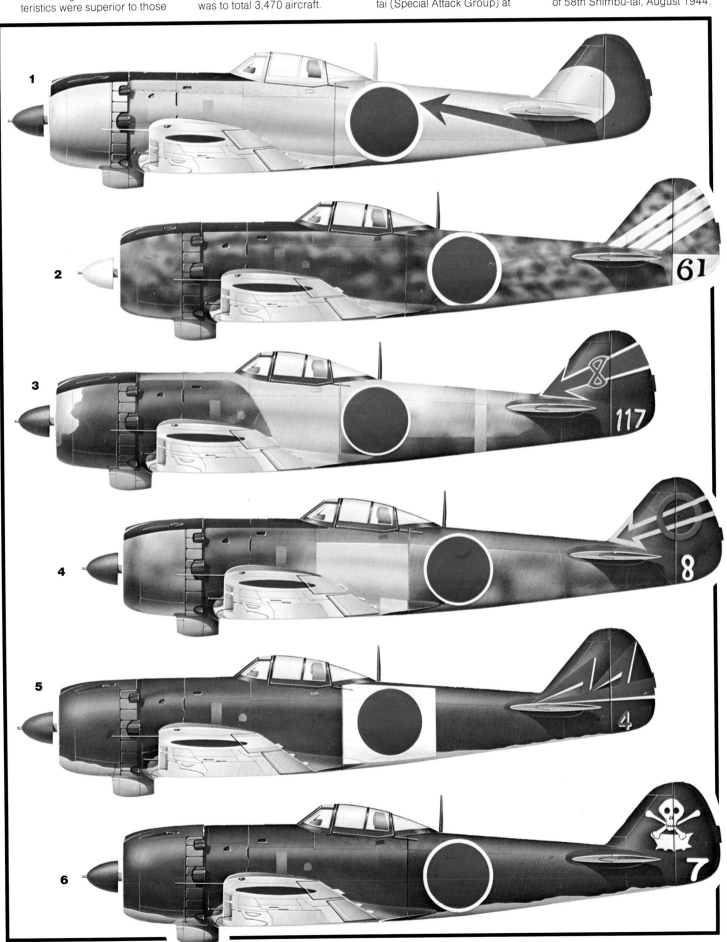

# Messerschmitt Me 262 (1944)

One of the comparatively few truly epoch-marking fighters in aviation's annals and arguably the most formidable warplane to attain service status in WWII, the Me 262 launched a new era in aerial warfare. First flown on turbojets alone (V3) on 18 July 1942, the Me 262 was to enter service with the Luftwaffe in the summer of 1944, and a total of 1,378 was to be completed. Despite its radicality and if marginally underpowered, the Me 262 was truly a pilot's aeroplane; responsive and docile with pleasant harmony of control. Although it was demanding on runway length, and its engines were temperamental, it offered a marked speed gain over any predecessor. (1) Me 262A-2a, I Gruppe/Kampfgeschwader 51, Achmer, in spring 1945. (2) Me 262A-2a/U1 of the Erprobungskommando (Test Detachment) Schenck, commanded by Maj Wolfgang Schenck, in autumn 1944. (3) Me 262A-2a (Werk-Nr 111 625, 9K+FH) of I/KG 51, Achmer, in spring 1945. (4) Me 262A-2a of 1./KG 51, March 1945. (5) Me 262A-1a/U3 of Einsatzkommando (Operational Detachment) Braunegg, Northern Italy, March 1945. (6) S-92 "Turbina" (Turbine), an Avia-assembled Me 262A-2, originally flown by 5th Fighter Sqdn (5.stihaci letka), Czech Air Force, in 1950-51, after re-coding (PL-01) for ground use.

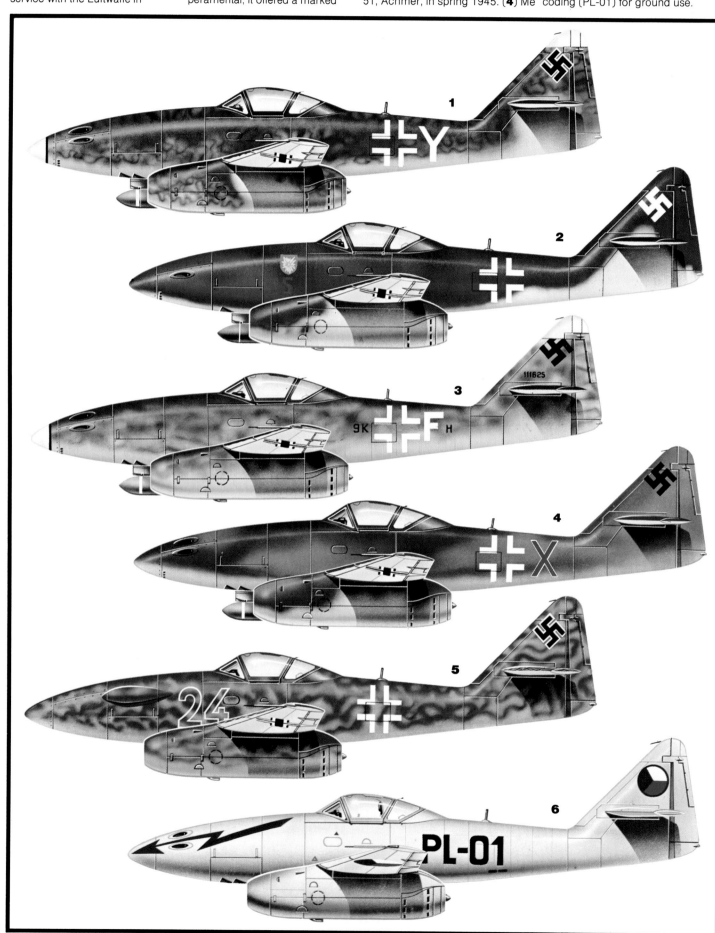

# Gloster Meteor (1944)

Aerodynamically less sophistic- ated than its contemporary, the Me 262, and the only Allied jet aircraft to see operational use in WWII, the Meteor was perhaps the most successful of western first-generation jet fighters. First flown on 5 March 1943, it achieved service status with the RAF at about the same time as the Me 262, but did not attain quantity production status so rapidly. In developed form, the Meteor offered a sound perform- ance, innocuous handling and a high standard of reliability. It was to remain first-line RAF equipment for 17 years and be exported to a dozen foreign air forces, 3,550 being built in the UK and 300 in the Netherlands. (**1**) Meteor F Mk 3 (EE270), No 245 Sqdn, Colerne, late 1945. (**2**) Meteor F Mk 3 (EE455) modi- fied for a world speed record attempt in November 1945. (**3**) Meteor PR Mk 10 (VS979) of No 541 Sqdn operating from Bückeburg, Germany, with 2nd Tactical Air Force, in 1952. (**4**) Meteor F Mk 8 (WF714) of CO, Sqdn Ldr Desmond de Villiers (hence decorative tail) of No 500 Sqdn, Royal Auxiliary Air Force, West Malling, Kent, 1954. (**5**) Meteor F Mk 8 of Eskadrille 742, Royal Danish Air Force, Karup, 1954. (**6**) Meteor U Mk 16 (WH284) target drone delivered to Llanbedr in June 1960.

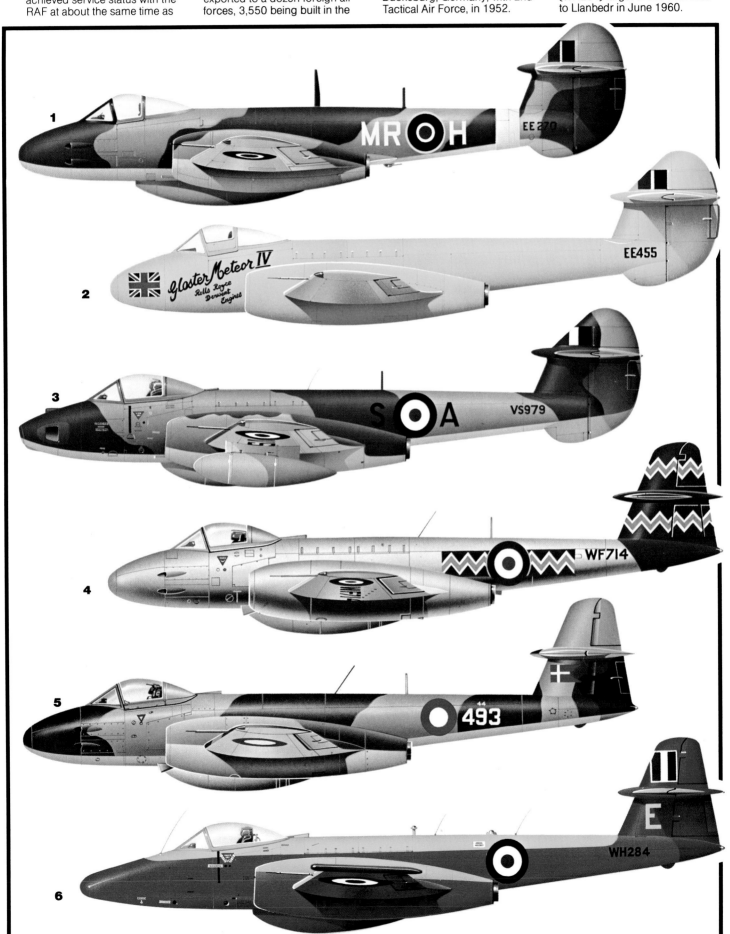

# Lockheed P-80 Shooting Star (1945)

Such was the tempo of fighter development in the immediate post-WWII years, that the P-80 Shooting Star saw barely five years of service before, in November 1950, its obsolescence was rendered manifest by the debut in Korean skies of the MiG-15. Indeed, so serious was the adverse performance disparity

that it was only the superior skill of its pilots which enabled it to survive encounters with the Soviet fighter. The first American jet aircraft to achieve major service status, the P-80 Shooting Star suffered high attrition during its early career. Built in the remarkably short time of 143 days, the first prototype,

the XP-80, flew on 9 January 1944, the first production P-80A being completed in February 1945. Early aircraft featured a highly polished light grey overall finish, but the scuffing and chipping to which this was prone resulted in a deterioration of performance and consequent standardisation on polished natural metal.

Redesignated F-80 after mid-June 1948, the Shooting Star served primarily in the ground attack and armed reconnaissance roles in Korea until mid-April 1953, 525 being ordered as P-80As (240 of which were either converted to or completed as P-80Bs) and a further 798 as P-80Cs, the latter being delivered 1948-49.

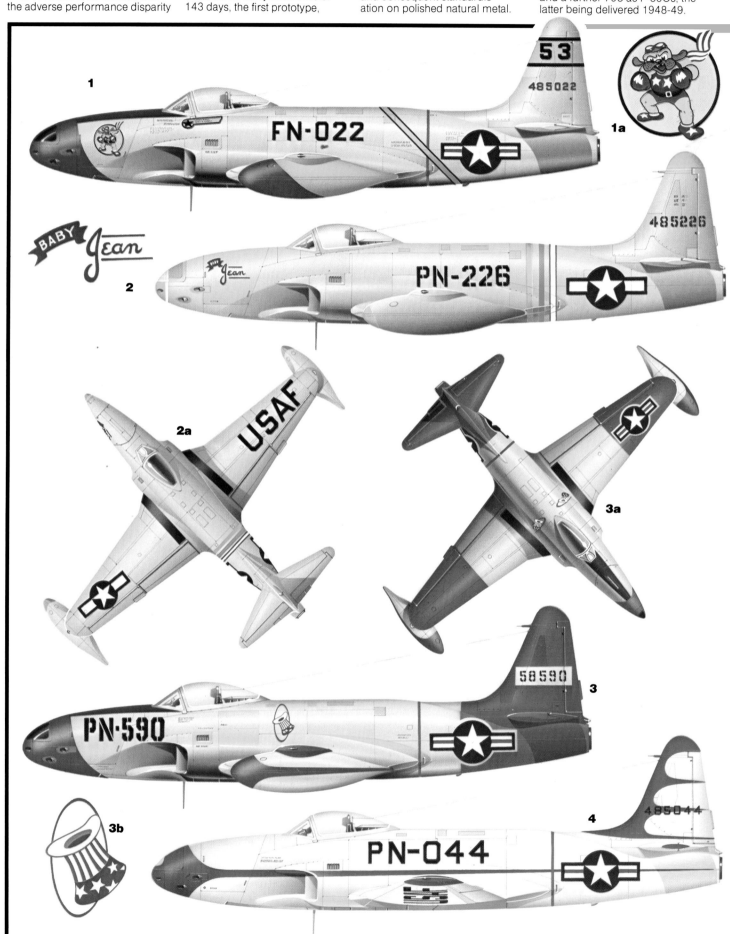

(1) P-80A-1-LO (44-85022) of the 62nd Fighter Sqdn, 56th Fighter Group, deployed to Germany, July 1948. (1a) Emblem of 62nd Sqdn (2) P-80A-1-LO (44-85226) of the 412th Fighter Group, 1946, this being the first unit to equip. Note light grey overall finish and P-80 "PN" buzz code retained until June 1948. (2a) Topside planview of PN-226. (3) P-80B-5 (45-8590) of 94th Fighter Sqdn, Ladd Field, Fairbanks, Alaska, 1947. Note the high-visibility markings. (3a) Topside planview of PN-590, and (3b) "Hat-in-the-Ring" emblem of the 94th FS. (4) P-80A-1 (44-85044) of Flight Test Division, Wright Field, 1948, with overall white finish. (5) P-80A-1 (44-85033) of 61st Fighter Sqdn, 56th Fighter Group, Selfridge Field, Michigan, in summer 1948. (5a) 61st FS emblem and (5b) 56th FG emblem, these appearing on port and starboard side of the nose, respectively. (6) P-80A-5 (44-85462) after conversion to QF-80F standard for pilotless operations. Note the arrester hook. (7) P-80C-5 (47-547) of 36th Fighter-Bomber Sqdn, 8th FBW, Korea, in 1949. (8) P-80A-1 (44-85088) serving for transitional training with Iowa Air National Guard. (9) RF-80A (44-85467), having been converted from P-80A-5 for photo-recce task. Note retention of fighter category "FT" buzz code.

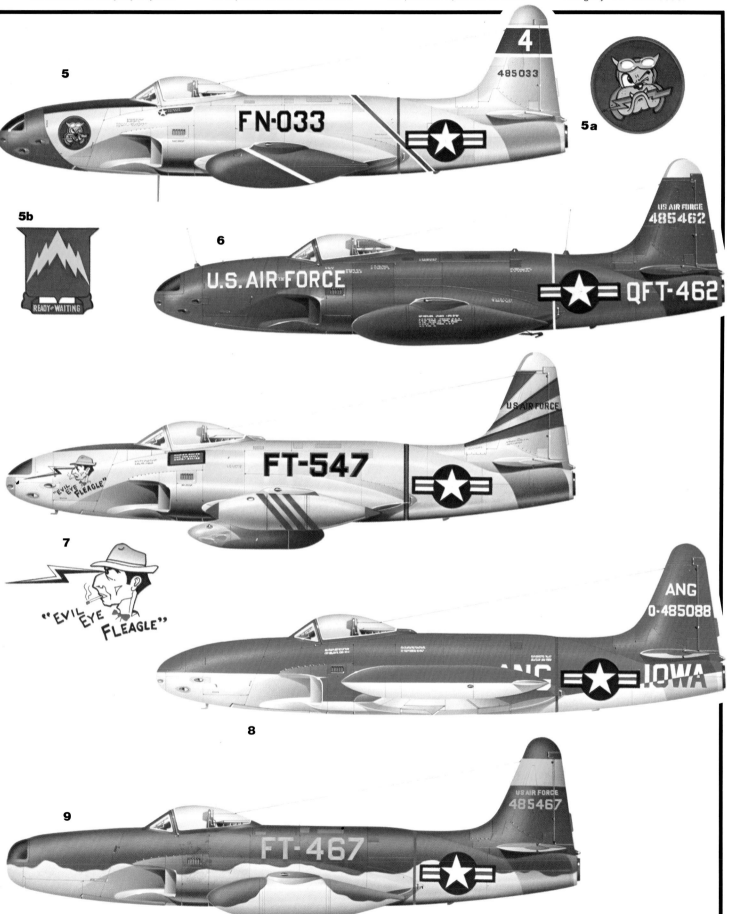

# English Electric Canberra (1951)

If longevity of service is any criteria, then the Canberra is to be judged one of the most successful jet combat aircraft yet flown. Making its RAF service debut in May 1951, it was continuing to fulfil a variety of tasks with the RAF 30 years later, in 1981, remaining first line equipment with no fewer

than eight foreign air forces. First flown on 13 May 1949 as the initial British essay in jet bomber design, the Canberra, in Mosquito bomber tradition, carried no defensive armament, relying instead on speed to evade interception. It was to emulate the Mosquito further in proving to be outstandingly versatile. The

Canberra was manufactured continuously for a dozen years, 902 being built in the UK, 503 being licence-built in the USA (as the B-57) and 56 more in Australia. (**1**) Canberra B 2 (WJ678) of No 100 Sqdn, Marham, 1978. Note the black-white shadowed single-letter fin code and squadron emblem (white skull with crossed

bones on circular green field) superimposed on black-and-yellow checkerboard. (**2**) Canberra T 4 (WJ861) of No 85 Sqdn at Binbrook, April 1971. Note polyurethane grey overall finish and Day-glo nose and tail bars, and wing leading edge. (**2a**) Hexagonal marking of No 85 Sqdn. (**3**) Canberra B 2 (WH640) of No 10

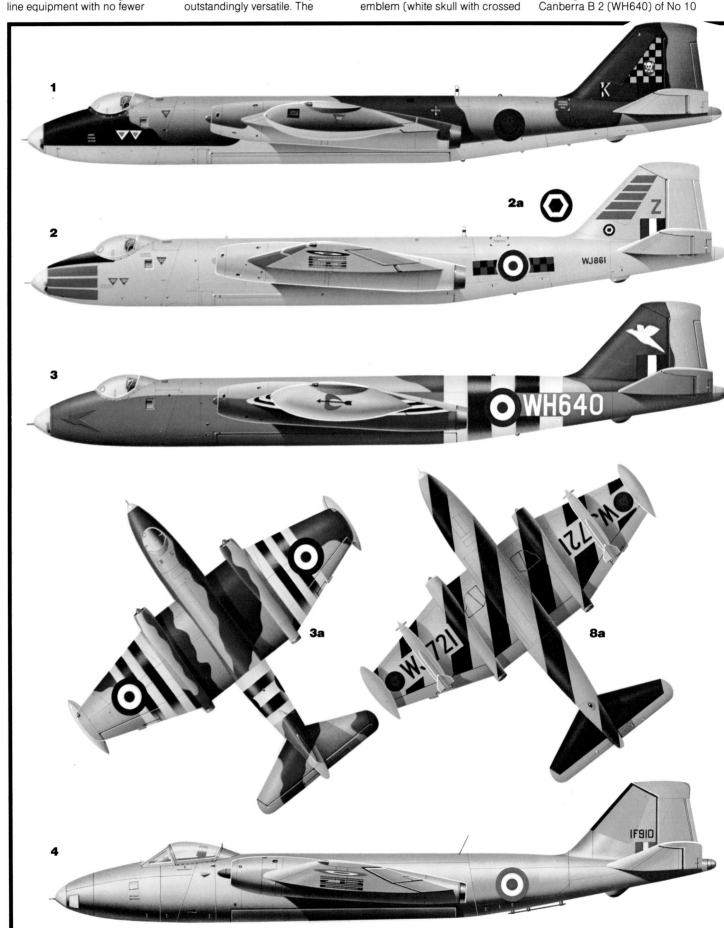

Sqdn deployed to Nicosia, Cyprus, in October 1956 for Suez campaign (home-based Honington, Suffolk). Note "Suez striping" comprising two black and three white (owing to temporary shortage of yellow paint) bands. The speedbird emblem of RAF Scampton (which was the unit's previous base) was retained on the nose, the white pheasant emblem of RAF Honington appeared on the tail, and the "Winged Arrow" emblem of No 10 Sqdn appeared on the tip tank. (**3a**) Upper surfaces of WH640. (**4**) Canberra B(I) 58 (IF910) of No 58 "Black Elephants" Sqdn, Indian Air Force, Agra, in 1959. (**5**) Canberra B(I) 12 (452) of No 12 Sqdn, SAAF, Waterkloof, 1975. Note PRU Blue overall finish. (**6**) Canberra B 52 (354) of the Imperial Ethiopian Air Force, Asmara, 1970. (**7**) Canberra B 2 (99+36 ex-WK130) of Erprobungs-stelle (test Centre) 61, Köln/Wahn, 1978-79, for cartographic tasks on behalf of the Military Geographic Office. (**8**) Canberra TT 18 (WJ721) of No 7 Sqdn, St Mawgan, Cornwall, 1974, and (**8a**) undersurfaces of same aircraft. (**8b**) The Ursa Major Constellation emblem of No 7 Sqdn. (**9**) Canberra B(I) 66 (F1028) of the Indian Air Force, 1970. (**10**) Canberra B 2 (2085), No 5 Sqdn, Rhodesian Air Force, New Sarum, 1970. Note post-UDI national insignia, later deleted.

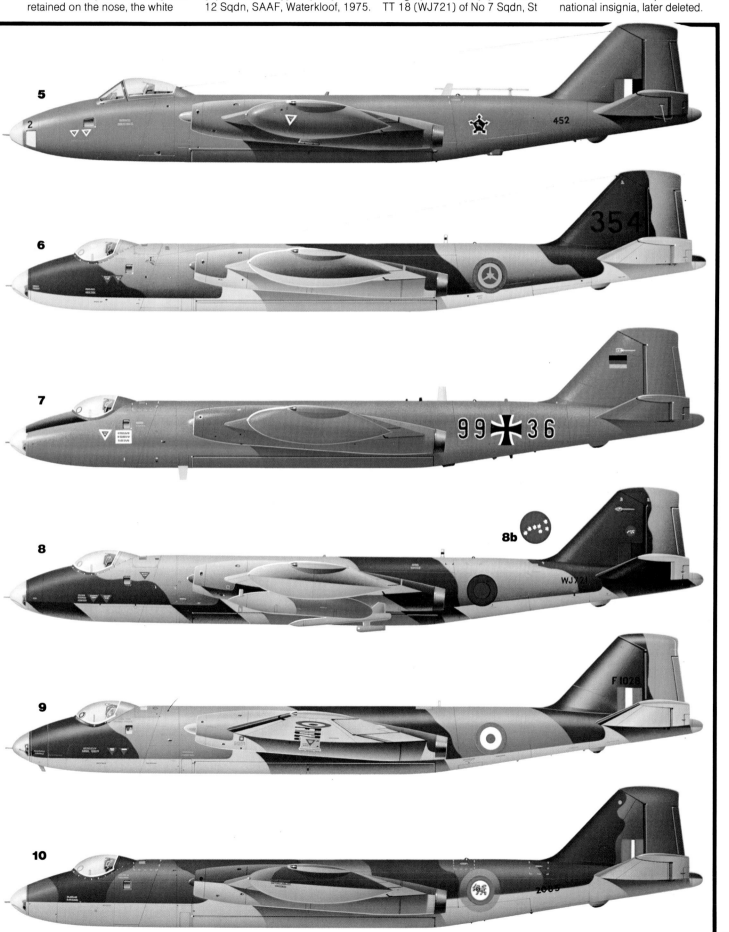

# Republic F-84F Thunderstreak (RF-84F Thunderflash) (1954)

Providing many of the vertebrae of NATO's European air power backbone from mid 'fifties until early 'seventies, the F-84F fighter-bomber and its tactical reconnaissance counterpart, the RF-84F, were demanding on field length and possessed what were, at the time of their debut, quite dauntingly high landing speeds. With external loads, the F-84F tended to wallow in the climb-out and lacked acceleration. It was also prone to high-speed stalling, but both F-84F and RF-84F were rugged and stable, the fighter-bomber being able to lift formidable stores loads. Evolved from the mating of the fuselage of the straight-wing F-84E Thunderjet with swept surfaces, a prototype (YF-84F) flew on 3 June 1950. After re-engining and major redesign, the F-84F entered production and joined the USAF inventory early 1954; 2,713 were built. The recce RF-84F derivative, with similar airframe but with wing root intake duct location, entered service almost simultaneously, a total of 715 being manufactured. (1) F-84F-51 (52-7166) of 1ère Escadrille, 2ème Wing, based at Florennes, Belgium, 1969. (1a) Topside planview of 52-7166. (2) F-84F (52-8842) of the 3e Escadrille ''Ardennes'', the 3e Escadre de Chasse, Armée de l'Air, home-based at Reims and

deployed to Akrotiri, Cyprus, during Suez operation, November 1956. Note black-and-yellow Suez ID striping and "Boar's Head" emblem of EC 3/3. (2a) Topside planview of 52-8842. Note yellow wingtips signifying 3e Esc. (3) F-84F-25 (53-6721) of "Getti Tonanti" (Thunderjet) aerobatic team of 5a Aerobrigata, Aero-

nautica Militare Italiana, Rimini, in 1960. Note that the "Goddess Diana" emblem of Aerobrigata appeared on starboard side. The Olympic symbol marked 1960 Rome venue of the Games. (3a) Starboard upper surfaces of 53-6721. (4) F-84F-25 (53-6657) of the "Diavoli Rossi" (Red Devils) 6a Aerobrigata aerobatic team,

AMI, Ghedi, 1958. (4a) Port upper surfaces of 53-6657. (5) RF-84F-26 (52-7327), No 112 Sqdn, 1st Tac Air Force, Türk Hava Kuvvetleri, Eskisehir, 1971. Note "Scorpion" emblem of No 112 Sqdn. (5a) Upper surfaces of 52-7327. (6) RF-84F-26 (52-7283) of 729 Eskadrille, Kongelige Danske Flyvevåben, Karup, 1969.

Note emblem of 729 ESK, and (6a) upper surfaces of 52-7283. (7 and 7a) RF-84F (51-1912) of 42ème Escadrille, Force Aerienne Belge, Bierset-Liège, 1971. (8) RF-84F (53-7633) of the 1e Escadrille "Belfort", 33 Escadre de Reconnaissance, Armée de l'Air, Luxeuil, 1966. Note "Battle Axe" emblem of the 1/33 Escadrille.

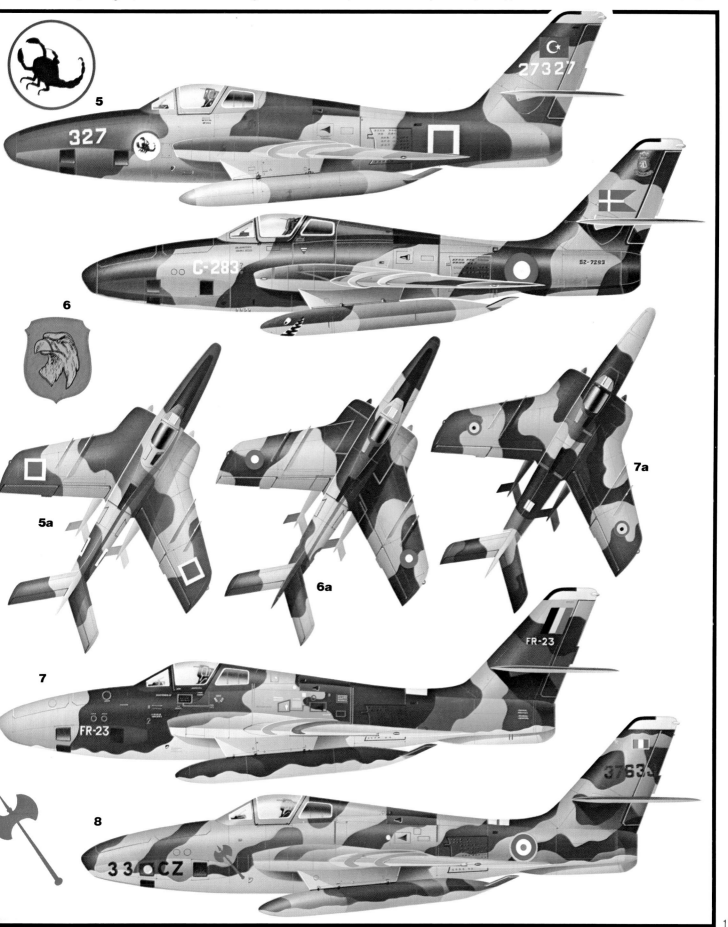

# Hawker Hunter (1954)

If greatness in a combat aircraft equates with outstanding service longevity, extreme operational flexibility combined with universal popularity, then the Hunter was indeed truly great and surely *the* classic fighter design of the 'fifties. It was aesthetically unsurpassed and a thoroughbred aircraft in every sense.

The Hawker Hunter was always a pilot's aeroplane, manifesting flawless handling and very few limitations, and it was extraordinarily robust. It saw almost two decades of first line RAF service, and as late as 1981, three decades after its first flight, it remained in the operational inventories of a number of air forces. Flown for the first time on 20 July 1951, the Hunter entered service (in its F Mk 1 version) in July 1954, and production continued into 1959, with a total of 1,972 being completed, of which 445 were built under licence in the Netherlands and Belgium. Of these, almost one-third were later to be refurbished and converted for a variety of roles for the RAF and Royal Navy, and for more than a dozen overseas customers. The Hunter's last operational roles with the RAF were those of ground attack fighter and reconnaissance fighter as the FGA Mk 9 and FR Mk 10 respectively, both of these being conversions of the final

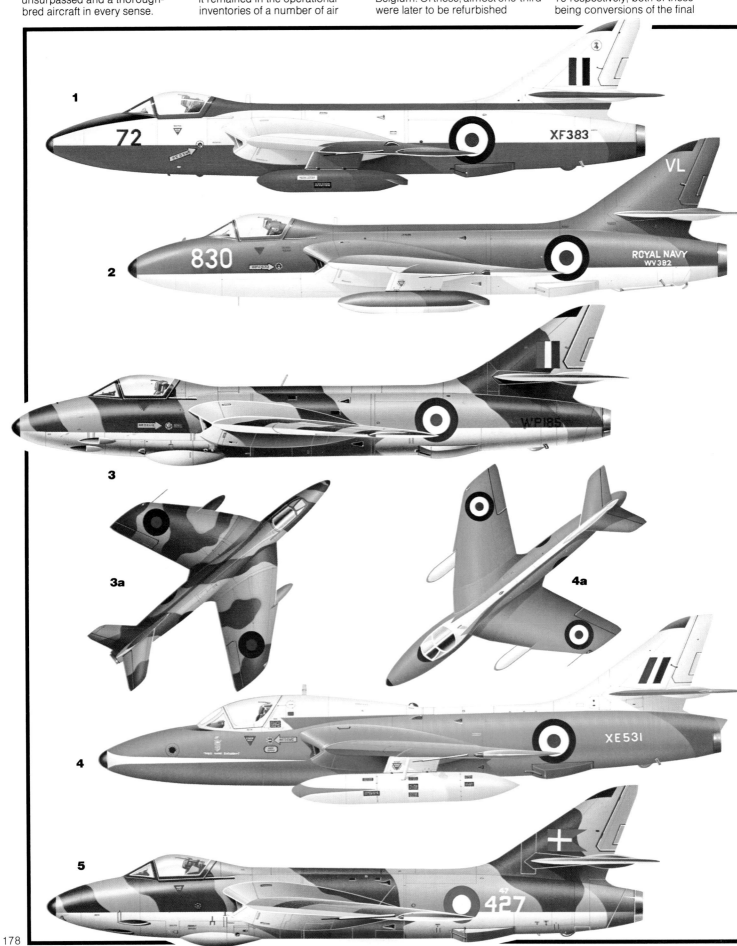

single-seat production model, the F Mk 6, and remaining in the first line operational inventory until the early years of the 'seventies. (**1**) Hunter F Mk 6 (XF383) of No 4 Flying Training School, RAF Valley, late 'seventies, for use by FTS's No 3 Sqdn in the high-speed low-level training role. Note the standard RAF training colour scheme. (**2**) Hunter GA Mk 11 (WV382) of Fleet Requirements & Air Direction Unit, Royal Navy, RNAS Yeovilton, late 'seventies. (**3**) Hunter F Mk 5 (WP185) in the standard RAF Fighter Command finish of the late '50s/early '60s. (**3a**) Upper surfaces of WP185. (**4**) Hunter Mk 12 (XE531) used by Royal Aircraft Establishment at Farnborough for equipment development trials (for example fly-by-wire control system tests undertaken in 1980-81). (**4a**) Upper surfaces of XE531. (**5**) Hunter Mk 51 (427) of 724 Eskadrille, Royal Danish Air Force, Aalborg, 1957. (**6**) Hunter F Mk 56 (BA360), Indian Air Force, 1960. (**7**) Hunter FGA Mk 78 (QA10) of Qatar Emiri Air Force, Doha, 1972. (**8**) Hunter F Mk 58, 1 Fliegerstaffel, Swiss Flugwaffe, 1968. (**9**) Hunter FR Mk 76A (708), Abu Dhabi Air Force, Sharjah, 1976. (**10**) Hunter F Mk 6 (L175), Lebanese Air Force, 1960. (**11**) Hunter T Mk 8M (XL602), Royal Navy, RNAS Yeovilton, 1980, for radar testing.

179

# North American F-100 Super Sabre (1954)

One of the true epoch-markers of military aviation's annals in being the first Western fighter capable of genuine level-flight supersonic performance, the F-100 Super Sabre was also noteworthy for the brevity of its prototype-to-production cycle. Flown in prototype form (YF-100A) on 25 May 1953, it appeared in production F-100A form barely five months later, on 29 October, and the first USAF Tactical Air Command unit to which the new fighter was assigned began to take delivery in September 1954. Shortly after its introduction, however, the F-100A was found to suffer inertia coupling which, producing uncontrollable yaw, was the result of inadequate directional stability. This was rectified by a major increase in vertical fin area, coupled with an increase in wing span, and the Super Sabre was subsequently to enjoy a long and particularly distinguished career. The F-100A was essentially an air superiority fighter and the F-100C that succeeded it featured in-flight refuelling and increased internal fuel derived from use of a "wet" wing which was also strengthened to permit six external ordnance stations, thereby suiting the Super Sabre for the fighter-bomber mission. The definitive single-seat model and penultimate production model of the Super Sabre

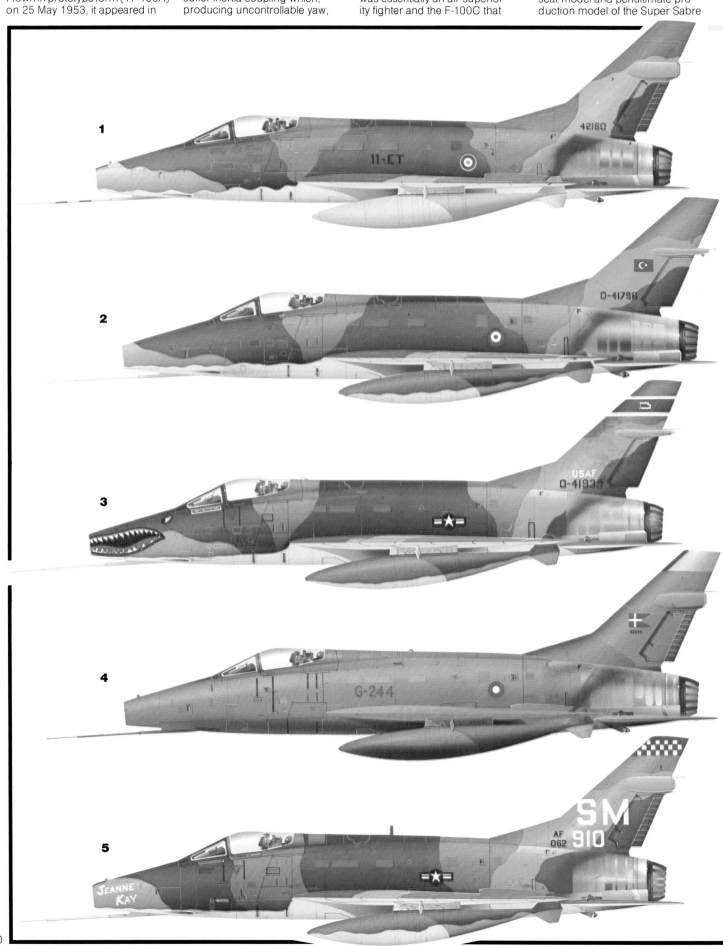

was the F-100D which was a more sophisticated and versatile fighter-bomber, the last version being the F-100F tandem-seater combining the fighter-bomber role with that of proficiency training. When production ended in October 1959, a total of 2,192 F-100s had been delivered to the USAF Tactical Air Command.

(**1**) F-100D-10 (54-2160) of Escadron 1/11 "Roussilon", Armée de l'Air, Toul, in 1972. (**1a**) Upper surfaces of -2160. (**2**) F-100C-5 (54-1798) of 111th Sqdn, Türk Hava Kuvvetleri, 1st Jet Air Base, Eskisehir, Turkey, 1973. (**2a**) Scrap view of -1798 upper port wing surfaces. (**3**) F-100C-20 (54-1939) of 127th Tactical

Fighter Sqdn of the Kansas Air National Guard. Note stylised map of Kansas on the tail band. (**4**) F-100D-15 (54-2244) of Esk 730, Kongelige Danske Flyvevåben at Skrydstrup, 1975. (**4a**) Scrap view of -2244 upper port wing surfaces. Note that matt green finish applied to Danish F-100s, which imparted a worn impression

(as illustrated) within a few months of application, was replaced by high-gloss finish with better anti-corrosion properties from 1979 until final withdrawal in 1981. (**5**) F-100D-6 (56-2910) of 308th Tactical Fighter Sqdn, 31st TFW, Tuy Hoa, Vietnam, 1970. (**5a**) Topside plan view of 308th TFS F-100D-6.

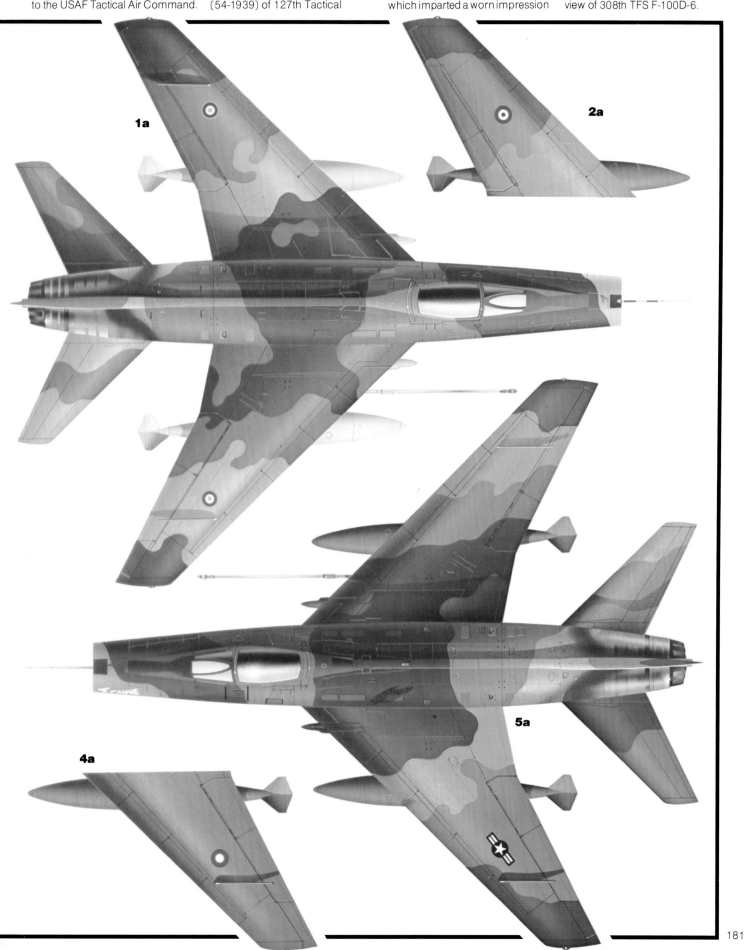

# Dassault Super Mystère (1958)

Claiming the distinction of having been the first combat aircraft produced in Western Europe capable of attaining supersonic speed in level flight, the Super Mystère suffered the misfortune of being overshadowed by the very much more spectacular Mirage (see pages 190-1) which, from the same stable, followed closely upon its heels. As a consequence, the Super Mystère enjoyed only a comparatively brief production life. However, the strictly limited quantity of fighters of this type built reflected in no way upon the intrinsic capabilities of the type, which was to see no fewer than 19 years of first-line service with France's Armée de l'Air. The first prototype, designated Super Mystère B1 and powered by the Rolls-Royce Avon engine, was flown on 2 March 1955, the first SNECMA Atar-powered model, the Super Mystère B2, following on 15 May 1956. Contracts followed for 180 production Super Mystère B2s, and the first deliveries (to Escadron 1/10 "Valois") began in May 1958. Twenty-four of the Super Mystère B2s were supplied to the Israeli Defence Force/Air Force (La Tsvah Hagana Le Israel/ Heyl Ha'Avir), attrition being made up from Armée de l'Air stocks and the type distinguishing itself in both the 1967 and 1973 Middle East conflicts.

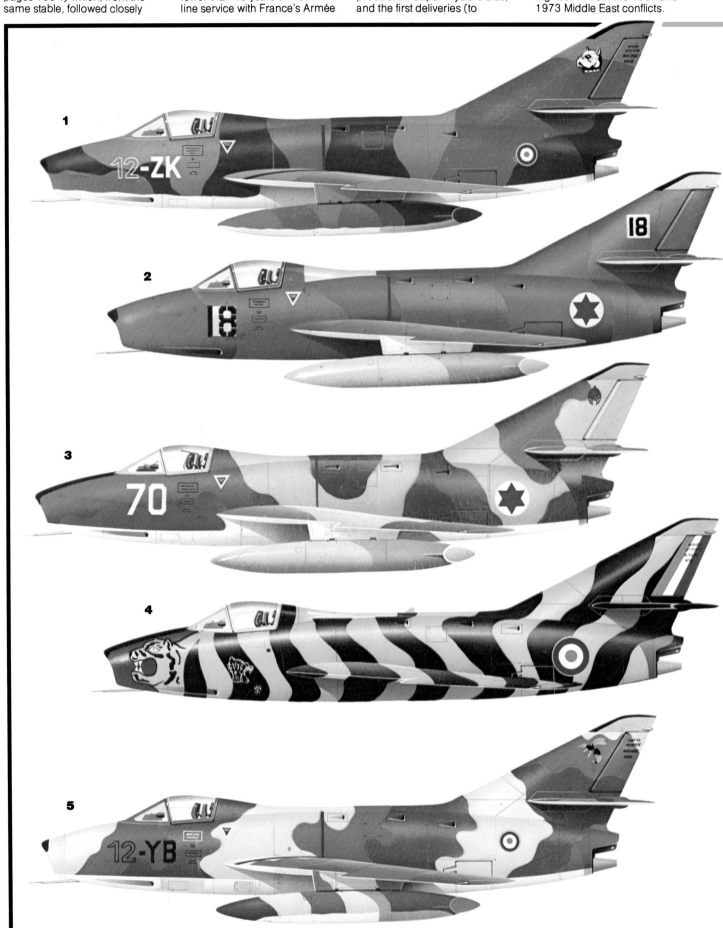

(**1**) Super Mystère B2 Nº113 of Escadron 2/12 "Cornouailles", Cambrai, summer 1972. (**1a**) Upper surfaces of 12-ZK with medium green, dark stone and chestnut brown disruptive camouflage. (**1b**) "Scorpion" emblem appearing on starboard and (**1c**) "Dog's Head" emblem appearing on port of tail fin of 12-ZK. (**2**) Super Mystère B2 of Israeli Heyl Ha' Avir at Hatzor, near Rehovot, south of Tel Aviv, summer 1972. Note natural metal skinning behind individual aircraft number. (**3**) Super Mystère B2 of Heyl Ha'Avir, Hatzor, 1972. Note camouflage scheme of green, tan and café au lait introduced from late 1971. (**4**) Super Mystère B2 Nº136 (12-YH of Escadron 1/12 "Cambrésis") specially painted for the "Tiger Meet" hosted at Cambrai, July 1972. (**5**) Super Mystère B2 Nº99 of Escadron 1/12 "Cambrésis" at Cambrai, autumn 1971. The Israeli-style three-colour (green, tan and café au lait) disruptive camouflage scheme is noteworthy, this having been applied to some Armée de l'Air Super Mystères to facilitate interchangeability with those of Heyl Ha'Avir prior to 1973 Middle East conflict. (**5a**) Upper surface planview of 12-YB. (**5b**) "Wasp" emblem on portside of tail fin of 12-YB, and (**5c**) "Tiger's Head" emblem appearing on starboard side.

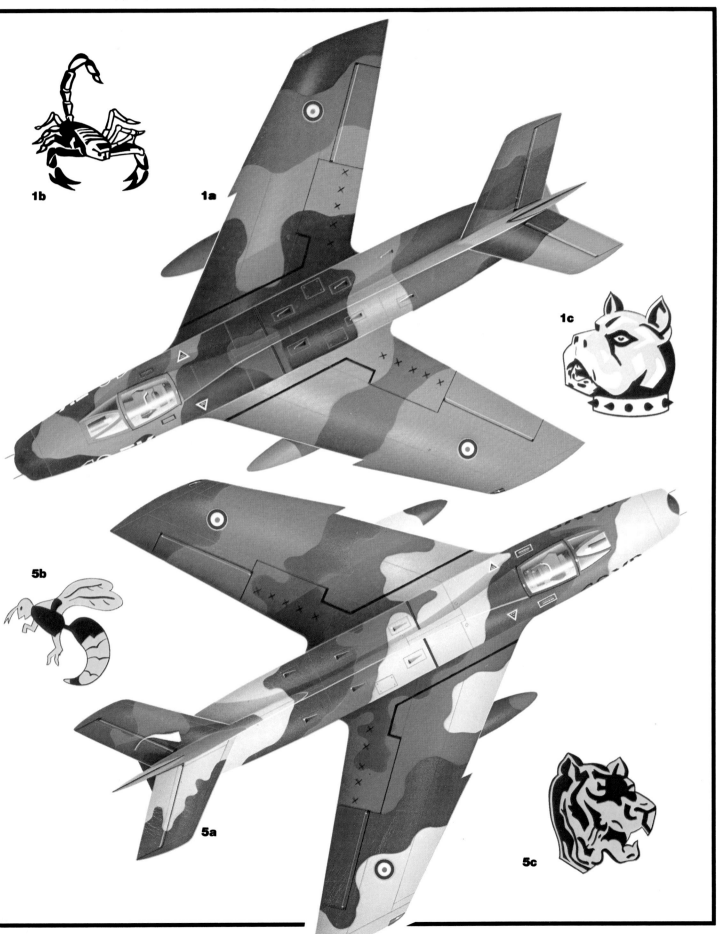

183

# Mikoyan-Gurevich Fishbed (MiG-21) (1959)

Providing many of the vertebrae of the Warsaw Pact's tactical air power backbone from the early 'sixties through the mid-'seventies, the MiG-21, known in the West as Fishbed, was for a long period to rank as the most widely-used fighter in the world. A fall-out of experience gained in the Korean conflict and an

outstanding lightweight fighter, the MiG-21 has been the subject of a complex genealogical process translating the unsophisticated MiG-21F Fishbed-C, which entered production in 1959, with light armament and simple radar ranging, into the MiG-21Mbis Fishbed-N all-weather dual-role fighter of the mid-'seventies,

retaining little more than a configurational similarity to the initial large-scale production model. An RD-9Ye-powered aerodynamic prototype, the Ye-4, flew on 14 June 1956, this becoming the Ye-5 in the following year when re-engined by the R-11, a production prototype, the Ye-6 with the R-11F-300 following in

1958, and entering production as the MiG-21. The Ye-7 of 1960 introduced a limited all-weather capability, being built in large numbers as the MiG-21PF Fishbed-D. An extremely agile fighter, but suffering an overly modest action radius, some 6,000 MiG-21s have been built, with production continuing in 1981 at

some 200 annually for export. (1) MiG-21PF Fishbed-D initial production series (note narrow-chord fin and lack of parabrake bullet fairing), early Frontal Aviation camouflage, circa 1964. (2) MiG-21FL (Type 77) Fishbed-D (C993) of the Indian Air Force "Red Archer" aerobatic team, 1970. (3) MiG-21FL Fishbed-D (C746) of Indian Air Force in camouflage applied on base during Indo-Pakistani conflict of December 1971. (4) MiG-21Mbis Fishbed-N of regiment assigned to Trans-Baikal Military District. Note the random pattern of dark green, sienna and light buff. (4a) Half-and-half plan view, and (4b) head-on view of the same aircraft. (5) MiG-21MF Fishbed-J of regiment assigned to Kiev Military District (5th Frontal Aviation Army), 1973-4. (5a) Symbol indicating unit of a prescribed standard of efficiency. (6) MiG-21MF Fishbed-J (7611), 7th Air Army, Czechoslovak Air Force, 1974. (7) MiG-21MF Fishbed-J (1502) of the same air army, with (7a) sqdn emblem. (8) MiG-21MF Fishbed-J (425) of 8th Fighter Regiment, 1st Air Defence Division, Marxwalde, Air Force of the German Democratic Republic, in 1975. (9) MiG-21PF Fishbed-D (C992) with cannon pack and haphazard camouflaging applied at Indian Air Force unit level during December 1971.

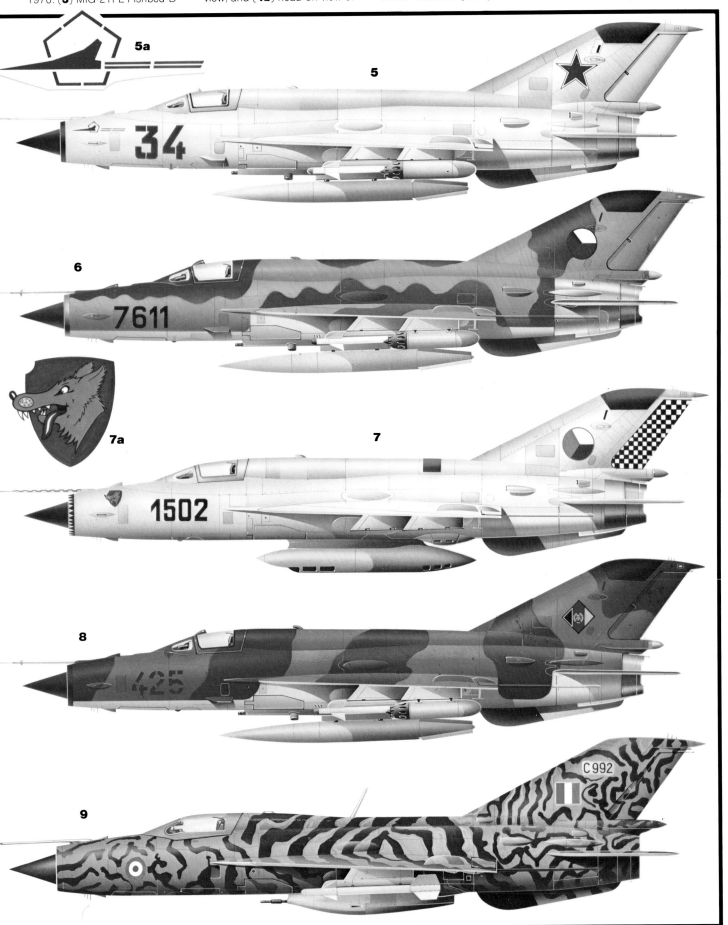

# Sukhoi Fitter (1959)

The Pavel Sukhoi-designed family of tactical fighters, assigned the reporting name Fitter in the West by the Air Standards Co-ordinating Committee, offers the most extraordinary example of incremental development in the history of combat aircraft design. The first prototype of this large single-seat warplane,

the S-1, was flown in 1955. An aerodynamically improved second prototype, the S-2, followed, and this, with further changes as the S-22, was ordered into large scale production in 1958 as the Su-7B, to become known in the West as Fitter-A. Various further modifications were introduced, resulting in the Su-7BM, the

Su-7BKL and the Su-7BMK, the two last-mentioned embodying changes enhancing rough-field capability. In 1966, an experimental version, the S-22I (Fitter-B) was flown, this having variable-sweep wing outer panels. A production derivative of this, the Su-17 (Fitter-C), with uprated engine and deepened dorsal spine, made

its appearance in service in 1971, being exported as the Su-20, this differing in equipment standard but being externally similar and therefore retaining the reporting designation Fitter-C. A longer nose with terrain avoidance radar and a laser ranger resulted in the Fitter-D, and an export Su-22

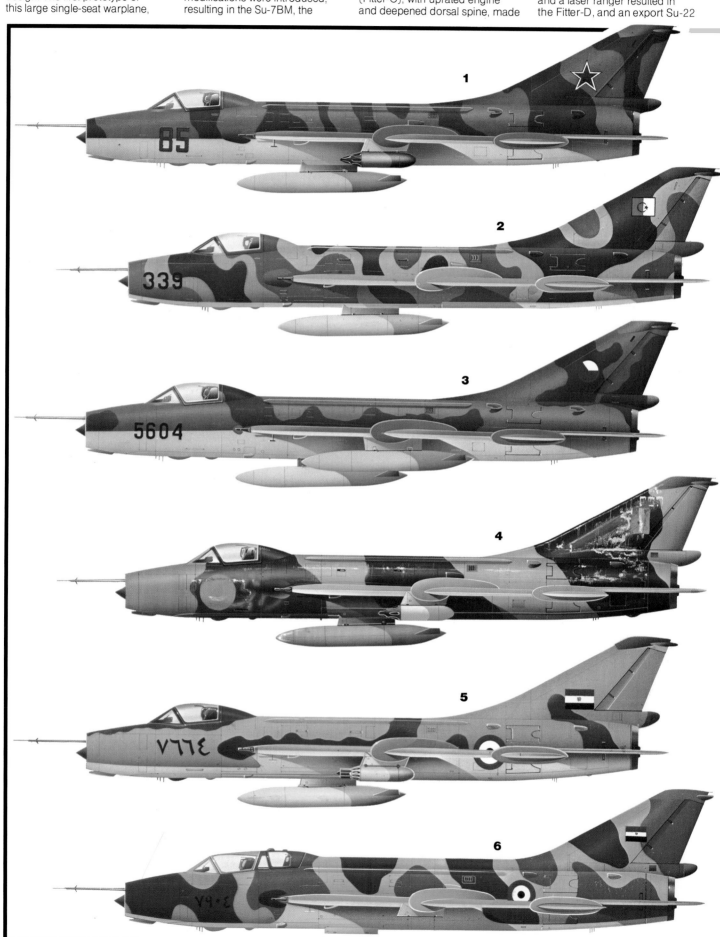

version with a larger-diameter rear fuselage became Fitter-F. Fitter-E was a two-seat trainer version introducing a drooped nose, and mid-1979 two further versions appeared in service— the two-seat Fitter-G with a deeper and broader fuel-housing dorsal fairing and a new vertical tail, and an equivalent single-

seater, Fitter-H. (**1**) Su-7BMK Fitter-A of a V-VS Frontovaya Aviatsiya regiment, Trans-Baikal Military District, 1978. (**2**) Su-7BM Fitter-A of the Algerian Air Force, 1977. (**3**) Su-7BMK Fitter-A of the Czechoslovak Air Force, in 1980. (**4**) Su-7BM Fitter-A of Indian Air Force during Indo-Pakistan conflict of December

1971. Note worn dark green and grey-green field-applied finish and largely obscured national insignia. (**5**) Su-7BM Fitter-A of Egyptian Air Force, 1976. (**6**) Su-7UM Moujik-A transition trainer of Egyptian Air Force, 1976. (**7**) Su-20 Fitter-C of the Polish Air Force, .1974. (**8**) Su-20 Fitter-C of 55th Strike Sqdn,

Egyptian Air Force, 1977. The planview (**8a**) of same aircraft shows min and max sweep angles. Note that the probes extending from the nose are depicted as seen from below. (**8b**) Head-on view of the same aircraft fully swept. (**9**) Su-20 Fitter-H of Libyan Arab Republic Air Force, Okba Ben Nafi Base, in 1980.

187

# McDonnell Douglas F-4 Phantom II (1960)

The most significant and most successful jet fighter of the 'sixties in the western hemisphere, the Phantom II was first conceived in 1954 as a shipboard attack fighter, flying for the first time on 27 May 1958. Characterised by a rather obese, bulbous fuselage, with sharply canted outer wing panels and a one-piece tailplane with pronounced anhedral, the Phantom II was scarcely an example of aeronautical pulchritude, but it was to prove supremely versatile and to enjoy two decades of continuous production. Being the first production aircraft with variable-area intakes and provision for a semi-recessed missile armament, the Phantom II entered the US Navy inventory (as the F4H-1F) late in 1960, and that service was to receive a total of 1,218 aircraft of this type (the USMC receiving a further 46) by the time deliveries of shipboard models terminated in December 1965. Meanwhile, the Phantom II had been adopted by the USAF Tactical Air Command, entering USAF service (as the F-4C) in 1963, and 2,640 being procured. Standard USAF models were exported to eight countries, and special versions were produced for the RAF and Luftwaffe. Licence manufacture also took place in Japan where 138 were added to the 5,211 built in the USA.

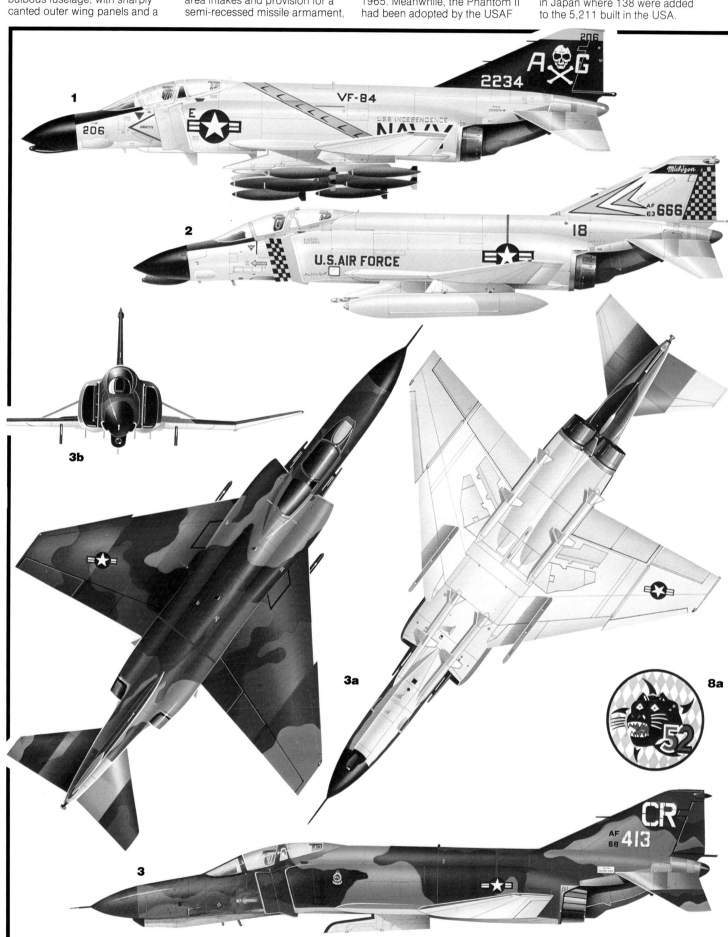

188

(**1**) F-4B (BuAer No. 152234) of US Navy Sqdn VF-84 "Jolly Rogers", USS *Independence*, 1965. Note light gull grey upper and glossy insignia white undersurfaces. (**2**) F-4C (63-666), 171st fighter-Interceptor Sqdn, Michigan Air National Guard, Selfridge ANGB, 1980. Note overall light grey air superiority finish. (**3**) F-4E (68-413) of 32nd Tactical Fighter Sqdn, 36th TFW, Soesterberg, Netherlands, 1970. (**3a**) Upper and lower planviews showing the dark green, medium green and tan camouflage and pale grey undersurfaces, and (**3b**) head-on view of 68-413. (**4**) Phantom FGR Mk 2 (XT912), No 23 Sqdn, RAF Wattisham, Suffolk, 1980. (**5**) F-4D (3-602), 306th Fighter Sqdn, of the Iranian Imperial Air Force, Meharabad, Tehran, 1970 (**6**) RF-4B (BuAer 153099), Reconnaissance Sqdn VMCJ-2, US Marine Corps, NAS Jacksonville, Florida, 1970. (**7**) RF-4E (57-6909) of the 501 Hiko-tai, Air Self-Defence Force, Hyakuri AB, Honshu, Japan, 1980. (**7a**) "Woodpecker" emblem of the 501 Hiko-tai. (**8**) RF-4E 35+79 (69-7526) of Aufklärungsgesch-wader 52, Federal German Luftwaffe, Leck, 1972. Note standard NATO finish of gloss dark sea grey, dark green and light grey. (**8a**) "Panther" emblem of AKG 52. (**9**) F-4E (187) of Israel Defence Force/Air Force during the Arab-Israeli conflict of October 1973.

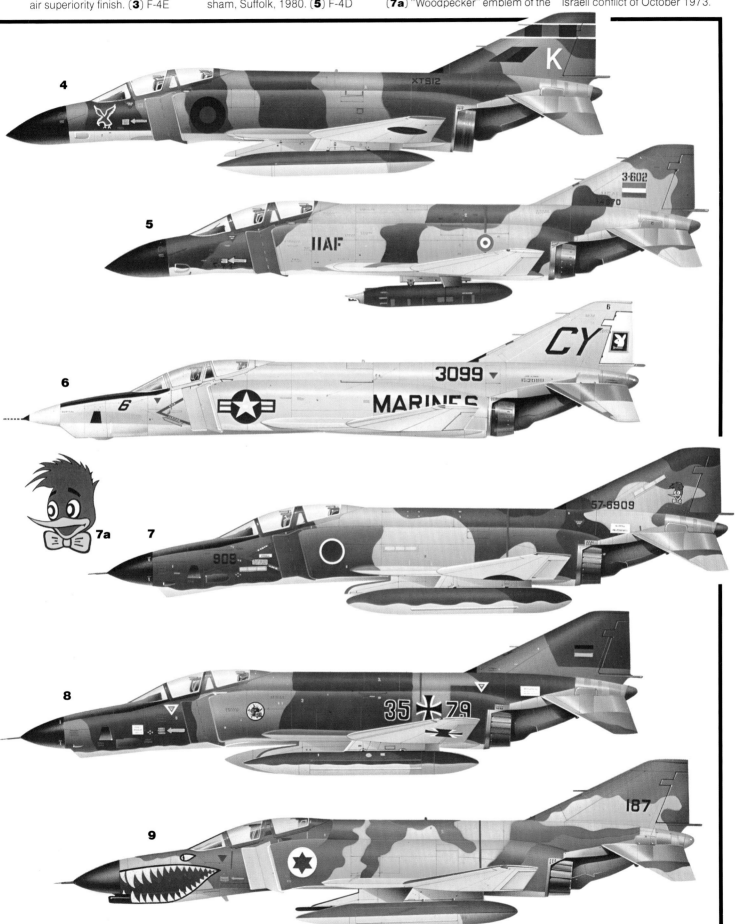

# Dassault-Breguet Mirage III (and 5) (1961)

One of a generation of bisonic fighters following in the wake of the Korean War, France's tailless delta Mirage III represented a dramatic advance in speed capability over the generation of fighters preceding it. Without doubt the most outstanding West European fighter of the 'sixties in terms of export success, and contemporaneous with the MiG-21 and F-104 Starfighter, the Mirage III was claimed to be the only production fighter capable of both flying at Mach 2.0 with air-to-air weapons and operating from less than 2,500ft (762m) of unpaved runway. The Mirage III first flew on 17 November 1956, and the initial production Mirage IIIC basic interceptor entered service in 1961, in which year the dual-role Mirage IIIE with increased fuel made its debut, followed, in 1967, by the simplified Mirage 5. The Mirage has established a record among Western combat aircraft for production longevity, orders for all versions of this delta fighter so far exceeding 1,400, with manufacture expected to continue into 1983. (**1**) Mirage IIICZ (811), No 2 Sqdn, South African Air Force, Waterkloof, 1974. HIgh-gloss disruptive camouflage in dark green and sand on upper surfaces. (**1a**) Emblem of No 2 Sqdn/Eskader 2. (**2**) Mirage IIIC (10-LE) of Escadron de Chasse

3/10 "Vexin", BA 188 Djibouti, 1980. (**3**) Mirage IIIEA (I-007) of I Escuadron de Caza, VIII Brigada Aérea, Fuerza Aérea Argentina, at José C. Paz AB, Buenos Aires. (**4**) Mirage 5COA (3029) of Escuadron de Caza, Fuerza Aérea Colombiana, at German Olana AB, Palanquero. (**5**) Mirage IIIEE of Escuadrón 112 of Ala de Caza 12, (Spanish) Ejército del Aire, at Manises-Valencia. Note Ala 11 emblem, the legend reading "Vista, suerte y al toro" (literally translating as "Sight, luck and to the bull"). (**6**) Mirage IIIE (4-BS) of Escadron de Chasse 2/4 "La Fayette", BA 116 Luxeuil, 1977. Note Sioux Indian Head emblem of Esc 2/4. (**7**) Mirage 5BA (BA28) of 2ème Escadrille de Chasseurs-Bombardiers at Florennes, Belgium. Note 2ème Esc "Comète" emblem. (**8**) Mirage 5M (M413) of 21 Wing, 2nd Tactical Air Group, Zaire Air Force, Kamina. (**9**) Mirage 5PA (70-411) of Operations Group South, Pakistan Air Force, Masroor, Mauripur. (**10**) Mirage 5SDE of Egyptian Air Force, 1975. Note wingtips in underside planview. (**11**) Mirage IIIO (A3-69), No 75 Sqdn, RAAF, at Butterworth, Malaysia, 1978. (**11a**) Emblem of No 75 Sqdn. (**12**) Mirage 5AD (513), United Arab Emirates Air Force, Abu Dhabi International Airport.

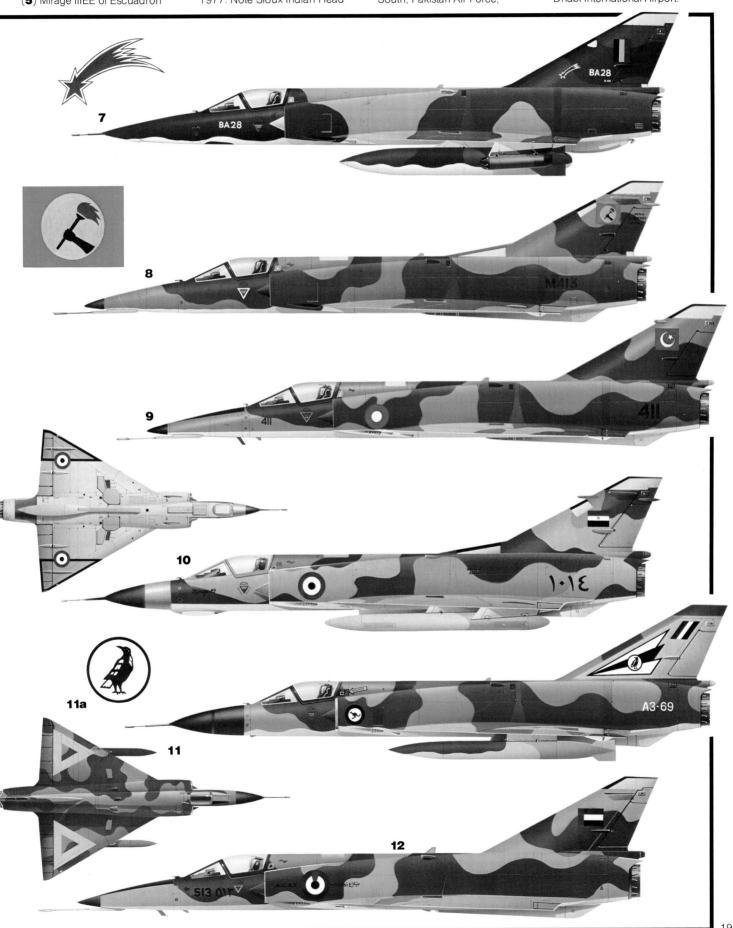

# BAC Lightning (1959)

Conceived as a specialised all-weather interceptor and unique among fighters in having twin engines vertically disposed and staggered to provide what was, at the time of its development, minimum transonic drag for maximum possible thrust, the Lightning first flew (as the P.1B) on 4 April 1957. Characterised by an exceptionally deep fuselage, much of which is occupied by intake ducting and tailpipes, the Lightning began to enter service at the end of 1959, soon establishing a reputation for superlative quality of handling. Production was completed in September 1972, with a total of 337 built, including 55 for export. (**1**) Lightning F Mk 2A (XN775) of No 92 Sqdn, Gütersloh, Germany, 1974. Note matt dark green upper and natural metal lower surfaces adopted autumn 1972 for German-based Lightnings. (**1a**) The "Cobra and Maple Sprig" emblem of No 92 Sqdn. (**2**) Lightning F Mk 3 (XP744), No 56 Sqdn, Wattisham, in 1965. (**2a**) "Phoenix-arising" emblem of No 56 Sqdn (just perceptible on the nose of XP744). (**3**) Lightning F Mk 6 (XR747) of No 5 Sqdn, Binbrook, 1979, in standard NATO dark sea grey and dark green camouflage. (**3a**) "Maple Leaf" emblem of No 5 Sqdn. (**4**) Lightning T Mk 5 (XS458) of Lightning Training Flight, Binbrook, and (**4a**) emblem of LTF.

# Saab Viggen (1972)

Of exceptional configuration in being a delta-winged canard, the Viggen (Thunderbolt) is the product of a "standardised platform" concept—a basic design more or less readily adaptable to fulfil a variety of roles. Viggen was first flown on 8 February 1967, and the initial production model, the AJ 37 which entered service with the Swedish Flygvapen in the summer of 1971, was optimised for the attack mission. Tandem two-seat training (SK 37) and reconnaissance (SH 37 and SF 37) variants were evolved as "first generation" Viggens, and a version optimised for the intercept role, the JA 37, is seen as a "second generation" model.

Having a more powerful engine, new systems and structural changes, the JA 37 Viggen began to enter service in 1980, and 149 of this version are following 180 "first generation" Viggens. (**1**) AJ 37 of F 15 (Hälsinge Flygflottilj), Söderhamn, South Norrland Military Command, 1980. (**2**) JA 37 of F 13 (Bråvalla Flygflottilj), Norrköping, East Sweden Military Command, 1980. (**2a**) Top planview of JA 37 showing elaborate three-tone green and stone upper surface camouflage pattern adopted for the Viggen mid-'seventies. (**2b**) Head-on view of JA 37 with AAMs and fuel tank. (**2c**) Emblem of F 13 Bråvalla Flygflottilj.

# Northrop F-5 (Tiger II) (1965)

Conceived as an attempt to halt the upward spiral in fighter size, weight and complexity, the F-5 began life as a company-sponsored project, with the first of three prototypes ordered for USAF evaluation flying on 30 July 1959. The programme was subsequently virtually "moth-balled" until selection of the

Northrop lightweight fighter in May 1962 as a counterair warplane for supply to favoured nations under the US Military Assistance Program. Service status of the F-5A and two-seat F-5B was attained early in 1965, 621 of the former and 134 of the latter being built by the parent company, plus 220 licence-built

(as CF-5 and NF-5) by Canadair and 69 (as SF-5) by CASA. An upgraded version optimised for air superiority, the F-5E Tiger II, flew on 11 August 1972, more than 1,100 (including equivalent two-seat F-5F) having been delivered by mid-1981, when a further development, the single-engined F-5G, was being built.

(1) F-5A (10534), 302nd Fighter Sqdn, Iranian Imperial Air Force, Mehrabad, 1969. (2) CF-5A, 433 Escadrille Tactique de Combat, Canadian Armed Forces, based at Bagotville, Quebec, in 1972. (3) F-5A of the No 1 Sqdn, Royal Jordanian Air Force, King Hussein Air Base, Mafraq, 1975. (4) F-5A-40 (01399) of 341 Mira

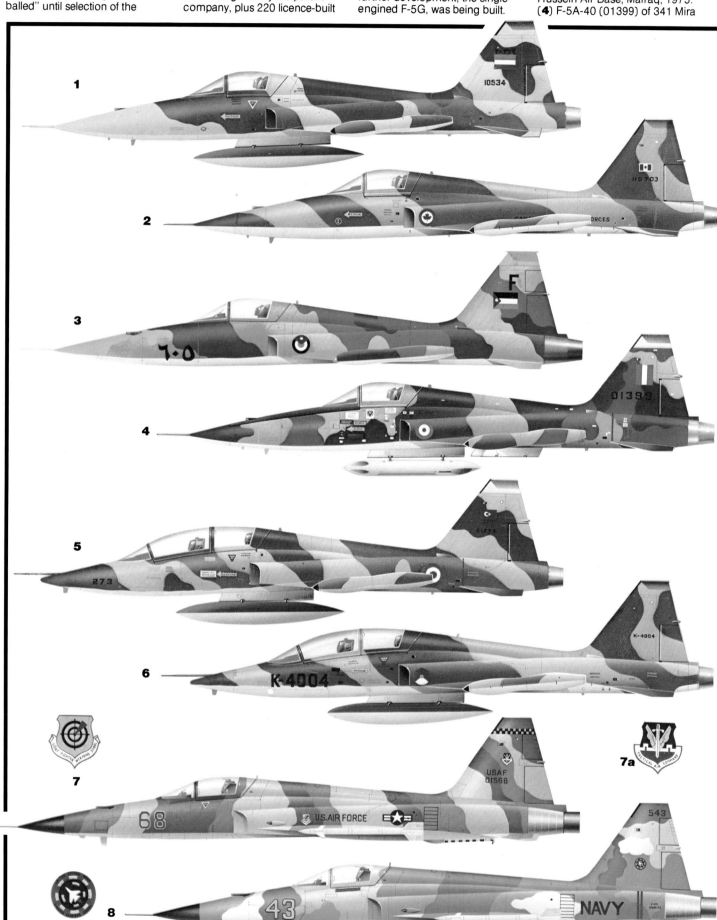

(Sqdn) of the 111ª Pterix Mahis (Fighter Wing), Hellenic Air Force, Achialos, 1971. (**5**) F-5B of 161 Filo (Sqdn), Türk Hava Kuvetleri, Bandirma, 1976. (**6**) NF-5B of Nr 313 Sqdn of the Koninlijke Luchtmacht, Twenthe, Netherlands, 1971. (**7**) F-5E (01568) of 64th Fighter Weapons Sqdn, 57th FWW, Nellis AFB,

Nevada, in "Aggressor" finish (one of nine used for dissimilar combat training). Note Fighter Weapons School emblem (intake trunk, (**7a**) and (**7b**) Tactical Air Command emblem (fin). (**8**) F-5E (159881) of US Naval Fighter Weapons "Top Gun" School, Miramar NAS, Calif. Note school emblem. (**9**) F-5E (1037) of No 7

Sqdn, Royal Saudi Air Force, Taif. (**10**) F-5E (4820) of 1º Esquadrão, 1º Grupo de Aviação de Caça, Fôrça Aérea Brasileira, Santa Cruz AFB, Rio de Janeiro. (**10a**) Topside of 4820 (**11**) F-5E (01545), 527th Tactical Fighter Training Aggressor Sqdn, based at Alconbury, Cambs. (**11a**) Upper surfaces of 01545. (**12**) F-5E

(00933) of Iranian Islamic Air Force. (**12a**) Topside of 00933. (**13**) F-5E (J-804) of Grupo 8, Fuerza Aérea de Chile, based at Antofagasta AFB. (**13a**) Topside view of J-804 showing unusual insignia arrangement. (**14**) F-5E (74-00959) "Chung Cheng" of the 2nd Fighter Wing, Nationalist Chinese Air Force, Taiwan.

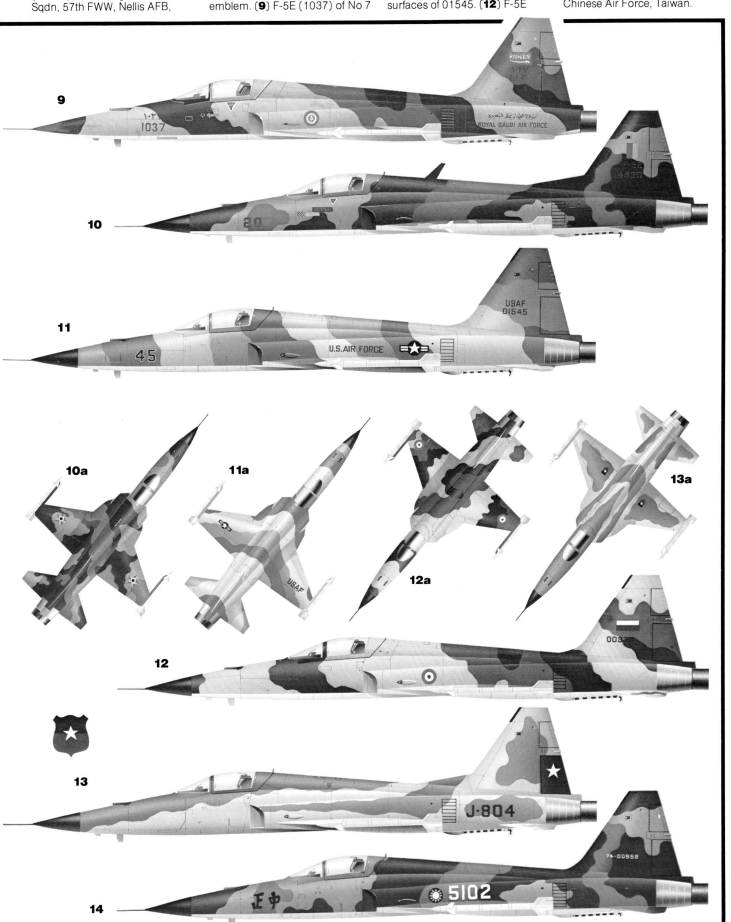

195

# Mikoyan-Gurevich Flogger (1971)

Numerically second in importance among current Soviet Air Force combat aircraft and rapidly overhauling the most numerous, its stablemate the MiG-21 (alias Fishbed), the Flogger is today a family of very closely related aircraft which, possessing an extensive commonality of both airframe and systems features,

now covers almost the entire spectrum of fighter tasks, from interception and air superiority to interdiction and ground attack. It was first introduced into service by V-VS squadrons in 1971 as a straight air combat fighter under the designation MiG-23 (Flogger-B), but the basic design has been progressively

developed to fulfil other tasks. A shift in emphasis from air defence to the more traditional tactical support tasks of the Frontovaya Aviatsiya resulted in evolution of two distinct Flogger versions optimised to differing degrees for the air-ground role. The first of these, the MiG-23B (Flogger-F), introduced a new

forward fuselage embodying a dropped nose to improve target acquisition and a modified power plant. The second, the MiG-27 (Flogger-D), features basically similar forward fuselage, but commonality with other Flogger family members was restricted to wings and tail surfaces, major changes being incorporated in

the remainder of the airframe and in the systems. The most recent service version of the MiG-27 (Flogger-J) features aerodynamic modifications to the wing fillets and a further modified nose. The air-air and air-ground versions of the MiG-23 have now been exported to more than a dozen countries.

(**1**) MiG-23MF Flogger-B of IAP-VO Strany regiment in overall light grey air superiority finish. The nose emblem indicates that the aircraft belongs to a unit that has achieved a prescribed level of merit. (**2**) MiG-23 Flogger-G based at Kubinka, west of Moscow, 1978. (**3**) MiG-23MF Flogger-B of the Air Force of the DDR, 1979.

(**4**) MiG-23 Flogger-E of Libyan Arab Republic Air Force, 1980. (**5**) MiG-23BM Flogger-F of the Algerian Air Force. Note that individual aircraft number conforms with ground line and not with line of flight as is usual. (**6**) MiG-23BM Flogger-F of the Czechoslovak Air Force, Pardubice, east of Prague, 1980.

(**7**) MiG-27 Flogger-D of V-VS Frontovaya Aviatsiya as part of Group of Soviet Forces in Germany, 1978. (**7a**) Planview of same aircraft depicting both upper and lower surfaces of port side. Note that brown tone can vary from light sand to deep café au lait. (**7b**) Head-on view with wings at minimum sweep.

# Dassault-Breguet Mirage F1 (1973)

Possessing no relationship to the delta-winged Mirages (see pages 190-1) other than a common design origin despite its name, the Mirage F1 was designed as a multi-role fighter. In its F1C form optimised for the all-weather air superiority mission and carrying no air-to-ground weapon delivery system, it is now the primary air defence fighter of France's Armée de l'Air, but it has also been exported as an all-altitude air superiority and all-weather attack fighter (F1E), as a dedicated ground attack aircraft with simplified avionics (F1A) and as a two-seat conversion trainer (F1B).

The first Mirage F1 prototype was flown on 23 December 1966, series production of the F1C version being ordered for the Armée de l'Air in 1969, with the first flying on 15 February 1973, and the first deliveries commencing (to Escadron 2/30) late in December of that year. By mid-1981, almost 450 had been delivered to the Armée de l'Air and to 10 export customers, and sufficient orders had been placed to sustain production until at least early 1984. A tactical reconnaissance version, the Mirage F1R, is under development and is scheduled to enter Armée de l'Air service in 1983, and the Mirage F1C-200 has a fixed flight refuelling probe.

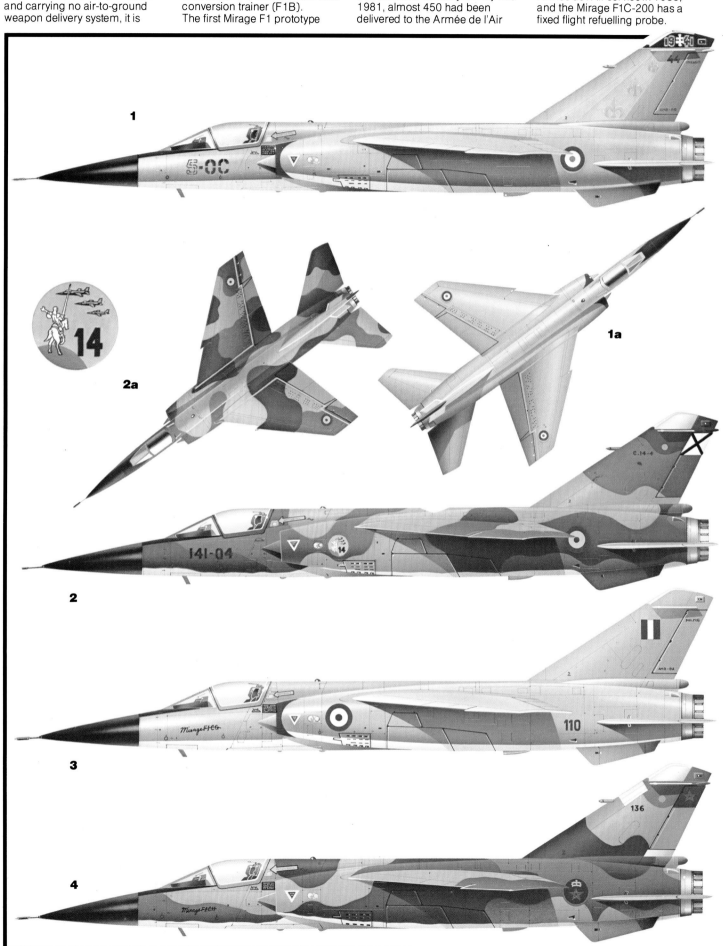

(1) Mirage F1C Nº 44, Escuadron 2/5 "Ile de France", BA 115, Orange-Caritat, in standard CAFDA (Commandement Air des Forces de Défence Aérienne) air superiority finish of dull blue-grey upper surfaces with natural metal underside. (1a) Upper surfaces of 5-OC. (2) Mirage F1CE of Escuadrón 141, Ala de Caza 14, of Spain's Ejército del Aire Albacete. (2a) Emblem of Ala 14 and upper surfaces of Mirage F1CE 141-04. (3) Mirage F1CG of 114ª Pterighe (Wing), Elliniki Aeroporia (Hellenic Air Force), Tanagra. (4) Mirage F1CH of Royal Maroc Air Force. (5) Mirage F1CZ of No 3 Sqdn, South African Air Force, Waterkloof. Note enlarged detail of No 3 Sqdn emblem. (6) Mirage F1CK of Kuwaiti Air Force. (7) Tail detail of current Armée de l'Air Mirage F1C units with scrap views of individual aircraft identification. Note that the arrows indicate differing emblems on port and starboard sides of vertical tail. Top row left to right, Nº 9 30-MF of 2/30 "Normandie-Niémen"; Nº 81 12-ZC of 2/12 "Cornouaille"; Nº 54 12-YH of 1/12 "Cambrésis"; Nº 19 5-NQ of 1/5 "Vendée"; and lower row, Nº 28 30-FF of 3/30 "Lorraine". Overall finish is similar to Nº 44 5-OC. (8) Mirage F1JA of Fuerza Aérea, Ecuatoriana at Guayaquil.

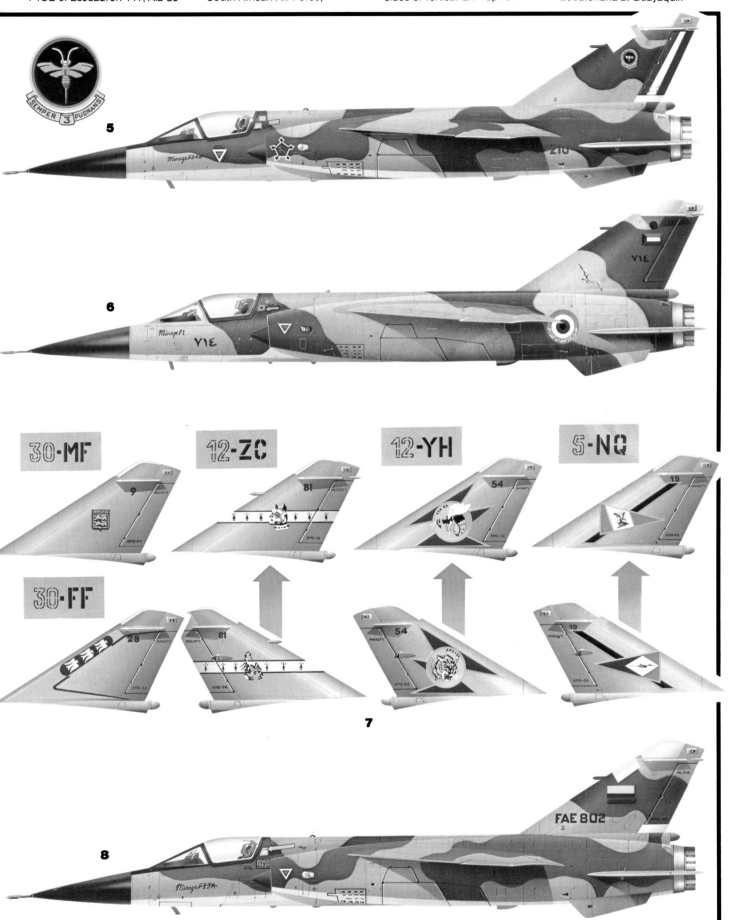

# Nancheng A-5 (Fantan) (1973)

Built at Nancheng, China, for the Air Force of the People's Liberation Army, the A-5, alias Kiang (Attack) 5, is also known by the western reporting name of Fantan. The A-5 is essentially a strike fighter derivative of the licence-built MiG-19 diurnal clear-weather interceptor, and it differs from its progenitor primarily in having a new fore fuselage with sharply pointed conical nose and lateral intakes in place of a nose pitot intake. The cockpit is moved forward and an internal ordnance bay has been introduced. The prototype of the A-5 is believed to have flown in 1970, with service introduction commencing in 1973. Substantial quantities of aircraft of this type—probably several hundred —have since been built.

(**1**) An A-5 of the AFPLA in the natural metal finish utilised by most aircraft of this type. The national insignia appears on the fuselage and upper wing surfaces only. (**1a**) Detail of underside of the nose showing asymmetric arrangement of nosegear doors and camera port. (**2**) A-5 in two-tone camouflage scheme of dark earth and mid green with azure blue undersurfaces as used in combat over Vietnam early 1979. (**2a**) Half-and-half planview of same aircraft illustrating the starboard upper and lower sides, and (**2b**) head-on view.

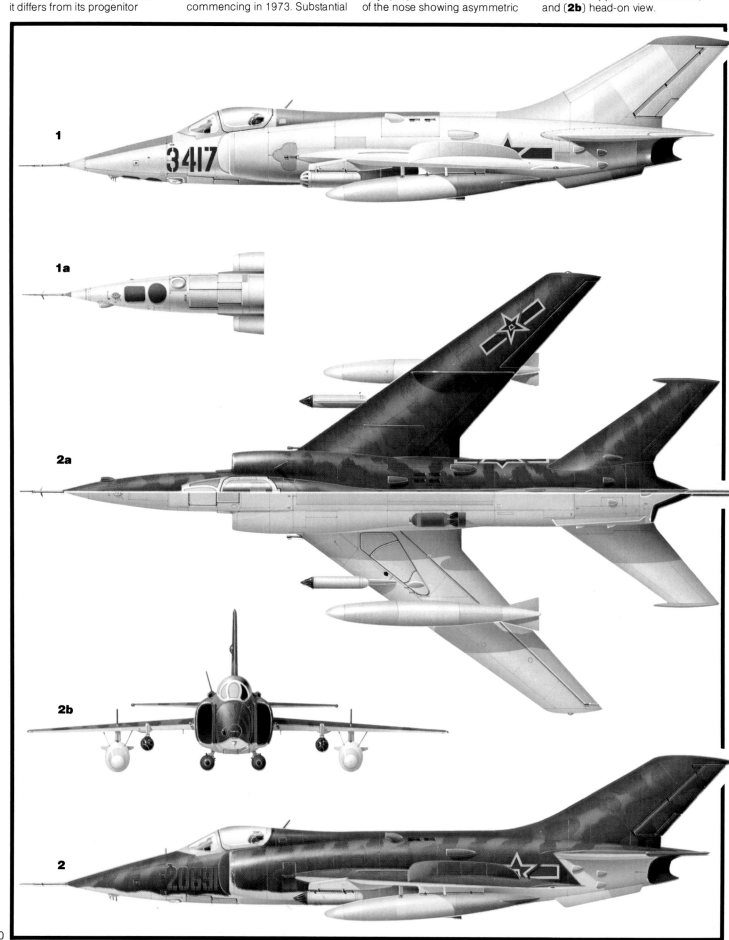

# IAI Kfir (1975)

Israel Aircraft Industries' Kfir (Young Lion) multi-role fighter affords one of the most extra-ordinary sagas in the annals of combat aircraft development. The successful mating of a French Mirage airframe (see pages 190-1) with a US General Electric J79 turbojet, the Kfir began to join the inventory of the air compon-

ent of the Israel Defence Force, Heyl Ha'Avir, in April 1975, and was followed by an improved version, the Kfir-C2 in 1976. The latter embodied modifications to improve combat manoeuvrability, these primarily consisting of canard auxiliary surfaces, dog-tooth wing leading-edge extensions and strakes on the nose.

(**1**) Kfir (718) of initial series with standard sand, tan and medium green upper surface finish and pale blue undersurfaces, in 1975-6. Note the black-outlined orange-yellow triangles for use as quick ID aids. (**2**) Kfir (725) of No 101 Sqdn, the premier Heyl Ha'Avir fighter unit, 1975-6. (**2a**) Emblem of No 101 Squadron.

(**3**) Kfir-C2 (871) in two-tone grey air superiority finish adopted by Heyl Ha'Avir in 1978. (**4**) Kfir-C2 (855) in standard dual-role finish, Hatzerim, in the Negev, July 1976. (**4a**) Half-and-half planview of 855 showing the starboard upper and lower surfaces with ID panels, and (**4b**) head-on view of 855.

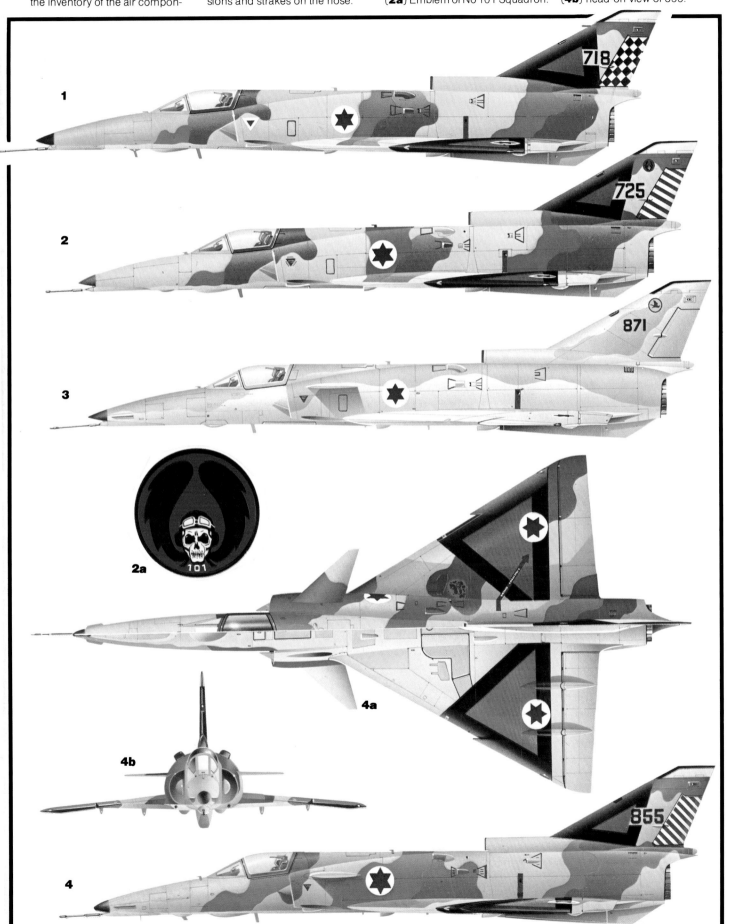

# British Aerospace Hawk (1976)

The first of the new generation of basic/advanced jet trainers with light attack capability to have achieved service status, the Hawk first flew on 21 August 1974, this being a pre-production aircraft built on production tooling—there being no prototypes as such—and the first production examples began to enter service (at RAF Valley) in November 1976. An outstandingly sturdy and manoeuvrable aircraft, the Hawk has replaced the Gnat Trainer and the Hunter in the RAF for advanced flying, weapon and radio navigation training. It is suitable for a variety of operational roles, however, and a substantial number of RAF Hawks are being modified to carry a pair of AIM-9L air-to-air missiles to supplement home defence fighter forces in an emergency. For the close air support role provision is made for two additional wing stores pylons (increasing the total to four). A 30mm Aden cannon and ammunition pack may be carried on the fuselage centreline, and the Hawk has also demonstrated its ability to carry a total external load of 6,500lb. In addition to the RAF, the Hawk has been supplied to the air arms of Kenya, Indonesia and Finland, and has also been ordered by the Zimbabwe Air Force for delivery in 1982.

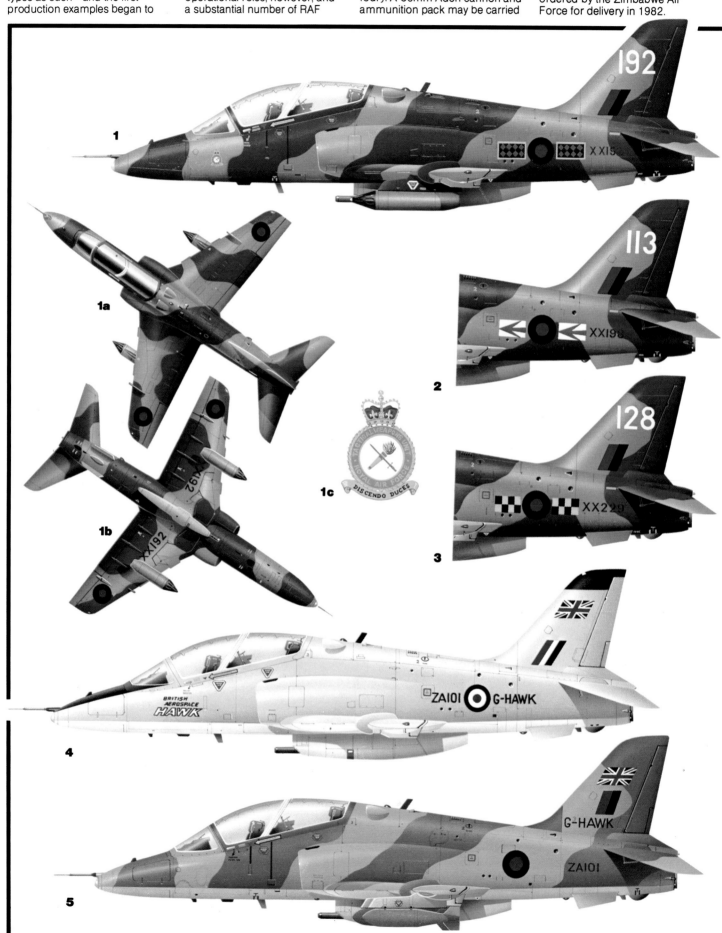

(**1**) Hawk T Mk 1 (XX192) of No 1 Tactical Weapons Unit, RAF Brawdy, South Wales, and bearing the insignia of No 234 Sqdn. (**1a**) Upper and (**1b**) underside of XX192. Note application of the disruptive camouflage to all surfaces (**1c**) Crest of Tactical Weapons Unit. (**2**) Rear fuselage detail of Hawk T Mk 1 (XX198) used by TWU with insignia of No 79 Sqdn. (**3**) Rear fuselage detail of Hawk T Mk 1 (XX229) used by No 2 Tactical Weapons Unit, RAF Chivenor, with the insignia of No 63 Sqdn. (**4**) Hawk Mk 50 demonstrator as painted in 1979 in US Navy grey/white finish with all lettering in dark blue (**5**) Hawk Mk 50 demonstrator in its original dark earth and stone camouflage with azure underside for Middle East demonstrations. (**6**) Hawk T Mk 1 (XX170) serving with No 4 Flying Training School, RAF Valley. Note crest of No 4 FTS carried on fin. (**7**) Hawk T Mk 1 (XX253) of RAF Red Arrows aerobatic demonstration team. (**8**) Hawk Mk 52 of Kenya Air Force at Nanyuki, 1981. Note scrap view of upper wing surface showing the national insignia. (**9**) Hawk Mk 53 of No 1 Training wing, Indonesian Armed Forces-Air Force. (**10**) Hawk Mk 51 of Hävllv 21, Satakunta Wing of Finnish Air Force, Pori, Gulf of Bothnia, 1981.

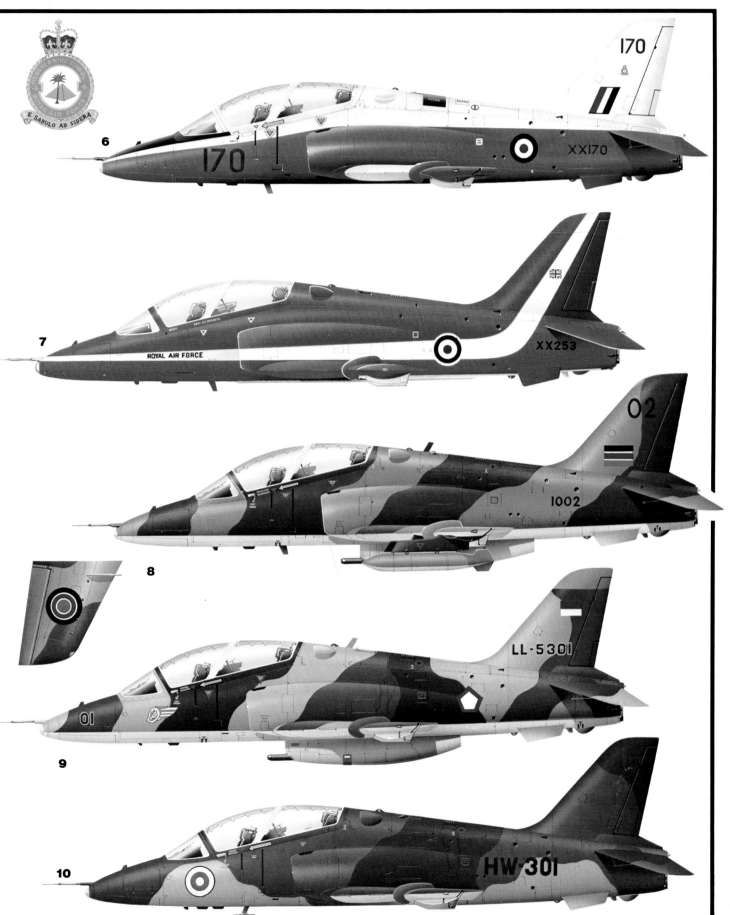

# Dassault-Breguet/Dornier Alpha Jet (1978)

Developed and manufactured under a co-operative programme by the French and Federal German aircraft industries, the Alpha Jet is, like the Hawk on the preceding pages, one of the new generation of basic/advanced jet trainers with light attack capability. First flown on 26 October 1973, the Alpha Jet is being manufactured to fulfil fundamentally different roles in service with the Armée de l'Air and the Luftwaffe, the former employing it for the training mission and the latter utilising it for the close air support and battlefield reconnaissance tasks. The Alpha Jet entered French service in the summer of 1978, achieving operation status in Germany two years later. Both French and German services are to procure 175 aircraft, and export contracts for Alpha Jets from Belgium, Egypt, Ivory Coast, Morocco, Nigeria and Qatar had been fulfilled or were in process of fulfilment by mid-1981. Although retaining its second seat, the Luftwaffe Alpa Jet is normally flown as a single-seater for the close air support role for which it is equipped with a centreline pod housing a 27mm cannon, two hardpoints under each wing carrying bombs or rocket pods. A total of 466 Alpha Jets had been ordered by mid-1981, with some 260 delivered.

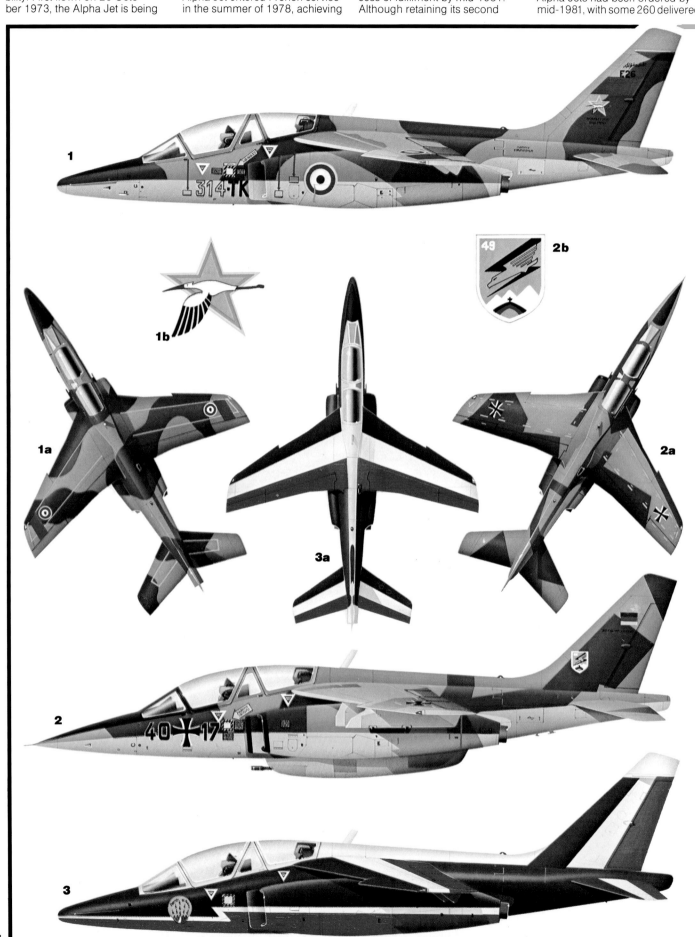

(1) Alpha Jet E of 314ᵉ Groupement École "Christian Martel", Armée de l'Air, Tours, in 1980. (1a) Upper surfaces of same aircraft. Note Dayglo panels indicating training role. (1b) The emblem of GE 314. (2) Alpha Jet A, Jagdbombergeschwader 49, Federal German Luftwaffe, 1980. (2a) Upper surfaces of the same aircraft, and (2b) the emblem of Jabo G 49. (3) Alpha Jet E of the Patrouille de France, the Armée de l'Air aerobatic team, 1980. (3a) Upper surfaces of the same aircraft. (4) Second prototype Alpha Jet E (F-ZWRX) in demonstration colours for the 1975 Paris Salon de l'Aéronautique. (5) Alpha Jet B of 7ème Escadrille, Centre de Perfectionnement, Force Aérienne Belge, Brustem, 1980. (6) Alpha Jet of the Force Aérienne de la Côte d'Ivoire, Abidjan, 1980. Note the retention of civil registration TU-VAG. (7) Alpha Jet (231) of Royal Moroccan Air Force, 1981. (8) Alpha Jet of Togo Air Force. Note retention of civil registration 5V-MBA. (9) Alpha Jet A (No 58) as demonstrated in the USA in September 1980. Note the French registration F-ZVLB on aft fuselage despite Luftwaffe emblem on port air intake (replaced on starboard intake by an Armée de l'Air roundel). The "Lockheed" legend on the nose indicates the US sponsorship.

205

# General Dynamics F-16 Fighting Falcon (1979)

First flown (YF-16) on 20 January 1974, the Fighting Falcon achieved service status with the USAF in 1979, with the Israeli and Belgian air forces, in 1980, and with the Dutch, Danish and Norwegian air forces during 1981. Production for European services is being undertaken in Belgium and the Netherlands, and USAF.

planning in mid-1981 called for the procurement of 1,388 Fighting Falcons (including 204 F-16B two-seaters), future recipients including Egypt and South Korea. (**1**) F-16A (79-0295) of the 4th Tactical Fighter Sqdn, 388th TFW, Hill AFB, Utah, 1981. (**1a**) Upper surfaces of 79-0295 in standard USAF two-tone grey air superior-

ity finish. (**1b**) 4th TFS emblem (on port side of the air intake), (**1c**) 388th TFW emblem (on the starboard side of the intake), and (**1d**) Tactical Air Command crest (on vertical fin). Note that the 388th "Lightning Flash" is repeated at tip of vertical surfaces, "HL" signifying Hill AFB. (**2**) F-16A temporarily in the

markings of No 306 Sqdn, KLu, Leeuwarden, Holland. 1980. (**2a**) The emblem of No 306 Sqdn. (**3**) F-16A (105), Israel Defence Force/Air Force, 1980. (**3a**) Upper surfaces of 105. (**4**) The F-16B (78-0096) evaluated at Hill AFB, 1980, in "European One" lizard camouflage scheme of two tones of green plus charcoal.

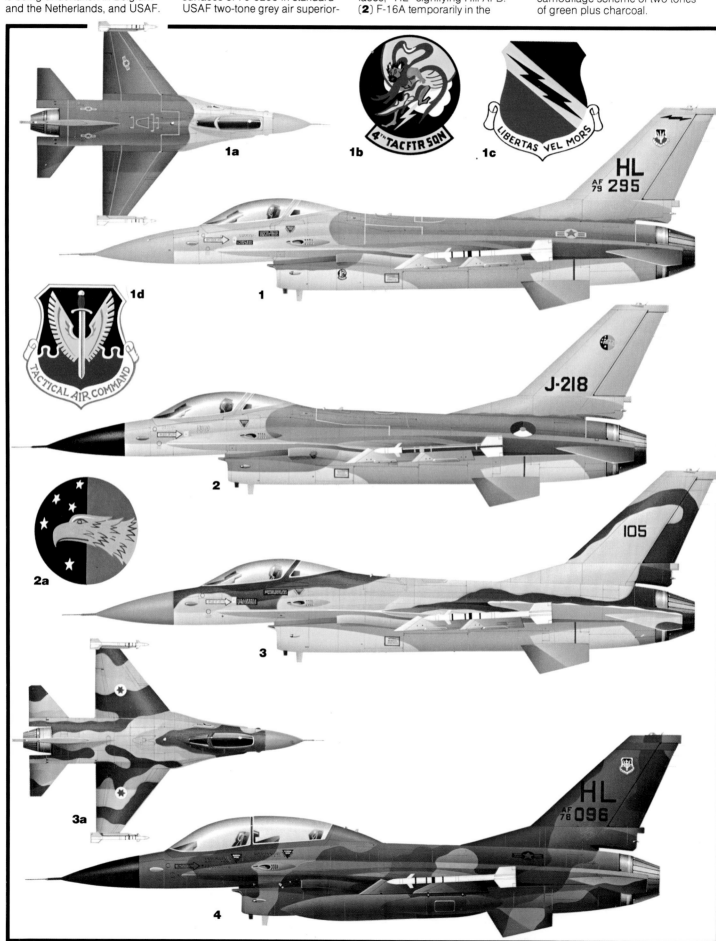

# Panavia Tornado (1981)

The result of an unprecedented multi-national (UK, Federal Germany and Italy) development and production programme, Tornado is a multi-role aircraft for close air support, interdiction counter-air strike and reconnaissance. First flown on 14 August 1974, Tornado entered service in 1981 with the Tri-National Tornado Training Establishment, and 385 (including 165 interceptors) are to be produced for the RAF, 212 for the Luftwaffe, 112 for the Marineflieger and 100 for Italy. (**1**) Tornado GR Mk 1 (ZA322) B-50 of the Tri-National Tornado Training Establishment (TTTE) at Cottesmore, 1981. (**1a**) Upper surfaces of ZA322 (fourth British production aircraft) with wings fully swept. (**1b**) Head-on view of Tornado GR Mk 1 in a representative configuration with wing and fuselage pylons, etc. (**2**) Tornado (4005) G-24 of Luftwaffe assigned to the TTTE. Note that dual control configuration is indicated by a tail number below 50. (**3**) Tornado P-02 (second German prototype) in Marineflieger finish as tested at Erprobungsstelle 61, Manching. Note Kormoran missiles. (**4**) Tornado P-14 (M.M.7001), the Italian pre-production aircraft, with TTTE marking applied solely for visit to Cottesmore on the occasion of the formal opening of the Establishment, 1981.

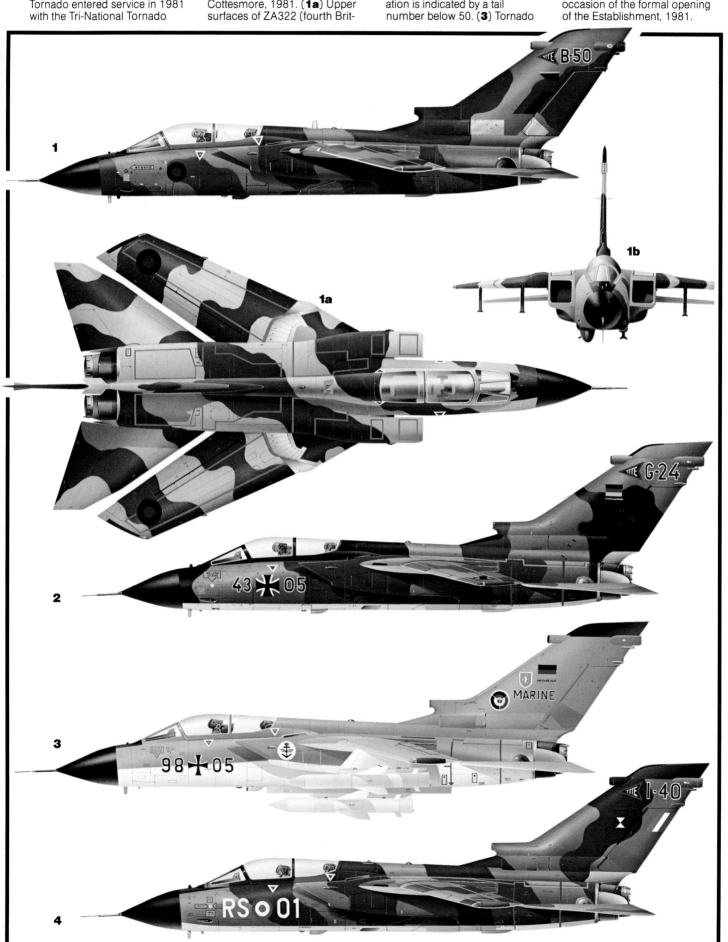